Handbook of Computational Sciences

Scrivener Publishing
100 Cummings Center, Suite 541J
Beverly, MA 01915-6106

Publishers at Scrivener
Martin Scrivener (martin@scrivenerpublishing.com)
Phillip Carmical (pcarmical@scrivenerpublishing.com)

Handbook of Computational Sciences

A Multi and Interdisciplinary Approach

Edited by

Ahmed A. Elgnar

Faculty of Computers & Artificial Intelligence, Beni-Suef University, Egypt

Vigneshwar M

Cybase Technologies, Coimbatore, Tamil Nadu, India

Krishna Kant Singh

Department of Computer Science and Engineering, Amity University, Uttar Pradesh, India

and

Zdzislaw Polkowski

The Karkonosze University of Applied Sciences, Poland

Scrivener
Publishing

This edition first published 2023 by John Wiley & Sons, Inc., 111 River Street, Hoboken, NJ 07030, USA and Scrivener Publishing LLC, 100 Cummings Center, Suite 541J, Beverly, MA 01915, USA
© 2023 Scrivener Publishing LLC
For more information about Scrivener publications please visit www.scrivenerpublishing.com.

Wiley Global Headquarters
111 River Street, Hoboken, NJ 07030, USA

For details of our global editorial offices, customer services, and more information about Wiley products visit us at www.wiley.com.

Limit of Liability/Disclaimer of Warranty

Library of Congress Cataloging-in-Publication Data

ISBN 978-1-197-6046-7

Cover image: Pixabay.Com
Cover design by Russell Richardson

Set in size of 11pt and Minion Pro by Manila Typesetting Company, Makati, Philippines

Printed in the USA

10 9 8 7 6 5 4 3 2 1

Contents

15 Robotic Arm: Impact on Industrial and Domestic Applications 323
Nidhi Chahal, Ruchi Bisht, Arun Kumar Rana
and Aryan Srivastava

16 Effects of Using VR on Computer Science Students' Learning
Behavior in Indonesia: An Experimental Study for TEFL   341
Muthmainnah, Ahmad Al Yakin, Luís Cardoso,
Ahmed A. Elngar, Ibrahim Oteir and Abdullah Nijr Al-Otaibi

Preface

This handbook explores computational methods that are found on the engineering side of computer science. These methods appear in worldwide applications and are the focus of research works that seek to apply them to meet current and future societal needs.

This volume pertains to applications in the areas of imaging, medical imaging, wireless and WS networks, IoT with applied areas, big data for various applicable solutions, etc. This text delves deeply into the core subject and then broadens to encompass the interlinking, inter–disciplinary, and cross-disciplinary sections of other relevant areas. Those areas include applied, simulation, modeling, real-time, research applications, and more.

In proportion with greater technological advancements come increased complexities and new intriguing issues that require micro-level analysis with strong consideration for future outcomes. Such analysis involves the use of computing hardware, networking, algorithms, data structures, programming, databases, and other domain-specific knowledge for the implementation of physical processes that run on computers.

Computational sciences can conglomerate with other cross- and inter-disciplines to evolve into something useful to humankind. A wide-ranging perspective is necessary for the evolution of a new paradigm. To accomplish this, the approach must involve highly advanced learning that includes research by scholars, scientists, engineers, medical practitioners, biologists, chemists, physicists, etc.; and it touches upon areas of physical-, biological-, and life science; many forms of computational science (physics, chemistry, neuroscience, mathematics, and biology), software engineering, arts and humanities, and more.

The editors wish to thank Scrivener Publishing and their team for the opportunity to publish this volume.

The Editors
May 2023

A Sensor-Based Automated Irrigation System for Indian Agricultural Fields

I.S. Akila[1] and Ahmed A. Elngar[2*]

[1]*Department of ECE, Coimbatore Institute of Technology, Coimbatore, Tamil Nadu, India*
[2]*Faculty of Computers and Artificial Intelligence, Beni-Suef University, Beni-Suef City, Egypt*

Abstract
The continuous monitoring of field conditions using an IoT system is essential to maintain the optimum levels of the field parameters like soil moisture and temperature and to increase productivity. Continuous monitoring and automation of irrigation to optimize field conditions is a challenge faced by the agriculture sector. The proposed work presents an IoT system that collects temperature and humidity data through the sensors, processes them, and automates the irrigation process based on the results. Considering the pragmatic feasibility of many conventional and modern approaches, this work proposes a simplified and economic solution to automate the process of irrigation amidst the challenges such as lack of skilled labor and overhead involved in the complexity of the existing solutions. The work could be extended to various geographical regions of the Indian landscape to make a comprehensive and all-inclusive solution for the automation of the irrigation process.

Keywords: Agriculture, irrigation, image processing, sensor, box-counting, fractal dimension

1.1 Introduction

Agriculture plays a major role in the Indian economy. Due to the unpredictable and inconsistent nature of factors that influence farming in India,

---

Corresponding author: elngar_7@yahoo.co.uk

Ahmed A. Elngar, Vigneshwar M, Krishna Kant Singh and Zdzislaw Polkowski (eds.) Handbook of Computational Sciences: A Multi and Interdisciplinary Approach, (1–22) © 2023 Scrivener Publishing LLC there arises a need to extend the technology into agriculture thereby increasing productivity. Across the wide scope of the Indian landscape, farmers employ several styles of agriculture that could be synthesized and enhanced with the invention of emerging technologies.

Optimum soil temperature and moisture levels should be maintained to augment crop growth. Macronutrient levels should also be maintained to adequacy for better yield. A smart monitoring platform is required to monitor field conditions continuously. An effective automated system would reduce human efforts to a great extent. This system facilitates smart monitoring of several parameters such as optimum water and other soil properties that cumulatively influence productivity in the primary sector.

The process of automation in the agricultural monitoring process is done by interfacing the required sensors to NI myRIO, which is supported by the LabVIEW platform. Image processing technique using a suitable box counting algorithm estimates the fractal dimension of the soil particles and further, it has been implemented to detect physical parameters of the soil.

Modern technology finds its applications in various fields for better outcomes. Agriculture, a significant field to be monitored and enhanced, has exploited technology to obtain higher productivity, growth, and yield rates. Hence reducing human effort and automating the process of irrigation by enabling remote access to field parameters would contribute to the betterment of yields in agriculture.

The rest of the chapter is organized as follows. Section 1.2 presents significant research works performed to automate the process of agricultural monitoring amidst their boundaries. Section 1.3 illustrates the proposed work of this chapter. Section 1.4 discusses the performance study and results of the work. Section 1.5 concludes the work and presents future possibilities for enhancement.

1.2   Literary Survey

Through the traces of modern technological advancements, shortage of skilled labor, and increasing demand, there is much research work focused on the automation of agricultural monitoring systems.

A.D. Kadage and J.D. Gawade [1] have designed and implemented a system to monitor field conditions continuously by interfacing sensors to a microcontroller and notifying the farmer through SMS (Short Message Service) when field conditions deviate from normal parameters. The system utilizes a GSM module and prompts commands from the farmer to take necessary action. However, their work has not considered network availability and related constraints. Thus, continuous monitoring is facilitated without emphasizing automating the process of irrigation.

Swarup S. Mathurkar and Rahul B. Lanjewar [2] proposed a system to develop a smart sensor-based monitoring system for the agricultural environment using a Field Programmable Gate Array (FPGA) which comprised of a wireless protocol, different types of sensors, microcontroller, serial protocol, and the FPGA with display element. The work was done using sensors that help in checking moisture, temperature, and humidity conditions. According to these conditions, farmers can schedule their work.

Bansari Deb Majumder, Arijita Das, Dibyendu Sur, Sushmita Das, Avishek Brahma, and Chandan Dutta [3] have attempted to develop an automated system that can measure different agricultural process parameters (like temperature, soil moisture, sunlight intensity, humidity, chemical contents, etc.) and control using PID controller. These parameters can be remotely monitored and controlled. With the help of MATLAB interfaced with NI LabVIEW, a virtual simulation of the entire process on the front panel is made feasible. Alarm systems are incorporated to generate the necessary alarm signal in case of the worst scenario to alert the farmer about the consequences. This will provide the farmer with a remote-control approach to looking after his land and crops. It will also increase the productivity of land through efficient control and will reduce human efforts through complete automation of the harvesting process.

Anastasia Sofou, Georgios Evangelopoulos, and Petros Maragos [4] proposed a system to examine the sophisticated integration of selected modern methods for image feature extraction, texture analysis, and segmentation into homogeneous regions. The experimental results in images are digitized under different specifications and scales demonstrating the proposed system's efficacy. Further, this work explores the possibilities of a smart agricultural monitoring system based on geographical constraints.

H.T. Ingale and N.N. Kasat [5] proposed a system for automatic irrigation by using sensors that would make farmers aware of the changing conditions of humidity levels to schedule the proper timing for irrigation. Due to the direct transfer of water to the roots, water conservation takes place and also helps to maintain the moisture to soil ratio at the root zone constant to some extent. Thus, the system is efficient and compatible with the changing environment. Also, the system saves water and improves the growth of plants. The influence of other climate parameters could be considered to improve the quality of the outcome in this work.

Rahul B. Lanjewar, Swarup S. Mathurkar, Nilesh R. Patel and Rohit S. Somkuwar [6] presented a sensor system to monitor and measure parameters such as temperature, soil moisture, and humidity. Further, the work done by M.K. Gayatri, J. Jayasakthi, and G.S. Anandha Mala [7] motivates the employment of the data obtained through emerging technologies such as the Internet of Things (IoT) and cloud computing to automate manual agricultural activities.

V. Vijay Hari Ram, H. Vishal, S. Dhanalakshmi and P. Meenakshi Vidya [8] presented a framework for regulating water supply in an agricultural field with a simple IoT model. Tanmay Baranwal, Nitika and Pushpendra Kumar Pateriya [9] proposed an IoT-based system for from the security perspective and further makes an example of using modern technologies to adopt and support traditional environments. In their work, Nikesh Gondchawar and R.S. Kawitkar [10] presented a GPS-based automation framework for a smart agriculture system.

Yijun Hu, Jingfang Shen, and Yonghao Qi [11] have predicted the growth of rice plants using fractal dimension parameters for the prediction of bio-mass of the rice and have proven to improvise the prediction model. P. Senthil and Akila I.S. [12] presented the Fire Bird V ATmega2560 robotic kit for the prediction of soil moisture and to determine the shortest path using Dijkstra's algorithm for the robotic kit movement and it was proven that the system was efficient in monitoring the moisture content of the soil.

I.S. Akila, A. Sivakumar, and S. Swaminathan [13] depict the work of extracting the texture of the plant using image processing techniques and the height of the plant was estimated using a virtual height measurement scheme. The works of [14, 15], and [16] discuss the use of IoT in agriculture, its issues, challenges, and solutions. They also depict different IoT architectures which are application specific.

From the literature survey, the features such as network constraint, distance viability, reliability, complex algorithms in image processing, increased human efforts and manual control are identified as predominant parameters to improve contemporary agricultural monitoring systems. Our work is proposed to overcome these real-time challenges through automated irrigation, remote access to field conditions, and simple image processing techniques for determining soil physical parameters.

1.3 Proposed System

1.3.1 System Architecture

The block diagram for our proposed system is shown in Figure 1.1. The work is aimed at automating the irrigation process by interfacing the nec-essary sensors, namely, the temperature sensor and moisture sensors to the

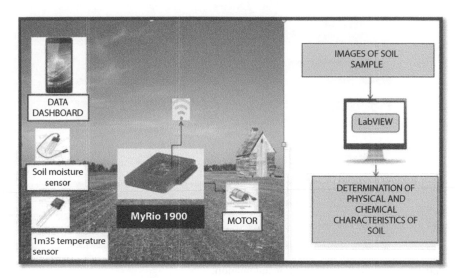

Figure 1.1 Proposed system architecture.

NI myRIO board with configured Wi-Fi (Wireless Fidelity) facility. When the power is supplied to myRIO, the temperature sensor monitors the soil temperature. If it exceeds 30°C, it will automatically turn on the motor. The temperature is displayed on the Data dashboard. Similarly, irrigation takes place when the moisture level violates the threshold range. When the temperature and moisture levels go below their respective threshold values, the motor remains off. The outcome of the sensors is used to automatically initiate the irrigation process.

1.3.2   Flow of Automated Irrigation

Figure 1.2 shows the flow of activities involved in the automation of the irrigation system. Initially, myRIO is configured and then interfaced with the appropriate sensors. The data are read from the sensor, and according to the threshold fixed, the automation control of ON/OFF the motor is done.

1.3.3   Interfacing Sensors

YL69 soil moisture sensor and LM35 soil temperature sensor are interfaced with the NI myRIO as per Table 1.1. The sensors are connected to the MXP connector pins of myRIO, where the MXP connector consists of both analogy and digital input and output pins with 5V.

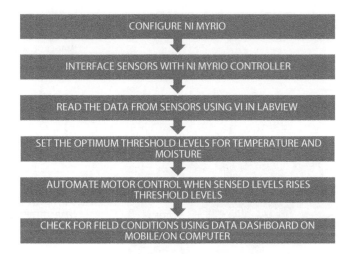

Figure 1.2 Process flow of irrigation automation.

Table 1.1 Connection specification.

S. no.	Sensors	Sensor connector pins	Myrio connector pins
1	Soil moisture sensor	Vcc	MSP DIO(5V)
		Ground	MSP DGND
		AO (analog output)	MSP AI0+
2	Soil temperature sensor	Vcc	MXP A1
		Analog output	MSP AI1+
		GND	MSP AI 1-

The optimum values for the soil temperature and moisture are fixed as the threshold as depicted in Table 1.2 which is compared to the sensed values of parameters.

Upon the comparison of the sensed values and fixed threshold values, the motor is initiated, and irrigation is done automatically. A DC motor is interfaced to MXP connector PIN 27 as shown in Figure 1.3.

The NI Data dashboard mobile application enables the implementation of network-shared variables. In the irrigation automation the motor status, temperatures in Celsius, and percentage of moisture status have been configured as shared variables as shown in Figure 1.4. They can be accessed by connecting to the Wi-Fi network in the configured myRIO as shown

Table 1.2 Threshold values for temperature and moisture.

S. no.	Parameters	Threshold values
1	Soil moisture content	50% of Moisture Value
2	Soil temperature	Up to 30° C

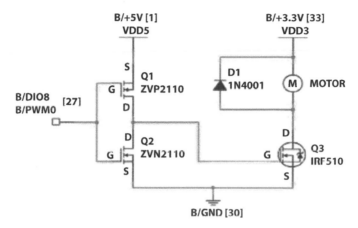

Figure 1.3 Circuit diagram of DC MOTOR.

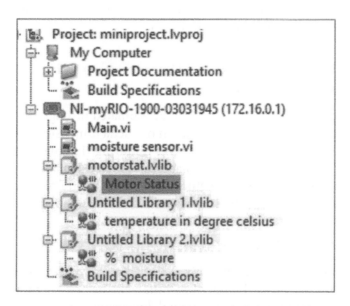

Figure 1.4 Project explorer window showing the network shared variables.

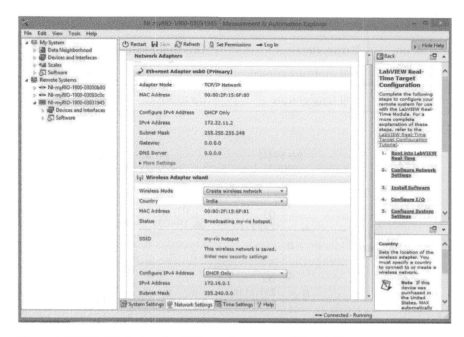

Figure 1.5 NI MAX window for Wi-Fi configuration on NI-myRIO.

in Figure 1.5. The NI Measurement and Automation Explorer provide a facility for configuring on-board Wi-Fi on NI myRIO. After the configuration of Wi-Fi, myRIO can be disconnected from the host computer and deployed to work as a stand-alone system.

1.3.4   Physical Characteristics Determination Using Image Processing

The physical characteristics of soil can be estimated through simple image processing techniques by the estimation of fractal dimension. As depicted in Figure 1.6 image processing involves capturing the images of the soil and converting them into binary images, and then calculating the average value using the box-counting method. The computed fractal dimension is used to estimate the value of the physical characteristics of the soil.

1.3.4.1   Fractal Dimension Estimation

Fractal dimension is a mathematical descriptor of image features which characterizes the physical properties of the soil. The box-counting method is one of the methods to estimate fractal dimensions.

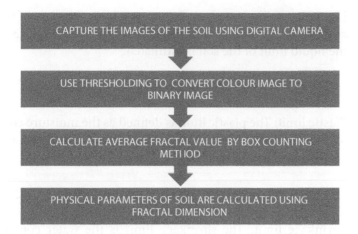

Figure 1.6 Process of physical parameter estimation of soil.

1.3.4.2 Box-Counting Method

The box-counting principle involves counting the number of ones covered by a specified box size in the binary image. It consists of the following steps:

1. Convert the color image to a binary image using color thresholding.
2. Extract the central 3x3 subarray
3. Count the number of 1's in the extracted array
4. Estimate the fractal dimension using the Eqn. [3.1]

$$FD = \log(N(S))/\log(1/S) \qquad (3.1)$$

where, Box size (S–3), Number of one's in that box.

1.3.4.3 Physical Parameters

The following physical characteristics of the soil are estimated to determine the quality of the soil content.

➢ Water content: Water content or moisture content is the quantity of water contained in the soil and is estimated using Eqn. [3.2].

$$w\% = -22.95X^3 + 28.84X^2 + 85.34X - 106.4 \qquad (3.2)$$

➤ Liquid limit: The Atterberg limits are a basic measure of the critical water contents of fine-grained soil using Eqn. [3.3] the liquid limit of the soil is estimated.

$$wL\% = 34.31X^3 - 10.62X^2 + 24.83X - 124.3 \qquad (3.3)$$

➤ Plastic limit: The plastic limit is defined as the moisture content at which soil begins to behave as a plastic material and is estimated using Eqn. [3.4].

$$wP\% = 185.9X^3 - 893.5X^2 + 1428X - 735 \qquad (3.4)$$

➤ Shrinkage limit: The shrinkage limit is the water content where the further loss of moisture will not result in any more volume reduction and is determined using the Eqn. [3.5].

$$wS\% = -144.8X^3 + 669.6X^2 - 1028X + 543.4 \qquad (3.5)$$

➤ Specific gravity: Specific gravity is defined as the ratio of the weight of an equal volume of distilled water at that temperature both weights taken in air and computed using the Eqn. [3.6].

$$G = 27.14X^3 - 127.4X^2 + 198.3X - 99.73 \qquad (3.6)$$

➤ Uniformity and curvature coefficient: The uniformity coefficient Cu is defined as the ratio of D60 by D10. So, when Cu is greater than 4–6, it is understood as a well-graded soil and when the Cu is less than 4, they are poorly graded or uniformly graded. Uniformly graded in the sense, that the soils have got the identical size of the particles and are determined using the Eqns. [3.7 and 3.8].

$$cc = 6.308 \, X3 - 25.73 \, X2 + 33.58 \, X - 13.13 \qquad (3.7)$$

$$cu = 125.2 \, X^3 - 608.7 \, X^2 + 985.9 \, X - 524.8 \qquad (3.8)$$

➤ Field density: Field density or density of field is expressed in lines of force per unit area of a cross-section perpendicular to lines of force and is estimated using the Eqn. [3.9].

$$Fd = -8.046X^3+32.64X^2-42.66+19.31 \qquad (3.9)$$

The formulae used for estimating physical characteristics are shown from Eqns. [3.2] to [3.9] where X stands for the fractal dimension of the image.

Thus, the system computes the features to determine the time to initiate the process of irrigation. This system reduces manual effort, increases productivity, and reduces water wastage.

1.4 Performance Studies

The results obtained from the performance evaluation of our proposed system are discussed below.

1.4.1 Experimental Environment

Figure 1.7 shows LabVIEW VI for interfacing the temperature sensor (lm35) and soil moisture sensor to NI myRIO. The analog output voltages from the sensors are converted to suitable temperature and moisture (in terms of percentage).

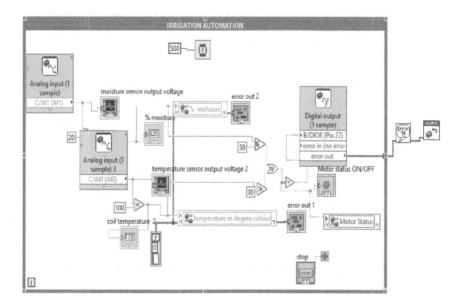

Figure 1.7 Block diagram for irrigation automation by monitoring soil temperature and moisture.

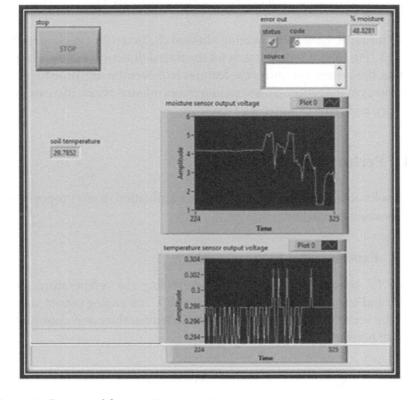

Figure 1.8 Front panel for irrigation automation.

The optimum threshold values of temperature and moisture are fixed. Any variation in soil temperature above threshold temperature (30° C) and drop in soil moisture content below 50% is detected and it turns on a motor that irrigates the field. The soil temperature, moisture levels and motor status have been configured as network-shared variables.

Figure 1.8 shows the front panel containing the output voltage waveforms of the temperature and moisture sensors. The numeric display of temperature and moisture in terms of Celsius and percentage moisture is also shown across time intervals.

1.4.2   Accessing Shared Variables from NI Data Dashboard

By connecting to the Wi-Fi network configured on myRIO, the values of shared variables for four different scenarios are given as follows and the results are presented in Figures 1.9–1.12.

Figure 1.9 Shared variables (T>30°C)-Motor ON.

Figure 1.10 Shared variables (M<50%)-Motor ON.

Figure 1.11 Shared variables (T<30°C and M>50%)-Motor OFF.

Figure 1.12 Shared variables (T>30°C and M<50%)-Motor ON.

1.4.2.1   Scenario 1

- Temperature above threshold (T>30°C)
- Moisture(M) within optimum range (51–100)%

1.4.2.2   Scenario 2

- Temperature below threshold (T<30°C)
- Moisture(M) outside optimum range (0-50)% (motor on)

1.4.2.3   Scenario 3

- Temperature and moisture within optimum range (T<30°C and M>50%)

1.4.2.4   Scenario 4

- Temperature and moisture outside the optimum range (T>30°C and M<50%)

The various values of temperature, moisture of soil, and motor status are shown in Table 1.3. It is obvious that motor is on when threshold conditions are violated.

Table 1.3 Tabulation of results for irrigation automation.

S. no.	Temperature (°C)	Moisture (%)	Motor status
1	32.715	60.059	ON
2	28.9	39.355	ON
3	28.8	85.93	OFF
4	30.762	33.105	OFF

1.5 Image Processing to Determine Physical Characteristics

The images of different soil samples, collected from various fields are processed using LabVIEW. The alluvial and red soil samples that were considered for analysis to determine physical characteristics are shown in Figure 1.13 (a) and (b).

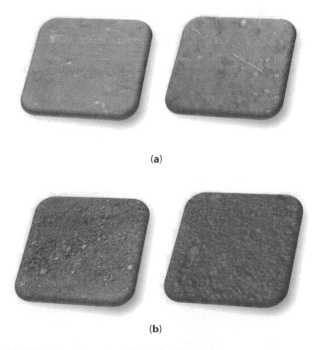

(a)

(b)

Figure 1.13 (a) Alluvial soil samples. (b) Red soil samples.

Figure 1.14 shows the LabVIEW VI for Image processing. As discussed, image processing involves reading the images of the soil and conversion to binary, and then applying the box-counting method to calculate the average value. The computed fractal dimension is used to estimate the value of the physical characteristics of the soil.

Figure 1.15 shows the results obtained on applying color thresholding to the image. The entire image has been converted into an array of pixels. The resized subarray shown is used for fractal dimension estimation by the box-counting method.

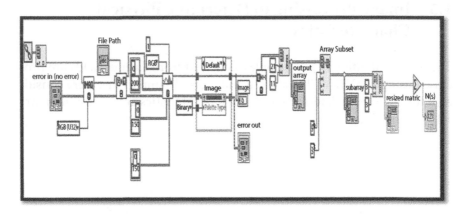

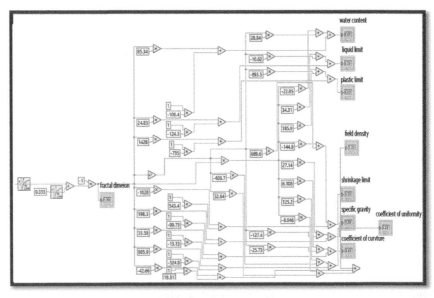

Figure 1.14 LabVIEW VI for image processing.

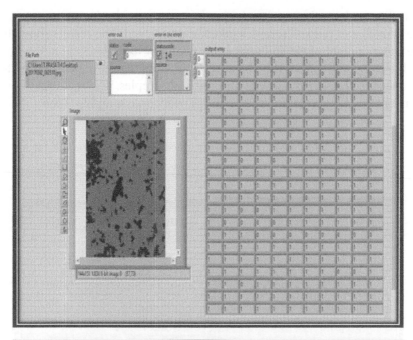

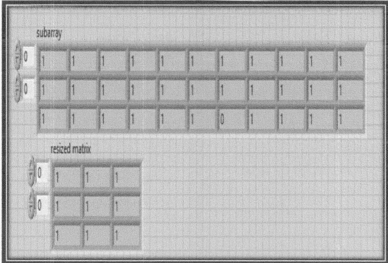

Figure 1.15 Front panel of color thresholding and subarray extraction.

In Figure 1.16, the results obtained for various physical parameters of the alluvial and red soil samples taken are displayed. The results show that the water content of the soil samples is relatively low.

Tables 1.4 and 1.5 list the physical parameters that have been estimated by image processing of alluvial and red soil samples. The readings shown were obtained by averaging the readings over three samples taken.

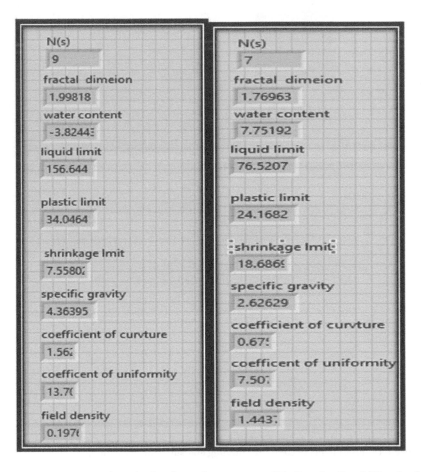

Figure 1.16 Front panel results for physical parameters of (i) alluvial soil and (ii) red soil.

Table 1.4 Physical characteristics of alluvial soil.

Soil tested: alluvial soil		
S. no.	Physical characteristic	Value obtained (averaged over 3 samples)
1	Fractal Dimension (FD)	1.57
2	Water content (%w)	4.39
3	Liquid limit (%l)	66.79
4	Plastic limit (%p)	25.18
5	Shrinkage limit (%S)	16.08
6	Specific gravity (G)	3.06
7	Coefficient of curvature (CC)	1.02
8	Coefficient of uniformity (Cu)	7.34
9	Field density (fd)	1.014

Table 1.5 Physical characteristics of red soil.

Soil tested: red soil		
S. no.	Physical characteristic	Value obtained (averaged over 3 samples)
1	Fractal Dimension (FD)	1.76
2	Water content (%w)	7.75
3	Liquid limit (%l)	76.52
4	Plastic limit (%p)	24.168
5	Shrinkage limit (%S)	18.686
6	Specific gravity (G)	2.62
7	Coefficient of curvature (CC)	0.675
8	Coefficient of uniformity (Cu)	7.507
9	Field density (fd)	1.443

1.6   Conclusion and Future Enhancements

1.6.1   Conclusion

From the results obtained, it is observed that the proposed system ensures enhanced productivity and safety, easier agriculture procedures, and simplified determination of physical characteristics as compared to conventional procedures. This research work focuses on developing a smart agriculture irrigation monitoring system for the Indian scenario.

1.6.2   Future Scope

The performance of the proposed system can further be tuned to accommodate fuzzy-based estimation of parameters to study the rapid changes in the climate. Also, the study can be extended to various regions of the Indian landscape considering the distinguishable challenges of these regions.

References

1. Kadage, A.D. and Gawade, J.D., A wireless control system for agricultural motor. *IEEE Trans. Emerg. Technol.*, 09, 722–725, 2009.
2. Mathurkar, S.S. and Lanjewar, R.B., Smart sensors based monitoring system for agriculture using field programmable gate array. *Int. J. Circuit Power Comput. Technol.*, 03, 339–342, 2014.
3. Majumder, B.D., Das, A., Sur, D., Das, S., Brahma, A., Dutta, C., Development of automated agricultural process monitoring and control technology. *IOSR J. Agric. Vet. Sci.*, 8, 38–44, 2015.
4. Sofou, A., Evangelopoulos, G., Maragos, P., Soil image segmentation and texture analysis: A computer vision approach. *IEEE Geosci. Remote Sens. Lett.*, 2, 394–398, 2005.
5. Ingale, H.T. and Kasat, N.N., Automated irrigation system. *Int. J. Eng. Res. Dev.*, 4, 51–54, 2012.
6. Lanjewar, R.B., Mathurkar, S.S., Patel, N.R., Somkuwar, R.S., Smart sensors based monitoring system for agriculture using field programmable gate array. *IEEE International Conference on Circuit, Power and Computing Technologies*, pp. 339–344, 2014.
7. Gayatri, M.K., Jayasakthi, Mala, G.S.A., Providing smart agricultural solutions to farmers for better yielding using IoT. *IEEE International Conference on Technological Innovations in ICT for Agriculture and Rural Development*, pp. 40–43, 2015.

8. Ram, V.V.H., Vishal, H., Dhanalakshmi, S., Meenakshi Vidya, P., Regulation of water in agriculture field using Internet of Things. *IEEE International Conference on Technological Innovations in ICT for Agriculture and Rural Development*, vol. 3, pp. 113–115, 2015.

9. Baranwal, T., Nitika, Pateriya, P.K., Development of IoT based smart security and monitoring devices for agriculture. *IEEE Cloud System and Big Data Computing*, vol. 02, pp. 597–602, 2016.

10. Gondchawar, N. and Kawitkar, R.S., IoT based smart agriculture. *Int. J. Adv. Res. Comput. Commun. Eng.*, 5, 838–842, 2016.

11. Hu, Y., Shen, J., Qi, Y., Estimation of rice biomass at different growth stages by using fractal dimension in image processing. *Appl. Sci.*, 1, 15, 7151, 2021, https://doi.org/10.3390/app11157151.

12. Senthil, P. and Akila, I.S., Automated robotic moisture monitoring in agricultural fields, in: *The Proc. of International Seminar on Intelligent Technology and Its Applications (ISITIA)*, Bali, Indonesia, pp. 375–380, 2018.

13. Akila, I.S., Sivakumar, A., Swaminathan, S., Automation in plant growth monitoring using high-precision image classification and virtual height measurement techniques, in: *The Proc. of International Conference on Innovations in Information, Embedded and Communication Systems (ICIIECS)*, vol. IV, pp. 564–567, 2017.

14. Kumar, S., Tiwari, P., Zymbler, M., Internet of Things is a revolutionary approach for future technology enhancement: A review. *J. Big Data*, 6, 111, 2019.

15. Alfonso, I., Garcés, K., Castro, H., Cabot, J., Self-adaptive architectures in IoT systems: A systematic literature review. *J. Internet Serv. Appl.*, 12, 14, 2021.

16. Zhao, J.-C., Zhang, J.-F., Feng, Y., Guo, J.-X., The study and application of the IoT technology in agriculture, *3rd International Conference on Computer Science and Information Technology*, Chengdu, pp. 462–465, 2010.

An Enhanced Integrated Image Mining Approach to Address Macro Nutritional Deficiency Problems Limiting Maize Yield

Sridevy S.[1*], Anna Saro Vijendran[2] and Ahmed A. Elngar[3]

[1]*Computer Science, Department of Physical Science & Information Technology, Agricultural Engineering College & Research Institute, Tamil Nadu Agricultural University, Coimbatore, Tamil Nadu, India*
[2]*School of Computing, Sri Ramakrishna College of Arts and Science Nava India Road, Peelamedu, Coimbatore, Tamil Nadu, India*
[3]*Faculty of Computers and Artificial Intelligence, Beni-Suef University, Beni-Suef City, Egypt*

Abstract

Agriculture has become much more of a means to feed ever-growing populations. Plants have become an indispensable energy source and are found to be an important solution to solve the problem of global warming. This chapter presents an integrated approach using image processing and mining to detect, quantify and classify plant diseases from maize leaf images in the visible spectrum. The proposed work can be able to determine single macro nutritional, multiple macro nutritional deficiencies determination, develop an expert decision support system, and analyzes spectral reflectance and RGB intensities of control which may then be useful to restrict the ineffective data to be processed in the design of suitable approaches. The experimental result is conducted on each stage and the result shows the more promising result on this proposed work while comparing the existing approaches.

Keywords: Agriculture, maize leaf, quantify, nutrient deficiency, spectral reflectance

*Corresponding author: sridevy.s@tnau.ac.in

Ahmed A. Elgnar, Vigneshwar M, Krishna Kant Singh and Zdzislaw Polkowski (eds.) Handbook of Computational Sciences: A Multi and Interdisciplinary Approach, (23–36) © 2023 Scrivener Publishing LLC

2.1   Introduction

Traditional agricultural management practices assume parameters in crop fields to be homogeneous, thus the output of pesticides and managing actions is not in relation to the demands [15]. The occurrence of deficiencies in plants is turning out to be an alarming condition in today's agricultural world. As plants become victims of unsettled climatic, environmental, and soil conditions, a nutritional imbalance is observed in these sensitive plants [16]. Precision agriculture integrating different modern technologies like sensors, information, and management systems aim to match agricultural input and practices to the spatial and temporal variability within a field. Thus, better use of resources and avoidance of great differences in yield quality and quantity due to small-scale site-specific differences can be attained. The aim of this study is to diagnose nutrient deficiency in maize with the help of variation in leaf color of the maize crop using Multivariate Image Analysis and Multivariate Image Regression Analysis. Further developing an expert system to give recommendations to the farmers based on the diagnosed nutritional deficiency.

2.2   Related Work

The contribution of several imaging techniques such as thermal imaging, fluorescence imaging, hyperspectral imaging, and photometric (RGB) feature-based imaging are notable. This section discusses existing work done on identifying nutritional deficiency in crops using image processing and image mining techniques.

Mutanga *et al.* [1] reported that phosphorus and potassium elements, which are responsible for both the photosynthetic process and the tissue composition of plants, affected reflection and absorption in the visible region of the spectrum. Bogrekci and Lee [2] reported that spatial variation in actual and predicted maps of phosphorus variability could be represented using diffuse reflectance spectroscopy in the UV, VIS, and NIR regions. Using the visible region of the spectrum i.e., red (500–600 nm) to green (600–700 nm) reflectance ratio Gamon and Surfus [3] suggested that prediction of anthocyanins content was possible. Horgan *et al.* [4] have shown that it is possible to identify a cultivar of carrot roots based on their color and shape using statistical analysis of digital images.

Du and Sun [5] using image segmentation evaluated several food quality assessment methods separating defects and infirmities in the food products. The efficiency of various segmentation algorithms applied for apple defects detection, pizza sauce separation, and detecting touching pistachio nuts was also studied. Puchalski *et al.* [6] developed an image processing system for detecting defects on the apple surfaces such as bruises, frost damage, and scabs from the combination of the images reported an overall accuracy of 96%. Besides, other work by Mizushima and Lu [7] proposed Otsu's method for apple defects detection and support vector machine for apple grading and sorting.

Pastrana and Rath [8] contributed a novel approach to segmenting plantlets suffering from the problem of occlusion, testing with plants having 2, 3, and 4 leaves. This method, by ellipse approximation, solved leaf complexities and found leaf clusters using active shape models. Another study by Cope *et al.* [9] reviewed various computational, morphometric, and image processing methods analyzing images of plants measuring leaf outlines, flower shape, vein structures, and leaf textures proposed a robust automated species identification system that could instigate people in botanical training and working expertise. The efficiency of the system can be increased by having a small number of classes and a restricted set of features improvements

Kelman and Linker [10] proposed 3D convexity analysis for shape and color analysis of the mature apple detection in tree images especially the Golden Delicious apple variety orchard under natural light conditions which accounted for 94% correctness when the edges were identified using the Canny filter. Kamalak Kannan and Hemalatha [11] provided an expert system about agriculture that helps the farmer to cultivate the crops for high yield and gives awareness about organic farming.

Pawan *et al.* [12] instigated the preprocessing of the input image using histogram equalization applied to increase the contrast in low contrast image, K-means clustering algorithm is used for feature selection, and finally, classification is performed using Neural-network. Thus, the image processing technique is used for detecting diseases on cotton leaves early and accurately which will be useful to farmers. Multispectral full-waveform light detection and ranging (LiDAR) instrument prototype was developed by Zheng Niu *et al.* [13] with four wavelengths and a supercontinuum laser as a light source was calibrated to investigate the biochemical parameters and fine structure of vegetation.

The objectives of the study done by Brent *et al.* [21] are to find specific regions of the spectral reflectance response curves of a soybean canopy that show genotypic differences and to determine factors that influence the spectral reflectance response curves of soybean cultivars by the specified breeding process. Vasudev *et al.* [22] in their work introduced the software Nitrate App which has revolutionized the method to find nitrogen content in Maize leaves. The methodology incorporated was to turn the manual process into a software application using image processing. Initially, the image of the Maize leaf is captured and preprocessed to remove the noise of the source image to extract the color and texture characteristics of maize leaves by utilizing RGB and the HSV model.

Ali *et al.* [23] applied a new technique based upon a commercially available hand-held scanner which overcomes the problems. An algorithm was developed to determine the chlorophyll content, using a Logarithmic sigmoid transfer function that non-linearly maps the normalized value of G, with respect to R and B. In [24] Selma *et al.* developed a remote-sensing system consisting of a helium balloon with two small-format digital cameras for the generation of classifiers based on different combinations of spectral bands and vegetation indices from original, segmented, and reflectance images in order to determine the levels of leaf nitrogen and chlorophyll in the bean. Sridevi and Anna Saro Vijendran in their survey [25] provided new insight into the detection of the nutritional deficiency of plants and explored the need for agricultural input rationalization. Besides, by adjusting agricultural practices like fertilizer and pesticide application environmental damage can be reduced to the site that demands profit maximization.

2.3   Motivation

The motivation of this proposed work is to develop an enhanced integrated approach using image mining for determining a nutrient deficiency in the maize leaf. It is performed by adapting proper color space for input images, removing the presence of noise, implementing smart algorithms to reduce the computational cost, and increasing accuracy and reliability by implementing unsupervised learning techniques and analysis to reveal insights into the relationship between spectra and RGB intensities.

2.4   Framework of Enhanced Integrated Image Mining Approaches to Address Macro Nutritional Deficiency Problems Limiting Maize Yield

The proposed architecture of this research work is shown in Figure 2.1. The dataset used in this work is maize leaf images according to the

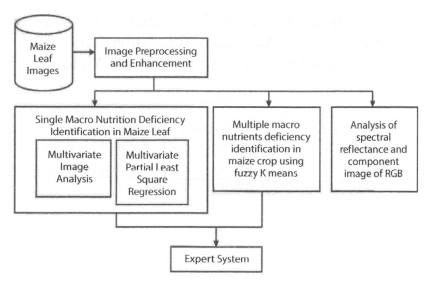

Figure 2.1 Proposed architecture.

recommendation given by AgriPortal of Tamilnadu Agricultural University, Coimbatore [14]. The images are preprocessed prior to the identification of the presence of deficiency. To determine the intensity and color variance near the edges of the objects the given input images are converted to HSV Color Transformation. Histogram equalization is applied to produce a gray map which increases the intensities that can be better visualized on the histogram. To perform better image analysis the important features are extracted using Independent Component Analysis (ICA). With the extracted Features four different phases are deployed in this research work. In the First and Second Phases Single Macro Nutrition Deficiency is determined using Multivariate [17] and Multivariate Partial Least Square Regression Analysis [18].

The third phase concentrates on the identification of multiple macronutrients deficiency which is observed by modeling fuzzy K-means [19]. In the fourth phase, the expert system is developed for end users namely the farmers which provide immediate and instant information on the possible nutrition deficiency affecting the life of maize with the consideration of several known symptoms supplied [20]. The final phase proposed to identify effective spectra ranges and significant component images of RGB intensities which may then be useful to restrict the ineffective data to be processed in the design of suitable approaches.

2.5 Algorithm – Enhanced Integrated Image Mining Approaches to Address Macro Nutritional Deficiency Problems Limiting Maize Yield

The sequence of steps may be as follows:

Algorithm: An Enhanced Integrated Image Mining Approach to Address Macro Nutritional Deficiency Problems Limiting Maize Yield
Input: Maize leaf images according to the recommendation given by AgriPortal of Tamilnadu Agricultural University

Procedure
  Begin
- Read an input image database
- Perform HSV transformation as per the following equation

$$mx_{(i,j)} = max(I_{R(i,j)}, I_{G(i,j)}, I_{B(i,j)})$$

$$min_{(i,j)} = min(I_{R(i,j)}, I_{G(i,j)}, I_{B(i,j)})$$

$$H(i,j) = \begin{bmatrix} \dfrac{60*(I_{G(i,j)}, I_{B(i,j)})}{mx-min} & I_{R(i,j)} > max(I_{G(i,j)}, I_{B(i,j)}) \\ \dfrac{180*(I_{B(i,j)}, I_{R(i,j)})}{mx-min} & I_{G(i,j)} > max(I_{R(i,j)}, I_{B(i,j)}) \\ \dfrac{300*(I_{R(i,j)}, I_{G(i,j)})}{mx-min} & I_{B(i,j)} > max(I_{R(i,j)}, I_{G(i,j)}) \end{bmatrix}$$

$$V(i,j) = [mx]$$

$$S(i,j) = \frac{[mx-min]}{mx}$$

Apply customized Filtering based on Threshold
- Generate Histogram for given input image
- Feature Extraction of image is done using ICA

$$x(t) = Mv(t) = D^{-1/2}E'v(t)$$

$$s(t) = Wx(t)$$

$$p[s_1(t),\ldots,s_n(t)] = \prod_{i=1}^{n} pi[s_i(t)]$$

- If method == Multivariate Image Analysis then
  - Unfold the color and spatial information of the image pixels to configure a matrix of raw data.

$$X_i = r_{(n,m)}, \; r_{(n-1,m-1)}, \; r_{(n-1,m)}, \; \cdots \; r_{(n,m-1)},$$

$$g_{(n,m)}, \; g_{(n-1,m-1)}, \; g_{(n-1,m)}, \; \cdots, \; g_{(n,m-1)},$$

$$b_{(n,m)}, \; b_{(n-1,m-1)}, \; b_{(n-1,m)}, \cdots, \; b_{(n,m-1)}$$

  - Multi-resolution is applied to capture defects and parts of defects, of different sizes with minimum computational cost.
  - T² values of pixels are then computed from the score matrix:

$$T_i^2 = \sum_{l=1}^{L} \frac{t_{il}^2}{s_l^2}$$

  - Post-processing is performed through simple morphological operations.
  - Predicting the Type of deficiency presented.
- Else if method == Multivariate Partial Least Square Regression image analysis then
  - Feature Extraction using standard deviation, variance, perimeter, energy, and entropy
  - Standard Deviation (σ) of pixel intensities in the block is defined as calculated using the function std () in the mat lab.

$$\sigma_i^{n-1} = \Sigma(x - \mu)$$

  - Variance (v) is the square of the standard deviation

$$v = \left(\sigma_i^{n-1} \right)^2$$

○ Perimeter (P) is defined as the distance around the block and computed using the formula

$$P = 2 * (H + W)$$

○ Energy (E) is defined as the sum of squared elements in the image and is also known as uniformity or the angular second moment.

z

$$\text{Energy (E)} = \text{sum } xi^2$$

○ Entropy- It is defined as a statistical measure of randomness that can be used to characterize the texture of the input image. It is calculated using the function entropy () in the mat lab.

$$Entropy = \sum_{i,j} P(i,j) logP(i,j)$$

○ Generate matrix
○ Linear Regression Matrix
○ Generate the diagonal matrix for regression
○ Perform the Normalization Process
○ Find the maximum Covariance
○ Predicting the type of deficiency
○ Suggestion by the expert system to the user
• end if
• If method== fuzzy K means-based macronutrients deficiency analysis, then
    ○ The first level of segmentation is done using k-means segmentation
    ○ Multi-color space-based feature extraction is used to extract the features from the deficient area of the maize leaf image

$$\sigma_i^{n-1} = \Sigma(x - \mu)$$

- o Based on extracted features the deficiency of leaves is classified as nitrogen deficiency or Potassium and Phosphorous deficiency based on fuzzy membership rules.
- o Second level segmentation using fuzzy k means clustering algorithm is used to segment the nutrient deficient part from the leaf images.

$$\mu_f(x) = min\left\{2 - 2\left(\frac{|f-x|}{\lambda}\right)1\right\}$$

- o Nutrient deficiencies are identified using a Fuzzy rule-based system
- if method== spectral reflectance of various macro nutritional deficiencies then
  - o Acquisition of Photometric images reading RGB values to identify spots of control and various deficiencies
  - o Reflectance measurement of identified sports of control and various deficiencies with GER1500 Radio spectrometer
  - o Data Pretreatment and preprocessing for scale correction and outlier removal
  - o Independent t-test to determine whether populations mean of control and deficiency spectra significantly differ
  - o Finding correlation to model the linear relationship between control spectra and R, G, and B intensity values individually.
  - o Finding a correlation to model the linear relationship between nitrogen deficiency spectra and RGB intensity values individually.
  - o Finding a correlation to model the linear relationship between potassium deficiency spectra and RGB intensity values individually.
  - o Infer the significant spectral wavelength and significant image component of RGB intensities of control and deficiency

  end if

End

Output: The type of Deficiency affected the maize leaf

Experimental Results

The experimental process of the proposed Enhanced Integrated Image Mining Approaches to Address Macro Nutritional deficiency problems has been deployed using MATLAB. Control and deficient leaf images are collected from experimental fields of Tamil Nadu Agricultural University, Coimbatore [13]. Totally 60 images are collected from open source. Out of these 30 images are considered for training purposes and 30 images for testing purposes (Figure 2.2).

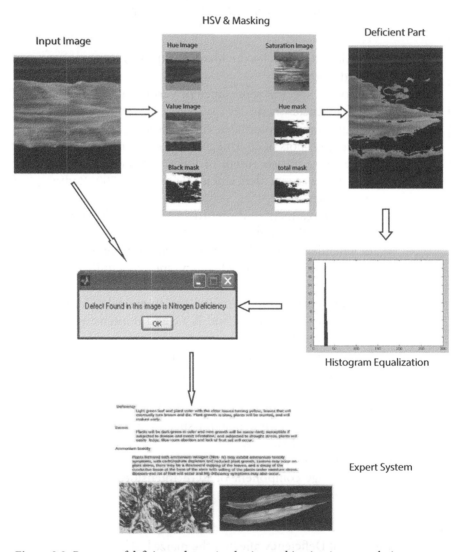

Figure 2.2 Presence of deficiency determined using multivariate image analysis.

In this chapter multiple macronutrients deficiency of nitrogen, phosphorous, potassium, and InV are detected using fuzzy k means shown in Figure 2.3.

The proposed work exhibits Spectral reflectance and component image of RGB analysis reveal insights into relationship between spectra and RGB intensities as in Figures 2.4 and 2.5.

Differences in spectral reflectance of the leaves were highly correlated (r) to red, green, and blue intensity values of nitrogen and K-deficient leaves. In nitrogen-deficient leaves, the highest r value (0.63–0.68) was observed

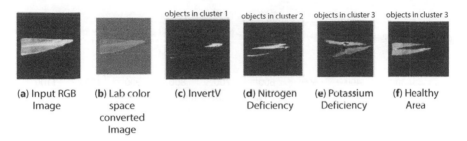

| (a) Input RGB Image | (b) Lab color space converted Image | (c) InvertV | (d) Nitrogen Deficiency | (e) Potassium Deficiency | (f) Healthy Area |

Figure 2.3 Multiple macronutrients deficiency identification in maize crop using Fuzzy K means.

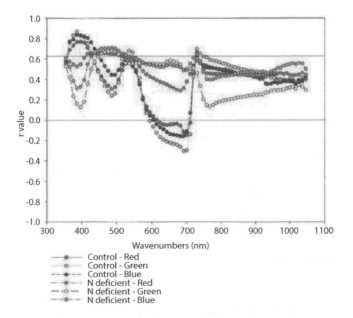

Figure 2.4 Significance spectra range for nitrogen deficiency.

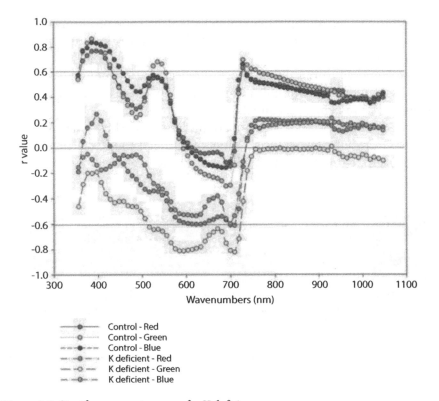

Figure 2.5 Significance spectra range for K deficiency.

in the VIS portion (blue: 420–520 nm) for red, green, and blue intensity values. However, the control leaves had the highest r value (0.63–0.83) from 400 to 420 nm (blue) for red, green, and blue intensity values (Figure 2.4).

For K deficient leaves, a significant negative relationship (R-value: -0.6 to -0.8) was observed in 500–720 nm (green and red) for Green intensity values; however, the Red and Blue intensity values were found to be non-significant for K deficient leaves (Figure 2.5). The control leaves had the highest r value (0.63–0.83) from 400–420 nm (blue) for Red, Green, and Blue intensity values (Figure 2.5).

2.6   Conclusion

The proposed work developed integrated novel techniques to address the nutritional deficiency problems limiting maize yield. This is one of the most essential problems to be solved in agriculture to feed hunger. This work put forth the pitfalls of the early research carried out over the last three decades and solved them by proposing innovative techniques for determining single and multiple micronutrient deficiencies and giving suggestions by developing an expert system. Also, the work is extended to model the relationship between spectral reflectance and RGB intensity values to suggest future research to be carried out in effective spectra ranges and significant component images of RGB intensities which may then be useful to restrict the ineffective data to be processed in the design of suitable approaches.

References

1. Mutanga, O., Skidmore, A.K., Prins, H.H.T., Predicting *in situ* pasture quality in the Kruger National Park, South Africa, using continuum-removed absorption features. *Remote Sens. Environ.*, 89, 393–408, 2004.
2. Bogrekci, I. and Lee, W.S., Spectral phosphorus mapping using diffuse reflectance of soils and grass. *Biosyst. Eng.*, 91, 3, 305–312, 2005.
3. Gamon, J.A. and Surfus, J.S., Assessing leaf pigment content and activity with a reflectometer. *New Phytol.*, 143, 105–117, 1999.
4. Horgan, G.W., Talbot, M., Davey, J.C., Use of statistical image analysis to discriminate carrot cultivars. *Comput. Electron. Agric.*, 31, 191–199, 2001.
5. Du, C.J. and Sun, D.W., Recent developments in the applications of image processing techniques for food quality evaluation. *Trends Food Sci. Technol.*, 15, 230–249, 2004.
6. Puchalski, C., Gorzelany, J., Zagula, G., Brusewitz, G., Image analysis for apple defect detection, detection. *Biosyst. Agric. Eng.*, 8, 197–205, 2008.
7. Mizushima, A. and Lu, R., An image segmentation method for apple sorting and grading using support vector machine and Otsu's method. *Comput. Electron. Agric.*, 94, 29–37, 2013.
8. Pastrana, J.C. and Rath, T., Novel image processing approach for solving the overlapping problem in agriculture. *Biosyst. Eng.*, 115, 106–115, 2013.
9. Cope, J.S., Corney, D., Clark, J.Y., Remagnino, P., Wilkin, P., Plant species identification using digital morphometrics: A review. *Expert Syst. Appl.*, 39, 7562–7573, 2012.
10. Kelman, E.E. and Linker, R., Vision-based localisation of mature apples in tree images using convexity. *Biosyst. Eng.*, 114, 174–185, 2014.
11. Kamalak Kannan, P. and Hemalatha, K., Agro genius: An emergent expert system for querying agricultural clarification using data mining technique. *Int. J. Eng. Sci.*, 1, 11, 34–39, December 2012.
12. Warne, P.P. and Ganorkar, S.R., Detection of diseases on cotton leaves using K-mean clustering. *Int. Res. J. Eng. Technol. (IRJET)*, 2, 4, 425–431, 2015.

13. Niu, Z., Xu, Z., Sun, G., Huang, W., Wang, L., Feng, M., Li, W., He, W., Gao, S., Design of a new multispectral waveform LiDAR instrument to monitor vegetation. *IEEE Geosci. Remote Sens. Lett.*, 2, 7, 1506–1510, 2015.

14. http://agritech.tnau.ac.in.

15. Steiner, U., Bürling, K., Oerke, E.C., Sensor use in plant protection. *Gesunde Pflanzen*, 60, 131–141, 2008.

16. Nisale, S.S., Bharambe, C.J., More, V.N., Detection and analysis of deficiencies in groundnut plant using geometric moments, World Academy of Science, Engineering and Technology, *International Journal of Agricultural and Biosystems Engineering*, 5, 10, 608–612, 2011.

17. Sridevy, S. and Vijendran, A.S., Analysis of maize crop leaf using multivariate image analysis for identifying soil deficiency. *Res. J. Appl. Sci. Eng. Technol.*, 8, 19, 2071–2081, 2014, ©Maxwell Scientific Organization.

18. Sridevy, S. and Vijendran, A.S., Maize leaf deficiency identification using multivariate partial least square regression. *Int. J. Appl. Eng. Res.*, 10, 8, 19441–19456, 2015, ©Research India Publications.

19. Sridevy, S. and Vijendran, A.S., *Multiple macro nutrients deficiency identification in maize crop using fuzzy K means*, Article in Press. *Int. J. Chem. Stud.*, 8, 6, 587–593, 2020.

20. Sridevy, S. and Vijendran, A.S., An evolving expert system for maize plant nutrient deficiency using image processing technique. *Int. J. Sci. Res., (IJSR)*, 5, 2, 70–77, 2016.

21. Christenson, B.S., Schapaugh Jr., W.T., An, N., Price, K.P., Fritz, A.K., Characterizing changes in soybean spectral response curves with breeding advancements. *Crop Sci.*, 54, 1585–1597, April 2015.

22. Sunagar, V., Kattimani, P., Padasali, V., Neetha, Estimation of nitrogen content in leaves using image processing. *Hiremath Proceedings of International Conference on Advances in Engineering & Technology*, Goa, India, 20th April-2014.

23. Ali, M.M., Al-Ani, A., Eamus, D., Tan, D.K.Y., A new image processing based technique to determine chlorophyll in plants. *American-Eurasian J. Agric. Environ. Sci.*, 12, 10, 1323–1328, 2012, © IDOSI Publications, 2012.

24. Abrahão, S.A., de Assis de Carvalho Pinto, F., de Queiroz, D.M., TerraSantos, N., de Souza, J.E., Determination of nitrogen and chlorophyll levels in bean-plant leaves by using spectral vegetation bands and indices. *Revista Ciência Agronômica*, 44, 3, 464–473, 2013.

25. Sridevy, S. and Vijendran, A.S., Survey report on image processing in agriculture. *Int. J. Inf. Technol., (IREIT)*, 3, 4, 1551–1560, 2015.

3

Collaborative Filtering Skyline (CFS) for Enhanced Recommender Systems

Shobana G.[1] and Ahmed A. Elngar[2]*

[1]Department of Information Technology, Sri Krishna College of Engineering and Technology, Kuniamuthur, Coimbatore, India
[2]Faculty of Computers and Artificial Intelligence, Beni-Suef University, Beni-Suef City, Egypt

Abstract

Collaborative filtering (CF) systems exploit previous ratings and similarity in user behavior to recommend the top-k objects/records which are potentially most interesting to the user assuming a single score per object. However, in various applications, a record (e.g., hotel) may be rated on several attributes (value, service, etc.), in which case simply returning the ones with the highest overall scores fails to capture the individual attribute characteristics and accommodate different selection criteria. To enhance the flexibility of CF, we propose Collaborative Filtering Skyline (CFS), a general framework that combines the advantages of CF with those of the skyline operator. CFS generates a personalized skyline for each user based on scores of other users with similar behavior. The personalized skyline includes objects that are good in certain aspects and eliminates the ones that are not interesting in any attribute combination. Although the integration of skylines and CF has several attractive properties, it also involves rather expensive computations. We face this challenge through a comprehensive set of algorithms and optimizations that reduce the cost of generating personalized skylines. We propose the top-k personalized skyline, where the user specifies the required output cardinality. We propose to Create an online web application to allow users to log in, view, search and upload videos. The videos can be uploaded by any user under different categories with a brief description of the movie. The purpose of this module is to form the base application for which we will apply the concept of skyline-based recommendation. We will allow the users to rate the movies on the site based on different attributes. The attribute ratings are

*Corresponding author: elngar_7@yahoo.co.uk

Ahmed A. Elgnar, Vigneshwar M, Krishna Kant Singh and Zdzislaw Polkowski (eds.) Handbook of Computational Sciences: A Multi and Interdisciplinary Approach, (37–68) © 2023 Scrivener Publishing LLC

collected for each user for each movie and stored in the database for later analysis. The rating data forms the basis of data collection for this project. This data is then analyzed to allow the recommendation system to finalize the recommendation list of items. By applying the concept of skylines, the skyline items for each attribute are computed for the logged-in user. The personalized skylines are computed. To be able to finalize the recommendation list by computing the top personalized skylines. The top list will differ for each user. Based on skyline computation results, the list of movies to be recommended are generated and displayed to the logged-in user.

Keywords: KE – Knowledge engineering, CF – Collaborative Filtering, CFS – Collaborative Filtering Skyline, ESC – exact Skyline Computation, ASC – Approximate skyline computation, D&C – Divide and conquer, BNL – Block nested loops

3.1 Introduction and Objective

Knowledge Engineering (KE) is an engineering discipline that involves integrating knowledge into computer systems in order to solve complex problems normally requiring a high level of human expertise. Knowledge engineering is a field within artificial intelligence that develops knowledge-based systems. Such systems are computer programs that contain large amounts of knowledge, rules, and reasoning mechanisms to provide solutions to real-world problems [1].

A major form of a knowledge-based system is an expert system, one designed to emulate the reasoning processes of an expert practitioner (i.e. one having performed in a professional role for very many years).

Collaborative filtering (CF) is the process of filtering information or patterns using techniques involving collaboration among multiple agents, viewpoints, data sources, etc. Popular CF systems include those of Amazon and Netflix, for recommending books and movies, respectively. Such systems maintain a database of scores entered by users for records/objects (books, movies) that they have rated [2].

Given an active user ul looking for an interesting object, these systems usually take two steps:

1. Retrieve users who have similar rating patterns with ul.
2. Utilize their cores to return the top-k records that are potentially most interesting to ul. Conventional CF assumes a single score per object.

However, in various applications, a record may involve several attributes. As our running example, we use Trip Advisor (www.tripadvisor.com), a site that maintains hotel reviews written by travelers. Each review rates a hotel on features such as Service, Cleanliness, and Value (the score is an integer between 1 and 5). The existence of multiple attributes induces the need to distinguish the concepts of scoring patterns and selection criteria. For instance, if two users um and un have visited the same set of hotels and have given identical scores on all dimensions, their scoring patterns are indistinguishable [3]. On the other hand, they may have different selection criteria; e.g., service may be very important to business travelers um, whereas un is more interested in good value for selecting a hotel for her/his vacation.

A typical CF system cannot differentiate between the two users and based on their identical scoring patterns would likely make the same recommendations to both. To overcome this problem, the system could ask each user for an explicit preference function that weights all attributes according to her/his choice criteria and produces a single score per hotel. Such a function would set apart um and un but would also incur information loss due to the replacement of individual ratings (on each dimension) with a single value. For instance, two (overall) scores (by two distinct users) for a hotel may be the same, even though the ratings on every attribute are rather different [4]. Furthermore, in practice, casual users may not have a clear idea about the relative importance of the various attributes. Even if they do, it may be difficult to express it using a mathematical formula. Finally, their selection criteria may change over time depending on the purpose of the travel (e.g., business or vacation).

3.1.1   Objective

(i)   To develop a user recommendation system based on collaborative filtering.

(ii)   To provide optimized recommendations by applying the concept of skylines to collaborative filtering.

(iii)   To give weightage to the individual attributes of a user's rating and not just the overall score.

(iv)   To use the Exact Skyline computation algorithm and Approximate Skyline Computation (ASC) algorithm to implement the recommendation system.

3.2   Motivation

Motivated by the above observations, we apply the concept of skylines to collaborative filtering. A record (in our example, a hotel) ri dominates another rj (ri; rj), if and only if ri is not worse than rj on any dimension, and it is better than rj on at least one attribute. This implies that ri is preferable to rj according to any preference function which is monotone on all attributes. The skyline contains all non-dominated records. Continuing the running example, assume that the system maintains the average rating for each hotel on every attribute. A traveler could only select hotels that belong to the skyline (according to the attributes of her/his choice). The rest can be eliminated, since for each hotel that is not in the skyline, there is at least another, which is equal or better on all aspects, independently of the preference function. In other words, the skyline allows the clients to make their own choices, by including hotels that are good on certain aspects and removing the ones that are not interesting on any attribute combination.

So far, our example assumes a single skyline computed using the average scores per attribute. However, replacing the distinct scores with a single average per dimension contradicts the principles of CF because it does not take into account the individual user characteristics and their similarities. To solve this problem, we propose collaborative filtering skyline (CFS), a general framework that generates a personalized skyline, Skyl, for each active user ul based on scores of other users with similar scoring patterns. Let si;m be the score of user um for record (e.g., hotel) ri; si;m is a vector of values, each corresponding to an attribute of ri (e.g., value, service, etc.). We say that a tuple ri dominates another rj with respect to an active user ul (and denote it as ri > rj), if there is a large number of pairs si;m > sj;n, especially if those scores originate from users um, un that are similar to each other and to ul. The personalized skyline Skyl of ul contains all records that are not dominated.

Like conventional CF, CFS involves expensive computations, necessitating efficient indexing and query processing techniques. We address these challenges through the following contributions: 1) we develop algorithms and optimization techniques for exact personalized skyline computation, 2) we present methods for approximate skylines that significantly reduce the cost in large data sets without compromising effectiveness, and 3) we propose top-k personalized skylines, which restrict the skyline cardinality to a user-specified number.

3.3   Literature Survey

Börzsönyi *et al.* introduced the skyline operator to the database literature and proposed two disk based algorithms for large datasets. The first, called D&C (for divide and conquer) divides the dataset into partitions that fit in memory, computes the partial skyline in every partition, and generates the final skyline by merging the partial ones. The second algorithm, called BNL, applies the concept of block-nested loops. SFS improves BNL by sorting the data. Other variants of BNL include LESS and SaLSa [5]. All these methods do not use any indexing and, usually, they have to scan the entire dataset before reporting any skyline point. Another set of algorithms utilizes conventional or multi-dimensional indexes to speed up query processing and progressively report skyline points. Such methods include Bitmap, Index, NN and BBS. All the above techniques consider that each tuple has a single representation in the system. On the other hand, in CFS a record is associated with multiple scores [6].

In addition to conventional databases, skyline processing has been studied in other scenarios. For instance, Morse et al. use spatial access methods to maintain the skyline in streams with explicit deletions. In distributed environments, several methods query independent subsystems, each in charge of a specific attribute, and compute the skylines using the partial results. In the data mining context, Wong et al. identify the combinations of attributes that lead to the inclusion of a record in the skyline [7]. The sky cube consists of the skylines in all possible subspaces. The compressed sky cube supports efficient updates. Sub-sky aims at computing the skyline on subspaces. Chan et al. focus on skyline evaluation for attributes with partially ordered domains, whereas Morse et al. considers low-cardinality domains. A dynamic skyline changes the coordinate system according to a user-specified point. The reverse skyline retrieves those objects, whose dynamic skyline contains a given query point. Given a set of points Q, the spatial skyline retrieves the objects that are the nearest neighbors of any point in Q [8].

All the above techniques consider that each tuple has a single representation in the system. On the other hand, in CFS, a record is associated with multiple scores. The only work similar to ours on this aspect is that on probabilistic skylines, which assumes that a record has several instances. Let si;m be an instance of ri, and sj;n an instance of record rj. Si denotes the set of instances of ri (resp., for Sj). There are in total jSij _ jSjj pairs (si;m, sj;n). In this model, a record ri dominates another rj with probability Pr½ri _ rj_ which is equal to the ratio of all pairs such that si;m>sj;n over jSij _ jSjj. Given a probability threshold p, the p-skyline contains the subset of records whose probability to be dominated does not exceed p. Pei et al. propose a bottom-up and a top-down algorithm for efficiently computing probabilistic skylines. Both algorithms utilize heuristics to avoid dominance checks between all possible instance pairs [9].

Lian and Chen extend these techniques to reverse skyline processing. The probabilistic skyline model was not aimed at CF, and it has limited expressive power for such applications. Specifically, the system outputs a single skyline for all users, instead of the personalized skylines of CFS. Furthermore, the query processing algorithms are inapplicable to CFS because they prune using minimum bounding rectangles without differentiating between scores of distinct users. On the contrary, CFS necessitates the inspection of the individual scores (and the corresponding users who input them) for the similarity computations. Let R be a set of records and S be a set of scores on the tuples of R, submitted by a set of users U [10].

Given an active user ul 2 U, CF can be formulated as the problem of predicting the score Si;l of ul for each record ri 2 R that she/he has not rated yet. Depending on the estimated scores, CF recommends to ul the k records with the highest rating. Existing systems can be classified in two broad categories: user-based and item-based. User-based approaches maintain the pair wise similarities of all users computed on their rating patterns. In order to estimate Si;l, they exploit the scores si;m of each user um who is similar to ul. Item-based approaches maintain the pair wise similarities of all records, e.g., two tuples that have received the same scores from each user that has rated both are very similar. Then, si;l is predicted using the scores Sj;l of the active user, on records rj that are similar to ri. Common [11].

Similarity measures include the Pearson Correlation Coefficient, Mean Squared Difference, and Vector Space Similarity. Content-based techniques maintain the pair wise similarities of all records, which depend solely on their features. For example, two documents maybe considered identical if they contain the same terms. Then, si;l is predicted using the ratings of the active user on records similar to ri. Note that these techniques do not fall in the CF framework because the scores are not considered either 1) for computing the similarity between two records, as in item-based approaches, or 2) for computing the similarity between users as in user-based methods. Hybrid techniques combine CF and content-based solutions [12]. One approach implements collaborative and content-based methods independently and combines their prediction. A second alternative incorporates some content-based (resp., CF) characteristics into a CF (resp., content based) system.

Regarding concrete systems, Grundy proposes stereotypes as a mechanism for modeling similarity in book recommendations. Tapestry requires each user to manually specify her/his similarity with respect to other users. Group Lens and Ringo were among the first systems to propose CF algorithms for automatic predictions. Several recommendation systems (e.g., Syskill & Webert, Fab, Filterbot, P-Tango, and Yoda) have been applied in information retrieval and information filtering. CF systems are also used by several companies, including Amazon and Netflix. It is worth noting that Netflix established a competition to beat the prediction accuracy of its own CF method, which attracted several thousand participants [10]. Moreover, CF has been investigated in machine learning as a classification problem, by applying various techniques including inductive learning, neural and Bayesian networks and, more recently, probabilistic models, such as personality diagnosis and probabilistic clustering.

Herlocker *et al.* review key issues in evaluating recommender systems, such as the user tasks, the types of analysis and data sets, the metrics for measuring predictions effectiveness, etc. Similar to user-based CF systems, we utilize similarity between the active user ul and the other users. However, whereas existing systems aim at suggesting the top-k records assuming a single score per object, CFS maintains the personalized skylines of the most interesting records based on multiple attributes. Unlike content-based systems, we do not assume a set of well-defined features used to determine an objective similarity measure between each pair of records. Instead, each user rates each record subjectively. 2 CFS permits the distinction of scoring patterns and selection criteria, as discussed in the introduction, i.e., two users are given diverse choices even if their scoring patterns are identical, which is not possible in conventional CF [11]. Furthermore, CFS enhances flexibility by eliminating the need for a scoring function (to assign weights to different attributes).

3.4   System Analysis and Existing Systems

Requirements Analysis is done to understand the problem which the software system is to solve. For example, the problem could be automating an existing manual process, or developing a completely new automated system, or a combination of the two. For large systems which have many features, and that need to perform many different tasks, understanding the requirements of the system is a major task. The emphasis in requirements Analysis is on identifying what is needed from the system and not how the system will achieve its goals. This task is complicated by the fact that there are often at least two parties involved in software development - a client and a developer [9]. The developer usually does not understand the client's problem domain, and the client often does not understand the issues involved in software systems. This causes a communication gap, which has to be adequately bridged during requirements Analysis.

In most software projects, the requirement phase ends with a document describing all the requirements. In other words, the goal of the requirement specification phase is to produce the software requirement specification document. The person responsible for the requirement analysis is often called the analyst. There are two major activities in this phase - problem understanding or analysis and requirement specification in problem analysis; the analyst has to understand the problem and its context. Such analysis typically requires a thorough understanding of the existing system, the parts of which must be automated.

Once the problem is analyzed and the essentials understood, the requirements must be specified in the requirement specification document. For requirement specification in the form of a document, some specification language must be selected (for example English, regular expressions, tables, or a combination of these). The requirements documents must specify all functional and performance requirements, the formats of inputs, outputs and any required standards, and all design constraints that exits due to political, economic environmental, and security reasons. The phase ends with validation of requirements specified in the document. The basic purpose of validation is to make sure that the requirements specified in the document, actually reflect the actual requirements or needs, and that all requirements are specified. Validation is often done through requirement review, in which a group of people including representatives of the client critically review the requirements specification.

   i.   A condition or capability needed by a user to solve a problem or achieve an objective.
   ii. A condition or capability that must be met or possessed by a system to satisfy a contract, standard, specifications, and other formally imposed document.

Note that in software requirements we are dealing with the requirements of the proposed system, that is, the capabilities that system, which is yet to be developed, should have. It is because we are dealing with specifying a system that does not exist in any form that the problem of requirements becomes complicated. Regardless of how the requirements phase proceeds, the Software Requirement Specification (SRS) is a document that completely describes what the proposed software should do without describing how the system will do it?. The basic goal of the requirement phase is to produce the Software Requirement Specification (SRS), which describes the complete external behavior of the proposed software. Given an active user ul looking for an interesting object, these systems usually take two steps:

   (i)   retrieve users who have similar rating patterns with ul;

(ii)   utilize their scores to return the top-k records that are potentially most interesting to ul

Conventional CF assumes a single score per object. However, in various applications a record may involve several attributes. As an example, consider a site that maintains hotel reviews written by travelers. Each review rates a hotel on features such as Service, Cleanliness, and Value (the score is an integer between 1 and 5). The existence of multiple attributes induces the need to distinguish the concepts of scoring patterns and selection criteria. For instance, if two users um and un have visited the same set of hotels and have given identical scores on all dimensions, their scoring patterns are indistinguishable. On the other hand, they may have different selection criteria; e.g., service may be very important to business travelers um, whereas un is more interested in good value for selecting a hotel for her/his vacation.

A typical CF system cannot differentiate between the two users and based on their identical scoring patterns would likely make the same recommendations to both. To overcome this problem, the system could ask each user for an explicit preference function that weighs all attributes according to her/his choice criteria and produces a single score per hotel. Such a function would set apart um and un but would also incur information loss due to the replacement of individual ratings (on each dimension) with a single value. For instance, two (overall) scores (by two distinct users) for a hotel may be the same, even though the ratings on every attribute are rather different [7]. Furthermore, in practice, casual users may not have a clear idea about the relative importance of the various attributes. Even if they do, it may be difficult to express it using a mathematical formula. Finally, their selection criteria may change over time depending on the purpose of the travel (e.g., business or vacation).

3.4.1   Drawbacks

- A record may involve several attributes.
- cannot differentiate between the two users with equal scores
- Incur information loss due to the replacement of individual ratings (on each dimension) with a single value.
- Casual users may not have a clear idea about the relative importance of the various attributes.
- Difficult to express it using a mathematical formula.
- Their selection criteria may change over time depending on the purpose of the travel (e.g., business or vacation).

3.5   Proposed System

Motivated by the above observations, we apply the concept of skylines to collaborative filtering. A record (in our example, a hotel) ri dominates another rj (ri;rj), if and only if ri is not worse than rj on any dimension, and it is better than rj on at least one attribute. This implies that ri is preferable to rj according to any preference function which is monotone on all attributes. The skyline contains all non-dominated records. Continuing the running example, assume that the system maintains the average rating for each hotel on every attribute. A traveler could only select hotels that belong to the skyline (according to the attributes of her/his choice). The rest can be eliminated, since, for each hotel that is not in the skyline, there is at least another, which is equal or better in all aspects, independently of the preference function. In other words, the skyline allows the clients to make their own choices, by including hotels that are good in certain aspects and removing the ones that are not interesting on any attribute combination.

3.5.1   Feasibility Study

The feasibility of the project is analyzed in this phase and business proposal is put forth with a very general plan for the project and some cost estimates. During system analysis the feasibility study of the proposed system is to be carried out. This is to ensure that the proposed system is not a burden to the company. For feasibility analysis, some understanding of the major requirements for the system is essential. Three key considerations involved in the feasibility analysis are

    (i)   Economical Feasibility
    (ii) Operational Feasibility
    (iii) Technical Feasibility

3.5.2   Economic Feasibility

This study is carried out to check the economic impact that the system will have on the organization. The amount of fund that the company can pour into the research and development of the system is limited. The expenditures must be justified. The developed system is well within the budget and feasible. It is normal for every organization to choose a system development only if there is a gain with respect to time and cost overhead. In the economic feasibility, the development cost of the system is evaluated weighing it against the ultimate benefit derived from the new system. It is found that the benefit that occurred from the new system is more than that cost and time involved in its development.

3.5.3   Operational Feasibility

The development of the system was started because of the requirements put forward by the management of the concerned end user. This system handles a large amount of data in an optimized way and does not need any user intervention. So, it is sure that the system developed is operationally feasible.

3.5.4   Technical Feasibility

Technical feasibility includes risk, resource availability, and technologies. Technical feasibility is the most difficult area to assess at the earlier stage of the system development process. Therefore, the process of analysis and definition of the proposed system was conducted in parallel with the assessment of technical feasibility. Since the misjudgment at this stage will be disastrous a cynical attitude was maintained throughout the evaluation of technical feasibility. The management provides the latest hardware and software facilities for the successful completion of the projects. With the latest hardware and software support, the system will perform extremely well as shown in Figure 3.1.

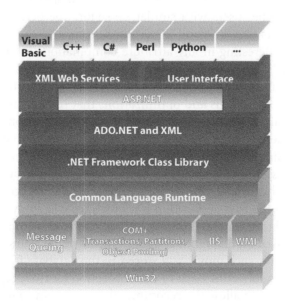

Figure 3.1 Skyline points.

The .NET Framework provides the necessary compile-time and run-time foundation to build and run .NET-based applications.

3.5.5   Problem Definition and Project Overview

Collaborative filtering systems utilize overall scores of other users to return the top-k records that are potentially most interesting to a user ignoring the multiple attributes associated with a user's rating. Applying the concept of skylines to collaborative filtering can improve user recommendation systems and provide precise results.

3.5.6   Overview of the Project

Collaborative filtering (CF) systems exploit previous ratings and similarity in user behavior to recommend the top-k objects/records which are potentially most interesting to the user assuming a single score per object. However, in various applications, a record (e.g., hotel) may be rated on several attributes (value, service, etc.), in which case simply returning the ones with the highest overall scores fails to capture the individual attribute characteristics and accommodate different selection criteria. To enhance the flexibility of CF, we propose Collaborative Filtering Skyline (CFS), a general framework that combines the advantages of CF with those of the skyline operator. CFS generates a personalized skyline for each user based on scores of other users with similar behavior. The personalized skyline includes objects that are good in certain aspects and eliminates the ones that are not interesting in any attribute combination. Although the integration of skylines and CF has several attractive properties, it also involves rather expensive computations. We face this challenge through a comprehensive set of algorithms and optimizations that reduce the cost of generating personalized skylines. We propose the top-k personalized skyline, where the user specifies the required output cardinality. We propose to Create an online web application to allow users to log in, view, search, and upload videos. The videos can be uploaded by any user under different categories with a brief description of the movie. The purpose of this module is to form the base application for which we will apply the concept of skyline-based recommendation. We will allow the users to rate the movies on the site based on different attributes. The attribute ratings are collected for each user for each movie and stored in the database for later analysis. The rating data forms the basis of data collection for this project. This data is then analyzed to allow the recommendation system to finalize the recommendation list of items. By applying the concept of skylines, the skyline items for each attribute are computed for the logged-in user. The personalized skylines are computed. To be able to finalize the recommendation list by computing the top personalized skylines. The top list will differ for each user. Based on skyline computation results, the list of movies to be recommended is generated and displayed to the logged-in user.

We assume records with attributes, each taking values from a totally ordered domain. Accordingly, a record can be represented as a point in the d-dimensional space (in the sequel, we use the terms record, point, and object interchangeably). The skyline contains the best points according to any function that is monotonic on each attribute. Conversely, for each skyline record r, there is such a function that would assign it the highest score. These attractive properties of skylines have led to their application in various domains including multi-objective optimization, maximum vectors, and the contour problem.

All the above techniques consider that each tuple has a single representation in the system. On the other hand, in CFS, a record is associated with multiple scores. The only work similar to ours on this aspect is that on probabilistic skylines, which assumes that a record has several instances. Let $s_i;m$ be an instance of r_i, and $s_j;n$ an instance of record r_j. S_i denotes the set of instances of r_i (resp., for S_j). There are in total $| S_i |.| S_j |$ pairs $(s_i;m, s_j;n)$. In this model, a record r_i dominates another r_j with probability $Pr[r_i > r_j]$ which is equal to the ratio of all pairs such that $s_i;m > s_j;n$ over $| S_i |.| S_j |$. Given a probability threshold p, the p-skyline contains the subset of records whose probability to be dominated does not exceed p.

Figure 3.2 shows a simplified version of the example, where the user component (i.e., the grayscale color information) has been eliminated. Each record instance corresponds to a rating; e.g., $s_1;1$, $s_1;2$, and $s_1;3$ are scores of r_1, whereas $s_4;2$, and $s_4;3$ are scores of r_4. $Pr[r_1 > r_4] = 1/3$ since

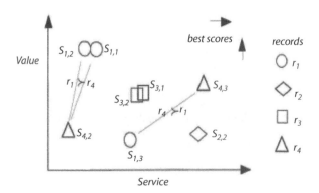

Figure 3.2 Skyline points.

there are two pairs (s1;1, s4;2), (s1;2, s4;2) out of the possible six, where r1 > r4. Conversely, Pr[r4> r1] = 1/6 because there is a single pair (s4;3, s1;3) such that r4 > r1. If p 1/6, neither r1 nor r4 is in the p-skyline because they are both dominated (by each other).

CFS necessitates the inspection of the individual scores (and the corresponding users who input them) for similarity computations. Let R be a set of records and S be a set of scores on the tuples of R, submitted by a set of user U. Given an active user ul 2 U, CF can be formulated as the problem of predicting the score si;l of ul for each record ri 2 R that she/he has not rated yet. Depending on the estimated scores, CF recommends to ul the k records with the highest rating.

Table 3.1 summarizes the frequently used symbols. Let R be the set of records and U the set of users in the system. The score si;m of a user um € U on a record ri € R is a vector of values3 (si;m[1], . . . , si;m[d]), each corresponding to a rating on a dimension of ri. Without loss of generality, we assume that higher scores on attributes are preferable. Any exact algorithm for computing personalized skylines should exhaustively consider all pairs of records: it is not possible to ignore a record during processing even if it is dominated because that particular record may be needed to exclude another record from the personalized skyline through another

Table 3.1 Symbols in algorithm.

Symbol	Definition
R	record set, $R = \{r_j\}$
U	user set, $U = \{u_m\}$
$s_{i,m}$	score on r_i given by u_m ($s_{i,m}[1],...,s_{i,m}[d]$)
$w_{m,n}^l$	weight of ($s_{i,m} \succ s_{j,n}$) with respect to u_l
$\sigma(u_m, u_n)$	similarity between users u_m and u_n
S_i	score set for record r_i
R_m	records reviewed by user u_m
$s_{i,m} \succ s_{j,n}$	dominance relationship between two scores
$r_i \nsucc r_j$	personalized dominance between r_i and r_j wrt u_l
θ_l	dominance threshold for user u_l
Sky_l	skyline set for u_l

personalized dominance relationship. Thus, optimizations proposed in traditional skyline algorithms, where transitivity holds, cannot be applied to our scenario. Instead, in the following, we present specialized algorithms for personalized skyline computation.

3.5.7   Exact Skyline Computation

Figure 3.3 illustrates the basic functionality of Exact Skyline Computation (ESC) for an active user ul. The input of the algorithm is threshold l. Initially, every record ri is a candidate for Skyl and compared against every other record rj. The variable Sum is used to store the weighted sum of each pair (si;m, sj;n) such that sj;n si;m. If Sum exceeds l, ri is dominated by rj and, therefore, it is excluded from the skyline. The set of users who have rated each record is obtained through the record table RT. The scores of these users and their similarities are retrieved through the user UT and similarity ST tables, respectively. Assuming that locating an entry in a hash table takes constant time,5 the worst case expected cost of the algorithm is $O(|Rj|2 \cdot |SAVG|2)$, since it has to consider all pairs (jRj2) of records and for each pair to retrieve all scores ($|SAVG|$) is the average number of ratings per record). Compared to conventional skylines, personalized skyline computation is inherently more expensive because of the multiple scores (i.e., instances) per record; for instance, the block-nested loop algorithm for conventional skylines, which compares all pairs of records (similar to basic ESC), has a cost $O(|Rj|2)$. Furthermore, pruning heuristics (e.g., based on minimum bounding rectangles) that eliminate records/

Basic ESC (user u_l, threshold θ_l) // computation of Sky_l for u_l
1. $Sky_l = \varnothing$
2. for each record r_i in R
3.   for each record $r_j \neq r_i$
4. $Sum=0$
5.   for each user u_m who has rated r_i
6.   for each user u_n who has rated r_j
7.   if $s_{j,n} \succ s_{i,m}$
8. $Sum=Sum + w^l_{m,n} / |S_i| \cdot |S_j|$
9.   if $Sum \geq \theta_l$
10.   skip r_i ; goto 2
11.   insert r_i into Sky_l // r_i is not dominated
12. report Sky_l

Figure 3.3 ESC algorithm.

instances collectively are inapplicable because CFS needs to consider the weights of individual score pairs. On the other hand, for several applications, the high cost is compensated by the fact the personalized skylines do not have to be constantly updated as new scores enter the system. Instead, it could suffice to execute the proposed algorithms and optimizations on a daily or weekly basis (e.g., recommend a set of movies for the night or the books of the week). For generality, we assume that the personalized skyline is computed over all attributes of every record. However, the proposed techniques can be adapted to accommodate selection conditions and subsets of attributes. In the first case (e.g., hotels should be in a given city), only records satisfying the input conditions are considered in Lines 2 and 3. In the second case (e.g., take into account only the service and value attributes), the dominance check in Line 7 considers just those dimensions. Depending on the application, the personalized skylines can be computed upon request, or pre computed during periods of low workloads (e.g., at night), or when the number of incoming scores exceeds a threshold (e.g., after 1,000 new scores have been received). Furthermore, given an incoming $s_i;l$, the CFS system can exclude r_i from Skyl (e.g., a subscriber of Amazon is not likely to be interested in a book that she/he has already read), or not (in Trip Advisor, a hotel remains interesting after the client has rated it).

3.5.8   Approximate Skyline Computation

ASC leads to minimal loss of effectiveness, but a significant gain of efficiency. The main difference with respect to ESC lies in the dominance test between two records r_i and r_j. Instead of iterating over all pairs of scores in S_i and S_j, ASC utilizes samples of size N. We show that ASC provides error guarantees related to N. Figure 3.4 summarizes ASC and the sampling process. Similar to ESC, the algorithm iterates overall record pairs r_i and r_j. However, for every $(r_i; r_j)$, only a sample (of size N) of the scores in S_i and S_j is used to determine dominance. For each sampled pair $(s_i;m; s_j;n)$, the variable Sum is incremented by 1, when $s_j;n$ $s_i;m$. After the sampling process terminates, if the average Sum=N is larger than the new threshold 0 l, r_j is expected to dominate r_i with high confidence. If no record can approximately dominate r_i, r_i is inserted into the personal skyline set Skyl. The complexity of ASC depends on the number of samples created for every record pair $(r_i; r_j)$. If 0 l is high, the necessary number of samples is small, and vice versa. Therefore, the approximate algorithm is expected to be significantly more efficient than the exact skyline computation when $N << |S_i|.|S_j|$ for all record pairs.

ASC (user u_l, threshold θ_l) // computation of approximate Sky_l
1. $Sky_l = \varnothing$
2. for each r_i in R
3.   for each record $r_j \neq r_i$
4. $Sum = 0$
5.   let θ'_l be the new threshold computed by Equation 5.3 and
        N be the number of samples: $N = 2\sqrt{1/\delta}/\varepsilon^2\theta_l$
6.   for each sample
7.   select user u_m with probability
$$|S_j| \cdot \sigma(u_m, u_l)/(|S_j| \cdot \sigma(u_m, u_l) + \sum_{m,n} \sigma(u_n, u_l))$$
8.   generate random number $rnd \in [0,1]$
9.   if $rnd < |S_j| \cdot \sigma(u_m, u_l) / (|S_j| \cdot \sigma(u_m, u_l) + \sum_{m,n} \sigma(u_n, u_l))$
10.   select user u_n with probability $1/|S_j|$
11.   else
12.   select user u_n with probability $\sigma(u_n, u_l)/ \sum_n \sigma(u_n, u_l)$
13.   if $s_{j,n} \succ s_{l,m}$
14. $Sum = Sum + 1$
15.   if $Sum/N \geq \theta_l$
16.   discard r_i
17.   insert r_i into Sky_l // r_i is not dominated
18.   report Sky_l

Figure 3.4 ASC algorithm.

3.5.9   Module Description

3.5.9.1   Modules

i) Movie Site Creation Module
The first module is to create an online web application to allow users to log in, view, search and upload videos. The videos can be uploaded by any user under different categories with a brief description of the movie. The purpose of this module is to form the base application for which we will apply the concept of skyline-based recommendation.

ii) User Community Rating
In this module, we will allow the users to rate the movies on the site based on different attributes. The attribute ratings are collected for each user for each movie and stored in the database for later analysis. The rating data forms the basis of data collection for this project. This data is then analyzed to allow the recommendation system to finalize the recommendation list of items.

iii) Skyline Computation and Movie Recommendation
By applying the concept of skylines, the skyline items for each attribute are computed for the logged-in user. The personalized skylines are computed

using two algorithms ESC and ASC. To be able to finalize the recommendation list by computing the top personalized skylines. The top list will differ for each user. Based on skyline computation results, the list of movies to be recommended is generated and displayed to the logged-in user.

3.5.10   Data Flow Diagram

Figures 3.5–3.8. shows the data flow diagram (DFD) is a graphical tool used for expressing system requirements in a graphical form. The DFD also known as the "bubble chart" has the purpose of clarifying system requirements and identifying major transformations that will become programs in system design. Thus, DFD can be stated as the starting point of the design phase that functionally decomposes the requirements specifications down to the lowest level of detail. The DFD consists of a series of bubbles joined by lines. The bubbles represent data transformations, and the lines represent data flows in the system.

The first step is to draw a data flow diagram (DFD). The DFD was first developed by Larry Constantine as a way of expressing system requirements in graphical form. A DFD also known as a "bubble chart" has the purpose of clarifying system requirements and identifying major transformations that will become programs in system design. So, it is the starting point of the design phase that functionally decomposes the requirements specifications down to the lowest level of detail. A DFD consists of a series of bubbles join by the data flows in the system.

The purpose of data flow diagrams is to provide a semantic bridge between users and systems developers. The diagrams are:

(i)   Graphical, eliminating thousands of words.
(ii) Logical representations, modeling what a system does, rather than physical models showing how it does it.

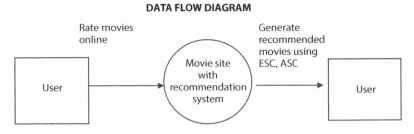

DATA FLOW DIAGRAM

Figure 3.5 DFD Level 0.

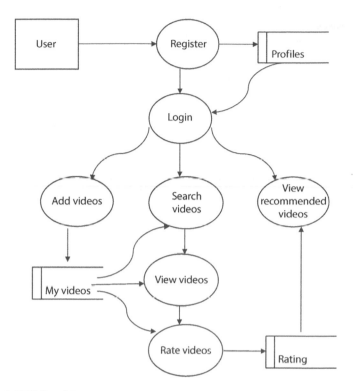

Figure 3.6 DFD Level 1.

(iii) Hierarchical, showing systems at any level of detail.
(iv) Jargon less, allowing user understanding and reviewing.
(v)   The goal of data flow diagramming is to have a commonly understood model of a system.

The diagrams are the basis of structured systems analysis. Data flow diagrams are supported by other techniques of structured systems analysis such as data structure diagrams, data dictionaries, and procedure-representing techniques such as decision tables, decision trees, and structured English.

The data flow diagram (DFD) is one of the most important tools used by system analysts. Data flow diagrams are made up of several symbols, which represent system components. Most data flow modeling methods use four kinds of symbols. These symbols are used to represent four kinds of system components processes, data stores, data flows, and external entities.

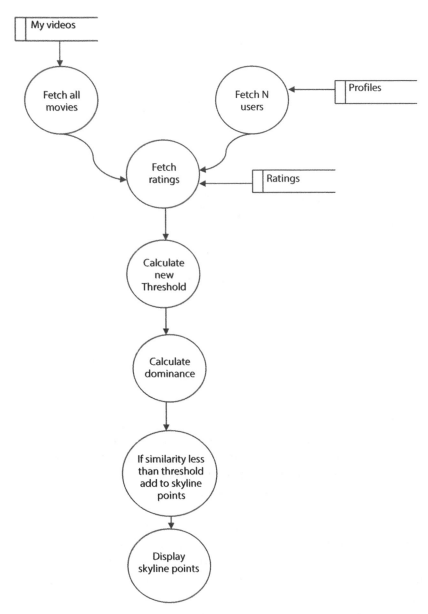

Figure 3.7 DFD for ASC algorithm.

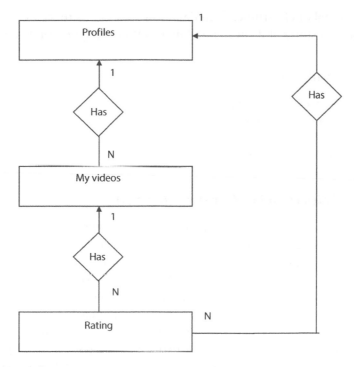

Figure 3.8 ER diagram.

3.5.10.1 External Entity (Source/Sink)

An external entity is a source or destination of a data flow, which is outside the area of study. Only those entities, which originate or receive data, are represented on a business process diagram. The symbol used is a rectangle containing a meaningful and unique identifier.

3.5.10.2 Process

A process shows a transformation or manipulation of data flows within the system. The symbol is used as a circle, which contains the function of the module.

3.5.10.3 Data Flow

A data flow shows the flow of information from its source to its destination. A data flow is represented by an arrow, with arrowheads showing the direction of flow. Information always flows to or from a process and may be written, verbal or electronic. Each data flow may be referenced by the processes or data stores at its head and tail, or by a description of its contents.

3.5.10.4   Data Store

A data store is a holding place for information within the system: It is represented by an open-ended narrow rectangle. Data stores may be long-term files such as sales ledgers or maybe short-term accumulations: for example, batches of documents that are waiting to be processed.

3.5.11   Rules Used For Constructing a DFD

The process should be named and numbered for easy reference. Each name should be representative of the process. The direction of flow is from top to bottom and from left to right. That is data flow should be from source to destination. When a process is exploded into lower-level details, they are numbered. The name of the data stores, sources, and destinations are written in capital letters. Process and data flow names have the first letter of each word capitalized. The DFD is particularly designed to aid communication. If it contains dozens of processes and data stores it gets too unwieldy. The rule of thumb is to explode the DFD into a functional level. Beyond that, it is best to take each function separately and expand it to show the explosion in a single process. If a user wants to know what happens within a given process, then the detailed explosion of that process may be shown.

Circles in DFD represent processes. Data Flow is represented by a thin line in the DFD and each data store has a unique name and a rectangle represents external entities. Unlike detailed flow chart, Data Flow Diagrams do not supply a detailed description of the modules but graphically describes a system's data and how the data interact with the system.

An arrow identifies the data flow in motion. It is a pipeline through which information is flown like the rectangle in the flowchart. A circle stands for a process that converts data into information. An open-ended box represents a data store, data at rest, or a temporary repository of data. A square defines a source or destination of system data.

3.5.12   Basic DFD Notation

Source or Destination of data   :

The process that transforms data flow   :

To represent data storage   :

Io represent Data flow   :

3.5.13   Profiles

No.	Field name	Data type	Size	Constraint	Notes
1	MYID	varchar	30	Primary key	User's ID
2	MYNAME	varchar	30	-	User's name
3	EMAIL	varchar	30	-	User's email
4	LOCATION	varchar	30	-	User's location
5	HOBBIES	varchar	30	-	User's hobbies
6	PASSWORD	varchar	15	-	User's password

The table contains information regarding users registering to the movie website. All the users are expected to register to the site and provide the details like supporting id, name, email, location, hobbies and password which are stored in this table.

3.5.14   Uploaded My Videos

No.	Field name	Data type	Size	Constraint	Notes
1	VID	int	-	Primary key	Video ID
2	USERID	varchar	30	Foreign key	User's id
3	VPATH	varchar	100	-	Video path
4	CATEGORY	varchar	30	-	Video category
5	ABOUTV	varchar	500	-	About video

The table contains information regarding videos uploaded to the movie website. Users are expected to register to the site and upload and watch videos. The video details like video id, user id, video path, video category, and short info about the video are stored in this table.

3.5.15   Rating My Videos

No.	Field name	Data type	Size	Constraint	Notes
1	VID	int	-	Primary key	Video ID
2	USERID	varchar	30	Foreign key	User's ID
3	ACTING	int	-	-	Rating for acting
4	CINEMA-TOGRAPHY	int	-	-	Rating for cinematography
5	MUSIC	int	-	-	Rating for music
6	CASTING	int	-	-	Rating for casting
7	STORY	int	-	-	Rating for story
8	AVGRATING	int	-	-	Average rating for the movie

The table contains information regarding rating of various users for videos uploaded to the movie website. Users registered to the site can rate videos. The video rating details like video id, userid, rating for five categories and the average rating are stored in this table.

S. no.	Test page	Test case	Expected result	Actual result
1.	Login.aspx	Click login without any data	Display entered username and password.	OK
2.	Login.aspx	Click login with incorrect username or password	Display invalid login/password	OK
3.	Login.aspx	Click login with correct username and password	Redirect to home. aspx	OK
4.	Login.aspx	Click on new user sign up link	Redirect to user registration page	OK
5.	Signup. aspx	Enter details and click on submit	Save user details to database	OK
6.	Home.aspx	After form loads	Display video search options	OK
7.	Home.aspx	Select a category and click on search	Display movies in the category	OK
8.	Home.aspx	Type a keyword and click on search	Display movies with given keyword	OK
9.	Home.aspx	Click on rate this video link	Redirect to the rating.aspx page	OK
10.	Home.aspx	Click on view rating link	Redirect to viewrating.aspx page	OK
11.	Rating.aspx	When form loads	Display rating if already rated	OK
12.	Rating.aspx	When users clicks on save after rating	Save the rating details to database	OK

(Continued)

(Continued)

S. no.	Test page	Test case	Expected result	Actual result
13.	Viewrating. aspx	When form loads	Display the rating average and total rating for the selected video	OK
14.	Myprofile. aspx	When form loads	Display the current user profile details	OK
15.	Myprofile. aspx	When user edits data and clicks update	Save the changed details to database	OK
16.	Myvideos. aspx	When user selects video and clicks upload button	Upload the video to videos folder on server and save the video details	OK
17.	Skyline. aspx	When user clicks on ESC link	Redirect to ESC. aspx	OK
18.	Skyline. aspx	When user clicks on ASC link	Redirect to ASC. aspc	OK
19.	ESC.aspx	When user clicks on calculate skylines	Display skyline videos for the logged in user using ESC algorithm	OK
20.	ASC.aspx	When a user clicks on calculate skylines	Display skyline videos for the logged-in user using ASC algorithm	OK

3.6   System Implementation

Implementation is the stage of the project where the theoretical design is turned into a working system. At this stage, the main workload and the major impact on the existing system shift to the user department. If the implementation is not carefully planned and controlled, it can cause chaos and confusion.

Implementation includes all those activities that take place to convert from the old system to the new one. The new system may be totally new, replacing an existing manual or automated system or it may be a major modification to an existing system. Proper implementation is essential to provide a reliable system to meet the organization's requirements.

The process of putting the developed system into actual use is called system implementation. The system can be implemented only after thorough testing is done and it is found to be working according to the specifications. The system personnel check the feasibility of the system. The most crucial stage is achieving a new successful system and giving confidence in the new system to the user that it will work efficiently and effectively. It involves careful planning, and investigation of the current system and its constraints on implementation. The system implementation has three main aspects. They are education and training, system testing, and changeover.

The implementation stage involves following tasks.

    (i)   Careful planning
    (ii) Investigation of system and constraints
    (iii) Design of methods to achieve the changeover
    (iv) Training of the staff in the changeover phase
    (v) Evaluation of the changeover method

3.6.1   Implementation Procedures

Implementation of software refers to the final installation of the package in its real environment, to the satisfaction of the intended users and the operation of the system. The people are not sure that the software is meant to make their job easier. In the initial stage, they doubt the software, but we have to ensure that the resistance does not build up as one has to make sure that.

The active user must be aware of the benefits of using the system

    (i)   Their confidence in the software built up
    (ii) Proper guidance is impaired to the user so that he is comfortable in using the application

Before going ahead and viewing the system, the user must know that for viewing the result, the server program should be running on the server. If the server object is not running on the server, the actual processes will not take place.

3.6.1.1   User Training

To achieve the objectives and benefits expected from the proposed system it is essential for the people who will be involved to be confident in their role in the new system. As the system becomes more complex, the need for education and training is more and more important.

Education is complementary to training. It brings life to formal training by explaining the background of the resources for them. Education involves creating the right atmosphere and motivating user staff. Education information can make training more interesting and more understandable.

3.6.1.2   User Manual

Once the implementation plan is decided, it is essential that the user of the system is made familiar and comfortable with the environment. Documentation providing the whole operations of the system is being developed. Useful tips and guidance is given inside the application itself to the user. The system is developed and user-friendly so that the user can work the system from the tips given in the application itself.

3.6.1.3   System Maintenance

The maintenance phase of the software cycle is the time in which software performs useful work. After a system is successfully implemented, it should be maintained in a proper manner. System maintenance is an important aspect of the software development life cycle. The need for system maintenance is to make it adaptable to the changes in the system environment. There may be social, technical, and other environmental changes, which affect a system that is being implemented. Software product enhancements may involve providing new functional capabilities, improving user displays and modes of interaction, and upgrading the performance characteristics of the system. So only thru proper system maintenance procedures, the system can be adapted to cope with these changes.

Software maintenance is of course, far more than "finding mistakes". We may define maintenance by describing four activities that are undertaken after a product is released for use.

3.6.1.4   Corrective Maintenance

The first maintenance activity occurs because it is unreasonable to assume that software testing will uncover all latent errors in a large software system. During the use of any large program, errors will occur and be reported to the developer. The process that includes the diagnosis and correction of one or more errors is called Corrective Maintenance.

3.6.1.5   Adaptive Maintenance

The second activity that contributes to a definition of maintenance occurs because of the rapid change that is encountered in every aspect of computing. Therefore Adaptive maintenance termed as an activity that modifies the software to properly interfere with a changing environment is both necessary and commonplace.

3.6.1.6   Perceptive Maintenance

The third activity that may be applied to a definition of maintenance occurs when a software package is successful. As the software is used, recommendations for new capabilities, modifications to existing functions, and general enhancement are received from users. To satisfy requests in this category, Perceptive maintenance is performed. This activity accounts for most of all efforts expended on software maintenance.

3.6.1.7   Preventive Maintenance

The fourth maintenance activity occurs when software is changed to improve future maintainability or reliability or to provide a better basis for future enhancements. Often called preventive maintenance, this activity is characterized by reverse engineering and re-engineering techniques.

3.7   Conclusion and Future Enhancements

3.7.1   Conclusion

This project proposes a collaborative filtering skyline (CFS), a general framework that generates a personalized skyline for each active user based on scores of other users with similar scoring patterns. The personalized skyline includes objects that are good in certain aspects and eliminates the ones that are not interesting in any attribute combination. CFS permits the distinction of scoring patterns and selection criteria, i.e., two users are given diverse choices even if their scoring patterns are identical, which is not possible in conventional collaborative filtering. We first develop an algorithm for exact skyline computation. Then, we propose an approximate solution, based on sampling, which provides confidence guarantees.

3.7.2   Enhancements

Further optimizations can be developed for the sampling calculations for the ASC algorithm to reduce the recommendation time calculation even lesser. Moreover, in real-time requirements like Netflix or Amazon, the algorithm can be split into two parts, one which is passive not requiring the live data of the user, and the other activities which depend on the data of the user. This can lead to a considerable improvement in performance.

References

1. Adomavicius, G. and Tuzhilin, A., Toward the next generation of recommender systems: A survey of the State-of-the-Art and possible extensions. *IEEE Trans. Knowl. Data Eng.*, 17, 6, 734–749, June 2005.
2. Balabanovic, M. and Shoham, Y., Fab: Content-based, collaborative recommendation. *Commun. ACM*, 40, 3, 66–72, 1997.
3. Bartolini, I., Ciaccia, P., Patella, M., Efficient sort-based skyline evaluation. *ACM Trans. Database Syst.*, 33, 4, 1–49, 2008.
4. Basu, C., Hirsh, H., Cohen, W.W., Recommendation as classification: Using social and content-based information in recommendation. *Proc. Conf. Am. Assoc. Artificial Intelligence (AAAI)*, 1998.
5. Börzsönyi, S., Kossmann, D., Stocker, K., The skyline operator. *Proc. 17th Int'l. Conf. Data Eng., (ICDE)*, 2001.
6. Breese, J.S., Heckerman, D., Kadie, C., Empirical analysis of predictive algorithms for collaborative filtering. *Proc. 14th Conf. Uncertainty in Artificial Intelligence (UAI)*, 1998.
7. Burke, R., Hybrid recommender systems: Survey and experiments. *User Model. User-Adapt. Interact.*, 12, 4, 331–370, 2002.
8. Chan, C.Y., Eng, P.-K., Tan, K.-L., Stratified computation of skylines with partially-ordered domains. *Proc. ACM SIGMOD*, 2005.
9. Chan, C.Y., Jagadish, H., Tan, K.-L., Tung, A., Zhang, Z., Finding k-Dominant skylines in high dimensional space. *Proc. ACM SIGMOD*, 2006.
10. Chomicki, J., Godfrey, P., Gryz, J., Liang, D., Skyline with presorting. *Proc. 19th Int'l. Conf. Data Eng., (ICDE)*, 2003.

11. Claypool, M., Gokhale, A., Miranda, T., Murnikov, P., Netes, D., Sartin, M., Combining content-based and collaborative filters in an online newspaper. *Proc. ACM SIGIR Workshop Recommender Systems*, 1999.

12. Cosley, D., Lawrence, S., Pennock, D.M., REFEREE: An open framework for practical testing of recommender systems using research index. *Proc. 28th Int'l. Conf. Very Large Data Bases (VLDB)*, 2002.

4

Automatic Retinopathic Diabetic Detection: Data Analyses, Approaches and Assessment Measures Using Deep Learning

Rinesh S.[1]*, Mahdi Ismael Omar[1], Thamaraiselvi K.[2], V. Karthick[3] and Vigneshwar Manoharan[4]

[1]*Department of Computer Science, Jigjiga University, Somali Region, Ethiopia*
[2]*Department of Computer Science, Malla Reddy College of Engineering, Hyderabad, Telangana, India*
[3]*Department of Computer Science and Engineering, Saveetha School of Engineering, Saveetha Institute of Medical and Technical Sciences, Chennai, Tamil Nadu, India*
[4]*R & D and Academic Initiatives, Cybase Technologies, Coimbatore, Tamil Nadu, India*

Abstract

The major cause of vision loss and blindness, diabetic retinal disease, affects millions of individuals globally. Although optical coherence tomography and fluorescein angiography are two well-known screening methods for identifying diseases, most people are unaware of them and do not have them performed when they should. The prevention of eyesight loss, which results from untreated diabetes mellitus among patients for an extended length of time, is greatly aided by early disease detection. The diabetic retinopathy dataset has been subjected to a number of machine learning and deep learning algorithms for classification and disease prediction, however most of them overlooked the element of data preprocessing and dimensionality reduction, leading to biased findings. A dataset on diabetes retinopathy was used in the current investigation; it was obtained from the UCI machine learning repository. After normalizing the raw data using the Standard Scalar approach, the most important dataset attributes are extracted using Principal Component Analysis (PCA). Reducing the number of dimensions is another function of the Firefly algorithm. A deep neural network model is given this compressed dataset for classification. Comparing the model's results to those

Corresponding author: rin.iimmba@gmail.com

Ahmed A. Elgnar, Vigneshwar M, Krishna Kant Singh and Zdzislaw Polkowski (eds.) Handbook of Computational Sciences: A Multi and Interdisciplinary Approach, (69–98) © 2023 Scrivener Publishing LLC

of other machine learning models currently in use reveals that the suggested model performs better in terms of accuracy, precision, recalls, sensitivity, and specificity.

Keywords: Diabetic Retinopathy (DR), Artificial Intelligence (AI), Deep Learning Algorithm (DLA), Deep Neural Networks (DNN), firefly

4.1   Introduction

A thin structural layer makes up the spherical retina, which is situated below the skull. How the retina functions involve the transmission of light through neural signals and coordination of the brain's visual information processing. The retina sits next to the optic nerve, and its central, dark oval region is known as the macula. In 2017, there are an additional 325 million people globally who are at risk of getting Type II diabetes, and this number is constantly growing [1]. Diabetes is a widespread disease that affects a large number of people globally. For diabetics between the ages of 20 and 74, hysterical diabetes, also known as diabetic retinopathy, can result in blindness [2]. Early detection is labor- and time-intensive and depends on trained readers for a good diagnosis. This presents a problem in places where there are typically few professional clinical facilities available. Furthermore, the subjective nature of DR testing methods greatly promotes reading error. In addition, considering the rise in the prevalence of both diabetes and the associated retinal issues around the world [3]. The demand for screening services can outpace manual diagnostic techniques. However, there are still issues with using CNNs in medical research. First, it can be challenging to find enough actual medical photos, particularly those for some rare disorders. Additionally, tagged medical data is often not widely available. Second, because DR characteristics are so intricate, they frequently interact with other lesions, making it difficult to spot DR's tiny lesions in low-quality pictures. Medical publications claim that fundus pictures are labeled manually, which is vulnerable to subjectivity. Third, when a single model is trained with a small amount of medical imaging data and unavoidable image noise, it is challenging to achieve high disease-detection accuracy. DR identification is challenging since lost follow-up, misunderstandings, and delayed treatment have occurred by the time reviewers submit their assessments, which usually happens a day or two later. By looking for lesions connected to the vascular anomalies brought on by the disease, clinicians can recognize DR. Although this strategy works, it has substantial resource requirements. Where there is a high prevalence of diabetes among the local population and DR detection is most necessary, there is frequently a dearth of the necessary knowledge and tools. By utilizing image categorization, pattern recognition, and machine learning, ongoing initiatives have progressed the creation of a thorough and automated DR screening approach. Several techniques that attempted to diagnose diabetic retinopathy have been tried in the past and more recently, in addition to our research. The first publication that was looked at was Development and Validation of a Deep Learning Algorithm for Detection of Diabetic Retinopathy in Retinal Fundus Photographs [4]. The automatic detection of diabetic retinopathy in retinal fundus images using a deep learning algorithm is discussed in this chapter. The data set was first scored by a group of 54 ophthalmologists, who assigned each image a score between 3 and 7, in order to prevent bias. High sensitivity and specificity were characteristics of the deep convolutional neural network. Automated diabetic retinopathy grading may benefit patients by improving early detection and treatment, screening program effectiveness, repeatability, and coverage, and eliminating access obstacles. There has to be a way to recognize referable diabetic retinopathy in order to increase the clinical utility of automated grading. Automated classification of diabetic retinopathy is one problem that has benefited from the application of machine learning, a branch of computer science that concentrates on teaching computers to recognize patterns in data. A sizable portion of research, however, has concentrated on "feature-engineering," which entails computing explicit features that are specified by specialists to develop algorithms intended to detect particular lesions or predict the presence of any degree of diabetic retinopathy [5]. Following these principles, picture preprocessing and classification move forward to boost the accuracy of the subsequent procedures. Beginning with the conversion of the specified image features to gray scale, the preprocessing of the image prepares it for future analysis. The imaging classification processes work to categorize the images in accordance with the features listed, producing the intended outcomes. The given retina image for the study considering diabetic retinopathy may be broken into numerous tiny sub-images for [6] the image-based techniques. For the purpose of acquiring improved images and correct data, noise reduction is also a part of the process. In order to reduce the necessity for such engineering, deep learning uses a vast data set of labeled samples to extract the most predictive properties from the photos themselves. This method uses the back-propagation optimization algorithm to show how internal machine parameters should be adjusted to provide the most accurate forecast of the intended image output. The algorithm employed in this study was trained using deep learning to identify referable diabetic retinopathy, and its performance was evaluated using two clinical validation sets.

4.2   Related Work

Fundoscopy, a medical procedure to view the retina, uses a sophisticated array of characteristics and localizations to help diagnose abnormal findings. The ability to recognize anomalies on the fundoscopic images, such as microaneurysms, tiny saccular capillaries outpouching, retina hemorrhages, and rupture blood vessels, makes the diagnosis of people with early-stage diabetic retinopathy extremely difficult. Depending on their study focus and area of interest, researchers have contributed significantly to the subject of diabetic retinopathy. Researchers have suggested and applied a variety of machine learning techniques, as evidenced by the linked work in the fields of medical sciences and machine learning; however there hasn't yet been a deep learning method comparison study for diabetic retinopathy. Thus, while taking into account the outcomes and optimizing for different machine learning methods for DR, the work completed proved to be a revolutionary technique. [7] Research by Rakshitha *et al.* illuminates the use of novel imaging transformation techniques, such as contourlet transform, curvelet transform, and wavelet transform, to enhance retinal images. As a result, their study compares these three picture modifications. Using color multi-scale uniform [8] LBPs (Local Binary Patterns), descriptors on the two advised hybrid and the five common color spaces, Vo *et al.*'s work analyzes discriminant texture properties. The features that were recovered can then be evaluated using the Fisher Linear Discriminant enhanced EFM. In contrast to other investigations, the study in [9] produced a deep learning system for the diagnosis of diabetic retinopathy. For the analysis, just a small subset of the higher resolution images was used. The results demonstrated that deep learning models could detect diseases at the right level of performance while also accounting for financial restrictions. The difference between retina with diabetic retinopathy and the normal retina is shown in Figure 4.1. With a focus on disease grading, the work in [10] introduced adjudication for the assessment of errors in diabetic retinopathy (DR). Deep learning techniques were employed in this process. The kappa score was calculated by comparing the model's sensitivities, accurateness, and area under the curve (AUC).

In the past, efforts to lessen the workload for ophthalmologists and to eliminate diagnostic differences among manual readers involved computer-aided diagnosis of diabetic retinopathy. Computer vision research was actively focused on automated approaches for detecting microaneurysms and reliably diagnosing diabetic retinopathy in patients' fundoscopic images. Previous studies using a variety of high bias, low variance digital image processing techniques were successful in identifying a common strategy for detecting subtle disorders, such as the use of top-hat algorithms to detect

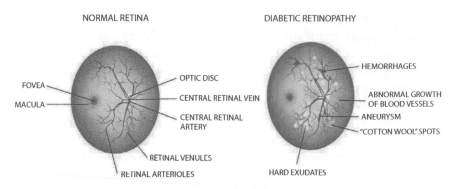

Figure 4.1 A distinction of normal retina and retinopathy with diabetics.

microaneurysms. In addition to Microaneurysms, there are a few other features that are effective at diagnosing diseases. Additional methods for determining microaneurysms and scoring DR, including as supporting vector machines, ensemble-based algorithms, and k-NN, have generated sensitivities and specificities that are 90% or higher using various extraction methods.

Using probability neural networks (PNN), Bayesian classifications, and supported vector machines, numerous researches have distinguished between diabetic retinopathy types NPDR and PDR (SVM). Images of blood vessel bleeding must be assessed using image processing methods and features created when input into the classifiers in order to differentiate between various DR disease kinds. The relevant research makes it abundantly clear that using different machine learning models and analyzing their results are at the heart of most research on diabetic retinopathy. Additionally, it should be emphasized that efforts to improve the safety of the diabetes Dataset of Retinopathy have received less attention, which could result in more precise results It is crucial to emphasize that the dataset's features determine how reliable the results generated by the machine learning model will be. On far larger private databases of 80,000 to 120,000 photos, previous CNN testing for DR fundus images found sensitivity and specificities in the 90% range for average or medium vs. moderate or severe binary categorization groups. However, class aggregation ratios graded for disease serve as a nontrivial foundation for precision measures for detecting four levels of DR, namely no DR (R0), mild (R1), moderate (R2), and extreme (R3). Stages R0 and R3 may reach great sensitivity, but R1 and R2's simulated recall rates are usually low. Experiments using publicly accessible data sets show that the relative difficulty of early-stage DR identification is the main cause of this. Additionally, current accuracies for R1 and R2 points are recorded as 0% and 41%, respectively. By comparing results with data from recently published studies, we will evaluate the sensitivity and specificity of our 4-ary classification model as well as analyze its effectiveness. Numerous studies have also discriminated between the PDR and NPDR subtypes of diabetic retinopathy using probabilistic neural networks (PNN), Bayesian classification, and support vector machines (SVM). The different DR circumstances can be categorized using images of blood vessel hemorrhages that were evaluated using image processing techniques, along with the resulting characteristics that were then fed into the classifiers [11]. It is plainly obvious from the related study that the use of numerous machine learning models and assessment of their effectiveness constitute the bulk of the work involved in diagnosing diabetic retinopathy. It has also been highlighted that initiatives to enhance the diabetic retinopathy dataset's quality, which might result in more accurate results, have gotten less attention. To improve the precision of the predictions made by machine learning models, the dataset's most crucial characteristics should be extracted and relevant dimensionality reduction techniques should be applied. In the current study, dimensionality reduction is accomplished using a two-layered method prior to applying a deep neural network model for classification. The planned study makes the following unique contributions: a) To improve the dataset's quality and ensure that it contains only the most important and helpful variables for training the suggested model; a three-layered, meticulous pre-processing technique is used. b) The time required to train ML-based models is greatly decreased by using PCA+Firefly. PCA seeks to preserve as much variety in a data collection as feasible while reducing the dimensionality of a set of various variables that are correlated with one another [12]. The algorithm transforms the data set's variable quantity into a fresh set of extraneous principal workings, arranged so that as one descends the hierarchy, less variation from the original variables is kept. As a result, there is the most variance from the original components in the first primary component. The main elements of the covariation matrix are its orthogonal eigenvectors.

4.3   Initial Steps and Experimental Environment

The PCA and Firefly algorithms utilized in the proposed model are discussed in this section. Also discussed is the suggested model's intricate architecture.

4.3.1   Analyzing the Principle Components

By lowering the dimensionality of a collection of several variables that are correlated with one another, PCA aims to preserve as much diversity as feasible [13]. The data set's variables are changed by the algorithm into a new set of extraneous principal workings that are arranged so that as one proceeds down the order, less variation from the original variables is preserved. The degree of variance from the original components is therefore largest in the first primary component. PCA requires a clambered dataset, and the approach recapitulates data-producing outcomes that are also complex to comparative grading. The major element is well-defined as a "linear grouping of observable variable quantity with appropriate weights". The outcome of PCA is composed of principal workings with statistics which are either less than or the same as the initial variables. Using PCA on a two-dimensional data set requires first normalizing the data. This is accomplished by extracting the respective means from each of the data set's constituent columns to produce a data set with a mean of zero. The second stage entails calculating the covariation matrix. A matrix of vectors must be created in order to create a feature vector. To calculate the principle components, the left multiplication of the scaled version of the data set is multiplied by the feature vector's transpose. The application of dimensionality reduction in computer vision, facial recognition, and picture compression is encouraged by the PCA idea. For pattern discovery of highly dimensional data, it also has a wide range of applications in data mining, bioinformatics, and psychology [14].

4.3.2   Firefly Algorithm

The "firefly procedure" is a swarm intelligence program that imitates the actions of fireflies in their natural environment. This study offers a brand-new classifier approach based on the firefly algorithm as a supervised learning technique.

Pseudo Code of Firefly Algorithm [15] is the first algorithm.

```
Begin
1) The objective function, f(x), is defined as (x1, x2,..., xd);
2) Produce a firefly population with initials xi I = 1, 2,..., n);
3) Create a formula for light intensity I that is linked to f(x) (for maxi-
    mizing issues, use I f(x) or I = f(x););)
4) Explain what the preoccupation coefficient is

Whereas (t MaxGroup) for j = 1: I (n fireflies) for I = 1: n (all n fireflies),
if (Ij > Ii),
Using exp(-r), vary attractiveness with respect to distance r;
shift the firefly from I to j;
Review fresh approaches and update light output;
ending if ending for j ending for I
To determine which fireflies are now the best, rank them.

end
```

4.4   Experimental Environment

Figure 4.2 shows the experimental setting for the suggested methodology. There are 19 contributing attributes in the dataset used in this study. These properties' values fall within a variety of ranges. This difference in the range of attribute values may cause some cases to be given different weights, which could lead to biased prediction results. The suggested method eliminates this unpredictability by preprocessing with a Normal Scaler method. The standard scaler approach converts the data into a common range in order to remove bias from the forecasts. The rectified data is then subjected to the Principal Component Analysis technique. The primary goal of PCA is to remove useless attributes from the DNN training set. In this work, the feature engineering process is strengthened even more by the use of the Firefly Optimization Algorithm, one of the well-known nature-inspired algorithms. The Firefly approach's key advantage is that it optimizes the parameters to quickly select the best ones while avoiding local minima. Because of these belongings, the Firefly procedure is the greatest choice for feature engineering when choosing the appropriate parameters to speed up training and enhance classification. The dataset is input to DNN for categorization of datasets relevant to diabetic retinopathy after dimensional reduction. The soft sign activation function and Adam optimizer were applied to all layers with the exception of the output. Due to the binary nature of the dataset for diabetic retinopathy, the output layer employed sigmoid activation function to classify the data. Using the Root Mean Square Propagation (RMSprop) error, backpropagation was performed. The dataset was divided into train and test sections in an 8:2 ratio. For each epoch, a batch of 64 data points was provided to the model, of which 80% were used to train the model and the remaining 20% to test it. By doing so, it was possible to delay testing the model after it had been trained on all but 20% of the data.

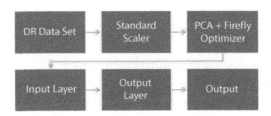

Figure 4.2 DNN-PCA model for diabetic retinopathy.

4.5   Data and Knowledge Sources

The collection consists of 36,125 high-resolution colored fundus images that have been labeled, classified into five classes, and shown in Table 4.1 to demonstrate the different disease phases. 5,000 of the 54,575 total test set photographs were used in this study. The images have been made available to the general public via EyePACs, an unrestricted tool for retinopathy testing. A qualified clinical expert has evaluated each image for the occurrence of diabetic retinopathy on a measure of 0 to 4 [16]. The class distribution in the original dataset for the number of images with the percentage of result is based on the No DR, Mild DR, Moderate DR, Severe DR, Proliferative DR and it is clearly illustrated in Figure 4.3. Different camera models and

Table 4.1 Class distribution in the initial dataset.

Class	Name	No. of images	Percentage
0	No DR	26810	74.48%
1	Mild DR	2543	7.96%
2	Moderate DR	5392	15.17%
3	Severe DR	883	2.58%
4	Proliferative DR	718	2.11%

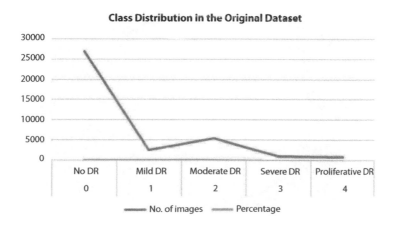

Figure 4.3 Class distribution in the original dataset.

setups were used to take the pictures in the dataset, which could have an effect on how the left and right retinas appear to the eye. In some images, the retina is shown anatomically, with the optic nerve for the right eye on the right and the macula on the left. Others are shown upside-down, much as they would look when examined through a microscope condensing lens during a standard living eye test. There is sound in the labels and the pictures. Pictures may be out of emphasis, contain artifacts, differ in quality, be underexposed, or be overexposed. The dataset's spread of placed heavy emphasis is seen in Table 4.1.

4.6   Data Preparation

The training images could not be used for training directly because of the non-standard image resolutions. To create a dataset that is consistent, the images were scaled down to 512 × 512 pixels of constant resolution. It used a lot of memory to train images with 512 × 512 pixel resolution on all three-color channels. The images were changed to a single channel due to this restriction. Green channel images were found to better preserve information than the other channel images after extensive testing. The photos were subjected to the histogram equalization technique in order to boost contrast uniformly across pixels. Each image was modified using Min-Max normalization to stop the convolutional neural network from detecting the underlying background noise in the image. The trained image with pixel resolution is shown as a unique image and it is illustrated in Figure 4.4.

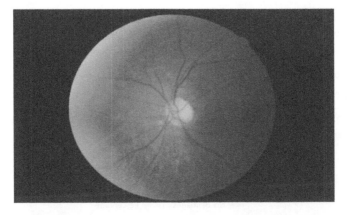

Figure 4.4 Unique image.

4.7   CNN's Integrated Design

The various deep network structures are revealed in Table 4.2. The link has a participation layer that accepts input in the form of 512×512 pixel pictures. The architecture is composed of five sets of convolutional combinations. Combining and dropout deposits are fixed on top of 1 another. Then, two sets of completely interconnected hidden layers with feature pooling are added. Next, the last production layer is used. To reserve the 3-D dimensions of the input and output volumes, zero-filling was applied in the convolutional layer. The Green channel image is given as input to the convolutional layer and pooling layers and the output is obtained as Histogram Equalization shown in Figure 4.5.

A. Constellation Layer
The architectures stack convolutional layers one on top of the other without using any spatial interpolation. As per Andrew Zisserman *et al.* [17], this permits designs with improved depth by broadening the receptive field, increasing the discriminativeness of the decision function, and reducing the number of trainable parameters.

B. Layering Pooling
A 2 × 2 filter and max-pooling were used in each layer of pooling. The input depth slice's 2 × 2 region will be the target of the MAX operation of the max-pooling layer.

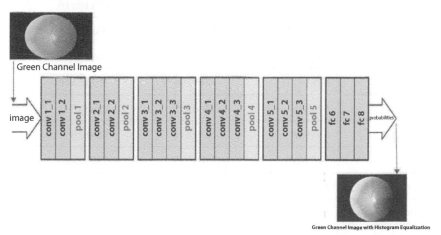

Figure 4.5 CNN architectures.

C. Layer Dropout
In [18], it is suggested that dropouts play a crucial role in reducing over-fitting in large networks and enhancing neural network performance in

Table 4.2 Three models' CNN architectures.

Layers	Model 1	Model 2	Model 3
input	1x512x512	1x512x512	1x512x512
conv 1	16x256x256	16x256x256	16x256x256
conv 2	16x256x256	16x256x256	16x256x256
pool 1	16x128x128	16x128x128	16x128x128
dropout 1	16x128x128	16x128x128	16x128x128
conv 3	32x64x64	32x64x64	32x64x64
conv 4	32x64x64	32x64x64	32x64x64
pool 2	32x32x32	32x32x32	32x32x32
dropout 2	32x32x32	32x32x32	32x32x32
conv 5	48x32x32	64x32x32	64x32x32
conv 6	48x32x32	64x32x32	64x32x32
conv 7	48x32x32	64x32x32	64x32x32
pool 3	48x16x16	64x16x16	64x16x16
dropout 3	48x16x16	64x16x16	64x16x16
conv 8	64x16x16	128x16x16	96x16x16
conv 9	64x16x16	128x16x16	96x16x16
conv 10	64x16x16	128x16x16	96x16x16
pool 4	64x8x8	128x8x8	96x8x8
dropout 4	64x8x8	128x8x8	96x8x8
conv 11	128x8x8	256x8x8	128x8x8
conv 12	128x8x8	256x8x8	128x8x8
pool 5	128x4x4	256x4x4	128x4x4
dropout 5	128x4x4	256x4x4	128x4x4
hidden 1	400	256	256

(*Continued*)

Table 4.2 Three models' CNN architectures. (*Continued*)

Layers	Model 1	Model 2	Model 3
maxout 1	200	128	128
dropout 6	200	128	128
hidden 2	400	256	256
maxout 2	200	128	128
output	5	5	5

supervised learning tasks. From the first to the fourth dropout layers, the dropout ratio climbed steadily from 0.1 to 0.4. The fifth- and sixth-layers' dropout ratios were held constant at 0.5.

Convolutional layers include: conv (number of filters x dimensions of the convolved matrix); pool (dimension of the pooled matrix); dropout (layer of dropout); fully connected hidden (number of hidden units); maxout (feature pooling); and output (layer of output) (output units corresponding to the 5 classes).

D. Layers that are Hidden and Include Pooling Layers

Four hundred units in both of the hidden layers of the initial model were fully connected, but it was only 256 for the second and third models.

E. Functions of Activation

The activation function used for the hidden and convolutional deposits was the leaking rectifier. Contrary to the conventional rectifier has a gradient that is non-zero for undesirable input, which frequently helps with union [19]. The class distribution following the class balancing with different stages of DR like No DR, Mild DR, Moderate DR, Severe DR, Proliferative DR is shown in Table 4.3.

Table 4.3 Class distribution following class balancing.

Class	Name	No. of images	Percentage
0	No DR	25810	35.65%
1	Mild DR	12215	16.87%
2	Moderate DR	26460	36.55%
3	Sever DR	4365	6.02
4	Proliferative DR	3540	4.89%

G. Methods for DR Discovery and Separation

Retinal structures are very useful in identifying diabetic retinopathy (DR). The class distribution for the number of images with the No DR, Mild DR, Moderate DR, Severe DR, Proliferative DR after class balancing is shown in Figure 4.6. In order to identify DR, many techniques have been tried to ascertain the retinal structures on the external of the eye. The methodologies for DR segmentation and identification are thoroughly examined in the next subsections. The DR detection and segmentation techniques are displayed in Figure 4.7 in accordance with the various retinal features.

H. Techniques for Segmenting Blood Vessels

The finding and separation of retinal blood vessels are essential for the identification and diagnosis of several retinal diseases, with age-related macular deterioration, high blood pressure, glaucoma, and diabetic retinopathy (DR). Additionally, when abnormal alterations in the cornea's vascular structure occur, retinal blood vessel detection and separation are crucial in the analysis of brain and heart illnesses. Studies on cornea's blood vessel separation are extra valuable and significant now that non-hostile fundus imagery is available. Figure 4.8 illustrates graphically how blood vessels were divided up and extracted.

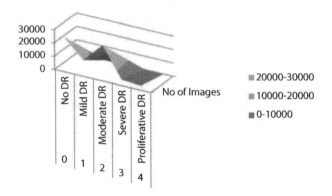

Figure 4.6 Class distribution after class balancing.

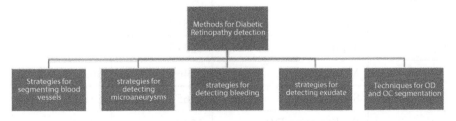

Figure 4.7 Retinal feature-based techniques for DR detection and segmentation.

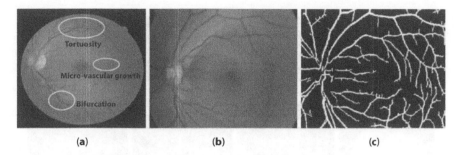

Figure 4.8 Changes in blood vessel structure (a), unique fundus image (b), and extracted vasculature (c) [20].

With the suggested approach, the author addressed augmentation and de-resounding problems by means of performance indicators such the superiority protection index, the operational comparison index, the highest signal to sound ratio, and the relationship coefficient. Cornea separation was also carried out by Leopold *et al.* [21], who gathered a variety of crucial performance metrics to determine the most effective method. With excellent performance, the authors segmented retinal fundus pictures using the Pixel BNN framework. The retinal datasets CHASE DB1, DRIVE, and STARE were used to test the developed system. The computational efficacy and efficiency of the suggested technique were assessed using the F1-score. In order to gradually improve image quality, Mahapatra *et al.* [22] developed a multi-stage assembly for medical image processing based on the trio loss function. The output excellence of the prior copy serves as an entry for the succeeding one in the trio damage purpose. High-quality pictures produced by the request of trio loss facilitate the diagnosis of cornea diseases from fundus pictures. Utilizing challenging datasets in blood vessel separation, X. Wang *et al.* proposed force detection and a arrangement outline for the categorization of Cornea vessels [23].

4.8   Preparing Retinal Image Data

The signs of DR were commonly mistaken for those of other eye conditions because of the complex anatomy of the Cornea. Various types of picture noise, such as low contrast, blurred lenses, black gaps on either side of the eyes, and insufficient light, were also apparent. The poor quality pictures made it difficult to clearly identify several minor lesions. As a result, some pre-processing was necessary. Some examples of low-quality data are provided in Figure 4.9 (b).

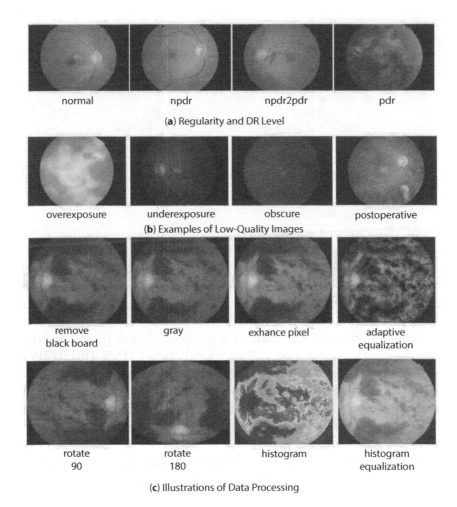

(a) Regularity and DR Level

(b) Examples of Low-Quality Images

(c) Illustrations of Data Processing

Figure 4.9 Examples of the dataset's poor quality and preprocessing images.

An algorithm was initially designed to remove the erroneous black space by deducting a specific number of pixels from each of the four edges for every picture because the black space significantly raises calculation costs. In order to match the input requirements of various models, we standardized the resolution by shrinking each image to the same size. The resolution of the photographs varied from 1631 to 1879 to 1823 to 1650. Additionally, we changed every image to greyscale in order to measure the bright intensity at individual pixel in a solo image. To improve the aesthetic impacts and uncover hidden information in the pictures with unduly brilliant or dim backgrounds and foregrounds, we cast off histogram equalization (HE). We used adaptive HE in each picture region as part of the preprocessing steps to progress local difference and authority delineation, which was previously proposed by Stark [24, 25]. Scientifically, the adaptive histogram equalization can be written as follows:

$$fc(u,v) = q(u - v, \alpha) - \beta q(u - v, 1) + \beta uq(d, \alpha)$$

$$q(d, \alpha) = \frac{1}{2} \sin(d)|2d|\alpha, \tag{4.1}$$

fc is known as an accumulation function, and HE is given if = 0. where 0 and 1. For dim photos, to improve the contrast effect over the entire image, we offered a contrast stretching algorithm. The following equation was used to run this algorithm:

$$I(x, y) = \frac{I(x, y) - Imin}{Imax - Imin} * 255 \tag{4.2}$$

I (x, y) represent the gray value of a single pixel in the original image, while Imin and Imax stand for the actual lowest and highest greyscale values of the actual picture, respectively.

4.9   Performance Evaluation

Figure 4.9 provides samples of dataset in pre-processing (c). The relative test was conducted using Xception. The binary task completed fine for the model. The sole pre-processing applied throughout the model's training was resizing. It was then put up against models that had been trained using every preprocessing technique. Up until 300 epochs, the model's accuracy without preprocessing was 94.79 percent. Even after precise turning, this model's accuracy did not go over this threshold. The model with pre-processing, on the other hand, converged nicely after 220 iterations and reached an accuracy of 95.68 percent. After fine turning, this accuracy rate increased to 97.15 percent (Figure 4.11). Details are shown in Figure 4.10 and Table 4.4.

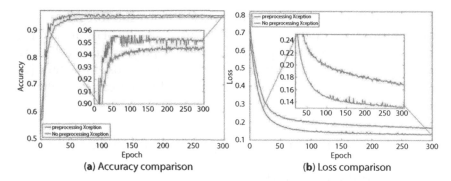

(a) Accuracy comparison   (b) Loss comparison

Figure 4.10 A comparison of the identification system's preprocessing before and after.

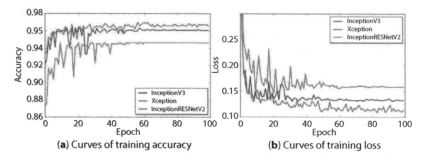

(a) Curves of training accuracy   (b) Curves of training loss

Figure 4.11 The training curves for the identification system's various parts.

4.10   Metrics

We assessed the models' validity and reliability as well as their groups. Trustworthiness refers to the mark of constancy gained through frequent tests beneath the similar situations. It can be evaluated by means of the Kappa worth. A Kappa > 0.8 specifies exceptional steadiness. Legitimacy indicates the grade of conventionality among restrained and real values, which is represented by the six system of measurement which is given in Equations 4.3 to 4.8.

In order to accurately assess the level of DR, a computer-assisted screening method uses machine learning to evaluate fundus images captured under different lighting and field-of-view conditions [26]. An automated system for identifying retinal images and the classification of DR is developed in [27]. Accurateness is expressed as a fraction of samples that were properly categorized. The proportion of accurately foreseen positives is known as precision. The accuracy of the classification of retinal images

Table 4.4 Ensemble metrics for the identifying systems.

Model	Accuracy	Precision	Sensitivity	Specificity	Auc	Kappa	F1_ score	Fβ_ score	Youden's index
Xceptiona	0.9521	0.9491	0.9321	0.9782	0.9551	0.9032	0.9523	0.9503	0.9101
Baseline:Resnet 50	0.9342	0.9333	0.9332	0.9351	0.9342	0.9231	0.9322	0.9223	0.9223
0:Xceptionb	0.9715	0.9711	0.9740	0.9683	0.9712	0.9424	0.9715	0.9712	0.9424
1:Inception V3	0.9354	0.9454	0.9454	0.9454	0.9354	0.9454	0.9454	0.9354	0.9522
2:IncepresV2c Ens(01)d	0.9456 0.9767	0.9556 0.9867	0.9556 0.9867	0.9556 0.9828	0.9456 0.9767	0.9556 0.9867	0.9556 0.9867	0.9456 0.9767	0.9343 0.9544
Ens(02)e	0.9522	0.9622	0.9622	0.9828	0.9522	0.9622	0.9622	0.9522	0.9522
Ens(12)f	0.9343	0.9543	0.9543	0.9543	0.9343	0.9543	0.9543	0.9343	0.9343
3:Ens(012)g	0.9716	0.9816	0.9816	0.9816	0.9716	0.9816	0.9816	0.9716	0.9716
Ens(012,01)h	0.9355	0.9455	0.9455	0.9455	0.9355	0.9455	0.9455	0.9355	0.9355
Ens(012,02)i	0.9457	0.9557	0.9557	0.9557	0.9457	0.9557	0.9557	0.9457	0.9457
Ens(0,01,02)j	0.9531	0.9631	0.9764	0.9631	0.9531	0.9631	0.9764	0.9531	0.9531
Ens(0,2,01,02)k	0.9332	0.9432	0.9432	0.9432	0.9332	0.9432	0.9432	0.9332	0.9332
Ens(0,1,01,02)l	0.9725	0.9625	0.9625	0.9625	0.9725	0.9625	0.9625	0.9725	0.9725

(Continued)

Table 4.4 Ensemble metrics for the identifying systems. (*Continued*)

Model	Accuracy	Precision	Sensitivity	Specificity	Auc	Kappa	F1_ score	Fβ_ score	Youden's index
Ens(0,01,02,3)m	**0.9767**	**0.9767**	0.9765	**0.9767**	**0.9767**	**0.9767**	0.9765	**0.9767**	0.9522
Ens(0,2,01,02,3)n	0.9347	0.9447	0.9447	0.9447	0.9347	0.9447	0.9447	0.9347	0.9343
Ens(0,1,01,02,3)	0.9520	0.9620	0.9620	0.9620	0.9520	0.9620	0.9620	0.9520	0.9716
Ens(0,01,02,012)p	**0.9767**	**0.9760**	0.9764	0.9543	**0.9862**	**0.9530**	**0.9769**	**0.9762**	0.9355

aXception = Performance evaluations prior to Xception preprocessing.

bXception = Performance evaluations following Xception's preprocessing.

c IncepresV2 = InceptionResNetV2.

dEns(01) = Xception and InceptionV3 averaged out.

eEns(02) = Xception and InceptionResNetV2 averaged.

fEns(12) = InceptionV3 and InceptionResNetV2 averaged.

gEns(012) = Time of getting, OriginsV3, and OriginsResV2 be around together.

hEns(0123,01) = normal of Ens(0123) and Ens (012).

iEns(0123,02) = normal of Ens(0123) and Ens (023).

jEns(0,023,02) equals the normal of Time of getting, Ens(023), and Ens (023).

kEns(0,23,02,12) equals the normal of Time of getting, OriginsResNetV2, Ens(02), and Ens (012).

lEns(0,1,2,01,02) equals the normal of Time of getting, OriginsV3, Ens(012), and Ens (023).

Time of getting, Ens(01), Ens(02), and Ens normal = mEns(2,02,12,3) (012).

Time of getting, OriginsResNetV2, and nEns(0,2,01,02,03) averaged across Ens(012), Ens(023), and Ens(03) (012).

oEns(0,1,01,02,3) is equal to the normal of Time of getting, OriginsV3, Ens(012), Ens(023), and Ens (012).

pEns(0,012,023,0123) is equal to the normal of Ens(012), Ens(023), and Ens (0123).

is based on the segmentation obtained by Fuzzy means clustering [28]. Because they are directly related to the effectiveness of the system, compassion and specificity are essential situation measures for recommendation results for early showing systems. Clinical research results have repeatedly shown that light therapy can be an effective treatment for both seasonal and major depressive disorder [29]. Owing to the unreliability of present automatic DR detection technologies, ophthalmologists are still need to screen DR directly utilizing retina pictures [30]. Specificity measures the proportion of properly identified true negatives, whereas sensitivity measures the percentage of correctly predicted positives. If the two measures are normally balanced, this balance can be visually represented by a receiver working typical arc with an AUC. The harmonic average of recall and precision is known as the F1 score. Good performance is indicated by an F1 score near 1. F1 score's weighted harmonic average is represented by F. The screening method displays more authenticity as the Youdens index gets closer to 1; the opposite connection is also true. The following is a presentation of these measures:

$$Accuracy = \frac{TP + TN}{TP + FP + TN + FN} \tag{4.3}$$

$$Sensitivity = \frac{TP}{TP + FN} \tag{4.4}$$

$$Precision = \frac{TN}{TN + FP} \tag{4.5}$$

$$F1\_Score = \frac{2TP}{2TP + FP + FN} \tag{4.6}$$

$$F\beta = \frac{(1 + \beta 2) \times Precision \times recall}{\beta 2 \times Precision + recall} \tag{4.7}$$

$$Youden's\ index = Sensitivity + Specificity - 1 \tag{4.8}$$
$$= \frac{TP \times TN - FN \times FP}{(TP + FP) \times (TN + FP)}$$

4.11   Investigation of Tests

The Genseral Institution for Medical Excellence in the UK recommends that a DR screening examination have a minimum compassion and specificity of 80.1% and 95%, respectively. The identification model did well in our study, with a compassion of 97.50%, specificity of 97.70%, and accurateness of 97.70%. The scaling model, on the other hand, attained a compassion of 98.10%, a specificity of 98.90%, and a correctness of 96.50%. The replicas therefore performed admirably on our facts. Early diagnosis of DR can decrease or halt the development of visual impairment; automated approaches can play a significant role in the screening for and identification of DR [31].

Diabetic retinopathy is a consequence of diabetes that can cause blindness if not detected in its initial phases [32]. Manual screening techniques exist, but they are laborious and ineffective when applied to a huge photographic database of patients [33]. However, in certain cases, the belongings of groups with multiple-group classification model were greater than individuals of uninteresting ensemble models. Early diagnosis has been demonstrated to be crucial in avoiding permanent vision impairment or blindness [34, 35]. The trials revealed that performance frequently rose with the strength of the base learner. We observed that several findings in the four-class studies began to worsen after the ensemble phase. Due to the fact that distinct improper novices with dissimilar pits might indirectly acquire various heights of semantic copy depiction, we predicted that the prototypical selection strategy used in the ensemble phase was mostly to blame for this degeneration. On the source of prototypical complementarity, the subsequent chances of these feeble novices can be combined to forecast the sensory system of unnoticed pictures. In contrast to the maximum technique in Table 4.4, the grading strategy was successful in our work since it greatly compact the modifications of the workings [36, 37].

4.12   Discussion

The following factors were taken into account while we designed the two ensemble models.

1. Integrated component strategy: The frameworks of the two classification tasks used the amount of session labels in the facts as a reference while they examined for the perfect grouping of module classifiers. We went through our experiments assuming that the fundamental elements were all independent. In the studies, we discovered that changing the

number of component classifiers at random will have a negative impact on the model's performance. Additionally, several component classifier method combinations were crucial for getting the highest addition presentation. Though, due to the variety of the real-world facts, the difficulty of the mission, and the level of freedom of the present module classifiers beneath the restriction of computational source necessities, defining the addition outline of a assumed usual classifier on actual data continues to be a stimulating delinquent.

2. Prototypical improvement: Given the tiny facts and deep replicas the scheme is using; the problem of gradient disappearance should be taken into consideration. Based on unverified layer-wise exercise, we presented a managed block-wise exercise method [38]. Respectively SDNN of a module classifier remained rummage-sale individually for a limited period of time, and it was accomplished utilizing tall near structures via the consistent pre-trained eye cartridge extractor model. After the SDNN had been individually skilled to produce a component classifier, it could be coupled with the matching feature extractor. The eye cartridge extractor module might be initialized with pre-trained heaviness, and the SDNN could use the best weight discovered after independent training as its pre-trained weight. After the training, the whole module classifier could be learned using adjustment. This exercise preparation resulted in a faster meeting of the entire organization module. To summation up, the module was separated into a number of exercise blocks, each with a suitable set of heaviness strictures. The component was then globally tuned to minimize the training cost and match the local ideal weight of each block.

3. There are numerous clear benefits: Primary, the repeatability and steadiness of analytic data may deliver doctors through information about the analytic procedure. Moreover, the 2 unique schemes might be rummage-sale to satisfy diverse request necessities. It's crucial to achieve high compassion and tall specificity when screening populations aimed at dangerous diseases in order to curtail False positive and negative outcomes. Not to mention, fast reporting of data from auxiliary diagnostic tests can improve doctors' performance.

4. A few restrictions: The ophthalmologist graders' clinical experience served as the foundation for the annotation

effort. As a result, the algorithm can behave differently when applied to photos that contain modest discoveries that the majority of clinicians are unable to detect. The nature of deep networks, which is another basic constraint brought on by the black box, is another issue. The specific features used to build the networks are unclear, but they are automatically picked up by the network from the photographs and grades that go along with them. To gain a better understanding of the variables that deep neural networks take into account while making predictions, research is now being conducted. It will be necessary to collect a big training dataset from other hospitals employing other kinds of cameras that includes tens of thousands of anomalous cases in order to improve the generalization of the models. In addition, by displaying the source regions of the features linked to a certain classification result and the strength of those features, the display of the features learned by CNNs might facilitate the understanding of diagnostic results. Additionally, using visualization, medical professionals can provide a precise diagnosis.

4.13   Results and Discussion

The fundus photography collection contained images taken under a wide range of lighting conditions from a diverse patient population. The lighting affects the pixel intensity values in the images and results in excessive variance that is unrelated to the categorization levels. A restricted contrast adaptive histogram equalization filtering approach was used with the OpenCV (http://opencv.org) module to address this issue. In Figure 4.10, the outcomes of this preprocessing stage are represented graphically. We found that and algorithm's accuracy rates were substantially same for the last two groups in the test (Figure 4.11). Our digital image preprocessing method increased the convolutional filters' ability to precisely recognize small features and microaneurysms, something the CNN had previously been unable to do. We speculate that this shift is caused by the impact of histogram equalization on the wise channel contrast. The accuracy percentage of the image classification methods BNN, DNN, CNN (VGGNET) is shown in Figure 4.12. The accuracy rates of BNN, DNN for image statistical data is shown in Figure 4.13. The testing and the training accuracy percentages of BNN, DNN, CNN (VGGNET) is illustrated in Table 4.5. The testing and the training accuracy rates of individual algorithms like BNN, DNN for image statistics is shown in Table 4.6.

Table 4.5 Accuracy percentages for processed image classification images by each algorithm.

Methods	Training	Testing
BNN	62.7	42
DNN	89.6	86.3
CNN (VGGNET)	76.4	78.3

Table 4.6 Accuracy rates of individual algorithms for image statistics.

Methods	Training	Testing
BNN	45.7	35.6
DNN	84.7	82.3

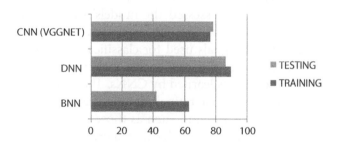

Figure 4.12 Accuracy percentages of each algorithm.

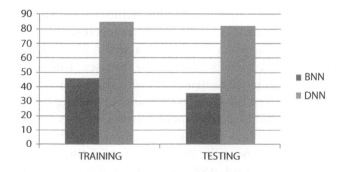

Figure 4.13 Accuracy rates of each algorithm for image statistical data.

4.14   Conclusions

The focus of the chapter is on offering a useful diagnostic model for diabetic retinopathy. Processing retinal imaging is essential for optimal performance. Statistics can reliably estimate the degree of severity; however, in the case of noisy images, the probability of having inaccurate data may result in reduced accuracy. When selecting the suitable structures from the photo, this is crucial for improved outcomes. Despite the fact that both the CNN and DNN models are efficient for images, in this case DNN outperforms Given that CNN's CPU training time affects the analysis, CNN for training accuracy and validation accuracy. In order to test a GPU system for a future work model, it can analyze more data to obtain better accuracy performance. A standalone software is useful for retinopathy detection. The standard and innovation of current eye care can be raised by utilizing the proposed model in conjunction with the NPDR screening algorithms. Finally, a new DeepDR grading and identification method was suggested, coupled with the development of a top-notch labelled medical imaging DR dataset. It has been established and studied that there is a correlation between the quantity of ideal component classifiers and the quantity of class labels. We assessed the models' validity and reliability using nine medical indicators. The outcomes showed that DeepDR performed as expected. The signals used for classification reside in a region of the image that is readily apparent to the viewer, according to visualizations of the characteristics learned by CNNs. The macroscopic features in moderate and severe diabetic retinal pictures are of a scale that can be classified by existing CNN designs, such as those found in the ImageNet visual database. On the other hand, the characteristics that separate moderate sickness from normal disease are found in less than 1% of the entire pixel volume, a level of subtlety that is frequently challenging for human interpreters to recognize. Slight details in medical imaging might be quite important for diagnosis. Fortunately, the architectures that are most frequently used have been enhanced to recognize macroscopic structures like those found in the ImageNet dataset. As a result, we might want a new model for using CNN models to diagnose diseases. This may be a two-stage lesion detection pipeline that starts with feature localization, moves on to classification, preprocessing to separate out diseases that are difficult to detect manually, and then rebalances network weights to take into consideration class imbalances common in medical datasets. Our long-term objectives include increasing the diagnosis of mild disease and shifting to the more difficult but advantageous multi-grade disease detection.

References

1. Solomon, S.D., Chew, E., Duh, E.J., Sobrin, L., Sun, J.K., VanderBeek, B.L., Wykoff, C.C., Gardner, T.W., Diabetic retinopathy: A position statement by the American Diabetes Association. *Diabetes Care*, 40, 412–418, 2017.

2. Aiello, L.P., The potential role of PKC β in diabetic retinopathy and macular edema. *Surv. Ophthalmol.*, 47, S263–S269, Dec. 2002.

3. Goh, J.K.H., Cheung, C.Y., Sim, S.S., Tan, P.C., Tan, G.S.W., Wong, T.Y., Retinal imaging techniques for diabetic retinopathy screening. *J. Diabetes Sci. Technol.*, 10, 2, 282–294, 2016, [PMC free article] [PubMed] [Google Scholar].

4. Gulshan, V., Peng, L., Coram, M., Stumpe, M., Wu, D., Narayanaswamy, A. *et al.*, Development and validation of a deep learning algorithm for detection of diabetic retinopathy in retinal fundus photographs. *JAMA*, 316, 22, 2402, 2016, http://dx.doi.org/10.1001/jama.2016.17216.

5. Mookiah, M.R.K., Acharya, U.R., Chua, C.K., Lim, C.M., Ng, E.Y.K., Laude, A., Computer-aided diagnosis of diabetic retinopathy: A review. *Comput. Biol. Med.*, 43, 12, 2136–2155, 2013.

6. Akram, M.U., Detection and classification of retinal lesions for grading of diabetic retinopathy. *Comput. Biol. Med.*, 45, 161–171, 2014.

7. Rakshitha, T.R., Devaraj, D., Prasanna Kumar, S.C., Comparative study of imaging transforms on diabetic retinopathy images. *Recent Trends in Electronics, Information & Communication Technology (RTEICT), IEEE International Conference on IEEE*, 2016.

8. Vo, H.H. and Verma, A., Discriminant color texture descriptors for diabetic retinopathy recognition. *Intelligent Computer Communication and Processing (ICCP), 2016 IEEE 12th International Conference on IEEE*, 2016.

9. Sahlsten, J., Jaskari, J., Kivinen, J., Turunen, L., Jaanio, E., Hietala, K., Kaski, K., Deep learning fundus image analysis for diabetic retinopathy and macular edema grading. *Sci. Rep.*, 9, 1–11, 2019.

10. Krause, J., Gulshan, V., Rahimy, E., Karth, P., Widner, K., Corrado, G.S., Peng, L., Webster, D.R., Grader variability and the importance of reference standards for evaluating machine learning models For diabetic retinopathy. *Ophthalmology*, 125, 1264–1272, 2018.

11. Lahmiri, S., High-frequency-based features for low and high retina haemorrhage classification. *Healthcare Technol. Lett.*, 4, 20–24, 2017.

12. Jolliffe, I.T. and Cadima, J., Principal component analysis: A review and recent developments. *Philos. Trans. R. Soc. A: Math. Phys. Eng. Sci.*, 374, 20150202, 2016.

13. Sapuppo, F., Umana, E., Frasca, M., La Rosa, M., Shannahoff-Khalsa, D., Fortuna, L., Bucolo, M., Complex spatio-temporal features in meg data. *Math. Biosci. Eng.*, 3, 697, 2006.

14. Mohsen, H., El-Dahshan, E.S.A., El-Horbaty, E.S.M., Salem, A.B.M., Classification using deep learning neural networks for brain tumors. *Future Comput. Inf. J.*, 3, 68–71, 2018.

15. Wang, H., Wang, W., Zhou, X., Sun, H., Zhao, J., Yu, X., Cui, Z., Firefly algorithm with neighborhood attraction. *Inf. Sci.*, 382, 374–387, 2017.
16. Diabetic retinopathy image dataset [Online]. Available: https://www.kaggle.com/c/diabetic-retinopathy-detection/data.
17. Simonyan, K. and Zisserman, A., Very deep convolutional networks for large-scale image recognition. *ICLR*, 2015.
18. Srivastava, N., Hinton, G., Krizhevsky, A., Sutskever, I., Salakhutdinov, R., Dropout: A simple way to prevent neural networks from overfitting. *J. Mach. Learn. Res.*, 15, 1929–1958, 2014.
19. Maas, A.L., Hannun, A.Y., Ng, A.Y., Rectifier non linearities improve neural network acoustic models. *Proceedings of the 30th International Conference on Machine Learning*, Atlanta, Georgia, USA, 2013.
20. Kaur, J. and Mittal, D., A generalized method for the detection of vascular structure in pathological retinal images. *Biocybern. Biomed. Eng.*, 37, 1, 184–200, 2017.
21. Leopold, H., Orchard, J., Zelek, J., Lakshminarayanan, V., PixelBNN: Augmenting the PixelCNN with batch normalization and the presentation of a fast architecture for retinal vessel segmentation. *J. Imaging*, 5, 2, 26, 2019.
22. Mahapatra, D., Bozorgtabar, B., Garnavi, R., Image super-resolution using progressive generative adversarial networks for medical image analysis. *Comput. Med. Imaging Graph*, 71, 30–39, Jan. 2019.
23. Wang, X., Jiang, X., Ren, J., Blood vessel segmentation from fundus image by a cascade classification framework. *Pattern Recognit.*, 88, 331–341, Apr. 2019.
24. Stark, J.A., Adaptive image contrast enhancement using generalizations of histogram equalization. *IEEE Trans. Image Process.*, 9, 5, 889–896, 2002.
25. Stark, J.A. and Fitzgerald, W.J., Model-based adaptive histogram equalization. *Signal Process.*, 39, 1–2, 193–200, 1994.
26. Roychowdhury, S., Koozekanani, D., Parhi, K., Dream: Diabetic retinopathy analysis using machine learning. *IEEE J. Biomed. Health Inf.*, 18, 5, 1717–1728, 2014.
27. Quellec, G., Lamard, M., Josselin, P.M., Cazuguel, G., Cochener, B., Roux, C., Optimal wavelet transform for the detection of microaneurysms in retina photographs. *IEEE Trans. Med. Imaging*, 27, 9, 1230–1241, 2008, [PMC free article] [PubMed] [Google Scholar].
28. Cai, W., Chen, S., Zhang, D., Fast and robust fuzzy c-means clustering algorithms incorporating local information for image segmentation. *Pattern Recognit.*, 40, 3, 825–838, 2007.
29. Li, X. and Li, X., The antidepressant effect of light therapy from retinal projections. *Neurosci. Bull.*, 34, 2, 359368, Apr. 2018.
30. Omar, Z.A., Hanafi, M., Mashohor, S., Mahfudz, N.F.M., Muna'im, M., Automatic diabetic retinopathy detection and classification system, in: *2017 7th IEEE International Conference on System Engineering and Technology (ICSET)*, 2017, October, IEEE, pp. 162–166.

31. Palavalasa, K.K. and Sambaturu, B., Automatic diabetic retinopathy detection using digital image processing, in: *2018 International Conference on Communication and Signal Processing (ICCSP)*, 2018, April, IEEE, pp. 0072–0076.
32. Pires, R., Jelinek, H.F., Wainer, J., Goldenstein, S., Valle, E., Rocha, A., Assessing the need for referral in automatic diabetic retinopathy detection. *IEEE Trans. Biomed. Eng.*, 60, 12, 3391–3398, 2013.
33. Paranjpe, M.J. and Kakatkar, M.N., Review of methods for diabetic retinopathy detection and severity classification. *Int. J. Res. Eng. Technol.*, 3, 3, 619–624, 2014.
34. Bravo, M.A. and Arbclácz, P.A., Automatic diabetic retinopathy classification, in: *13th International Conference on Medical Information Processing and Analysis*, 2017, November, vol. 10572, SPIE, pp. 446–455.
35. Gangwar, A.K. and Ravi, V., Diabetic retinopathy detection using transfer learning and deep learning, in: *Evolution in Computational Intelligence*, pp. 679–689, Springer, Singapore, 2021.
36. Szegedy, C., Liu, W., Jia, Y., Sermanet, P., Reed, S., Anguelov, D., Erhan, D., Vanhoucke, V., Rabinovich, A., Going deeper with convolutions, in: *Proceedings of the IEEE Conference on Computer Vision and Pattern Recognition*, pp. 1–9, 2015.
37. Ju, C., Bibaut, A., van der Laan, M., The relative performance of ensemble methods with deep convolutional neural networks for image classification. *J. Appl. Stat.*, 45, 15, 1–19, 2018.
38. Bengio, Y., Lamblin, P., Popovici, D., Larochelle, H., Greedy layer-wise training of deep networks. *Adv. Neural Inf. Process. Syst.*, 153–160, 2007.

5

Design and Implementation of Smart Parking Management System Based on License Plate Detection

Pallavi S. Bangare[1], Sanjana Naik[1], Shashwati Behare[1], Akanksha Swami[1], Jayesh Gaikwad[1], Sunil L. Bangare[1], G. Pradeepini[2] and Ahmed A. Elngar[3]*

[1]Department of Information Technology, Sinhgad Academy of Engineering, Pune, India
[2]CSE, Koneru Lakshmaiah Educational Foundation (KL University), Green Fields, Vaddeswaram, Guntur, A.P., India
[3]Faculty of Computers and Artificial Intelligence, Beni-Suef University, Beni-Suef City, Egypt

Abstract

There has been a major problem addressed about the parking slots in the metropolitan cities recently as there is a very limited space available reserved for parking as such. The major issue with vehicle parking is that the various malls and shopping complexes have very limited space and on the other hand the number of vehicles has drastically increased these days. Due to the rapid increase in vehicle density especially during the peak hours of the day, it is a difficult task for the drivers to find a parking space to park their vehicles. There has been a variety of research done before to address this issue. The proposed system makes use of advanced techniques for automating the parking reservation for various places using number plate recognition and android application with IoT integration for informing the parking availability status. The proposed system makes use of python Open CV for image processing and android for parking availability checks and booking. Image processing is used for vehicle number plate recognition at entry and exit through which in and out the time of parking is carried out. The proposed system gives 96% accuracy on tested images captured in real-time.

Keywords: Zigbee, RFID, WSN, IR sensor, ultrasonic sensor, Internet of Things, smart phone

*Corresponding author: elngar_7@yahoo.co.uk

Ahmed A. Elgnar, Vigneshwar M, Krishna Kant Singh and Zdzislaw Polkowski (eds.) Handbook of Computational Sciences: A Multi and Interdisciplinary Approach, (99–120) © 2023 Scrivener Publishing LLC

5.1   Introduction

In recent research in metropolitan cities along with an increase in population, there is high vehicle density on roads. Hence this leads to annoying issues for the drivers to park their vehicles as it is very difficult to find a parking slot. The drivers usually waste time and effort and end up parking their vehicles finding a space on the streets through luck. In the worst case, people fail to find any parking space, especially during peak hours and festive seasons. However, in the current parking system, a better but not optimal solution is being provided. It does not provide an economic benefit or vehicle refusal services and there is no resource reservation mechanism leading to a queuing system which is again time-consuming. It also lacks provide large-scale parking system. There are android applications available where the cost is calculated from the time the parking slot has been booked which is not economically beneficial for the users. Parking Guidance and Information (PGI) systems for better parking management are also available. PGI systems will provide drivers with effective information on parking within controlled areas and lead them to empty parking slots [2, 3]. And parking management system is also available which is using ZigBee technology [4]. S. L. Bangare *et al.* [9] work related to Intelligent Video Surveillance system and P. S. Bangare *et al.* [10, 11] work related to Accident monitoring system was also studied.

Current sensing technologies make monitoring implementable. The second is effective wireless communication between a vehicle and an allocation center. The third is the center must be able to implement a reservation that guarantees a specific parking spot to a driver. This is achievable through existing wireless technology interfacing a vehicle with hardware that makes a spot accessible only to the driver who has reserved it. A softer scheme is using a red/green light system placed at each parking spot, where red indicates that the spot is reserved and only the vehicle is assigned as shown in Figure 5.1.

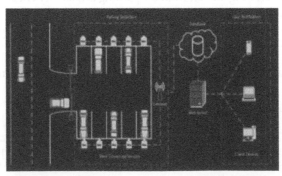

Figure 5.1 Typical car park system [1].

5.2   Literature Survey

5.2.1   Cloud-Based Smart-Parking System Based on Internet-of-Things/Technologies

This chapter provides a unique algorithm that increases the capability of the current cloud-based smart parking system [1] and it also develops a network architecture based on the Internet of Things technology. This system helps the users to find a free parking space with minimal cost based on new performance metrics which are automatic. These metrics will calculate the user spaces in each car park. To enhance parking management, an intelligent parking system was developed which reduced the purpose of hiring people to maintain the parking system [1]. This chapter proposes an effective cloud-based Smart parking system based on the Internet of Things. The data that includes the vehicle's GPS location and distance between car parks and the number of free parking spaces in car parks will be sent to the data center. Here the data center is presented as a cloud server that calculates the costs of a user parking request and this information is regularly updated and is made available to the vehicles in the network at any time. In this proposed system, each car park is an IoT network, and it operates independently of a regular car park. This paper implements a system model with wireless access in an open-source physical computing platform based on Arduino with RFID technology. It uses a smartphone that acts as a user interface between the cloud and the vehicles to check the feasibility of the proposed system [1].

5.2.2   A Cloud-Based Intelligent Car Parking System

A cloud-based intelligent car parking system is described in this paper. It is considered an important component of an Intelligent Transport System (ITS) for smart cities, there are three layers in the car parking system: sensor-, communication-, and application layer. In the implementation part, a sample car parking service for a university campus was proposed as shown in the architecture. The related IoT sub-system includes the following layers sensor layer, communication layer, and application layer. Using cloud-based intelligent parking system car parking services with the proposed platform can be implemented. It can be used on any private parking space. As result, the system development follows the personal software process (PSP) methodology. Methods used for the PSP are either test-driven or feature-driven. When a user/car enters the University campus through one of its gates, the car parking mobile app, installed on the user's mobile phone, will send an automatic HTTP request through the gates access point toward a web server, and a JSON response will be returned, containing information about the best available car parking lot. For a GPS-enabled mobile phone, a Route Utils generates the steps that must be followed by the driver and displays them on Google Maps [2].

5.2.3   Research and Implement of the Intelligent Parking Reservation Management System Based on ZigBee Technology

With the increasing development of the economy and city modernization level, traffic congestion and parking have become major social issues due to the increasing amount of vehicle density. In order to overcome this parking issue, a smart parking system has been proposed in this paper which is composed of a ZigBee network that sends the user-requested information to a PC through a coordinator and further updates the database. Using the internet, the parking information is provided to the application layer to make it convenient for the people seeking the parking position with the help of web services. The system consists of a mobile client and server-side parking lot. The client requests the server for parking information through a web-service interface. Then the server searches for the requested information in the available database and returns the required information to the client using the web-service interface. The real-time update status is available to the mobile client to ensure the correctness of the required information in the process [3].

5.2.4   Zigbee and GSM-Based Secure Vehicle Parking Management and Reservation System

In this research, the author has proposed a system in which the Parking lot vacancy module uses ZigBee along with PIC. Security Feature: The exit password must be entered else the user is not allowed to get out of the parking bay as the barrier gate will not get open until the correct exit password is entered. But the major drawback of the system is that The GSM and SMS module makes the system expensive. The SMS containing the entry/exit password to the parking lot may not be received due to network congestion [4].

5.2.5   Car Park Management with Networked Wireless Sensors and Active RFID

The main advantage of the gate management model is its low cost and simplicity over the lot management model. Gate management service: Another use of RFID tags is gate management. For example, a gate can be opened automatically using an RFID reader and the vehicle's tag at the gate. But the major drawback of the system is that No driver guidance systems to guide towards the parking lot [5].

5.2.6 Automated Parking System with Bluetooth Access

The system uses the user's mobile's Bluetooth for identification and registration. The vehicle is transported to the parking location with the help of a rack and pinion mechanism for linear motion. It automatically detects the unique registration number stored in the Bluetooth chip to check if the new vehicle is to be parked. It cannot be used in the existing parking system. The whole parking lot is to be designed with mechanical components such as rack and pinion mechanism [6].

5.2.7 Smart Parking: A Secure and Intelligent Parking System

A smart parking system is suggested, by using the secured wireless network and sensor communication, Smart-Parking is an intelligent parking service application as well as a novel security/privacy aware infrastructure. First, vehicles on the road can view and reserve a parking spot. The parking process can be an efficient and non-stop service as well as parking service is an intelligent service. New vacant parking spots and advertisements for discounts on parking fees can be distributed to the cars passing by also the parking process has been created as a stochastic process. Not only maintenance work can be scheduled but also the revenue of the parking site can be predicted. New business promotions can be broadcasted to all vehicles passing by the parking site through wireless networks [7, 8].

5.3 Proposed System

As per the survey done for the various systems proposed previously, the major factor that comes as the reason have major shortcomings is that the hardware cost drastically increases for most of the systems due to wear and tear and limited life span of the sensors too. So, in the proposed system, as per the research done, we tried to avoid any sort of data sensors and still achieve the efficiency highest possible with the combination of image processing and machine learning to manage the possible crowd for car parking as shown in Figure 5.2.

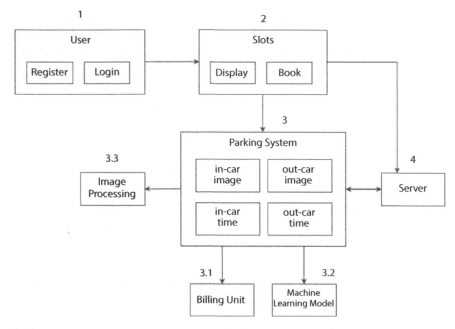

Figure 5.2 Proposed architecture.

5.3.1 Methodology

The system is divided into sub-systems which are the 'FULL' display system, image acquisition, plate number recognition, auto direction system, and auto payment system. Firstly, data is acquired from IR sensors of each parking space to count the availability of parking spaces in the parking area. Then, the image of the car is acquired at the entrance to be analyzed. During this time, time entering, and license plate reference numbers are recorded for future transaction. Secondly, the image acquired from hardware components by Camera are analyzed in data analysis part where mostly done in MATLAB. The image of the car is analyzed for its license plate numbers for future reference. The time entering is analyzed during car exiting to calculate the fees of parking. Plus, the data acquired from IR probes of each parking space is calculated for the calculating free parking spaces. The 'FULL' sign is expected to be displayed through Application display. Other information to be displayed is fees accumulated according to specific parking rate. The fee is likely displayed on the desktop computer interface.

The direction system also expected to be having information display where it is used to guide drivers to nearest free parking space. In addition, the auto parking system needs interface and management systems to communicate with drivers and system's developers. Firstly, the barrier gate is managed to be opened when the main program acquired the license plate reference, and it is recorded. And after some time, delayed, the barrier gate will close again. Then, all the output need no physical interactions will be managed app. However, for software development and calculation, the desktop computer will be used. System's developers and maintenance would have to use the desktop computer to manage the systems. IoT system has the IR sensors mounted for the slot to determine the slot status whether the slot is empty or occupied. This slot status of the IR sensors is sent to the server for displaying it to the user while booking the parking slots.

The proposed system working is as follows:

(i)   The user is allowed to register from the android application and login to the application to search for the parking slot availability of the specific place.

(ii)   Once the user registers and logs in to the application, user then gets the access to view the available parking count and if available can book the parking for specific place by providing the vehicle details for which the parking has to be reserved.

(iii)   Once the user does the booking for the parking, users parking charges start getting applied from the booking time itself as 1 parking gets reserved for the user and so that count is reduced from the count displayed to other users.

(iv)   When the user's car reaches the destination i.e. parking entry, the image acquisition system i.e. camera at the entrance captures the license plate of the from the car image and recognizes the number plate for which the booking status can be checked. If the booking is found, the car's in time is recorded.

(v)   After some time when the car has to exit, at the exit gate, the user's car image is again captured to check the vehicle number plate and check the charges for the vehicle based on the booking time of the parking of the vehicle.

(vi)   Also, when the vehicle is parked in the slot, the sensors determine the vehicle availability and inform the server with the help of IR sensors and Arduino board.

5.3.2   Vehicle Number Plate Recognition Technique

Firstly, the car image is captured. Then, the system should extract the number plate of the car alone for the segmentation of character purpose. This plate localization algorithm is based on combining morphological operation sensitive to specific shapes in the input image with a good threshold value by which the license plate is located. A big percentage of localization of License plates is achieved by the technique mentioned below.

a) Image Input
Take car image as input.

b) Otsu Adaptive Thresholding
In the first stage, the input image is converted first to a binary image using an adaptive threshold method that help cope with the dynamic changes of illumination conditions during the binarization of the image. Therefore, the Otsu's algorithm is applied which is an efficient and simple method. S. L. Bangare *et al.* work for Otsu was referred [12].

c) Connected Component Analysis
The Connected Component Analysis technique (CCAT) is performed to detect rectangles in the image which are taken as a generated license plate candidate.

d) Edge Detection
The edge detection is applied inside the generated candidates to search for the closed curves in the candidates generated. If the number of the closed curves is more than three, the candidate detected is a license plate and the closed curves detected are taken as a character. If it not the case, no license plate is detected.

5.4 High Level Design of Proposed System

5.4.1 Data Flow Diagram

Figure 5.3 show the Data Flow Diagram level 0.

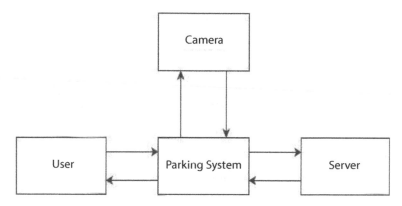

Figure 5.3 DFD level 0.

Figure 5.4 show the Data Flow Diagram level 1.

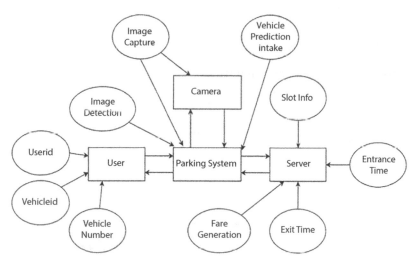

Figure 5.4 DFD level 1.

Figure 5.5 show the Data Flow Diagram level 2.

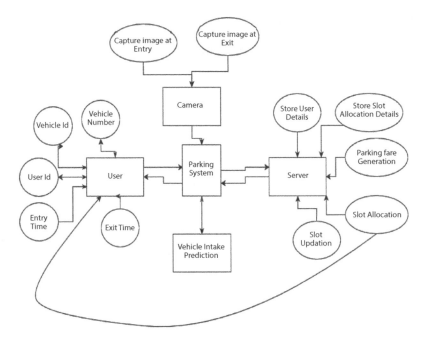

Figure 5.5 DFD level 3.

5.4.2 UML Diagrams

a) Class diagram as shown in Figure 5.6.

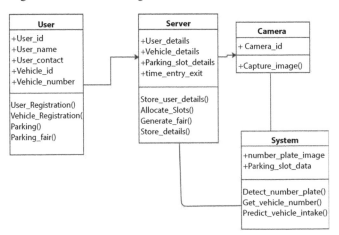

Figure 5.6 Class diagram.

b) Figure 5.7 show the use case diagram.

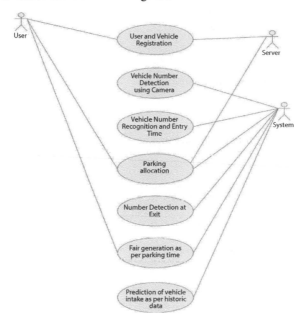

Figure 5.7 Use case diagram.

c) Figure 5.8 show the sequence diagram.

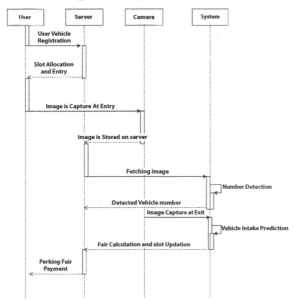

Figure 5.8 Sequence diagram.

d) Activity diagram as shown in Figure 5.9.

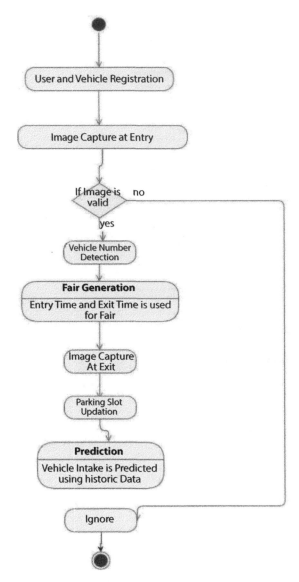

Figure 5.9 Activity diagram.

5.5   Project Requirement Specification

5.5.1   Software Requirements

(i)   OS Requirements: Windows 7 onwards
(ii)   Android Studio
(iii) Java JDK 1.8 onwards
(iv)   MySQL server
(v)   Wamp Server
(vi)   Pycharm

5.5.2   Hardware Requirements

(i)   Android Processor (Android Mobile)
(ii)   HC05 Bluetooth Module
(iii) Web Cam for car plate image capture
(iv)   Server (Laptop or PC for Server Software Operations)
(v)   Wireless Internet connectivity.

5.6   Algorithms

The proposed system comprises of 4 major entities

(i)   Arduino For IR Sensor Controller
(ii)   IR Sensors
(iii) Server
(iv)   Android User Application

The proposed system works in the following way

(i)   Firstly, the car image is captured. Then, the system should extract the number plate of the car alone for the segmentation of character purpose. This plate localization algorithm is based on combining morphological operation sensitive to specific shapes in the input image with a good threshold value by which the license plate is located. A big percentage of localization of License plates is achieved by the technique mentioned below.

(ii)   Image input: Take car image as input.
(iii) Otsu Adaptive Thresholding: In the first stage, the input
       image is converted first to a binary image using an adaptive
       threshold method that help cope with the dynamic changes
       of illumination conditions during the binarization of the
       image. Therefore, the Otsu's algorithm is applied which is
       an efficient and simple method Connected Component
       Analysis: The Connected Component Analysis technique
       (CCAT) is performed to detect rectangles in the image
       which are taken as a generated license plate candidate
(iv)   Edge Detection: the edge detection is applied inside the
       generated candidates to search for the closed curves in the
       candidates generated. If the number of the closed curves is
       more than three, the candidate detected is a license plate
       and the closed curves detected are taken as a character. If
       it not the case, no license plate is detected.

(1) This variance can further compound the complexity for an algorithm
to ascertain what area of a vehicle constitutes a license plate and what area
is not. Therefore, the algorithm must rule out a vehicle's mirror, headlight,
bumper etc. In general, algorithms look for geometric shapes of rectangular proportion. However, since a vehicle can have many rectangular objects
on it, further algorithms are needed to validate that the identified object
is indeed a license plate. To accomplish this, key components of the algorithm look for characteristics that would indicate that the object is a license
plate. The algorithm searches for a similar background color of unified
proportion and contrast as a means to differentiate objects on a vehicle.
Vehicles are moving objects and their rate of velocity must be accounted
for in the algorithm's design. This speed creates further complexity as a
license plates image is angularly skewed and subjected to refractory issues
from light changes.

(2) Components of algorithms that adjust for the angular skew of the
license plate image to accurately sample, correct, and proportionally recal-
culate to an optimal size as shown in Figure 5.10.

Figure 5.10 License plate sizing sequence.

5.7   Proposed System Results

a. Figure 5.11 show the User Registration and Login.

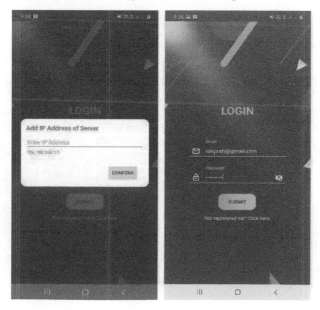

Figure 5.11 User Login and registration.

b. Figure 5.12 show the user dashboard.

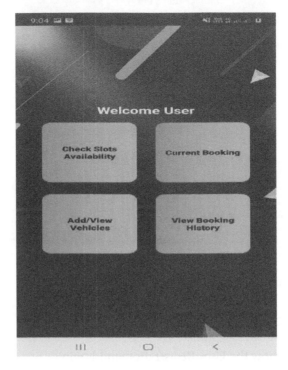

Figure 5.12   User dashboard.

c. Adding vehicle details as shown in the Figure 5.13.

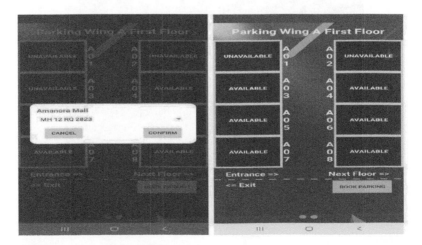

Figure 5.13   Adding vehicle details.

d. Check Available Slots

User can check the availability of the registered parking premises and as per the availability, user can choose the premises to travel and then book the slot as shown in Figure 5.14.

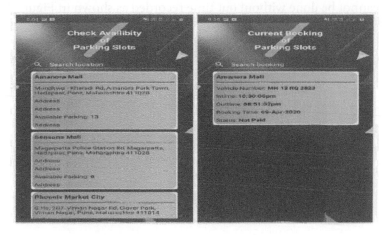

Figure 5.14 Check available slot.

e. Make Parking Booking

Figure 5.15 show the Search for the mall and make the booking for the slot displayed on the screen. While booking the slot, user can also choose the vehicle for which the booking is to be done.

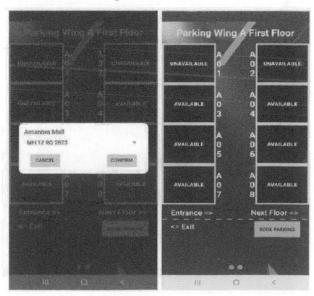

Figure 5.15 Parking booking.

f. Parking payment cannot be done without out time from server
User once makes the booking and enters the premises, he cannot make the payment, until users out time from the web cam is recorded. If user tries to make the payment without out time recorded, user is informed that payment cannot be done without out time recorded as shown in Figure 5.16.

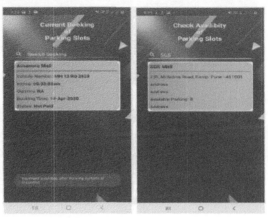

Figure 5.16 Parking booking: out time.

g. Making Parking Payment
Figure 5.17 show the user can see the current unpaid bookings and whenever exiting from the premises, can make the payment from the app for the selected booking.

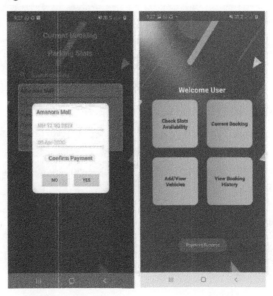

Figure 5.17 Parking payment.

h. Image recognition from license plate as shown in Figure 5.18.

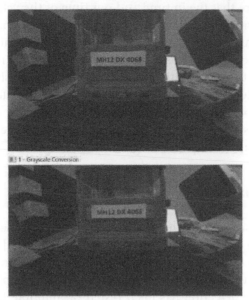

Figure 5.18 Vehicle license plate pre-processing.

i. License plate extraction as shown in the Figure 5.19.

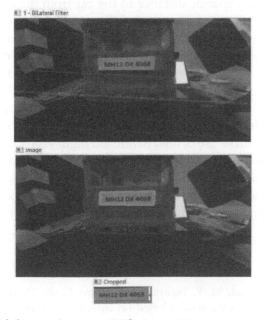

Figure 5.19 Vehicle license plate recognized.

The vehicles license plate is captured at the entry and exit of the parking area to make sure that the in time and out time of the vehicle is recorded properly for payment calculation. The proposed system has makes use of edge detection and thresholding technique for determining the number plate of the vehicle and so the accuracy of the system gained is comparatively high with the combinational logic of image processing with thresholding. The system was tested on 100 images for vehicle number plate recognition before it was used in the proposed system and out of 100 image 96 images were correctly recognized. So, the system gives overall 96% accuracy for license plate recognition.

5.8   Conclusion

As in the proposed system, the development of an automatic parking system with license plate recognition, parking lots status and guidance parking system and electronic billing system is successfully implemented. The performance of the developed of algorithms for license plate localization and license plate detection has been tested on multiple images captured with the webcam and real time images of the license plates and has been found to be achieving the accuracy of 96%. Recognition is acceptable range. The developed algorithms accurately localize and recognize the number plates with specific distance of the car from the capturing device to maintain the efficiency. Electronic billing system performance is also acceptable and recommended for commercial use. The proposed gives the high-end advantage that system gets completely automated, saves manual errors, and gives parking availability information on fingertips through the application. The proposed system can be further extended to make use of high definition night vision cameras to make sure that the system can also work efficiently in the day and night time. The proposed system can be further extended to make use of high definition night vision cameras to make sure that the system can also work efficiently in the day and night time. The proposed system has the limitation of quality of camera and the angle of camera set for capturing the vehicle image at entry and exit which makes the system dependent and which can further be worked upon.

References

1. Pham, T.N., Tsai, M.-F., Nguyen, D.B., Dow, C.-R., Deng, D.-J., A cloud-based smart-parking system based on Internet-of-Things technologies. In *IEEE Access*, vol. 3, pp. 1581–1591, 2015.

2. Ji, Z., Ganchev, I., Droma, M.O., Zhang, X., A cloud-based intelligent car parking services for smart cities, IEEE, 2014, 978-1-4673-5225-3/14/$31.00.
3. Shiyao, C., Ming, W., Chen, L., Na, R., The research and implement of the intelligent parking reservation management system based on ZigBee technology. *2014 Sixth International Conference on Measuring Technology and Mechatronics Automation*, IEEE, 2014, 978-1-4799-3435-5/14 $31.00.
4. Sayeeraman, A. and Ramesh, P.S., Zigbee and GSM based secure vehicle parking management and reservation system. *J. Theor. Appl. Inf. Technol.*, 37, 2, 31st March 2012.
5. Karbab, E., Djenouri, D., Boulkaboul, S., Bagula, A., Car park management with networked wireless sensors and active RFID, IEEE, 2015, 978-1-4799-8802-0/15/$31.00.
6. Singh, H., Anand, C., Kumar, V., Sharma, A., Automated parking system with bluetooth access. *Int. J. Eng. Comput. Sci.*, ISSN 2319-7242, 2014.
7. Al-Kharusi, H. and Al-Bahadly, I., Intelligent parking management system based on image processing. *World J. Eng. Technol.*, 2, 55–67, 2014, Published Online May 2014 in SciRe.
8. Yan, G., Yang, W., Rawat, D.B., Olariu, S., Smart parking: A secure and intelligent parking system, in: *2008 11th International IEEE Conference on Intelligent Transportation Systems*. 2008.
9. Bangare, S.L., Tribhuwan, R.F., Shukla, K.M., Jain, S.A., Vispute, R.G., Intelligent video surveillance system based on machine learning. *J. Eng. Sci.*, 11, 7, 410–416, July/2020, ISSN 0377-9254.
10. Bangare, P.S., Petare, Y.S., Chaudhari, A.P., Jadhav, R.D., Bangare, S.L., Survey on accident monitoring system. *Int. J. Inf. Comput. Sci.*, 6, 4, 8–18, 2019.
11. Bangare, P.S., Petare, Y.S., Chaudhari, A.P., Jadhav, R.D., Bangare, S.L., Pradeepini, G., Patil, S.T., Developing accident monitoring system using wireless application. *Int. J. Inf. Comput. Sci.*, 6, 4, 1–7, 2019.
12. Bangare, S.L. and Patil, S.T., Reviewing Otsu's method for image thresholding. *Int. J. Appl. Eng. Res. (IJAER)*, 10, 9, 21777–21783, 2015, ISSN 0973-9769.

A Novel Algorithm for Stationary Analysis of the Characteristics of the Queue-Dependent Random Probability for Co-Processor-Shared Memory Using Computational Sciences

Nandhini Varadharajan[1], Vigneshwar Manoharan[2], Rajadurai[3] and Ahmed A. Elngar[4*]

[1]R & D - Bharath Labs, Bharath Corporate, Coimbatore, Tamil Nadu, India
[2]R & D and Academic Initiatives at CBAS Corp, Coimbatore, Tamil Nadu, India
[3]Government Arts College, Hudco Colony, Peelamedu, Coimbatore, TN, India
[4]Faculty of Computers and Artificial Intelligence, Beni-Suef University, Beni-Suef City, Egypt

Abstract

The implication of Queuing Theory is a probability random process applied along with Mathematical models for the allocation of resources using operational research. In an Operating system, there are several processes that will be in a queue or waiting for instructions. Then they are allocated for resource utilization by various operating system algorithms and methods. When these processes are about to enter for processing, there may lot many times and batch processing involved. Similarly, there are load-balancing servers that are implied for queuing up the process and allocating the resources, and balancing the load to the servers. This is a computational sciences model designed by implying Queue dependent random probability for co-processors which would be for a shared memory system.

Keywords: Stationary analysis, queue-dependent random, balancing, probability, computational sciences

Corresponding author: elngar_7@yahoo.co.uk

Ahmed A. Elgnar, Vigneshwar M, Krishna Kant Singh and Zdzislaw Polkowski (eds.) Handbook of Computational Sciences: A Multi and Interdisciplinary Approach, (121–136) © 2023 Scrivener Publishing LLC

6.1   Introduction — Processor-Shared Service Queue with Independent Service Rate Using Probability Queuing Theory

An M/M/2 retrial queuing system where customers arrive according to a Poisson process with a rate $\lambda>0$. Any primary arrival who finds all servers busy upon arrival leaves the system facility immediately and joins the orbit. Figure 6.1 shows the retrial queue. The control policy is to access the server from in the orbit, and 0 when the orbit is empty. Any primary arrival or retrial who finds an idle server is served immediately. The successive times are assumed to be mutually independent and exponentially distributed with parameter $v>0$ [1]. The input stream of primary arrivals, service times, and intervals between repeated attempts are assumed to be mutually independent. State–transition diagram. The state of the system at time t can be described by the dimensional process

$$X(t) = \{(C(t), N(t)) \,|\, t \geq 0\}$$

Where C (t) denotes the number of busy servers at time t and, N (t) denotes the number of customers in the orbit at time t.X is an irreducible Markovian process whose state space S is the product of finite set $\{0, 1, 2\}$ and half-line, i.e. $S = \{0, 1, 2\} \times Z+$. In many queuing situations, blocked customers do not leave the system. Instead, they may come back to the service facility after a random time and retry for service [2]. Queues in which customers are allowed to conduct retrials have wide practical use in telephone switching systems and in a telecommunications network. Here considering, the M/M/2 retrial queue in which customers arrived according to Poisson stream with rate $\lambda>0$ at a service facility consisting of two identical exponential servers. A customer who finds both the servers busy is obliged to leave the service area temporarily but he comes back after an exponentially distributed amount of time. Between trials, a customer is said to be in "ORBIT". The results show finds that the steady-state probabilities for the M/M/2 queue with state-dependent service rate. The service rate v_1 if one server is busy and v_2 if both the servers are busy, also illustrate the numerical example.

6.2   The Applications of Queuing Models in Processor-Shared Memory

Queuing theory is an important branch of applied probability, and it involves the mathematical study of "queues" or waiting lines. The formation of a waiting line is a common phenomenon that occurs whenever the current demand for a service exceeds the current capacity to provide that service. Decisions regarding the amount of service to be provided are made frequently in industry and elsewhere. Since it is frequently impossible to accurately predict when the units will arrive to seek service and/or how much time will be required to provide that service, these decisions are often difficult ones [3]. Providing too much service capacity would involve excessive costs. On the other hand, not providing enough service capacity would cause the waiting line to become excessively long at times. Excessive waiting also is costly in one sense, whether it is the social cost or the cost of lost customers. Therefore, the ultimate goal is to achieve an economic balance between the cost of service and the cost associated with waiting for that service. The first study on waiting lines (queue) was "The theory of probabilities and telephone conversations" by A.K. Erlang in 1909, which aimed to answer a number of questions concerning the number of service channels to be provided in the context of random demand for such services. Queues are essentially studied with the objective of improving the behavior of the system as a whole.

6.3   The Basic Structure of Queuing Models

A system consisting of a servicing facility, a process of arrival of customers who wish to be served by the facility, and the process of service is called a queuing system. The term "customer" may refer to, for example, a machine arriving at an inspection center or a person arriving at a booking center in a railway station. Customers are selected for service by certain rules, known as queue discipline [4]. The service for the customers is performed as per the queue discipline by the service station, after which the customers leave the system. Figure 6.1 shows the typical queuing process.

Figure 6.1 A typical queuing process.

6.4   Characteristics of Queuing System

The basic characteristics of a queuing system are

    a) The arrival pattern of customers
    b) The service pattern of servers
    c) The queue disciplines
    d) The system capacity
    e) The number of servers

6.5   The Arrival Pattern of Customers

The pattern in which the arrival takes place may be from a particular behavior in a bulk (group) or in single. In such a situation, not only the time between successive arrivals viz., inter arrival time of the batches may be stochastic, but also the number if customers in the batch. The stationary arrival process does not involve variation of the probabilistic structure with respect to time, whereas the non-stationary arrival process does involve variation of the probabilistic with respect to time. Balking can be defined as the behavior of the customer on examining the length of the queue and thereby skipping it without joining. Customers leaving the queue impatiently, after having waited for some time for service, without getting service are called reneged customers.

6.6   The Service Pattern of Servers Queue Discipline, System Capacity, and the Number of Servers

Most importantly, a probability distribution is needed to describe the sequence of customer service times. Services may also be single or batch. One generally thinks of one customer being served at a time by a given server, but there are many situations where customers may be served simultaneously by the same server, such as a computer with parallel processing, sightseers on a guided tour, or people boarding a train. The service process may be depending on the number of customers waiting for service. The situation in which service depends on the number of customers waiting is referred to as a state-dependent service. Service can be stationary or non-stationary with respect to time. The dependence on time is not to be confused with dependence on the state. The former does not depend on the number of customers in the system, but rather on how long it has been in operation. If the service rate is high, it is very likely that some customers will be delayed by waiting in line. In general, customers arrive and depart at irregular intervals. Hence, the queue length will assume no definitive pattern unless arrivals and services are deterministic [5]. A probability distribution for queue length will be the result of two separate process-arrivals and services-which are mutually independent. For the customers who are waiting for service, the procedure by which customers are selected for service is termed queue discipline. The "First in first out" (FIFO) is the most commonly used service discipline following the natural law. "Last in first out" (LIFO) is also followed in many occasions. Such a queue discipline is followed in the inventory system, where there is no obsolescence of stored units, since the last arrived unit is easier to reach. In a "service in random order" (SIRO), the customers are assigned priorities while they enter the system. The customers with higher priority are selected for service before those with lower priority, whatever may be their time of arrival to the system. The number of customers, who can be accommodated in the queue and at a service center put together, is called the system capacity [6]. It may be finite or infinite. The number of servers in a queuing model can be finite or infinite. In case of more than one server, depending upon the nature and requirement of the service, the servers may be arranged in series or parallel or combination of both. In a single server model, there will be only one server, whereas in a multi-server model, there will be more than one parallel server. The queuing system which has many servers in series is called multistage queuing system.

6.7   Kendall's Notation

Kendall's notation is most widely used to represent a queuing system. According to this notation, a queuing system is denoted as A/B/X/Y/Z., Where A denotes the inter-arrival time distribution of the customers from the source population; B stands for the service time distribution of the given service facility; X is the number of servers; Y is the capacity of the system, and Z stands for the queue discipline is FIFO, then the system is denoted as A/B/X without mentioning Y and Z. For example, the notation M/M/2/∞/ FIFO indicates a queuing process with exponential inter-arrival times, exponential service times, two parallel servers, no restriction on the maximum number allowed in the system, and first –come, first –served queue discipline [7]. In many situations, only the first three symbols are used. Current practice is to omit the service-capacity symbol if no restriction is imposed (Y=∞) and to omit the discipline if it is first come, first served (Z=FIFO).

6.8   The Formation of Retrial Queues as a Solution

Queuing systems with repeated attempts are characterized by that a customer who finds all the servers are busy when they arrive. They do not like to leave the service area. They repeat their request after some random time. Between their trials, the blocked customers join in a pool of unsatisfied customers called "ORBIT". When a telephone caller when dialing a number (say, public utility) gets a busy signal (finds the telephone facility busy because it is already engaged by another caller). In such cases the caller repeats his call after a random amount of time; other callers also do the same. These callers become sources of repeated calls and remain in an "ORBIT", while a fresh caller (called a primary caller) who finds the facility free immediately gets the facility. These considerations bring into focus the need for a new queuing system, which is called the "retrial queuing system" as shown in Figure 6.2.

6.9   The Stationary Analysis of the Characteristics of the M/M/2 Queue with Constant Repeated Attempts

Consider an M/M/2 retrial queuing system at which customers arrive according to a Poisson process with rate $\lambda > 0$. Any primary arrival who finds all servers busy upon arrival leaves the system facility immediately and joins the orbit. Figure 6.1 shows the retrial queue. The control policy to access to the server from in the orbit, and 0, when the orbit is empty. Any primary arrival or retrial who finds an idle server is served immediately. The successive times are assumed to be mutually independent and exponentially distributed with parameter $v > 0$. The input stream of primary arrivals, service times and intervals between repeated attempts are assumed to be mutually independent. State – transition diagram is shown in Figure 6.3. The state of the system at time t can be described by the bidimensional process.

$$X_{(t)} = \{(C(t), N(t)) \mid t \mid \geq 0\}$$

where
      C (t) denotes the number of busy servers at time t and
      N (t) denotes the number of customers in the orbit at time t.
      X is an irreducible Markovian process whose state space S is the
          product of finite set $\{0, 1, 2\}$ and half-line, i.e. $S = \{0, 1, 2\} \times Z_+$

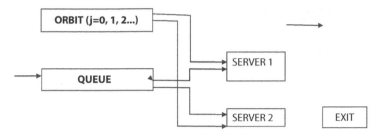

Figure 6.2 Retrial queues.

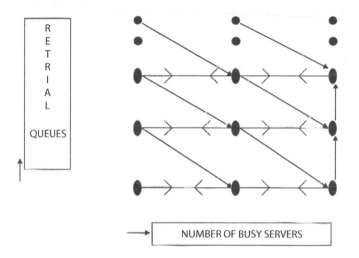

Figure 6.3 Number of busy servers.

Define the limit distribution

$$P_{ij} = \lim_{t \to \infty} P \ \{ \ (C \ (= i, N \ (t) = j, t)) \} \ ; \ i = 0, 1, 2, 3$$

$$P_{ij} = \lim_{t \to} P \ \{ \ (C \ (= i, N \ (t) = j, t)) \} \ ; \ j = 0, 1, 2, 3$$

Which for a standard Markov process always exist?
The steady state equations are

$$(\lambda + \mu \ (1 - \delta_{j0}) \ P_{0j} \ = \nu \rho_{1j} : j \geq 0 \tag{6.1}$$

$$(\lambda + \nu + \mu \ (1 - \delta_{j0}) \ P_{1j} \ = \lambda \ P_{0j} + 2 \ \nu \ P_{2j} + \mu \acute{P}_{0j+1} \ ; j \geq 0 \tag{6.2}$$

$$(\lambda + 2v) \, P_{2j} = \lambda \, P_{1j} + \mu \, P_{1,j+1} + \lambda \, P_2, j - 1 \, (1 - \delta \, j0) \, ; \, j \geq 0 \quad (6.3)$$

Where δ is Kronecker's delta

$$\delta_{j0} =$$

$$\delta_{jo} = \left\{ \begin{array}{l|l} 1 & 1; j = o \\ 0 & o; j \neq o \end{array} \right\}$$

6.10   Computation of the Steady-State Probabilities

Theorem 4.9.1 A Necessary and sufficient condition for the ergodicity of the M/M/2 constant retrial queue is

Which for a standard Markov process always exist? The steady state equations are

$$(\lambda + \mu \, (1 - \delta_{j0}) \, P_{0j} = v\rho_{1j} \, ; j \geq 0 \quad (6.4)$$

$$(\lambda + v + \mu \, (1 - \delta_{j0}) \, P_{1j} = \lambda P_{0j} + 2vP_{2j} + \mu P_{0,j+1} ; j \geq 0 \quad (6.5)$$

$$(\lambda + 2v) \, P_{2j} = \lambda P_{1j} + \mu P_{1,j+1} + \lambda P_{2,j-1} \, (1 - \delta_{j0}) ; j \geq 0 \quad (6.6)$$

Where δ is Kronecker's delta

$$\delta_{jo} = \left\{ \begin{array}{l|l} 1 & 1; j = o \\ 0 & o; j \neq o \end{array} \right\}$$

$$\frac{\lambda(\lambda+\mu)^2}{2v\mu(\lambda+v+\mu)} < 1$$

Proof
From Equation (6.3), we get

$$P_{1j} - \frac{(\lambda+\mu(1-j_0))P_{0j}}{N} \quad (6.7)$$

Using (6.5) and (6.7) we can express the probabilities $\{P_{2j}\}$ in terms of the sequence $\{P_{0j}\}$

$$2\,v\,P_{2j} = (\lambda + v + \mu\,(1 - \delta_{j0}))\,P_{1j} - \lambda P_{0j} - \mu P_{0,j+1}$$

$$2\,v P_{2j} = (\lambda + v + \mu(1 - \delta_{j0})) - \left(\frac{(\lambda + \mu(1 - \delta_{j0}))P_{0j}}{v}\right) - \lambda P_{0j} - \mu P_{0,j+1}$$

$$2\,v P_{2j} - \left(\frac{\left((\lambda^2 + \lambda\,\mu(1 - \delta_{j0}) + \lambda v + v\,\mu(1 - \delta_{j0})P_{0j} + \lambda\mu(1 - \delta\,jo)\right) + \mu^2(1 - \delta\,jo)^2}{v}\right)$$
$$P_{0j} - \lambda P - \mu P_{0j}$$

$$2\,v P_{2j} = \left(\frac{\left((\lambda + \lambda\,\mu(1 - \delta_{j0}) + \lambda v + v\,\mu(1 - \delta_{j0})P_{0j} + v\mu(1 - \delta\,jo)\right)Poj) - \lambda v Poj}{v}\right) - \mu P_{0j}$$

$$2\,v P_{2j} = \left(\frac{\left(\lambda + \mu(1 - \delta_{j0})^2 + \lambda v + v\,\mu(1 - \delta_{j0}) - (1 - \delta\,jo)\right) - \lambda v)}{v} P_{0j}\right) - \mu P_{0j}$$

$$P2j - \left(\frac{(\lambda + \mu(1 - \delta_{j0})^2 + v\,\mu(1 - \delta_{j0}))}{v} P_{0j}\right) - \frac{\mu}{2v} P_{0j+1} \qquad \text{(II)}$$

By substituting equation I and II in equation 6.6, I get the following

$$(\lambda + 2\,v)\,P_{2j} = \lambda\,P_{1j} + \mu\,P_{1,j+1} + \lambda\,P_{2,j-1}\,(1 - \delta_{j0})\,;\,j \geq 0$$

Since

$$P_{1j} = \left(\frac{\lambda + \mu(1 - \delta_{j0})}{v} P_{0j}\right) \qquad \text{(I)}$$

$$P_{2j} - \left(\frac{(\lambda + \mu(1 - \delta_{j0}) + v\,\mu(1 - \delta_{j0}))}{2v2}\right) P_{0j} - \frac{\mu}{2v} P_{0,j+1} \qquad \text{(II)}$$

$$P_{1,j+1} = \left(\frac{\lambda + \mu(1 - \delta j+1, o)}{v} P_{0,j+1}\right)$$

$$P_{2,j-1} = \left(\frac{(\lambda + \mu(1-\delta_{j-1,0}) + v\,\mu(1-\delta_{j-1,0}))}{2v2} \right) P_{0,j-1} - \frac{\mu}{2v} P_{0j}$$

By substituting all these values in Equation (6.6) then

$$\lambda + 2v \left(\frac{(\lambda + \mu(1-\delta)^2 + v\,\mu(1-\delta_{j0}))}{2v2} \right) P_{0,j} - \frac{\mu}{2v}$$

$$P_{0j+1} = \lambda \left(\frac{\lambda + \mu(1-\delta jo)}{v} P_{0,j} \right) + \mu \left(\frac{\lambda + \mu(1-\delta j + 1,0)}{v} P_{0,j+1} \right)$$

$$+ (1 - \delta jo\lambda\, \frac{(\lambda + \mu(1-\delta j - 1,0)^2 + v\,\mu(1-\delta_{j\_1,0}) P_{0,j-1})}{2v2} - \frac{\mu}{2v} P_{0,j}$$

Collecting P_{0j} on L.H.S and the remaining on the R.H.S

$$(\lambda + 2v) \left(\frac{\lambda + \mu(1-\delta))^2 + v\,\mu(1-\delta)}{2v2} P_{0,j+1} \right)$$

Taking L. H. S. and solving

$$\boxed{\alpha_j \quad \frac{\lambda\lceil (\lambda + \mu(1(1 \quad _j))^2 + v\mu(1 \quad _j); j \geq 00}{2v}}$$

$$\frac{(2\,v\,[\lambda^{2\ +}\ 2\lambda\mu(1-\delta_{j0}) + \mu(1-\delta_{j0})^2] - 2\,v\lambda^2 - 2v\lambda\mu(1-\delta_{j0}) + \lambda v\mu(1-\delta_{j0}))}{2v^2 * p_{0j}}$$

$$\frac{(2\,v\,[\lambda^{2+}\ 4\,v\lambda\mu(1-\delta_{j0}) + 2\,v\mu^2(1-\delta_{j0})^2] - 2\,v\lambda^{2-} 2\,v\lambda\mu(1-\delta_{j0}) + \lambda\,v\,\mu(1-\delta_{j0}))}{2v^2 * p_{0j}}$$

$$\frac{(3\lambda\mu(1-\delta_{j0}) + 2v\mu^2(1-\delta_{j0}) + 2\,v\mu^2(1-\delta_{j0})^2 + 2\,v^2\mu(1-\delta_{j0})}{2v^2}$$

Using the condition $\displaystyle\sum_{(i,j)} P_{ij} = 1$, by adding P_{0j}, P_{1j}, P_{2j} and equating to 1.

$$\left(\frac{2v[\lambda^2 + 2\lambda\mu(1-\delta_{j0}) + \mu(1-\delta_{j0})^2] - 2v\lambda^2 - 2v\lambda\mu(1-\delta_{j0}) + \lambda v\mu(1-\delta_{j0})}{2v^2}\right)P_{0j}$$

$$\left(\frac{2v\lambda^2 + 4\lambda\mu(1-\delta_{j0}) + 2v\mu^2(1-\delta^{j0})^2 - 2v\lambda^2 - 2v\lambda\mu(1-\delta_{j0}) + \lambda v\mu(1-\delta_{j0})}{2v^2}\right)P_{0j}$$

$$\left(\frac{3\lambda v\mu(1-\delta_{j0}) + 2v\mu^2(1-\delta_{j0})^2 + 2v^2\mu(1-\delta_{j0})}{2v^2}\right)$$

$$\left(\frac{3\lambda\mu}{2v}\frac{\mu^2(1-\delta_{j0})}{v} + \frac{v\mu}{v}\right)(1-\delta_{j0})$$

Taking $\dfrac{\mu}{v}$ and $(1-\delta_{j0})$ as common

$\therefore$L.H.S.

$$(\alpha_j + \beta_j)\,P_{0j}$$

Taking R.H.S. and solving

$$\left(\frac{\lambda\mu}{2v} + \mu + \frac{\lambda\mu}{v} + \frac{\mu^2(1-\delta_{j+1,0})}{v}\right)P_{0,j+1} = \frac{\mu}{v}\left(\frac{\lambda}{2} + v + \lambda + \mu(1-\delta_{j0})\right)$$

$$\left(\frac{\lambda\mu}{2v} + \mu + \frac{\lambda\mu}{v} + \frac{\mu^2(1-\delta_{j+1,0})}{v}\right)P_{0,j+1} = \frac{\mu}{v}\left(\frac{\lambda}{2} + v + \lambda + \mu(1-\delta_{j0})\right)$$

$$\beta_{j1} - \frac{\mu}{v^2}\left(\frac{3\lambda}{2} + v + \lambda + \mu(1-\delta_{j0})\right)$$

$\therefore$The equation (6.7) becomes

$$(\alpha_j + \beta_j) = P_{0j} = \alpha_{j-1}P_{0,j-1}(1-\delta_{j0}) + \beta_{j+1},P_{0,j+1}; j \geq 0$$

The sequence $\{P_{0j}\}$ is a birth and death process with birth parameter α_j and death parameter β_j

$$S_1 = \sum_{j=1}^{\infty}\prod_{k=o}^{j-1}\frac{\alpha_k}{\beta_{k+1}}$$

$$S_2 = \sum_{j=1}^{\infty} \left(\alpha_j \prod_{k=o}^{j-1} \frac{\alpha_k}{\beta_{k+1}} \right)^{-1}$$

Defining

$$\alpha = \frac{\lambda((\lambda+\mu)^2 + \nu\mu)}{2\nu^2}$$

$$\beta = \frac{\mu}{\nu} \left(\frac{3}{2}\lambda + \nu + \mu \right)$$

$$\gamma = \frac{\lambda^3}{2\nu^2}$$

Then it follows that

$$S_1 = \frac{\lambda}{\beta} \sum_{j=o}^{\infty} \left(\frac{\alpha_j}{\beta_j} \right)$$

$$S_2 = \frac{1}{\beta} \sum_{j=1}^{\infty} \left(\frac{\beta_j}{\alpha_j} \right)$$

Consequently, S1<∞ if and only if α<β, and S2<∞ if and only if β<α. Hence the classification of the states in birth and death processes guarantees that {P0j} is ergodic in and only if α<β; null recurrent if and only if α=β, transient if and only if α>β

α<β if and only if

$$\frac{\lambda(\lambda+\mu)^2}{2\nu\mu(\lambda+\nu+\mu)} < 1$$

$$\left(\frac{\dfrac{\lambda(\lambda+\mu)^2}{2\nu^2} + \dfrac{\lambda\nu\mu}{2\nu^2}}{\dfrac{\lambda\mu}{\nu} + \dfrac{\mu}{\nu}(\lambda+\nu+\mu)} \right) < 1$$

$$\frac{\lambda(\lambda+\mu)^2}{2\nu^2} \frac{\nu}{\mu(\lambda+\nu+\mu)} < 1$$

$$\frac{\lambda(\lambda + \mu)^2}{2\nu\mu\,(\lambda + \nu + \mu)} < 1$$

This gives the theorem. Since the stationary probabilities for the birth and death sequence $\{P_{0j}\}$ are given by

$$P_{oj} = P_{oo} \prod_{k=o}^{j-1} \frac{\alpha_k}{\beta_{k+1}}$$

$$P_{oj} = P_{oo} \frac{\alpha_0 \cdot \alpha_1 \ldots \ldots \alpha_{j-1}}{\beta_1 \cdot \beta_2 \ldots \ldots \beta_j}$$

$$P_{oj} = P_{oo} \frac{\gamma\alpha_{j-1}}{\beta_j}$$

$$P_{oj} = \left(\frac{\gamma\alpha}{\beta}\right)^j P_{oo}; j \geq 1$$

It follows (I), (II) and the normalizing condition $\sum_{(i,j)} P_{ij} = 1$ the following theorem.

Theorem 2.2

Under the stability assumption, the stationary distribution of the state of the sever and the number of customers in orbit is given by

$$P_{0j} = \frac{\lambda^2}{(\lambda + \mu)^2 + \nu\mu}\left(\frac{\lambda[(\lambda + \mu)^2 + \nu\mu]}{2\nu^2} \frac{2\nu^2}{\mu[(\nu + 2\nu)\lambda + 2\nu(\nu + \mu)]}\right)$$

$$p_{0j} = (\lambda + \mu)^2 + \nu\mu\left(\frac{\lambda^2(\lambda[(\lambda + \mu)^2 + \nu\mu])^i}{\nu\mu[3\lambda + 2(\nu + \mu)]}\right) P_{00}; j \geq 1$$

$$P_{1j} = \frac{\lambda + \mu(1 - \delta_{j0})}{\nu} P_{0j}; j \geq o$$

$$P_{2j} = \left(\frac{(\lambda + \mu(1 - \delta_{j_o}))^2 + \nu\mu(1 - \delta_{j0})}{2\nu^2}\right) P_{0j} \frac{\mu P_{0,j+1}}{2\nu}; j \geq o$$

$$p_{2,j} = \frac{(\lambda + \mu)^2 + \nu\mu}{2\nu^2} P_{0j} - \frac{\mu}{2\nu} P_{0,j+1}$$

=1, by adding P_{0j}, P_{1j}, P_{2j} and equating to 1.

Using the condition $\displaystyle\sum_{(i,j)} P_{ij}$

$$+ \mu)(\lambda + 2v))$$

Then finally we define the Poo as

$$P_{00} = \frac{2v\mu(\lambda+v+\mu) - \lambda(\lambda+\mu)^2}{\mu(2v(\lambda+v)+(\lambda+\mu)(\lambda+2v))}$$

6.11   Application of Retrial Queues

Queuing systems with repeated attempts of queues with returning customers are characterized by the following features. A request finding all servers busy upon arrivals leaves the service area but after some random time repeats his demand. Queuing models are often used for the performance analysis of computer and communication systems. In case of many real life systems, retrial queues can be applied in the performance modelling for example in modelling magnetic disk memory systems, cellular mobile networks, computer networks and local-area networks with non-persistent CSMA/CD(CARRIER SENSE MULTIPLE ACCESS WITH COLLISION DETECTION) protocols and Star topology.

6.12   Conclusion

Is this study we obtain the steady state probabilities for M/M/2 queue with constant repeated attempts and for M/M/2 retrial queue with state dependent service rate. In M/M/2 state dependent service rate model, I made a study on the variation of probabilities when the number of customers in the orbit changes. By keeping the value of λ, μ, v1, and v2 as constant and changing the value of j, I find the changing probabilities for idle serve, one server as busy, both the servers are busy (P0j, P1j, P2j) respectively. The Table 6.1 and Table 6.2 shows the value of different probabilities for different number of customers in the orbit.

Table 6.1   Number of customers in the orbit.

λ	1
μ	2
V_1	1
V_2	2

Table 6.2   Variations of probabilities.

j	P_{0j}	P_{1j}	P_{2j}
0	0.024476	0.024476	0.119658
1	0.014957	0.044872	0.073124
2	0.009141	0.027422	0.044687
3	0.005586	0.016758	0.027309
4	0.003414	0.010241	0.016689
5	0.002086	0.006258	0.010199
6	0.001275	0.003824	0.006233
7	0.000779	0.002337	0.003809
8	0.000476	0.001428	0.002328
9	0.000291	0.000873	0.001422
10	0.000178	0.000533	0.00869
11	0.000109	0.000326	0.000531
12	0.000066	0.000199	0.000325
13	0.000041	0.000122	0.000198
14	0.000025	0.000074	0.000121
15	0.000015	0.000046	0.000074

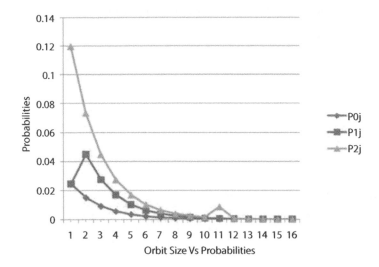

Orbit Size Vs Probabilities

References

1. Dudin, A.N. and Dudina, O.S., Analysis of multiserver retrial queueing system with varying capacity and parameter. *Mathematical Problems in Engineering,* 2015, Article 180481, 12, 2015. https://doi.org/10.1155/2015/180481.
2. Dimitriou, I., A mixed priority retrial queue with negative arrivals, unreliable server and multiple vacations. Intelligent Systems and Networks Group, Department of Electrical and Electronic Engineering, Imperial College, London, *Appl. Math. Model.,* SW7 2BT, UK, 37, 1295–1309 2 April 2012, https://doi.org/10.1016/j.apm.2012.04.011.
3. Artalejo, J.R., Steady State Analysis of an M/G/1 queue with repeated attempts and two-phase service. *Qual. Technol. Quant. Manag.,* 1, 189–199, 2004.
4. Garg, R.L. and Sing, P., Queue dependent servers queueing system. *Microelectron. Reliab.,* 33, 2289–2295, 1993.
5. Gross, D. and Harris, C.M., *Fundamentals of queueing theory,* Third Edition, John Wiley and Sons, 2018.
6. Kleinrock, L., *Queueing systems,* vol. 1, Theory John Wiley, New York, 1975.
7. Medhi, J., *Stochastic models in queueing theory,* Second Edition, Academic Publishers, 1991.

Smart e-Learning System with IoT-Enabled for Personalized Assessment

Veeramanickam M.R.M.[1], Visalatchi S.[1] and Ahmed A. Elngar[2*]

[1]*Department of Information Technology, Shri Vishnu Engineering College of Women (A), Andhra Pradesh, India*
[2]*Faculty of Computers and Artificial Intelligence, Beni-Suef University, Beni-Suef City, Egypt*

Abstract

Sharing classroom notes is an effective way of utilizing IoT technology with the e-learning concept. The learning system can be built to benefit the students with a smart system for hands-on notes sharing services. e-Learning benefits the teaching process by being equipped with a computer and enhanced software to share teaching notes to create a smart campus. IoT-enabled Smart campus will give effective transit of e-notes data from one point to another point. Our objectives are to create easily shareable notes sharing using Applications software to collect notes from regular teaching activities and which allow us to share via IoT-enabled medium to access within the network limit.

Keywords: Internet of Things, Raspberry Pi, e-Learning, personalized assessment

7.1 Introduction

The Internet of Things is the adhoc or permanent connectivity of physical objects or things integrated with electronic devices, and sensors, using things will exchange data with the device administrator, working cluster head, and any other associated devices in the network. Each internet of Things is a unique address identity via its assimilated computing system

---

Corresponding author: elngar_7@yahoo.co.uk

Ahmed A. Elgnar, Vigneshwar M, Krishna Kant Singh and Zdzislaw Polkowski (eds.) Handbook of Computational Sciences: A Multi and Interdisciplinary Approach, (137–152) © 2023 Scrivener Publishing LLC

network but can interoperable inside the connected Internet system. Internet of Things can influence the everywhere of e-learning implementation usage. You will discuss specific examples of how "IoT can enrich interactive learning, games-based learning, and on-demand learning to improve the overall learning experience" [1]. As we can study today's trends in the industry by what means e-learning is progressing using upcoming technology from the existing old methodology to a further modern society as well as collaborative blended learning design, and how the Internet of Things helps in that evolution.

One can discover n number of design cases that will enhance an indication of the importance of IoT fits within existing learning systems and a performance model and the way it will influence any field in the future.

"The fundamental components which make the internet of things reality are:

(i)   Hardware – Constructing the physical objects reactive by interacting and giving objects the ability to retrieve data and respond according to the instructions.
(ii) Software – Letting the data collection, storage, processing, manipulating, and instructing.
(iii) Communication Infrastructure – Furthermost important is communication among all infrastructure objects which consists of various protocols & technologies on which enable to exchange data between two physical objects each other" [2].

Internet of things projects are the best to learn about skills necessary to build IoT applications that can be deployed. To start with any internet of things platform, first of all you will need a platform. What better to get started than Raspberry Pi. "Raspberry Pi is a small kit credit card-sized single-board computer developed by Raspberry Pi foundation for the teaching and learning of basic computer science subjects in schools" [3]. There are hundreds of reasons why you should build your internet of things application on this platform. The major reason is the freedom of the open-source community and excellent community support.

All major IoT tech companies working to capture IoT markets by 2020 for revenue and paradigm shift in their business trends also. Big things are going to change in business as tech giants focus shift too. Apple and Google are top runners as per figure records as shown in Figure 7.1.

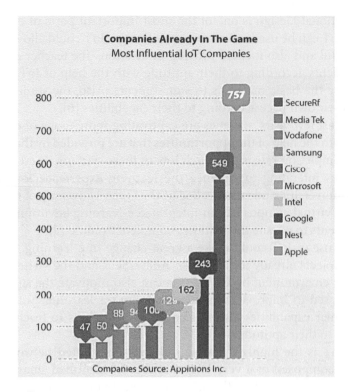

Figure 7.1 IoT company influence [4].

7.2   Literature Study

The author discussed the way to improve the e-learning platform and design features with IoT technology. Some of the ways to share e-notes sharing using the Google Drive platform, e-mail communication, different subjects of video lectures, etc. some own disadvantages are there using the old platform. With the help of IoT platforms and sensors can collect information within the campus, widely using technologies for RFID tags and also process it for further useful ways [5]. "International Joint project as initiated among Argentina & Brazil. This model is the context-aware based environment and culture-concerned design feature of a model which integrates into two different distinct e-learning using Adapt Web, i.e., E-Teacher + SAVER environment. SAVER is Software Virtual para Education Remote environment" [6–8].

Instructional Design is one of the most important parts of e-learning. And the IoT can be used in Instructional Design. IoT could allow students to be playful and also it could provide motivation. The teacher could also teach students according to their aptitude with the help of IoT. Teachers can choose the basic materials to suit students. Also, the students could learn at their own pace according to their capabilities [6].

In the last few years, societies are captivating more usage of e-learning courses with the help of the opportunities that are provided by the Internet. But the completion rate is too much low in these systems. There is a work in progress intending to enhance the learning experience for distance learning university students enrolled at the Open University of Catalonia. The UOC virtual campus has an integrated e-learning environment. This helps students to pursue their studies completely online [9].

So, the use of IoT could make a great change in e-learning. There are various projects already initiated like Adapt-SUR and the virtual campus e-learning environment by UOC. This can also motivate the student and could be used to improve the student's desire for learning. Students can learn at their capabilities also this could help teachers to teach students according to their aptitude.

"The IoT is the highly dynamic radically distributed networked system. It is composed of a very large number of identified smart objects" [10] many interconnects with each other object nodes, and also with end users or any other entities in the network model. Entering the era of IoT, the use of small, chip and flexible computer hardware allows end-user programming to become present. Raspberry Pi is one of these hardware. It is a fully customized and programmable computer board. With the help of the emerging trends in user programming, non-professional end-users get an opportunity to make changes in the products according to their needs [11].

There are various e-learning systems that are being practiced in use today in teaching and learning. But the actual application and usage with modern design features are very low due to the lack of actual current usage study. Hence the usage of the IoT platform leads to a great change in model smart e-learning systems.

7.3   Architecture Model

In this proposed system the notes that a teacher writes on the scribble pad are collected using Raspberry Pi which is analyzed by the scribble pad coordinates. Whatever data is collected by the Raspberry Pi is stored on the Server that is Web Server/FTP Server. The server is connected to the Raspberry Pi from which it fetches the data, stores it, processes it, and provides it to students in notes format whenever requested as shown in Figure 7.2.

The web application displays all the contents whichever has been uploaded by the admin/teacher to date. Students who missed the lectures or who don't get the concept at the lecture can access the subject notes easily and learn from them. Students who want to access other professor session lectures can easily do the same using this system.

As all concerned subjects' lectures can be accessed based on access permission to given students users for any subject notes. The proposed system is used to share notes among students who are registered. Apart from this, the students can also upload his/her notes which have been requested by any registered member, but the notes will be only available to everyone if and only if the notes are approved by the admin/teacher.

As the major, part, this project is concerned with how to construct all teaching and learning content as a digital base and easy accessibility among students and all other learners using IoT in a synchronized manner by a few minutes delay to the end-users.

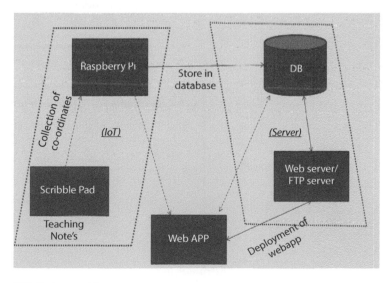

Figure 7.2 System architecture.

Figure 7.3 shows the activity diagram for the proposed system. Activity diagrams are the perfect tool for mapping processes and workflows. Figure 7.3 activity diagram shows all the activities that are carried out by the system.

The activity diagram shows the flow of the system which includes activities like writing the notes, storing notes; logging in to the web app, downloading and uploading the classroom notes and logging out, etc. Activities are nothing but the tasks that are performed by the system.

The component diagram (Figure 7.4) is used from UML. The functionality of all working systems as describes the components placed in a working model for those functionalities. The major components of the system as shown in the above diagram are Web App, Server, Scribble Pad, Raspberry Pi, FTP, etc.

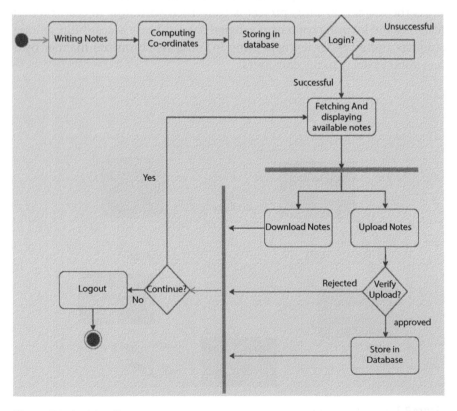

Figure 7.3 Activity diagram.

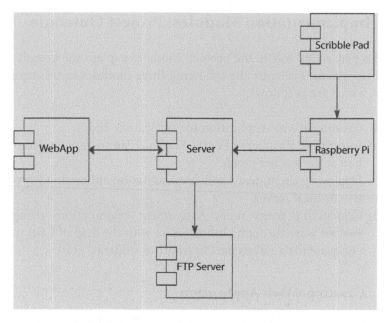

Figure 7.4 Component diagram.

7.4   Assessment Technique: CBR Algorithm

Case-based reasoning module for this assessment is used to understand students' marks and learning analysis for online analysis technique. The overall students' progress and assessments based on this grade will be assigned to the students. Also, this could be helpful for the teacher to analyze how much a student needs to be trained. In CBR, to evaluate the learning ability of a student by assigning grades to him/her summative assessments are used, as summative assessment covers a wider area of the course, as well as the level of the generalization, which is better in the summative assessment than the formative assessment.

This module provides the required corrective mechanism whenever there is failed students to pass grades keep them in multiple training, and assessments, to improve the better predict of probability. In this case, the CBR module finds an equivalent case for the corrective mechanism. Also, the learner could study the other available notes to improve his knowledge about the failed test and apply for the test again. This corrective mechanism helps the student to improve their knowledge about the part of studies that they found harder to learn. And help them to understand and learn things easily and improve their grades.

7.5   Implementation Modules: Project Outcome

Modules play a vital role in the project. Modules explain the overall working of the system. There are the following three modules in this proposed system, which are as follows:

a) Creating a Web Application for the learner end.
b) Integrating Raspberry Pi and Scribble Pad to generate content at the teacher's end.
c) Deploying client host a web application on either cloud system or local server.
d) Conducting many more Assessment examinations using various ways through Online Exam with the help of CBR to complete the analysis part to improve students' grades.

7.5.1   Creating a Web Application

This module is for creating a User Interface so a user can access the complete e-learning platform. The learners are allowed to upload (after approval), view notes that are available in the database, and download those notes. A teacher can do the same things (uploading these e-notes with help of administrator accesses by applications usage, and the teacher can approve students' notes as a content generation. Also, the web app could be used to access the notes that are uploaded directly from the input notes scribble pad through Raspberry Pi.

Figure 7.5 below is the startup homepage of the developed IoT based application which was received in a Mobile phone. The resultant start up page is thus exhibited as shown in Figure 7.6. The application can be even carried out to standalone systems, hand held systems, and also Mobile phones in particular.

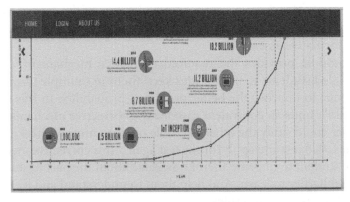

Figure 7.5 Homepage.

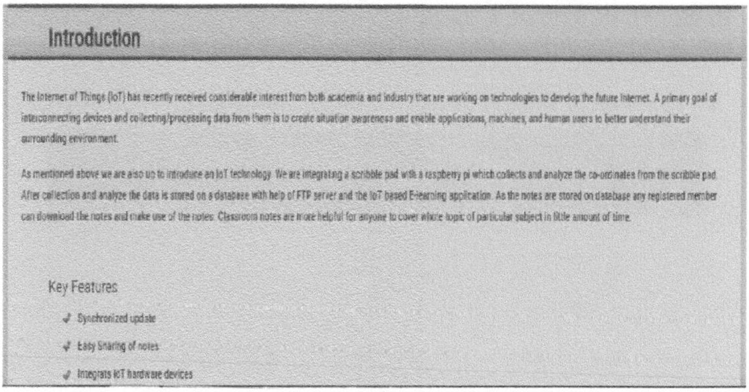

Figure 7.6 Homepage – e-learning platform introduction.

Figure 7.7 exhibits the online page where the online page exhibits the example notes available online. This exhibits the pages of the available online pages where materials like the presentations, other docs which might be a document format, picture format, etc., can be made available.

Figure 7.7 Download notes.

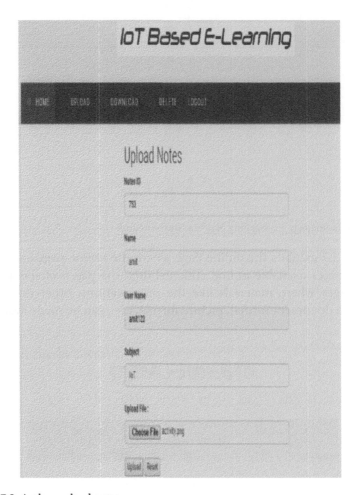

Figure 7.8 Author upload notes.

Figure 7.8 exhibits the online page where the author can upload contents online through this login authorized by the system. The authorized person will be able to upload the contents and direct the end users – students, seminars or conference attendees, etc., and help them to access the necessary contents made available on the IoT-based e-learning model.

7.5.2 Integrating Raspberry Pi and Scribble Pad

The scribble pad is used to write those contents for teacher helps to store the data in the form e-notes. To do all this firstly the contents written on scribble pad need to be get detected and after that to be stored. To do this we use a small computer i.e. the Raspberry Pi. In this module, we do the coding for integrating the Scribble pad with the Raspberry Pi. So that the coordinates of written data on the Scribble pad get detected and with the help of it Raspberry Pi detects what the written word or content is and after that stores that data in the database as shown in Figure 7.9.

The Raspberry Pi is a suitable great platform to build any simple Internet of the Things Application project. Raspberry is growing tremendously faster to use any IoT Domain. This Raspberry Pi IoT project is cheaper in terms of Cost due to availability Card Size Operating System in affordable price figure; to build our application we can impart IoT using Raspberry Pi to make accesses of student's sharable e-notes data anywhere in the network due to the simple connectivity of the system with scribble pad.

Figure 7.9 "Raspberry Pi 3 Model B kit" [12].

Scribble Pad Inputs
↓
Raspberry Pi Connecting Medium
↓
Store Data-Integrated Device
↓
Sharing E-Notes Data to Server for Uploading in the Websites
↓
Students Can Access Synchronized Classroom e-Notes Using an e-Learning Platform Web Application

7.5.3   Deploying Web App over Internet/FTP Server

In this module, the designed web app is deployed on the Internet/FTP server. So that anyone registered user within the network will be able to access the uploaded notes very easily. This gives an efficient and faster way of sharing notes.

7.5.4   Assessment Technique – Online Exam

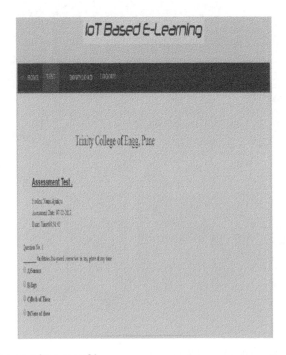

Figure 7.10 Test questions page 01.

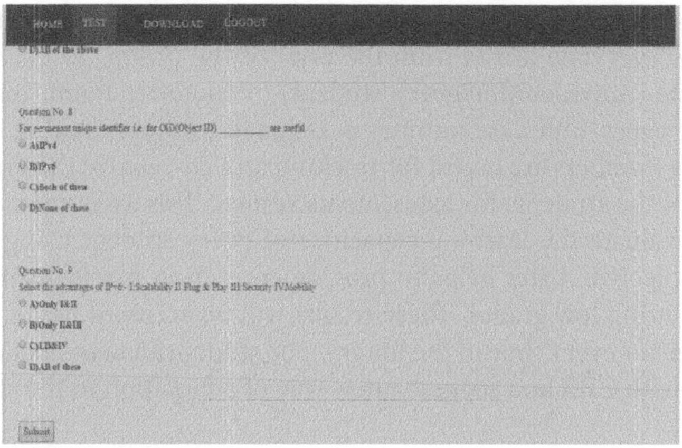

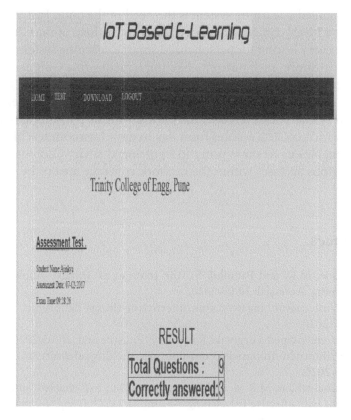

Figure 7.11 Test questions page 02.

Figure 7.12 Test assessment result page.

Figures 7.10, 7.11 and 7.12 are case-based assessments useful to understand how everyone learns from the pool of the group. So enables us to concentrate individual for every student, to motivate them, make them learn. The every-time case number is assigned to that initiating new case. These case numbers are useful for tracking and co-relative the growth and progress of the students for assessments results. This assessments analysis helps to evaluate the learning capacities of every student using the CBR module objective. Later helps to provide correction mechanism students who are getting low grades. These results will be accessed based on memory storage for every time in the library. The student's assessment similarity of results with CBR and suggest a new way of adaptation to the student.

7.6   Conclusion

The IoT-enabled e-learning system is the need of the hour. Faster Delivery of notes at a lower cost can be carried out with the help of the CBR model. This helps every learner for personalized smart e-learning system based on CBR. In the future, such outcome like implements, this CBR assessments analysis study with Machine learning features is the future scope. The main outcomes are easily shareable notes from one end to another end, anywhere, everywhere, by everyone, by sharing with help of this applications software which collects e-notes from day to day classroom teaching activity. This enables us to share using IoT-enhanced smart Campus medium to able various accesses within the network coverage area or by the cloud systems.

References

1. Kharade, M.K. and Pattathil, S., The Internet of Things—Applications in eLearning, Accessed: 10/05/2020.
2. http://internetofthingswiki.com/internet-of-things-definition/, Accessed: 10/05/2020.
3. https://en.wikipedia.org/wiki/Raspberry_Pi, Accessed: 10/05/2020.
4. http://internetofthingswiki.com/internet-of-things-definition/, Accessed: 10/05/2020.
5. Veeramanickam, M.R.M. and Mohanapriya, M., IoT enabled futures smart campus with effective E-Learning: i-Campus. *GSTF J. Eng. Technol. (JET)*, 3, 4, 81–87, April 2016.

6. Matsuo, K., Barolli, L., Xhafa, F., Kolici, V., Koyama, A., Durresi, A., Miho, R., Implementation of an E-learning system using P2P, web and sensor technologies. *Proc. of AINA*, pp. 800–807, 2009.

7. Domingo, M.G. and Forner, J.A.M., Expanding the learning environment: Combining physicality and virtuality – The Internet of Things for eLearning. *Proc. of IEEE 10th International Conference on Advanced Learning Technologies (ICALT)*, pp. 730–731, 2010.

8. Gasparini, Eyharabide, V., Schiaffino, S., Pimenta, M.S., Amandi, A., de Oliveira, J.P.M., Improving user profiling for a richer personalization: Modeling context in E-learning, in: *Intelligent and Adaptive Learning Systems: Technology Enhanced Support for Learners and Teachers*, Chapter 12, pp. 182–197, 2012.

9. Jhorman Andres Villanueva, V., Jack Daniels Marquez, F., Zeida Maria Solarte, A., Dvalos, A.G., Architecture for integrating real objects with virtual academic communities. *2015 Fifth International Conference on E-Learning*, April 2015, pp. 385–391, DOI 10.1109/ECONF.2015.74.

10. Vermesan, O., European Research Cluster on the Internet of Things, [Online]:http://www.internet-of-things-research.eu/about_iot.htm Accessed: 10/05/2020, 2010.

11. Gawande, S.V. and Deshmukh, P.R., Raspberry Pi technology. *Int. J. Innov. Emerging Res. Eng.*, 5, 4, 37–40, April 2015, image retrieved from https://www.raspberrypi.org/products/raspberry-pi-3-model-b/ dated on 18 Jan 2017.

12. Stan, K. and Williams, C., Raspberry Pi as a platform for the Internet of Things projects: Experiences and lessons. Association for Computing Machinery, New York, NY, USA, 2017.

8

Implementation of File Sharing System Using Li-Fi Based on Internet of Things (IoT)

**Sunil L. Bangare[1], Shirin Siddiqui[2], Ayush Srivastava[2], Avinash Kumar[2],
Pushkraj Bhagat[2], G. Pradeepini[3], S. T. Patil[4] and Ahmed A. Elngar[5]***

*[1]CSE, Dept., Koneru Lakshmaiah Educational Foundation (K. L. University),
Green Fields, Vaddeswaram, Guntur, A.P., India and Department of Information
Technology, Sinhgad Academy of Engineering, Pune, India
[2]Department of Information Technology, Sinhgad Academy of Engineering, Pune, India
[3]Dept. of Computer Science & Engineering, Koneru Lakshmaiah Educational
Foundation (K. L. University), Green Fields, Vaddeswaram, Guntur, A.P., India
[4]Dept. of Computer Engineering, V. I. T., Pune, India
[5]Faculty of Computers and Artificial Intelligence, Beni-Suef University,
Beni-Suef City, Egypt*

Abstract

In the past, the data transmission speed was limited to only 50kbps, namely, the wired ARPANET connection which was limited to only the US military in the 1960s, and now we have an easily accessible speed of up to 100Mbps. But, there is no stopping here, we can still cross the line and reach the unbelievable speed of transmission of up to 224 GB per second. Yes, that's right, which is equal to downloading 18 movies in the blink of an eye, by not using Radio frequency waves but using LIGHT FIDELITY. It is known as Li-Fi. Li-Fi is the new upcoming technology where the medium of transmission is light, and provides a super-fast speed of transmission of data with being eco-friendly to the environment without producing any harmful radiation to humans and other living creatures. So, with help of light as a medium, by using LED we can easily transfer and receive any text, audio, image, and video files. Like radio waves, visible light is part of the electromagnetic spectrum. The difference is that viable light

Corresponding author: elngar_7@yahoo.co.uk

Ahmed A. Elgnar, Vigneshwar M, Krishna Kant Singh and Zdzislaw Polkowski (eds.) Handbook
of Computational Sciences: A Multi and Interdisciplinary Approach, (153–184) © 2023 Scrivener
Publishing LLC

has a spectrum 10,000 times larger than radio waves. This means Li-Fi has the potential for enormous capacity. Instead of transmitting information via one data stream, visible light would make it possible to transmit the same information using thousands of data streams simultaneously. The world's ever-growing desire for more data at faster rates is pushing Wi-Fi's capacity to its limits. Wi-Fi is achieved by transmitting data through radio waves, but can only transfer so much at a time. By 2019, it was estimated that the world will be exchanging roughly 35 quintillion bytes of information each month, which we have already passed. Because radio frequencies are already in use and heavily regulated, that data is going to struggle to find a spot in line. Wi-Fi is simply running out of space. Capacity is only part of the problem. Wi-Fi is not a terribly efficient solution. The base stations responsible for transmitting radio waves only function at about 5% efficiency, most of the energy being used to cool the stations. For those transmitting sensitive data, security is also a problem, as radio waves travel through solid objects such as walls and doors.

Keywords: ARPANET, radio frequency, light fidelity, Li-Fi, LED

8.1   Introduction

8.1.1   Motivation

The Wi-Fi technology uses a Radio Frequency spectrum that not only exhibits harmful radiations but is also running out of space. By 2019, it was estimated that the world will be exchanging roughly 35 quintillion bytes of information each month, and the estimates for 2030 suggest an unbelievable amount of 572 Zettabytes. Even with the advancements and optimizations done using the 5G technology, there will come a time when Radio Frequency loses its capacity and become all the more harmful for human beings. The Li-Fi Technology will overcome this effect as it uses visible light as a source that is non-hazardous and has an unbelievably high speed of transmission of up to 224 GB per second. Since the frequency of Visible Light is much more than Radio waves the speed of data transfer is also increased to a considerable extent. This technology can help in enabling the internet-of-things (100 times more devices) significantly enhanced secure wireless communication (reduced interception of signals) enhanced energy efficiency by combining data communication and illumination (100 times energy reduction) and complete elimination of health concerns.

The main purpose of this chapter is to make an application that would enable file sharing from one device to another using light as a medium, live video streaming, audio, image, files, text, and anything that could be transferred using the Li-Fi Application that we propose to make.

8.1.2 Problem Statement

Implementation of File sharing System using Li-Fi, based on the Internet of Things (IoT) which includes transferring a file which can be in form of a text, audio, image, or video file from one device/system to another which is possible with the help of light acting as a medium between both the devices without producing harmful radiation, using self-built hardware equipment at home for testing purposes and trying to achieve the maximum speed that can be attained using equipment to show a proof of concept and build the software to transfer almost any kind of data over Visible Light as the medium.

8.1.3 Background

Li-Fi is a revolutionary technology that uses modulation of visible light to transmit a high volume of data. Visible Light Communication (VLC) is an umbrella that integrates all the technologies used for communication using visible light as the medium. The photo phone was a device that transmits speech using a beam of light wirelessly invented on February 19, 1880, by Alexander Graham Bell and his assistant Charles Summer Tainter. Li-Fi uses basic principles of VLC yet uses a two-way communication network protocol providing high connectivity speed. In the year 2006 Professor Harald Hass and his team of researchers started research on VLC technology. They demonstrated the usefulness of Li-Fi during a TED Talk in the year 2011. It was at that moment the term Li-Fi term was invented. The TED talk was entitled Wireless Data from Every Lightbulb. Li-Fi was named in reference to previous technology Wi-Fi (Wireless Fidelity). VLC technology was exhibited in 2012 using Li-Fi. By August 2013, data rates of over 1.6 Gbit/s were demonstrated over a single color LED. In September 2013, a press release said that Li-Fi, or VLC systems in general, do not require line-of-sight conditions. In October 2013, it was reported that Chinese manufacturers were working on Li-Fi development kits. In April 2014, the Russian company StinsComan announced the development of a Li-Fi wireless local network called Beam Caster. Getting better control of the light emitted from organic LEDs (OLEDs) could lead to faster links between the Internet and mobile devices, according to a Scottish researcher. Anyone who has tried to use the Wi-Fi on a crowded airplane or a packed hotel conference room knows it can be maddeningly slow; there usually isn't enough bandwidth. Some researchers, notably Harold Haas, head of the mobile communications group at the University of Edinburgh, have proposed an alternate system-Fi that rapidly flickers room lighting to send signals. To get even more bandwidth out of such a system, it would help if there were an easy way to break the light up into different colors, using individual wavelengths to send different signals. Their current module transfers data at 1.25 gigabytes per second but foresees boosting speeds up to 5 GB/second in the near future.

8.2 Existing System/Related Work

8.2.1 SHARE It

Share It is a cross-platform with over more than 500 Million users worldwide. It can be run on iOS, Android, PC, and Mac allowing us to transfer data consisting of video, audio, files like contacts, word documents, XML files, etc. from one device to another. It is 200 times faster than any Bluetooth inbuilt device with a speed of approx. 20 Mb/sec.

8.2.2 Super Beam

It makes sharing files (and entire folders) between Android devices a breeze. It uses Wi-Fi direct technology or whatever Wi-Fi connection available to transmit data at very high speeds.

8.2.3 Xender

Xender - It has an ability to transfer data of any size and format without using cellular data or Wi-Fi between two mobile devices either Android or iOS. The Team has also worked on the powerful feature "Connect To PC" that integrates devices to transfer files like mobiles to PC or to Smart TV.

8.3 Literature Survey

This section provide a Literature Survey as shown in Table 8.1 and Table 8.2.

Table 8.1 Literature survey.

Sr. no.	Reference	Seed idea/work description	Problems found	Any other criteria
1	[1]	Huffman Coding Technique for image compression	• Implements on gray scale images and can be improved using adaptive Huffman code • Increases Space complexity of data.	• This paper's work supports the compression of BMP, GIF, JPEG image files. • It is a minimal redundancy code.
2	[2]	Integrated Li-Fi(Light Fidelity) For Smart Communication Through Illumination	• In this paper they are going to use DE-9 Serial RS232. • Prototype used is not bidirectional.	In this paper it is vividly specified how Li-Fi is Better than Wi-Fi.
3	[3]	Design of Li-Fi Transceiver	• On-Off Keying encoding style data transmission. • Does not support Multi-user access. • Speed achieved is 115,200 bps only.	Limitations of the research can be removed by using better end devices.

(Continued)

Table 8.1 Literature survey. (*Continued*)

Sr. no	Reference	Seed idea/work description	Problems found	Any other criteria
4	[4]	Image Encoding and Decoding using Base64 technique and it's wireless transmission using Li-Fi	• This technique increases the size of encoded data by more than 33%. • Max distance achieved is 1 meter.	• Not efficient in case of big file transmission. • Time complexity is high.
5	[5]	Subaquatic Message Transmission Using Li-Fi	• Prototype used is not bidirectional and is used for the broadcast purpose. • Inefficient information about Multi-user access.	On-Off Keying Encoding style is used to transmit data. Speed attainable in Gbps.
6	[6]	Subaquatic Data Transmission using Li-Fi	• Proposed system is useful for underwater communication at a faster speed in Gbps.	Using this paper as a base we can improve the pace of transmission with more security.

Table 8.2 Literature survey.

Sr. no.	Reference name	Application	Description	Benefits
1	[1]	Hospital management Patient Monitoring	Temperature, heartbeat, glucose, and respiration sensors capture data from the human body. PIC16F877A changes signals into a digital format and feeds them into Li-Fi module which then sends the data in light form. The light is picked up at the receiver end by the photo sensor. The information received is then presented graphically on a computer.	Avoids frequent contact with the human body and medical equipment.
2	[2]	Vehicle Toll Collection System	The transmitter circuit is installed in every vehicle and a setup is used to send useful encrypted data such as vehicle number, personal identification number and payment gateway password via LED. The Li-Fi receiver with a photo-detector mounted in the middle of the road at tollbooth senses any variations in the light transmitted from LED. An intelligent processor at the receiver side automatically processes the payment using the type of vehicle by means of a wallet linked to the vehicle number and sends a confirmation for the toll deduction through SMS to the user.	Technology can help conserve fuel and create an environmentally friendly environment.

(Continued)

Table 8.2 Literature survey. (*Continued*)

Sr. no.	Reference name	Application	Description	Benefits
3.	[3]	Automatic product identification and intelligent shopping billing	The system has four sections: namely one that identifies products, one that serves as a trolley and a server for billing and payments. In product identification, each product is attached to an RFID tag which contains its details and a unique 14-digit ID. The Trolley consists of an LCD display, LiFi transceiver, a microcontroller where the remaining product details are stored and an RFID reader. The reader can detect all products added to the trolley and updates list if one or more products are removed. LiFi in the trolley communicates with the server Li-Fi and updates the information if needed.	Convenience when shopping. We can significantly reduce the queue or even eliminate its purpose by implementing this process.

(Continued)

Table 8.2 Literature survey. (*Continued*)

Sr. no.	Reference name	Application	Description	Benefits
4	[4]	Smart Transportation Framework	Evaluates the relationship between the speed of the lorry fleet and the transformation time of the traffic lights. The VLC transmitter is installed on the roadway intersection. It transmits traffic management data in real time. The receiver is fixed on each vehicle and decides whether the smart vehicle will move straight ahead or make a turn depending on the message it receives.	The result is significant in proactively reducing accidents caused by repeated lorry acceleration ad deceleration.
5	[5]	Li-Fi network grid system	The system composes of the grid server software and the grid client software with Li-Fi based interaction connections. The grid client software is activated on each client PC. The grid server program comprising of applications for event management and resource management is activated on the server computer. The server monitors different specifications such as storage capacity and computing power linked to the collective resources and activities on the network.	Monitoring specifications such as storage capacity and computing power linked to the collective activities on the network. It uses cheaper and faster speed connectivity resulting in simple implementation and enhanced functionality.

(*Continued*)

Table 8.2 Literature survey. (*Continued*)

Sr. no.	Reference name	Application	Description	Benefits
6	[6]	Beaconing network for interior location application	An LED driver modulates the light discharged by each LED and each LED transmits a specific beacon ID. A camera is used in the detector and the picture sequence is used to identify pixels corresponding to the beacon IDs. Pixels sensed are used to locate image blobs corresponding to each beacon.	determining unknown position using localization method.

8.4   Proposed System

Our proposed system consists of an application that helps us to perform the implementation of a file sharing system using Li-Fi, based on IoT which will include text, audio, image, and video files. Alongside Li-Fi the software application also focuses on the compression of data using a compression technique that efficiently reduces the size of data by approx 70% [7] to enhance the speed of transmission maintaining the quality of data unaltered. The use of Li-Fi advances this application as it cuts off the use of radio frequency waves practiced under traditional methods of file/data sharing methods. The use of Li-Fi is very beneficial in places such as hospitals as radio waves are harmful to the human body thus avoiding the use of radio frequency cultivated data transmission method [8]. The speed of light plays a vital role in Li-Fi as light travels at a very high speed giving a tremendous reduction in time required while transferring data. Also, Light as of its nature cannot penetrate through opaque objects like walls, wooden furniture, and many more which enhances the security of data and avoids the chances of data getting any kind of unethical access without actually putting much effort into the software application to maintain the security of data. S. L. Bangare *et al.* [9] proposed Li-Fi system which is the base for this work.

Given below is the architecture of our system which includes a pipeline of our proposed idea:

8.4.1   Input Data

This input data can be in the form of text, audio, image, or a video file which we have to transmit to the other device. This data is transferred from the computing device with which we wish to share the data, by browsing on the computing device and selecting from the local files system [10].

8.4.2   Conversion to Binary Encoded Information

This file that we want to transfer gets converted to the binary encoded information. In this process, pixels with the same magnitude form clusters and we perform compression to those clusters using the Optimal Huffman Algorithm. The advantage of using this compression is that it reduces error formation [11].

Huffman codes are optimal when probabilities of the source symbols are all negative powers of two. Examples of a negative power of two are $1/2, 1/4, 1/8$ etc.

The conclusion can be drawn from the following justification.

Suppose that the lengths of the Huffman code are $L=(l_1,l_2,...,l_n)$ for a source $P=(p_1,p_2,...,p_n)$ where n is the size of the alphabet.

Using a variable length code to the symbols, l_j bits for s_j, the average length of the code words is (in bits):

$$\bar{l} = \sum_{j=1}^{n} l_j p_j = l_1 p_1 + l_2 p_2 + \cdots + l_n p_n$$

The entropy of the source is –

$$H = \sum_{j=1}^{n} p_j \log \frac{1}{p_j} = p_1 \log \frac{1}{p_1} + p_2 \log \frac{1}{p_2} + \cdots + p_n \log \frac{1}{p_n}$$

This equation holds if and only if $l_j = -\log_2 p_j$ for all $j = 1, 2, ..., n$, because l_j has to be an integer (in bits). Since the length l_j has to be an integer (in bits) for Huffman codes, $-\log_2 p_j$ has to be an integer, too. Of course, $-\log_2 p_j$ be an integer unless p_j is a negative power of 2, for all $j=1, 2, ..., n$.

In other words, this can only happen if all probabilities are negative powers of 2 in Huffman codes, for l_j has to be an integer (in bits). For example, for a source = (1/2,1/4,1/8,1/8), Huffman codes for the source can be optimal.

8.4.3   Led Driver

This LED driver is used to flash that binary information which can be sensed at the other end [12].

There is an ampLi-Fier circuit just before the LEDs are placed, this increases the intensity of the electrical impulses and then transfers them to the LED. Like how the light blinks, with a flash that is the system's highest voltage is considered as 1 and with no flash that is with the system at 0 voltage the data is considered as 0. Now, this is happening at a very high speed. In our system, we have achieved a speed of 3600 baud rate, which is just for demonstration purpose of the capability of the Li-Fi System [13].

8.4.4   Photo Diode Receiver

This photodiode receiver is used to sense the message which is sent by the LED driver and can be used for further processes. This Receiver is sensitive to the presence of photons and immediately gets charges as light hits the surface of the receiver, the signal received at the surface is yet weak and cannot be decoded back to its original binary form. Hence, it then undergoes the ampLi-Fication stage in the next few sections as mentioned below [14] -

a) Double-Stage Inverting AmpLi-Fier
Double stage inverting ampLi-Fier is the higher version of single stage inverting ampLi-Fier. It helps in retaining the signal without any loss, whereas if we use a single-stage inverting ampLi-Fier there are chances of fading away of signals and reduction in quality [15].

b) Binary Information to Original Message
In this stage the binary information which was sent at the start of the Transmission, that binary information gets converted back into the original message which can be a text, image, audio, or video. We decode with help of the Optimal Huffman algorithm which is explained in the earlier section. This stage is important in encoding the entire data into streams of binary data to facilitate the transfer of the data from the transmitter to the receiver [16].

c) Output Signal
This is the final stage where we get the message which was sent by the sender initially. The sender transmitted this in the binary state and then was received at the receivers end to finally be decoded and converted to its original form and understood at the receiver end [17].

8.5   Workflow

The workflow of the Li-Fi application is divided into two parts [18]:

  (i)   Transmitter section
  (ii)   Receiver section

i) Transmitter Section
Here, we will be able to have the input in four forms that are text, image, audio, and video. These varieties of input get converted into binary that is in the form of 0's and 1's. For a document, the initial stage is to compress the input data into transferable content [19]. The main aim of the text compression algorithmic rule is to scale back the degree of the information. The foremost ordinarily used compression algorithmic rule is Huffman secret writing, this algorithmic rule makes use of data on the frequency of characters to assign variable-length codes to characters. Given below are the steps in which this is achieved [20].

a) Base64

Base64 encoding helps us to convert bytes that contain binary or text data to ASCII characters. By encoding the data, we improve the possibilities of it being processed correctly by different systems. Base64 arise from a specific Multipurpose Internet Mail Extension (MIME) content transfer encoding. Each Base64 digit in binary mean exactly 6 bits of data. Three 8-bit bytes which mean a total of 24 bits can that's why it's represented by four 6-bit Base64 digits [21].

Figure 8.1 – Explanation

Figure 8.1 shown above explains the overall workflow of the Transmitting section at a very basic level. The transmission starts with the intention to transfer some kind of Input data, which can be either text, an Image, Audio, or Video [22]. This data then goes to the second step of transmission where conversion of the data is done after detection to binary information encoded with 1's and 0's. The final Transmission process takes place through high-power LED Lights and an ampLi-Fier circuit attached to it. This results in the LED's blinking at a particular baud rate which varies from systems capacity to hardware functionality. This blinking is so fast that not even a naked human eye can detect it transferring data [23].

b) Base64 Encoding

Base64 encoding is a type of transformation of bytes into ASCII characters. We have 64 characters that represent numbers. The Base64 character set contains [24]:

   (i)   26 uppercase letters
   (ii) 26 lowercase letters

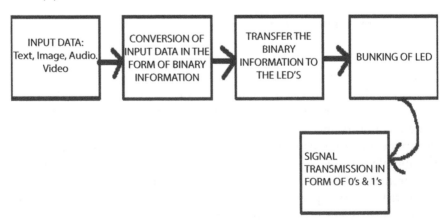

Figure 8.1 Transmitter side workflow.

(iii) 10 numbers

(iv) + and/for new lines

c) Working of Base64

If we want to perform Base64 encoding a string we would follow these steps [25]:

(i)   Take the ASCII value of each character in the string.

(ii) Calculate the 8-bit binary equivalent of the ASCII values

(iii) Convert the 8-bit chucks into 6 bits.

(iv) Convert the 6-bit binary groups to their respective decimal values.

(v)   Using a Base64 encoding table, assign the respective Base64 character for each decimal value.

d) Base64 Encoding Table 8.3.

Table 8.3 Base64 encoding table.

Value	Char	Value	Char	Value	Char	Value	Char
0	A	16	Q	32	G	48	W
1	B	17	R	33	H	49	X
2	C	18	S	34	I	50	Y
3	D	19	T	35	J	51	Z
4	E	20	U	36	K	52	0
5	F	21	V	37	L	53	1
6	G	22	W	38	M	54	2
7	H	23	X	39	N	55	3
8	I	24	Y	40	O	56	4
9	J	25	Z	41	P	57	5
10	K	26	A	42	Q	58	6
11	L	27	B	43	R	59	7
12	M	28	C	44	S	60	8
13	N	29	D	45	T	61	9
14	O	30	E	46	U	62	+
15	P	31	F	47	V	63	/

e) Example

Suppose we have the word "**And**".

ASCII values of these characters are **65,110,100**. In binary 8 bits equivalent it becomes:

01000001	01101110	01100100
65	110	100

Now we reinterpret these 3 bytes as 64 segments, each **6** bit segments can hold the value between 0 and 63, which becomes [26]:

010000	010110	111001	100100
16	22	57	36

decimal values of the above code

These values are used to derive the encoded character that represents our outputs [27].

Now we look up the values on the Base64 index table. And the output characters of our examples are **QW5k.**

Image compression is a technique applied to digital images, with a purpose to reduce its size without losing relevant information to cut short their storage space and increase transmission [28].

f) Huffman Coding – Base of JPEG Image Compression

Huffman coding can be used to compress all the types of data. Huffman coding can be performed for compressing an image, text file and many more data resulting into high compression ratio [29]. Suppose we have a 5×5 image with 8-bit color, i.e. 256 different colors. The not compressed image will take $5 \times 5 \times 8 = 200$ bits as shown in Figure 8.2.

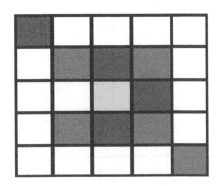

Figure 8.2 Image representation of 5×5 pixels.

First, we count how many times each color is occurring [30].

Then we sort the colors in order of priority based on decreasing or increasing frequency. This will look like this as shown in Figure 8.3:

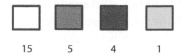

Figure 8.3 Frequency of pixels.

Now we put colors together to form a tree such that the colors farthest from the root are the least frequent. The colors are joined in pairs, with a node forming a connection [31]. A node can be connected to either a node or a color. In reference to the above example, the tree might look like this as shown in Figure 8.4:

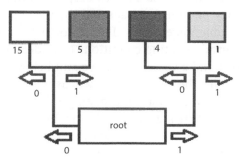

Figure 8.4 Huffman optimal tree.

This is known as a Huffman tree. It can be used for encoding and decoding as well. Each color is encoded as follows. We create codes by traveling from the root to each color. If we move right towards the node, we write "1", and if we move left, we write "0". This process gives a Huffman code as in Table 8.4 in which each symbol is assigned a bit code such that the most frequently occurring symbol has the shortest code, while the least occurring symbol is given the longest code [32].

Table 8.4 Huffman coding table.

Color	Frequency	Bit code
	15	00
	5	01
	4	10
	1	11

Using the variant is preferable in our example. This provides better compression for an image. This binary information gets transferred to the LED's with the help of Arduino and as soon as these LED's receives the information, they start blinking. And send the information in the form of 0's and 1's. If the LED blinks that mean 1 is getting to the authorized other system and if the LED doesn't blink that means 0 is getting to the authorized other system. And this is how the signal gets transmitted from one system to the other system [33].

ii) Receiver Section

Figure 8.5 – Explanation

[Figure 8.5 explains the overall workflow of the Receiver section at a very basic level. After the Transmission process is completed, on the other end, i.e. the receiver end there is a photoreceptor, in our case solar panel. These low-frequency photons are captured on the solar panel and then transmitted to a Double Stage AmpLi-Fier circuit, where thresholds are set according to the outside lighting conditions to understand the difference between a value of 1 and a value of 0 above and below the threshold. The circuit first ampLi-Fies the signals and then uses an operational ampLi-Fier to again understand this data and distinguish them as 1 and 0. After making the weak signal strong we decode this binary information to the Original Data by using the decoding algorithms and then display the final output on the screen which was initially transferred using the transmission section.]

a) Signal Reception

The information which was sent in the form of LED blinks from the sender site gets received over here at the receiving end. Here the signal which was

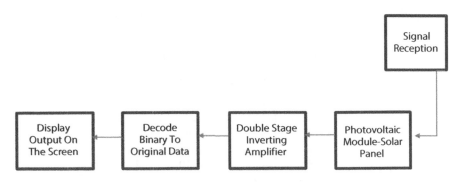

Figure 8.5 Receiver side workflow.

received was in the form of 0's and 1's which was nothing but ON blinks and OFF blinks, respectively [34].

b) Photovoltaic Module/Solar Panel
Solar panel is used informally for a photo-voltaic module. Photovoltaics are the transformation of light into electricity using semiconducting materials that manifest the photovoltaic effect. Photo-voltaic cells utilize sunlight as a source of energy and generate direct current electricity. A photovoltaic system recruits solar modules, each encompassing a number of solar cells, which produces electrical power.

c) Two-Stage Inverting AmpLi-Fier
Inverting ampLi-Fier keeps the signal safe from any kind of distortion and immunes the signal which makes the signal strong for transmission, so this is the main motive behind using a double-stage inverting ampLi-Fier.

d) Decode Binary to Original Data
After performing two-stage ampLi-Fication the binary signal which was in the form of binary representation i.e. in the form of 0's and 1's gets converted back into the information sent by the authorized sender in the form of text, video, audio, and image.

e) Display the Original Message on the Screen
Once the successful transmission of this message is done, it is then displayed on the screen after the conversion of the binary message back to its original digital form that was either an image a text or a video.

8.6   Proposed Solution

8.6.1   Hardware Setup

Figure 8.6 shows the Implementation of hardware to transmit data through light. The data here refers to string, plain text files, images of any extension, and videos. Li-Fi can transmit data within the line of sight based on an illuminous object's position. Data is initially compressed and converted to byte array format before transmission. This takes place at the backend of the application and then the file is sent via the computer's serial port to Arduino.

Arduino programming is applied to read the data in form of byte array. Initial baud rate is set to 1200 baud initialized within the Arduino code and

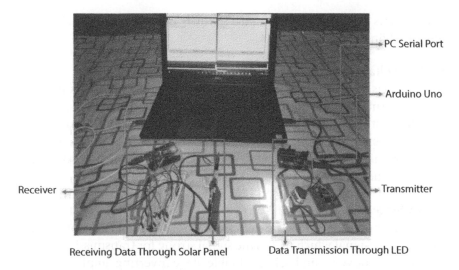

Figure 8.6 Li-Fi hardware implementation.

can be changed manually. The distance between LED and photo-voltaic receiver i.e. solar panel will bring a change in the speed of transmission. Speed of transmission depends on the hardware material used, data size, baud rate with which the data is getting transmitted and hardware used. The hardware setup consists of Computer, Serial port connection, Arduino Uno, power source, LED chip, and solar panel.

8.6.2 Transistor-Transistor Logic Serial Communication

The compressed data is sent to computer's serial port in form of byte array. TTL serial communication transmits data from there to Arduino. The prescribed voltage in TTL transmission may vary from 0V to 5V. 5V here is the maximum level TTL can attain. During transmission, voltage frequency may vary from 0V to Vcc, and often it is set to 3.3V–5V. The data is transmitted in a sequential manner and at the other end, the UART rebuilds the data received.

8.6.3 Arduino Uno

The ATmega328P dataset-based Arduino Uno is a microcontroller board. It has a USB connection, an ICSP header, reset button, and power jack along with the microcontroller to support it. It is connected to the PC in our project using a USB cable. The Arduino Uno is getting the input in byte array format and converts the data into binary format to transfer it. Conversion to binary gets settled automatically and doesn't need manual programming. The power supply in our project is the battery connected with LED to supply power.

i) Light Emitting Diode (LED)
The LED used in the chapter is 12V and blinks with a frequency of 1.2Hz. It is transmitting the data in binary format. Digital 1 Commands the LED to switch on and digital 0 commands the LED to switch off. This takes place using simple Arduino programming. Sending large binary data like this creates a phenomenon of LED flickering very fast that human naked eyes can't detect and data gets transmitted within a very less time frame.

ii) Photo-Voltaic Receiver – Solar Panel
Solar panel is receiving the data from LED's blinking i.e., On and Off as 1 and 0. The information received is converted to direct current using solar panels. The solar panel used during the demonstration is cost-friendly and works well with the transmission.

iii) Serial Transmission
The Arduino at receiver side is connected to solar panels and reads the binary information received. It then sends the data to the serial port of the computer using USB cable. The protocol with which this communication happens is called the UART Protocol. UART is a hardware communication protocol that uses asynchronous serial communication with configurable speed. Asynchronous means there is no clock signal to synchronize the output bits from the transmitting device going to the receiving end. Two UART's communicate directly with each other The transmitting UART converts the parallel data coming from the controlling device like the CPU (in our case from CPU to the Microcontroller Arduino) into serial form to the receiving UART, which then converts the serial data back to parallel data to the receiving device.

8.7   Software Implementation

8.7.1   Video Transmission

Video is combination of multiple images bind up together in a sequential manner. Frames/sec rate is the frequency with which images in a sequential manner called frames appear on the screen. Thus like image transmissions, we encoded video files and then compression is performed on them before transmission takes place.

8.7.2   Text/Text File Transmission

The user interacts with the Front end to select a text file. At this stage, we have achieved the transmission of the .txt file and will be enhancing it to other formats in further development. Text file of any size firstly gets compressed and the byte array is generated from it. This byte array is further given as input to the computer's serial port.

Figure 8.7 – Explanation
[Figure 8.7 shown beow is the computational execution, or the software execution of the entire hardware apparatus made. This is the demonstration of the textual data sent over light as a medium. As seen first the string "My name is Ayush Srivastava" is converted into its compressed form using

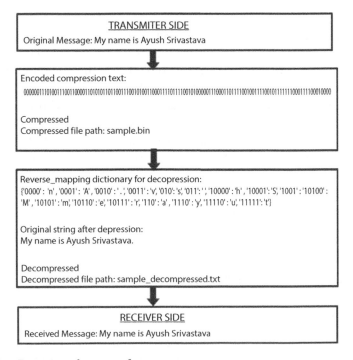

Figure 8.7 Execution of text transfer.

the optimal Huffman encoding algorithm, and upon transmission at the other end it is decompressed again and converted back to its original text.]

8.7.3   Audio Transmission

Nevertheless Base64 or Huffman Algorithm is working individually in the chapter. It's the combined efforts of both modules integrated together that give the desired output with less complex code, hence software cost can be restricted at a lower rate. The audio file is getting transferred through Li-Fi in the same way as all other files. First, we convert it to a Base64 byte array and then data is compressed using Huffman Algorithm before transmission. In the chapter, we implemented the transfer of audio files with all the extensions of file type.

8.7.4   Image Transmission

Image Transmission is different from transmitting text over a network. This is because the image is a two-dimensional figure such as a map, a graph, or a pie chart and is a combination of pixels in two dimensions. To reduce coding complexity, we have encoded the image first and then the encoded data is compressed into a byte array to be understood back at the receiver's end. At the receiver end, it is then decompressed using the same decompression algorithm and then converted to its original form and displayed on the recipient's computational device.

Below you will find the diagrammatic representation of the same concept mentioned in image transmission case.

Indoor Map-Reading System Using Li-Fi – Bonus Project
Figure 8.8 – Explanation
[Figure 8.8 shown below explains the overall workflow of the image transmission section. The image is first converted to its base 64 form encoding, since the encoding is quite large it is compressed using the Huffman compression algorithm. It is then transferred through light from the transmitter to the receiver and upon reception at the receiver's end, it is first decompressed to its base 64 encoding form and then converted back to its original image form and displayed on the recipient computational device.]

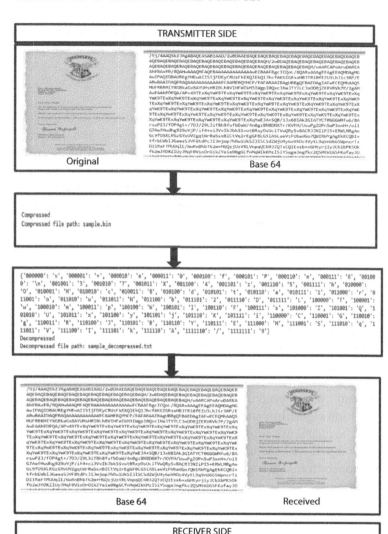

Figure 8.8 Image transfer module.

8.8   Block Diagram – Indoor Navigation System Using Li-Fi

Indoor map – reading system is a demonstration of an information/data transfer-based application that can be helpful in places like shopping malls, office buildings, and residents. Visually challenged people can get help using the application at places like this. This chapter has been added to demonstrate Data transfer applications in fields other than file sharing

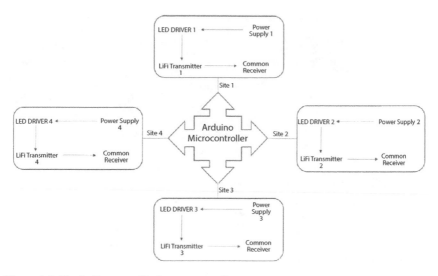

Figure 8.9 Block diagram of indoor map reading system.

applications contributing an important up thrust to make information exchange useful in various ways.

Figure 8.9 – Explanation
[Figure 8.9 shown above shows the overall demonstration of Li-Fi based Indoor Navigation map reading system, The hardware Apparatus is the same as mentioned above. This is shown as a demonstration to show that this same concept has application even in the indoor navigation system. Every room is adjusted to a unique light signal, and whenever the person (receiver) comes under the influence of this signal it understands and then maps it to the specific room which was sending this unique signal and understands where its current position is at, and from this position, it navigates the user to different locations.]

8.9   Implementation

All the hardware components required are the same as that of the Li-Fi File Transfer Application. We have used four transmitters and one common receiver for the mapping function here. Each transmitter is attached to each individual site facility. The transmitter at one site keeps transmitting data continuously until the light has been put off. The continuous loop of data transmission consists of unique code to identify which site the user is present at the moment as shown in Figure 8.10.

Figure 8.10 Demonstration of indoor map reading system.

Every time the solar receptor is placed in direct contact of LED transmitting data, the receiver displays the message and also gives a audible information as of which site the user is in. For example, is the user is at room "1", LED will transmit the unique code as "1". When the receptor is at direct line of sight it gives an audible message as "You are in room 1. Move left to go to room 2. Move right to go to room 3. Go straight to room 4." As shown in Table 8.5.

8.10   Unicode Transmission

Table 8.5 Unique code table.

Room 1	01000001
Room 2	01000010
Room 3	01000010
Room 4	01000100

Figure 8.11 Demonstration of placement of LED in room.

The unique code is generated so that there is no possibility of error. Each code is designed in manner to be received without having any confusion of intersection while giving the correct output. As the LED driver spreads light everywhere in our designed prototype, the information can be retrieved from any position within the room. Although it does depend from area to area, we installed one LED strip for one room in our prototype. As shown in Figure 8.11.

8.10.1   Receiver – Solar Panel

In the Map-reading system above, solar panels are used to receive data which further sends the information to our software module via Arduino UNO. A mobile application receives the data collected and it gets displayed on the screen.

8.10.2   Text to Speech

Map-reading with the help of Li-Fi will be very beneficial in the case of visually impaired people. The data received gets displayed on the mobile phone screen and then further the text-to-speech software module converts the text into audible command. Improvements can be done further in the demonstrated side project as above by enhancing the functionality of light to be able to determine the exact location of a person within the room and specifying by what angle the movement of the person should take place in order to have accurate results.

8.11   Conclusion

The Li-Fi Technology will overcome these drawbacks which are posed by the Wi-Fi technology and disadvantages because it uses visible light so that it doesn't produce any harmful radiation to the environment and the Human Body. This study has found that Li-Fi is way better than Wi-Fi because Li-Fi does not use radio waves and provides larger bandwidth. It is totally based on VLC. It cannot be hacked and is faster than Wi-Fi. From all these advantages of Li-Fi over Wi-Fi, file sharing would become safer and faster.

With the dynamic increase in Li-Fi technology, there is a lot of scope for development with the above-demonstrated projects. Li-Fi within an indoor facility can be used for multiple screen sharing instead of stage performance which makes it difficult for people sitting at back to see it properly. With the evolution, Li-Fi can cover many aspects of technological issues that involve indoor navigation systems also, as demonstrated above in the paper. With the use of proper hardware and efficient integration, the cost can achieve even lesser cost than our project claims at the moment. Improvement in the compression algorithm can also be made by doing some complex changes but that might increase the cost of the product. The File sharing application implemented can be made platform independent (i.e., OS, Devices like a computer or mobile Independent) by open sourcing the application with few other technical implications.

Although there's still a long way to make this technology a commercial success, it promises great potential in the field of wireless internet. A significant number of researchers 15 and companies are currently working on this concept, which promises to solve the problem of lack of radio spectrum, space, and low internet connection speed. By deployment of this technology, we can migrate to greener, cleaner, safer communication networks. The very concept of Li-Fi promises to solve issues such as, the shortage of radiofrequency bandwidth and eliminates the disadvantages of Radio communication technologies. Li-Fi is the upcoming and growing technology acting as a catalyst for various other developing and new inventions/technologies. Therefore, there is a certainty of the development of future applications of the Li-Fi which can be extended to different platforms and various walks of human life.

References

1. Shaikh, A.A. and Gadekar, P.P., Huffman coding technique for image compression. *Int. J. Adv. Comput. Technol.*, 4, 4, 1585–1587, April-2015.
2. Mahendran, R., Integrated Li-Fi (Light Fidelity) for smart communication through illumination. *2016 International Conference on Advanced Communication Control and Computing Technologies (ICACCCT)*, Embedded System Technology S.A Engg College, Chennai.
3. Goswami, P. and Shukla, M.K., Design of a Li-Fi transceiver, *Wireless Engineering and Technology*, 8, 44, 71–86, October 31, 2017.
4. Meshram, B.M. and Deshmukh, V.M., Image encoding & decoding using Base64 technique and it's wireless transmission using Li-Fi. *Int. J. Future Revolution Comput. Sci. Commun. Eng.*, 4, 4, 541–545, April 2018.
5. Xalxo, D.K. and Muralidharan, V., Subaquatic message transmission using Li-Fi. *Int. J. Trendy Res. Eng. Technol.*, *(IJTRET)*, 2, 2, 2, 22–25, April 2018.
6. Isik, M.F., Haboglu, M.R., Yatrasi, B., Applicability of Li-Fi for industrial automation. *Int. J. Electron. Electr. Eng.*, 5, 1, 21–25, February 2017.
7. Vasuja, M., Mishra, A.K., Chauhan, U.S., Chandola, D., Kapoor, S., Image transmission using Li-Fi. *2018 Second International Conference on Inventive Communication and Computational Technologies (ICICCT)*, Coimbatore, pp. 287–292, 2018.
8. Kiran, D. and Murulanilini, LI-FI: An emerging technology for healthcare. *Asian I Int. J. Trendy Res. Eng. Technol.*, *(IJTRET)*, 2, 2(2), 8(S1), 38–40, April 2018.
9. Bangare, S.L., Srivastava, A., Siddiqui, S., Kumar, A., Bhagat, P., File sharing application using Li-Fi. *Mukt Shabd J.*, UGC Care List Group - I J., 9, 6, 5179–5187, 2020/6.
10. Bandela, P., Nimmagadda, P., Mutchu, S., Li-Fi(Light Fidelity): The next generation of wireless network. *Int. J. Adv. Trends Comput. Sci. Eng.*, 3, 1, 132–137, 2014, Special Issue of ICETETS 2014 - Held on 24-25 February, 2014 in Malla Reddy Institute of Engineering and Technology, Secunderabad–14, AP, India.
11. Rastogi, S., Li-Fi: A 5G visible data communication *Int. J. Sci. Res.*, *(IJSR)*, 5, 9, 335–337, 2016.
12. Abdul-Wadood, D.N., George, L.E., Rasheed, N.A., Diagnosis of skin cancer using image texture analysis. *Int. J. Sci. Eng. Res.*, 5, 6, 155–161, June-2014.
13. Naeem, H., Ullah, F., Naeem, R.M., Khalid, S., Vasan, D., Jabbar, S., Saeed, S., Malwaare detection in industrial internet of things based on hybrid image visualization and deep learning model. *Ad Hoc Net.*, 105, 102154, 2020.

14. Dutta, S., Sharma, K., Gupta, N., Bodh, T.V., A new paradigm in wireless communication. *International Journal of Innovative Research in Computer and Communication Engineering (IJIRCCE)*, 1, 8, 1654–1658, 2013.

15. SchnichiroHaruyama, Visible light communication, recent activities in Japan. *Smart Spaces: A Smart Lighting ERC Industry-Academia Day*, BUPhotonics Center, Boston University, *The Bio-Electromagnetic Research Initiative (BEMRI)*, Feb 8, 2011.

16. Aldarkazaly, Z.T., Younus, M.F., Alwan, Z.S., Data transmission using Li-Fi technique. *Int. J. Adv. Sci. Technol.*, 29, 03,

17. Condliffe, J., Is Li-Fi ready to establish itself as the new Wi-Fi? *Tetrahedron*, 2822, 2011.

18. O'Brien, D., Le Minha, H., Zeng, L., Faulkner, G., Chou, H.H., Lee, K., Jung, D., Oh, Y.J., Won, E.T., Visible light communication: Recent progress and challenges. *Wireless World Research Forum*.

19. Rani, J., Chauhan, P., Tripathi, R., Li-Fi (LightFidelity)-the future technology in wireless communication. *Int. J. Appl. Eng. Res.*, 7, 11, 1–4, 2012.

20. Jamieson, I., 2010, http://www.bemri.org/visible light communication vlc systems.html.

21. Goyal, M., Saproo, D., Bhagashra, A., New epoch of wireless communication: Light fidelity. *Int. J. Innovative Res. Comput. Commun. Eng.*, 1, 2, 267–271 April 2013.

22. Khan, L.U. Visible light communication: Applications, architecture, standardization and research challenges. *Digit. Commun. Netw.*, 3, 2, 78–88, 2017

23. Matheus, L.E.M., Vieira, A.B., Vieira, L.F., Viera, M.A.M., Gnawali, O., Visible light communication: Concepts, applications and challenges, in: *IEEE Communications Surveys & Tutorials*, vol. 21, no. 4, pp. 3204–3237, Fourthquarter 2019.

24. Rahaim, M.B., Vegni, A.M., Little, T.D.C., A hybrid radio frequency and broadcast visible light communication system, in: *IEEE Global Communications Conference (GLOBECOM 2011) Workshops*, pp. 792–796, 5-9, Dec. 2011.

25. Marsh, G.W. and Kahn, J.M., Channel reuse strategies for indoor infrared wireless communications. *IEEE Trans. Commun.*, 45, 1280–1290, Oct. 1997.

26. Chen, C., Tsonev, D., Haas, H., Joint transmission in indoor visible light communication downlink cellular networks, in: *Proc. of the IEEE Workshop on Optical Wireless Communication (OWC 2013)*, Dec. 9, 2013, IEEE.

27. Stefan, I., Burchardt, H., Haas, H., Area spectral efficiency performance comparison between VLC and RF femtocell networks, in: *Proc. of International Conference on Communications (ICC)*, pp. 1–5, June 2013.

28. Prakash, R. and Agarwal, P., The new era of transmission and communication technology: Li-Fi (Light Fidelity) LED & TED based approach. *Int. J. Adv. Res. Comput. Eng. Technol. (IJARCET)*, 3, 2, 285–290, February 2014.

29. Karthika, R. and Balakrishnan, S., Wireless communication using Li-Fi technology. *SSRG Int. J. Electron. Commun. Eng.*, *(SSRG-IJECE)*, 2, 3, 32–40 March 2015.

30. Khandal, D. and Jain, S., Li-Fi (Light Fidelity): The future technology in wireless communication. *Int. J. Inf. Comput. Technol.*, 4, 16, 7–14, 2014.
31. Huang, Q., Li, X., Shaurette, M., Integrating Li-Fi wireless communication and energy harvesting wireless sensor for next generation building management. *International High Performance Building Conference*, Purdue University.
32. Noshad, M. and Brandt-Pearce, M., Hadamard coded modulation for visible light communications, in: *IEEE Transactions on Communications*, vol. 64, no. 3, pp. 1167–1175, March 2016.
33. Tsonev, D., Sinanovic, S., Haas, H., Novel unipolar orthogonal frequency division multiplexing (U-OFDM)for optical wireless communication, in: *Proc. of Vehicular Technology Conference*, VTC, Spring 2012.
34. Ekta, and Kaur, R., Light "fidelity (Li-Fi)-A comprehensive study. *Int. J. Comput. Sci. Mob. Computing*, 3, 4, 475–481, April 2014.

9

Survey on Artificial Intelligence Techniques in the Diagnosis of Pleural Mesothelioma

Ushasukhanya S.[1*], S.S. Sridhar[1] and Ahmed A. Elngar[2]

[1]SRM University, Kattankulathur, Chennai, India
[2]Faculty of Computers and Artificial Intelligence, Beni-Suef University, Beni-Suef City, Egypt

Abstract

Malignant mesothelioma (MM) is a vigorously progressing Tumor that results from mesothelium cells of various parts of the body in which pleura usually suffers. The important causes of MM are exposure to a mineral called asbestos, radiation, simian virus 40 infections, and also genetic disposition. The diagnosis of MM at the early stage plays a very important role in patient survival. Artificial intelligence techniques like PNN, and MLNN have been used so far in the classification of benign and malignant MM. The aim of the proposed work is to analyze all the artificial intelligence techniques used so far in the diagnosis of malignant mesothelioma. It also analyses Improved MTiling constructive neural network and SVM methods which could be further used in the diagnosis of malignant mesothelioma.

Keywords: Classification, malignant mesothelioma, accuracy, MTiling

9.1 Introduction

Cancer is a chronic disease with abnormal cell growth which progresses by invading the healthy cells of the body. There are more than 200 types of cancer, and these are caused by several reasons like lifestyle, environmental

---

Corresponding author: ushasukhanya.s@ktr.srmuniv.ac.in

Ahmed A. Elgnar, Vigneshwar M, Krishna Kant Singh and Zdzislaw Polkowski (eds.) Handbook of Computational Sciences: A Multi and Interdisciplinary Approach, (185–196) © 2023 Scrivener Publishing LLC

factors, and inherited genetics. Among various types of cancers, Lung cancer also known as lung carcinoma is a type of cancer with a low survival rate. Malignant Mesothelioma is a rare kind of cancer that develops in the mesothelium cells of various parts of the body like the lungs, abdomen, heart, and testicles. Pleural mesothelioma is a type of cancer that develops in the pleura of the lungs. It is diagnosed mostly in the third stage of cancer, and the patient survives only for 9 to 12 months after diagnosis. Exposure to a mineral called asbestos, radiation, simian virus 40 infections, and also genetic disposition are the causes of MM. Asbestos fibers when inhaled, become embedded in the lining of the lungs causing harmful inflammation of the pleura resulting in mesothelioma. The highest per capita incidence of malignant mesothelioma in the world is among the aboriginal people of Western Australia and a now-closed asbestos mine may be to blame. There have been a few published reports of mesotheliomas that developed after people were exposed to high doses of radiation to the chest or abdomen as the treatment for another cancer. Some lab studies have suggested that SV40 infection might cause mesothelioma. Malignant mesothelioma has to be diagnosed at an earlier stage to avoid low survival rates and hence classification is crucial.

Brause *et al.* [1] stated that the task of learning to diagnose makes the physician confronted. Certain basic difficulties that physicians experience are listed out here:

- Valid diagnosis requires experienced cases which are attained in the middle of the physician's career.
- Even for experienced physicians, the diagnostic capability is the same as newcomers when they handle rare cases like mesothelioma.
- Principally, pattern recognition systems resemble statistic computers, but humans don't. Though humans recognize patterns or objects very easily, they fail when probabilities must be assigned to observations.
- The diagnosis of rare diseases is becoming quite challenging as the new results disqualify the older treats, new cures, and new drugs are being introduced day by day.

Pleural mesothelioma being a rare disease faces almost all the difficulties stated above by Brause. Diagnosis of Pleural Mesothelioma is done by various methods like X-Ray, CT scan, PET-CT, MRI, and Biopsy. Mass screening is done by CT scan, which is a promising method for cancer detection. The long-term safety of the computerized tomography method is not established due to the risk of exposure to radiation. The use of microarray data is an alternative approach but is quite expensive. Hence, features from the CT scan images are used for the early detection of cancer. Malignant mesothelioma is always confused with benign mesothelioma which can also form in the pleural surroundings of the lungs. It is called benign fibrous mesothelioma, but it might not be visible in CT as this tumor does not start from mesothelial cells. Fibrous mesothelioma is usually benign, and about 1 in 10 are cancerous as shown in Figure 9.1.

Classification, an important tool of data mining has been used to classify the benign and malignant cells of mesothelioma. The usage of artificial intelligence methods for classification purposes in the medical field has been increasing recently. Features extracted from malignant mesothelioma patients and benign cells are used here for classification. These features are; age, gender, city, asbestos exposure, type of MM, duration of asbestos exposure, diagnosis method, keep aside, cytology, duration of symptoms, dyspnea, ache on chest, weakness, the habit of cigarette, performance status, White Blood cell count (WBC), hemoglobin (HGB), platelet count (PLT), sedimentation, blood lactic dehydrogenase (LDH), Alkaline phosphatase (ALP), total protein, albumin, glucose, pleural lactic dehydrogenase, pleural protein, pleural albumin, pleural glucose, dead or not, pleural effusion, pleural thickness on tomography, pleural level of acidity (pH), C-reactive protein (CRP), class of diagnosis. The chapter describes the various classifiers used in classifying benign and malignant cells of mesothelioma in related work, followed by the implementation of MTiling in the classification of MM in the proposed methodology.

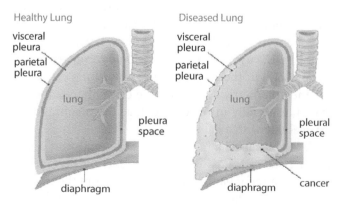

Figure 9.1 Healthy and MM-affected lung.

9.2   Methods

National Institute for Health Research (NIHR) has highlighted the research into mesothelioma as a high priority- which is funded by the PSP. It is an unusual and often fatal form of cancer with very poor survival rates. The main cause of Pleural Mesothelioma is asbestos which gets embedded in the pleura of the lungs. Pleura have two layers, visceral pleura and parietal pleura. These two layers contact and slide over each other when we breathe with the help of fluid present in between them. As the body's immune system tries to rid of the asbestos fibers out of the body, it causes permanent scarring and toughening of the nearby tissue. As the disease progresses, the lining of the lung thickens. This results in the formation of tumors making the blood vessels leak, resulting in pleural effusion [2]. This shows the statistics of MM with 90% of the pleural mesothelioma patients having lung fluid build-up, 79% having shortness of breath, 64 % having chest pain, 36% having a dry cough, and 30 % having weight loss.

Research for the classification of MM is carried out by measuring the levels of mesothelin, a protein present in the samples. Automatic diagnosis methods are carried out in which features are extracted from CT scan images of patients. Zhen J. Wang et al. [3] suggested that CT is the most sensitive modality widely used for the diagnosis of Mesothelioma. The primary imaging modality used for the evaluation of MPM is the computerized tomography technique. The invasion of the pericardium results in nodular pericardial thickening or pericardial effusion which is explicit in CT findings. Interlobar fissure thickenings and pulmonary metastases of MPM are also apparent as nodules and masses which rarely, diffuse miliary nodules are identified in CT images. Despite the limitations of its accuracy being suboptimal, CT remains the imaging study of choice for the initial evaluation of patients with MPM. Furthermore, the accuracy of tumor detection is enhanced by multi-detector row CT with multiplanar reformatting capability. The use of three-dimensional reconstruction of CT data is shown to be useful in the staging of neck and lung cancer as well. It is credible that the volumetric CT technique can enhance the visualization of tumor extent, especially in regions such as the diaphragm that may be strenuous to evaluate with axial imaging.

Brims et al. [4] proposed a model for the classification of patients with high and lower risks of MPM using a simple, clinically relevant decision tree. The dataset is a set of parameters collected from the time of diagnosis which includes age; sex; date of diagnosis; histological findings; symptoms at presentation, including dyspnea, chest pain, and weight loss, ECOG PS, routinely performed hematological investigations and biochemical investigations and date of death. A chi-square significance test at each split in the decision tree was used with either categorical or non-discrete variables which divide it into two at the place of best fit. Despite its advantages of being extremely fast at classifying unknown records, handling continuous and distinct attributes well, and working with recurrent attributes being fair enough, it still suffers. Small variations in the data lead to different-looking trees, sub-trees being duplicated several times and as expected, the performance of the model not being strong on an external data set are the few corns of this model.

A neural network is a "tie-in" computational system in which the computational systems written are procedural. One of the important aspects of a neural network is its ability to learn. Several artificial neural network techniques like PNN, MLNN, and LVQ structures have been used for the classification of benign and malignant mesothelioma. Among feed forward and backpropagation algorithms, backpropagation is identified as a strong tool for the training of MLNN structures and is extensively used in resolving many practical problems.

Orhan Er *et al.* [5] proposed a model for the classification of benign and malignant mesothelioma using various neural network techniques. They used the same dataset with 34 features for classification. PNN was implemented in the first stage of the study with one real-valued input vector in the input layer, a single hidden layer, and two outputs with an index of two classes in the output layer. Here output layer uses a 'winner takes all attitude to compare the probability density of each condition in the output layer. In the second stage of the study, the MLNN with two hidden layers was used. The steepest descent method to modify the weights was used here and hence, it suffers from a slow convergence rate and often yields suboptimal solutions. At the third stage of this study, a learning vector quantization neural network was used for the MM's disease diagnosis which had a multi-layered structure. He finally concluded that the most suitable neural network structure is the PNN structure for classifying MM's data. Though PNN is well suited for the classification of MM, it requires more memory space which is a key point to be considered.

Ascertaining appropriate neural network architecture is quite challenging and suffers from two opposing objectives. Firstly, the decision boundary has to be adequately defined and for this, the network must be large enough. Secondly for improved generalization, the network must be as small as possible. All the ANN classifiers suffer from balancing these two objectives except CONN. A constructive algorithm learns the topology in a style specific to the problem rather than learning on pre-specified network topology and at the same time its generalization capability is much better. Tiling, tower, pyramid, upstart, and sequential are the various CONN algorithms for constructing and training the neurons.

Dr. S.S. Sridhar *et al.* [6] suggested that out of various CONN algorithms; multi-category tiling architecture (MTiling) is the best for its various advantages out of which a few are listed below

- Guaranteed convergence does not require the input patterns to be projected, normalized, or quantized as the network itself is a vector quantizer.
- A reliable representation of the training set is ensured
- As the neurons are only trained, it is faster than other constructive algorithms.

They proposed a new MTiling CONN architecture that constructs a layered network of threshold neurons through MTiling algorithm as shown in Figure 9.2. This algorithm constructs layers of master neurons to classify maximum patterns along with ancillary neurons to address the misclassifications. MTiling architecture was found to behave better than other constructive neural networks when used with an improved adaptive learning strategy. It was implemented with an unsupervised learning strategy on datasets of binary patterns for achieving better performance in terms of generalization capability, faster convergence and less connection thereby requiring less storage as reported in [7].

The elimination of unnecessary network elements in the neural network architecture was done by network pruning. Parekh *et al.* [8] studied the

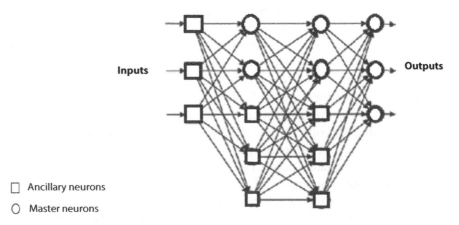

Inputs   Outputs

☐ Ancillary neurons
○ Master neurons

Figure 9.2 MTiling architecture.

applications of pruning techniques of MTiling to handle the real-valued pattern attributes and multiple output classes. Pruning with dead neurons, correlated neurons and redundant neurons are the three simple methods of MTiling algorithm that were discussed. Groups of one or more ancillary neurons were trained at a time in an attempt to make the current layer faithful. He considered a dataset of 2 spirals (2sp), BUPA liver disorder (liver), image segmentation (seg), Wisconsin diagnostic breast cancer (wdbc), and wine recognition (wine). For runs with and without network pruning, the number of neurons pruned, the total time for pruning, the network size, and the total training time, and the generalization performance over the 10 runs were recorded. The winner-take-all (WTA) strategy was used to compute the outputs for datasets involving more than two pattern classes. The experimental results demonstrated a moderate to significant reduction in the network size. It must be noted that these improvements come at an additional cost of identifying the neurons that can be pruned. He concluded that the additional time spent in pruning was a small fraction of the total training time of the MTiling network. Although there was a reduction in network size, the generalization performance of the networks seemed to remain nearly the same with or without pruning.

In the last decade, a growing trend is eminent in the use of other supervised learning techniques, like SVMs and BNs, towards cancer prediction and prognosis performance. Support vector machine depends on the structural risk minimization (SRM) principle founded on the statistical learning theory, which enhances generalization capabilities. Exarchos KP *et al.* [9] proposed a predictive model for breast cancer recurrence within five years after surgery. An initial dataset of 193 variables was selected out of which, only 14 features were considered based on their clinical knowledge. The authors employed SVM, ANN, and Cox-proportional hazard regression for producing the models and to find the optimal one. On considering accuracy, sensitivity, and specificity as the metrics for the efficiency of the classifier, the authors claimed that BCRSVM outperformed ANN and Cox regression models with an accuracy of 84.6%, 81.4%, and 72.6%, respectively.

Xuangao *et al.* [10] proposed a model for the classification of mediastinal lymph nodes. They used the Gaussian radial basis function (RBF) as the kernel function of the support vector machine (SVM). From PET images twenty-two-dimensional texture eigenvectors, 512-dimensional multi-resolution histogram eigenvectors from CT images, and 534-dimensional combined eigenvectors from the PET and CT images. He developed SVM models for CT, and PET, and combined PET/CT images, and labeled them as SVM1, SVM2, and SVM3, respectively. He obtained a sensitivity result of 96% for PET/CT images. Their study was actually limited by a small number of malignant lymph nodes. The composition of benignity and malignancy in training sets, extraction of texture eigenvectors, and formation of final SVMs would have been affected by the low proportion of malignant lymph nodes. Besides, a synchronous manual way of segmentation was done in the extraction of lymph nodes which would have hindered the performance of SVM.

Yuan Sui *et al.* [11] proposed a novel SVM classifier model merged with random under-sampling (RU) and SMOTE. They proposed an SVM classification algorithm for lung nodule recognition (RU-SMOTE-SVM) and created a database with 150 nodules and 908 non-nodules from CT images of lungs. Eight features were extracted from each sample for training and testing. They were able to balance the training samples and remove noise and duplicate information in the training sample thereby retaining only the useful information to enhance data utilization effectiveness. The pulmonary nodules classification under the unbalanced data gets ultimately improved by the performance of the RU-SMOTE-SVM algorithm. The average classification accuracy was found to be 81.57% in the classification of lung nodules.

Swati *et al.* [12] developed a CAD system for the diagnosis of lung cancer using an SVM classifier. A hyperplane in which the distance from it to the nearest data point was maximum on each side was selected. This is called the maximum margin hyperplane and it defines a linear classifier which is known as a maximum classifier hence the classification was done using a linear classifier of SVM. The data set consists of 25 diseased lung computer tomography image JPEG images of size196x257 out of which 7 features were considered for the proposed method. SVM provides an accuracy of 92.5% in the classification of benign and malignant lung tumors. The drawback of this system is the usage of a small database which could have hindered the accuracy of the system.

9.3 Analysis

The methods discussed above are summarized in Tables 9.1 and 9.2. The traditional method used so far, its advantages and disadvantages, and Improved MTiling and SVM methods used in the diagnosis of various other carcinomas are explicitly mentioned with its models and methods for analysis [13–15].

Out of the various methods used, the random search method yields the highest accuracy in spite of its increased memory utilization [16–17].

Table 9.1 Performance of ANN techniques for mesothelioma.

ANN techniques	Methods	Advantages	Disadvantages
PNN	Random search method	96.3% accuracy	Increased memory utilization
Decision tree	Chi-square significance test	94.5% sensitivity	Small variations in the data lead to different-looking trees Sub-trees being duplicated
MLNN	The non-linear sigmoid activation function	94.41% accuracy	Requires tuning a lot of parameters for achieving targeted accuracy

Table 9.2 Performance of Mtiling and SVM.

ANN technique	Models	Methods	Advantages
MTiling	Constructive neural network with improved adaptive learning strategy	Faster than other constructive neural networks	Reduced training time with no misclassifications
SVM	Predictive model for breast cancer recurrence	BCRSVM	BCRSVM outperformed ANN and COX regression models
SVM	Predictive model for mediastinal lymph nodes	Gaussian radial basis function of SVM	96% of sensitivity
SVM	Predictive model for lung nodule recognition	RU-SMOTE-SVM	Classification accuracy of 81.57% was achieved
SVM	Model for diagnosis of lung cancer	The linear classifier of SVM	92.5% accuracy in recognition of lung carcinomas

Table 9.2 discusses the usage of improved Mtiling and SVM classifiers in the diagnosis of various carcinomas. It is evident from table 2 that Mtiling and SVM will certainly provide higher classification accuracy in the diagnosis of malignant mesothelioma than the other traditional methods used so far.

9.4   Conclusion

Malignant mesothelioma, an occupational disease with less survival time after prognosis, faces a tough challenge in early diagnosis. In this study, the diagnosis of pleural malignant mesothelioma using various artificial techniques has been discussed. The chapter also analyses MTiling and SVM methods which have been used in the classification of various other tumors. These methods overcome the issues faced by traditional artificial techniques used so far in the diagnosis of malignant mesothelioma. In the future, we would like to implement an improved adaptive MTiling neural network for the diagnosis of malignant mesothelioma. SVM which provides better classification accuracy than other traditional ANN methods has been used in the diagnosis of various carcinomas and can certainly serve as a promising tool for the classification of malignant and benign mesothelioma. Features of Improved MTiling and SVM can also be combined together for enhancing the accuracy of classification rate as future work.

References

1. Brause, R.W., Medical analysis and diagnosis by neural networks. *International Symposium on Medical Data Analysis*, pp. 1–13, 2001.
2. Kancherla, K. and Mukkamala, S., Feature selection for lung cancer detection using SVM based recursive feature elimination method, Springer, pp. 168–176, 2012.
3. Wang, Z.J., Reddy, G.P. *et al.*, Malignant pleural mesothelioma: Evaluation with CT, MR imaging, and PET. *Educ. Exhibit-Contin. Med. Educ.*, 24, 1, 105–119, 2004.
4. Brims, F.J., Meniawy, T.M. *et al.*, A novel clinical prediction model for prognosis in malignant pleural mesothelioma using decision tree analysis. *J. Thorac. Oncol., Elsevier*, 11, 4, 573–582, 2016.
5. Erl, O., ÇetinTanrikulu, A., Abakay, A., Use of artificial intelligence techniques for diagnosis of malignant pleural mesothelioma. *Dicle Tip Dergisi*, 42, 1, 5–11, 2015.

6. Sridhar, S.S. and Ponnavaikko, M., New constructive neural network architecture for pattern classification. *Int. J. Comput. Electr. Eng.*, 3, 1, 843–848, February, 2011.

7. Sridhar, S.S. and Ponnavaikko, M., Improved adaptive learning algorithm for constructive neural networks. *Int. J. Comput. Electr. Eng.*, 3, 1, 1793–8163, 2011.

8. Parekh, R. *et al.*, Pruning strategies for the MTiling constructive learning algorithm. *Int. Conf. Neural Netw. IEEE*, 3, 1960–1965, 1997.

9. Er, O. *et al.*, An approach based on probabilistic neural network for diagnosis of Mesothelioma's disease, Elsevier. *Comput. Electric. Eng.*, 38, 75–81, 2012.

10. Kourou, K. *et al.*, Machine learning applications in cancer prognosis and prediction. *Int. J. Adv. Res. Comput. Sci. Software Eng.*, 6, 6, 1–8, June 2016.

11. Gao, X., The method and efficacy of support vector machine classifiers based on texture features and multi-resolution histogram from (18)F-FDG PET-CT images for the evaluation of mediastinal lymph nodes in patients with lung cancer. *Eur. J. Radiol.*, 84, 2, 312–317, 2015.

12. Sui, Y., Computer-aided lung nodule recognition by SVM classifier based on combination of random undersampling and SMOTE. *Comput. Math. Methods Med.*, 2015, 13, 2015, Article ID 368674.

13. Tidke, S.P. *et al.*, Classification of lung tumor using SVM. *Int. J. Comput. Eng. Res.*, 2, 5, 1254–1257, 2012.

14. Engchuan, W., Pathway activity transformation for multi-class classification of lung cancer datasets. *J. Neurocomputing*, 165, C, 81–89, October 2015.

15. Firmino, M. *et al.*, Computer-aided detection (CADe) and diagnosis (CADx) system for lung cancer with likelihood of malignancy. *Biomed. Eng. Online*, 15, 1, 2, 2016.

16. Luciano, C., CT signs, patterns and differential diagnosis of solitary fibrous tumors of the pleura. *J. Thorac. Dis.*, 4, 2, 112–113, 2012.

17. https://archive.ics.uci.edu/ml/datasets/Mesothelioma%C3%A2%E2%82%AC%E2%84%A2s+disease+data+set+

10

Handwritten Character Recognition and Genetic Algorithms

Magesh Kasthuri[1]* and Vigneshwar Manoharan[2]

[1] Wipro Limited, Bengaluru, India
[2] R & D and Academic Initiatives, CBAS Corp, India

Abstract

Handwriting recognition principally entails optical character recognition. However, a complete handwriting recognition system also handles formatting, performs correct segmentation into characters, and finds Offline character recognition. The field of character recognition is classified into Online and offline recognition based on the way recognition is carried out. Off-line handwriting recognition involves the automatic conversion of text in an image into letter codes, which are usable within computer and text-processing applications. The data obtained by this form can be regarded as a static representation of handwriting. Off-line handwriting recognition is comparatively difficult, as different people have different handwriting styles. There are two major techniques and devices in this regard called OCR and ICR. OCR, which is termed Optical Character Recognition, is based on a legacy model where character recognition is based on optical scanning. ICR, which is termed Intelligent Character recognition, is a modern engine, which has a different pattern of character recognition including but not limited to handwritten character recognition. In addition, as of today, OCR engines are primarily focused on machine-printed text, and ICR is for hand "printed" text. Though there are many OCR/ICR engines available today, supporting handwriting character recognition from multi-language is a greater challenge and costly task even today. This chapter discusses the stages in handwritten character recognition in both offline and online character recognition and explains how Genetic algorithms can help develop an AI-based Character recognition system.

Keywords: Handwritten, recognition, genetic algorithms, OCR, ICR

---

*Corresponding author: magesh.kasthuri@wipro.com

Ahmed A. Elgnar, Vigneshwar M, Krishna Kant Singh and Zdzislaw Polkowski (eds.) Handbook of Computational Sciences: A Multi and Interdisciplinary Approach, (197–224) © 2023 Scrivener Publishing LLC

10.1   Introduction

Language identification and interpretation of handwritten characters are challenges faced in various industries. For example, it is always a big challenge in data interpretation from cheques in banks, language identification, and translated messages from the ancient script in the form of manuscripts, palm scripts, and stone carvings to name a few.

Therefore, there is a need for greater accuracy in offline handwriting recognition of such handwritten text. Also, displaying the confidence of recognition helps the user to decide if this can be taken as an acceptable threshold or improvised with further noise reduction or manual correction process.

Soft computing is the area in the field of computer science where hard and complex tasks are accomplished with low cost or high benefit (in time and investment) with one or more in-exact solution techniques. It is not a single area of research or a process of study whereas it is commonly accepted and included in numerous computational and research areas including

    (i)   Neural Networks
    (ii)   Fuzzy system
    (iii) Evolutionary computing like Genetic Algorithms
    (iv) Swarm Intelligence
    (v)   Cognitive Reading
    (vi) Chaos theory

The trend of research in Cognitive Reading has become so popular in programming area in the field of Computer science from late 1990s when scientists and researchers show more interest in computational approaches that are complex in nature to derive from a known algorithm or solution. For instance, in the research area of Biology, medicine, and human management sciences there are various problems where we need Cognitive Reading to deliver a complex and in-exact solution when there is no polynomial time to arrive at an exact solution.

Human reading is a nearly analogous cognitive process to OCR that involves the decoding of printed symbols into meanings/characters/words/ sentences. Researchers in the field of Artificial Intelligence are interested to know how readers extract visual information and how it is related to words/sentence and meanings. One of the questions they are trying to solve is that – How recognition of a word is done by recognizing its characters or its holistic shape. Even more, interestingly, the question which opens many research ideas is how are humans able to read words when it is written in multiple languages (language identification and interpretation)? For many years, researchers in the field of cognitive learning and linguistics have extensively studied these questions and a large number of theories and reading models exist that explain different aspects of visual word recognition or reading.

Cognitive reading is one of the key principles used in Genetic algorithms where stroke-based character recognition is done based on a probable combination of stroke groups segmented for a given character set.

10.2   Recognition Framework for a Handwritten Character Recognition

From cognitive theories of computing, two primary strengths of the human brain are

1. Massive interconnection of various data stored in brain.
2. Parallel-processing architecture.

Neural network is based on such theories of the human brain and intelligence and hence forms an alternative computational approach called artificial neural network (ANN).

In a Handwritten character recognition system, the major challenge is in mimicking a neural network system into an artificial system to enable the system to think and decide based on the analysis it has done which is a simulation of the human brain. For example, the brain function of a child won't be matching to the decision system of supercomputer as the child can recognize its parent despite make-up change or haircuts. It is always a difficult task for a computer to perform such recognition even if we train multiple times. A user can enable more permutations and combination of the system to increase the accuracy of recognition. This is one the key reason that even after thirty years of dynamic and deep research in the artificial intelligence field, computers fall short of the expectations of intelligence we have of them. Like this, there are many problems to be addressed by artificial intelligence like speech and image recognition, robotics, vision, and combinatorial optimization, which is quite challenging and different from conventional computational methods.

Another challenge in ANN in simulating the human brain is that it has to process based on intuition or deeper insight into the problem based on historical approach of solving the problem. In other words, ANN is somewhat like a trained monkey which is trained to take right decision based on empirical reasoning without explicit verbalization of the problem. Please note that the monkey has its own mind and decision making power or native neural networks and also capable of solving tasks on its own with more complex solution than any task one might train the monkey to do, but it is not in the scope of simulating the natural system.

10.3   Offline Character Recognition

There are many researches done for offline character recognition using various neural network based solution and some of them are specific to a language (egg: Devanagari, Urdu, Arabic) and some of them are specific to handwritten character recognition but none of these researches provide a unified solution for multi-language based character recognition and none of them provides a solution which is cost effective in terms of training and cost effective in terms of accuracy in recognition rate.

Performance of single-algorithm systems drops precipitously as the quality of input decreases. In such situations, a human subject can continue to perform accurate recognition, showing only a gradual decrease in reliability. Collaboration between separate algorithms proves beneficial, in that such systems will allow a gradation of recognition levels expressed as probabilities or loose guesses to be passed from one level to the next. More specifically, a front-end system will perform some useful first-order basic processing. Then a second level of processing will be engaged which will judge whether to assimilate the results of the first process, extend them and proceed to the next stage with a positive recognition, or to dismiss them and re-invoke the first level again while asking for modifications.

Handwriting recognition is a widely implemented technology to electronically identify handwritten text. In online handwriting recognition, text written on a touch surface of an electronic touch device is dynamically recognized based on the movements of a writing device (digital pen, a finger, or a stylus) and presented to the user after each continuous stroke such as a character or word is entered. Therefore, the user is able to edit a character or a word in the event of incorrect recognition of text by the electronic device as soon as it is presented to the user. On the other hand, in offline handwriting recognition, recognition of characters occurs by identifying characters from an image of handwritten text instead of the user writing on a touch surface. Here, the recognized text is presented to a user only when the entire handwritten text represented in the image is recognized.

10.4   Literature Review

Filip Lundqvist *et al.* define Automatic script recognition and orientation detection are two important preprocessing steps during OCR. Script recognition determines the written script on the page to use an appropriate character recognition algorithm [1].

It is necessary when the OCR system does not have prior knowledge about the language on the page or the page is written in more than one script [2]. Orientation detection detects and corrects the deviation of the document's orientation angle from the horizontal direction [3]. This step is also required because if document images are wrongly oriented, the subsequent processing steps like layout analysis and character recognition will fail to work correctly since usually both assume pages to be in the correct orientation [4].

Also, this is very important for a handwritten document where orientation highly differs from person to person [5] and decides the character to be recognized if it is wrongly recognized for orientation. Based on this technique, natural image distortions can be handled efficiently with 95% accuracy [6] in character recognition.

Gulshan Goyal *et al.* takes about the process of handwritten character recognition where usually OCR systems are developed for a particular script or language, and they can recognize characters that belongs to that particular script or language. A script can be defined as a set of characters used to provide the graphical representation of a certain language or group of languages. Languages in the world are typeset in many different scripts [7].

A script may be used by only one language or it can be shared by more than one language [8]. A typical example is the Arabic script that is used for writing several languages of Asia [9] and Africa [10], such as Arabic, Persian, Pashto and Urdu. Usually, in multi-script or multilingual environment, OCR systems require to recognize characters irrespectively of their script class.

However, building an OCR system that could read characters from all scripts is very difficult. A brute-force solution [11] would be to train an OCR classifier on more than one script by adding individual characters from all the scripts in the training process. But this is a time-consuming operation [12] and has boundary limits that it cannot define generic solution for any handwritten character recognition [13].

However, this would lead to more classification errors [14] due to increase in the number of character classes. In addition, the features required for character recognition usually depend on structural properties of the writing which generally differs from one script to other.

Another solution [15] is to combine character or word level classifiers for different languages or scripts and recognition of a particular character or word is done by its respective classifier. But, this requires a prior knowledge of the script for application of appropriate classifiers. Automatic script recognition methods [16] give the prior knowledge about the script or language of a document for selecting a suitable character classifier.

Manisha Ch N *et al.* defines a method where Script recognition of multi-script documents in which different paragraphs, text lines or words in a page are written in different scripts. Some examples [17] include ancient multi-script documents, multilingual dictionaries, and books with line by line or column wise translation in different languages. In digital libraries, script recognition also helps in indexing, retrieval, and sorting of documents when dealing with multi-script environment.

This work presents a novel application of convolutional neural network (CNN) for automatic script recognition in multi-script document images. The method works at connected component level which is considered as characters of a particular script in a document image. The CNN acts as a discriminative learning model, where suitable features for script recognition are automatically extracted and learned.

The method is evaluated on English-Tamil, Tamil-English, English-French and English-German based multi-script document images and also single script document image like English or Tamil sentences. Hence this solution is one of the key applications in digital library in language detection, character recognition and automatic translation to combine them together into a unified solution which is very unique in nature in this research.

Joseph *et al.* evaluated various popular character recognition techniques *viz* OCR-optical character recognition that has processing functionality to convert any form of image automatically like written text [18] or printed text or even handwritten texts which is mapped to a form which can be electronically analyzed and organized into computer readable segmented image collection.

They are transformed from optically scanned image to binarized format which can be used to create suitable form of image pattern and can be used to analyze later. There are numerous feature recognition techniques available in practice which can be used to examine and to recognize characters based on captured/predetermined patterns stored in data store or historical record or trained data.

But all these techniques when carefully experimented has high dependency on standard fonts in case of printed text [19] or intensive training to capture many combinations of data sets for handwritten characters. Also due to text formation in handwritten text, there are noise [31] in recognition (reduced accuracy) due to change in size like reduction, magnification, or rotation (transformation of source image), different lighting condition (display condition), resolution limitation (device capability), perspective distortions (device fault), arbitrary orientation (manual error) and also poor quality of characters due to non-uniform illumination conditions during image acquisition (which can be considered as manual mistakes). Hence, it is a high demand in IT industry for a system for character recognition and a unified method to achieve the same seamlessly and automatically.

Borgo, Rita, *et al.* explains real-time application of these techniques by doing research study and practical application of offline character recognition methods in various industrial applications. Here is the example where Handwriting Recognition techniques [20] can prove to be solution for enhancing banking which satisfies the Visually Challenged person and may prove to be best banking solution. In order to build loyalty and drive profitability, banks need to offer a non-stop interactive banking environment. To achieve this, banks need to increase their business agility by anticipating customer needs and offer an engaging user experience. The automatic processing of bank cheques involves extraction and recognition of handwritten or user entered information from different data fields on the cheque such as courtesy amount, legal amount, date, payee and signature. Hence, Automatic bank cheque processing systems are needed not only to counter the growing cheque fraud menace but also to improve productivity and allow for advanced customer-service.

The Automatic Cheque Processing System employed in Next Generation Banking may prove to be novel technology gaining the customers satisfaction (good - will) and recognition of skilled forgery by efficient validation techniques.

Chacko AM *et al.* has published different research papers on Automatic recognition of handwritten characters and one such key application is Handwritten dates present on bank cheques is also very important in application environments where cheques will not be processed prior to the dates shown. In countries like India, a cheque cannot be processed after six months of the date written on it.

Verification of the hand printed signature present on a paper cheque is the most important challenge as the signature carries the authenticity of the cheque as explained by Chen *et al.* [21]. Character recognition, the process of converting the gray or binary images that contain textual information to electronic representation of characters that facilitate post-processing including data validation and syntax analysis is done to preserve the authenticity and avoid forgeries.

MacKenzie *et al*. proposes a graffiti-based usability system for human-computer interaction in processing empirical solution for character segmentation and noise reduced character recognition system. In this system, the key advantage highlighted is noise reduction by manual training and re-processing in order to achieve higher quality of recognition [22–24].

Sundaramoorthy *et al*. talks about various applications of genetic algorithm in combination with Fuzzy logic for synthesis and application of character segmentation and handwritten character training and recognition system using neural network-based solution [25].

Anita Mary *et al*. work on numerical recognition system to automate bank document processing explains a technique in which the courtesy amount recognition part is done by touching numeral segmentation and digit recognition. While writing courtesy amount, the digits may touch each other [26]. As a result, the touching numerals have to be successfully segmented before the recognition task. There are two types of approaches used for segmentation of touching numerals it involves local and global. Cutting points between the two touching numerals are extracted in local approaches, and in global approaches, significant splitting points are detected after analyzing the numeral string as whole.

The accuracy in recognizing constituent digits plays a big role in the recognition accuracy of the handwritten courtesy amount numeral string. After successful segmentation of individual digits from the numeral string, they have to be correctly recognized to get the value of the cheque. The digit recognition techniques can be grouped into neural network-based techniques. The legal amount recognition part is accomplished by guideline removal, amount segmentation and word recognition.

Anitha Mary *et al*. discusses about systems using Fuzzy neural network in character identification for cheque processing in Banks. In India, the courtesy amount is located on the right half of the cheque. A box is detected by identifying the cross-section points where horizontal and vertical lines meet [27]. Another method used for extraction in uses fuzzy membership values, entropy, energy and aspect ratio as features, which are fed into a fuzzy neural network (FNN) for the identification of a field.

In English texts, words are separated by apparent space, but the letters within a word are not well separated, so words can be considered as natural units to recognize [27]. In Chinese and Japanese texts, a sentence separated by punctuation marks is an integral unit because there is no difference between the inter-word and inter-character gaps [28]. Word or sentence recognition, or generally, character string recognition, faces the difficulty of character segmentation: the constituent characters cannot be reliably segmented before they are recognized [29].

Ashutosh Aggarwal *et al.* proposed a system [30] using analytical approaches, where each handwritten word of the legal amount is recognized by recognizing its constituent characters. A word is segmented into components like characters or graphemes (part of a character) first.

In global approaches, the entire word is considered as a single unit (pattern), and recognition is done without any sort of character-level segmentation. As the legal amount words written in English language can be case sensitive as shown in Figure 10.1, the size of the lexicon for word-level recognition can go up significantly.

Umal Patel *et al.* explains their work [31] in which words which are normally in complex patterns and having great variability in handwriting styles, handwritten word segmentation is handled. Handwritten word recognition can be greatly aided by a lexicon of valid words, which is usually dependent on the application domain. For example, as shown in below Figure 10.2, there are 33 different words that may appear in the so-called legal amounts on bank checks. Hence, the lexicon for this application is small and static (it is constant in all the instances).

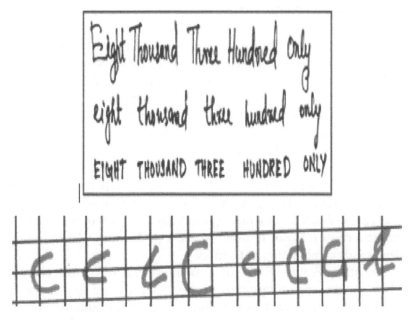

Figure 10.1 Different styles of handwritten character writing.

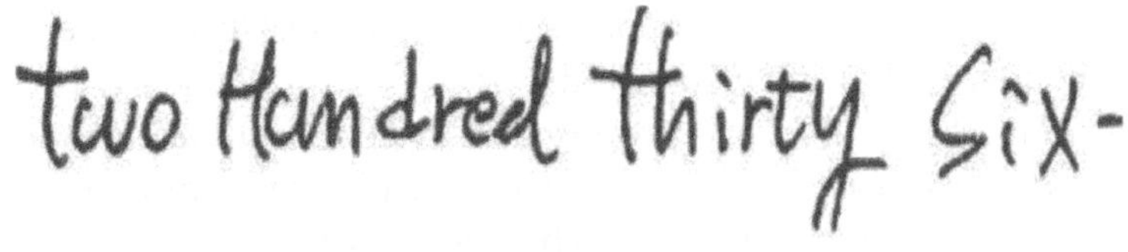

two Hundred thirty Six-

One	Two	Three	Four	Five
Six	Seven	Eight	Nine	Ten
Eleven	Twelve	Thirteen	Fourteen	Fifteen
Sixteen	Seventeen	Eighteen	Nineteen	Twenty
Thirty	Forty	Fifty	Sixty	Seventy
Eighty	Ninety	Hundred	Thousand	Dollars
Dollar	and	Only		

Figure 10.2 Lexicon character sets for bank cheque recognizer.

10.5   Feature Extraction

In pattern recognition, feature extraction is one the key term used and such feature can be characterized by steps of process to differentiate one type of object from another in a more meaningful and concise manner than is represented in the raw structure. So, it is always an important task in the pre-definition stage to define meaningful features which helps to develop a processing engine called a good recognizer, as it is well known that a common or generalized solution is not feasible.

In most of the cases, these features are usually defined based on the experience and/or intuition of the system designer. Depending on the type of problems given, there are numerous ways and a lot of variety of such features can be defined in extracting methods and ways of representation. In practical cases it is not unusual where a problem involving hundreds and thousands combination of features.

So far, other Feature Extraction methods can recognize characters based on matrix representation of strokes. So, there are chances of error prone detection in handwritten character recognition due to shape differences in the strokes of characters. The idea of Genetic algorithm is to take cells of strokes in the matrix during character recognition process to minimize the error detection and improvise the character recognition technique. This also saves time in training more and more combinations of characters.

In all current language detection process using neural networks, any system can detect only one language of the content. If the content is in mixed languages (representing multiple language content) then the accuracy of language detection and further processing of translating the content may require manual intervention as one has to decide if the recognition is correct before giving for translation.

Linear combination of feature vectors, simple selection using the discrimination power of features, Principal component analysis and sequential forward/backward data selection are common approaches to avoid the feature selection problem.

10.6   Pattern Recognition

Pattern recognition is one of the key areas of application of neural networks and it is termed as the ability to recognize a pattern on its own using its knowledge base. Genetic algorithm follows automatic training process to improve its knowledge base, but the key success lies in that the pattern must be recognized even when that pattern is distorted. Practically, it is used in human life in many ways.

A vehicle driver driving a car should be able to accurately recognize a traffic signal and react to it. This is one of the complex and critical pattern recognition procedure practiced by numerous drivers in day to day life. Even though, not all traffic signal looks like same or it can be altered depending on the time of day or the season, the task for the driver is to recognize it properly.

For instance, there are many variations of these traffic signals exist in roads it is not a hard task for a human driver. But when someone writes a program to mimic this operation (to write a computer program that accepts an image and tells if it is a traffic signal), then it would be a very complex task.

Off-line character recognition often involves scanning a form or document written sometime in the past. This means the individual characters contained in the scanned image will need to be extracted. Tools exist that are capable of performing this step however, several common imperfections in this step. The most common being characters that are connected together are returned as a single sub-image containing both characters.

Neural network recognizers learn from an initial image training set. The trained network then makes the character identifications. Each neural network uniquely learns the properties that differentiate training images. It then looks for similar properties in the target image to be identified. Neural networks are quick to setup; however, they can be inaccurate if they learn properties that are not important in the target data.

10.7   Noise Reduction

In an offline character recognition system, Noise reduction would be based on language in which character is written. For example, Hindi characters will have specific strokes where noise reduction is based on strokes used whereas Telugu language is based on shapes and curve notation which can be used for noise reduction. In mixed language content, it is always challenging to do noise reduction as there would be more than one language representation.

In a mixed-language handwritten content scenario, this gets complicated for languages with similar scripts or strokes. For example, if the user assumes Hebrew document as Latin document and find a Latin translator the outcome of the translation would be wrong. And since, in the case of offline interpretation, the user do not provide immediate feedback, there opportunity to correct such misinterpretation is impossible.

Image recognition is based on a technique where recording and matching of image characteristics such as size, segmented groups (strokes) and character interpretation is carried out. Both recording of an image and its subsequent matching with other images will be carried out through a series of stages of processing. There are six major such stages of processing as explained below.

The purpose of such processing step is to convert an image's graphic form into a binarized format which can be accessible and retrievable from a conventional and easy to process group of attribute (indexed store) and at the same time maintains relationship among the segmented group which helps to retain all information necessary to describe the image's characteristics.

The six stages involved in the processing of image in genetic algorithm-based character recognition are:

(i)   Image creation
(ii)   Image markup or reduction
(iii) Segment group storage
(iv)   Searching for segment group

(v)   Matching key stroke
(vi)   Character interpretation

10.8   Segmentation

With some exceptions, most Character recognition methods are based on segmentation-based character recognition approaches, in which words are segmented into isolated characters and each character is segmented further into strokes or group of strokes and characters are recognized individually from strokes. However, in case of degraded and low-resolution text in both handwritten and printed text-based image, character segmentation is problematic and the performance of character segmentation significantly affects character recognition accuracies.

Sophisticated character segmentation techniques have been proposed in past by many researchers, but achieving a good segmentation on various kinds of degradations is still a hard problem. Some other methods take into account word level information and recognize complete words without character segmentation. These methods are generally referred as "holistic word recognition methods" because they do not directly process the characters, but use global word level features like T-junctions, b-loop, d-loop, ascenders and descenders information for the recognition of entire word.

However, a drawback of whole word recognition is that it necessarily limited to small vocabularies and are useful only in applications with small static lexicons. Recognition based segmentation is another strategy to avoid the segmentation problem during character recognition process. In these methods input image is divided into many overlapping pieces, resulting into over-segmentation of the image. Usually a hypotheses graph is made using a single character classifier and segmentation boundaries can be drawn using some dynamic programing-based procedures.

From last two decades, model-based approaches such hidden Markov models (HMMs) have been very popular due to their ability to do segmentation free recognition. HMMs have been proved very successful in automatic speech recognition where segmentation is also a key issue.

Over the past years, many HMMs based text recognition approaches has been presented for machine printed, handwritten and cursive script recognition. However, HMMs unable to model contextual information completely because of independent observation assumption during state transitions. Another problem of HMMs is the lack of discriminative capabilities, while discriminative models generally give better performance for recognition task.

10.9   Pre-Processing

Pre-processing is almost one of the basic step in every text recognition system. Usually it is used to remove noise and different variations in the data. It may include binarization, noise removal, skew correction, image enhancement and data normalization etc. In genetic algorithm-based character recognition, pre-processing is used to normalize height of text line images.

This is done by rescaling image height of each input text line image to a fixed line height. The normalization process takes care of the image aspect ratio and the image width is rescaled proportional to the new image height.

Figure 10.3 shows an example text line image in original and after image height normalization. Screen rendered text lines are normalized to the height of 20 pixels and this value is determined empirically over the training dataset. Automatic training is adjusting these pre-determined text position, size and weight into various combinational values based on adjacent cell and strokes associated with the first identified stroke.

Image pre-processing involves the following steps are handled in the pre-processing stage to improvise the recognition rate of the system.

1. The input image should contain only segmented handwritten characters from a scanned document.
2. Skew detection & correction
3. Background noise removal
4. Skeletonization

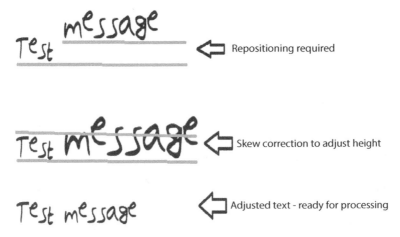

Figure 10.3 Preprocessing.

10.10   Hybrid Recognition

Since mixed language recognition for handwritten character is always complex and requires multiple iteration of training, using a Hybrid recognition technique would provide better accuracy due to its variant in processing technique.

Artificial neural networks (ANNs) have also been applied to various document image analysis and recognition tasks and good character recognition accuracies have been reported. But most successful application of ANNs are limited to the recognition of isolated characters or digits (e.g. Number plate recognition system in vehicle).

Combination of HMMs and ANNs has also been used effectively in various text and speech recognition problems and is generally referred as hybrid recognition approach.

Development of hybrid systems using HMMs and ANNs usually requires addressing two design issues. The first issue concerns with the architectural aspects of ANNs and HMMs, viz

1. How structure of the HMMs (discrete or continuous, character or word level HMMs) should be selected, and what kind of ANNs paradigm (multilayer perceptrons, radial basis or time delay neural networks etc.) should be used.
2. The second issue concerns how these two modules can be best trained together.

In past many hybrid HMMs/ANNs systems have been revealed using different kinds of HMMs and ANNs structures. In most of the hybrid systems, ANNs are used to augment HMMs either as an approximation of the probability density function or as a neural vector quantizer.

Some other hybrid approaches use ANNs to obtain observation probabilities for HMMs. These hybrid approaches either require combined training criteria for ANNs and HMM, or they use complex neural network architectures like time delay neural networks (TDNNs) or space displacement neural networks (SDNNs).

10.11   Applying Genetic Algorithm

Though there are various algorithms available from neural network processing in the field of handwritten character recognition like feature extraction, markov chain/markov theory, Bayesian process, Back propagation network algorithms Wavelets based character recognition, to name a few, Genetic algorithm is intended in a combination of neural networks with genetic algorithms as this process helps in minimizing the correction/mistake in character recognition and stores a large volume of processing patterns (trained data) and helps in easily and quickly identify characters from various combinations of patterns matching from the trained data.

A simple example of flow of process in Genetic Algorithm based system is shown in Figure 10.4. Genetic Algorithm is a very good means of optimizations in such problems in handwritten character recognition.

They help to optimize a desired property by generating templates of data based on hybrid solutions from the presently existing solutions. These hybrid solutions are added to the Knowledge base and may be used to generate more hybrids. This process is called training the network. These solutions may be better than previously generated solution templates. All this is based on genetic operators, which are basically defined in the beginning and applied over the problem.

Off-line handwriting recognition involves the automatic conversion of text in an image into letter codes which are usable within computer and text-processing applications. The data obtained by this form is regarded as a static representation of handwriting. Off-line handwriting recognition is comparatively difficult, as different people have different handwriting styles. And, as of today, OCR engines are primarily focused on machine printed text and ICR for hand "printed" text. There is no OCR/ICR engine that supports handwriting recognition as of today.

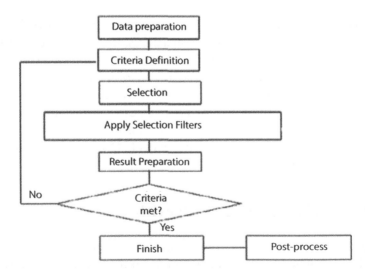

Figure 10.4 Flow of process in genetic algorithm.

Off-line handwriting recognition involves the automatic conversion of text in an image into letter codes which are usable within computer and text-processing applications. The data obtained by this form is regarded as a static representation of handwriting.

Neural network recognizers learn from an initial image training set. The trained network then makes the character identifications. Each neural network uniquely learns the properties that differentiate training images. It then looks for similar properties in the target image to be identified. Neural networks are quick to setup; however, they can be inaccurate if they learn properties that are not important in the target data.

A stroke is not limited to a continuous line segment. A stroke may also include a portion of a character that has a discontinuity in its representation. For example, an English alphabet 'i' may also be considered as a single stroke according to some embodiments in spite of a discontinuity in its representation because there is no sudden change in angle in any portion of this alphabet.

Therefore, there is need for greater accuracy in offline handwriting recognition of such handwritten text. Hence displaying the confidence of recognition helps the user to decide if this can be taken as acceptable threshold or improvise with further noise reduction or manual correction process.

Handwritten character recognition using Soft computing methods like neural networks is always a big area of research for long time and there are multiple theories and algorithms developed in the area of neural networks for handwritten character recognition.

For an offline handwritten character recognition system, it is not only because of numerous variation of writing styles of different individuals but also for the complex nature of character variation in different languages, automatic recognition of handwritten characters still poses some potential problems to the researchers.

The research framework for a genetic algorithm driven Character recognition system is design science: it is characteristic for design science to aim to answer people's needs by constructing and evaluating new technological products. The products of design science can be categorized into four types: constructs, models, methods and implementations. In this research a new construct, multi-language character set is evaluated; it will be determined if the construct works and whether or not it is an improvement compared to another older product: IRIScan OCR recognition system.

The operating environment of an artefact can cause unwanted side effects if designers are not familiar enough with the background where the artefact will operate.

Another problematic part of design science deals with evaluation and its intended use. In order to be able to evaluate the construct of design science, it is necessary to set evaluation criteria for it. The evaluation criteria for the construct in this particular study, the multi-language character set, is a recognition accuracy of near to 100%, where every character that a user draws is recognized correctly, and no extra attention to the recognition itself is required. This can prove to be impossible, though, since even people themselves often have problems in interpreting text written by others.

10.12   Multilingual Characters

God is great,
Everything is by the grace of god

10.12.1   Multilingual Characters – Hindi

Multilingual characters - Hindi as shown in Figure 10.5.

भगवान महान है,

सब कुछ भगवान की कृपा से है

bhagavaan mahaan hai ,
sab kuchh bhagavaan kee krpa se hai

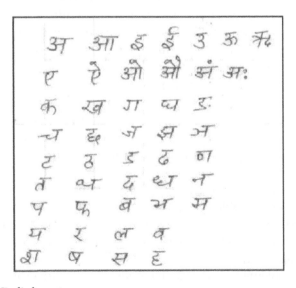

Figure 10.5 Hindi characters.

10.12.2   Multilingual Characters – Tamil Language

Multilingual characters - Tamil language as shown in Figure 10.6.

கடவுள் பெரியவர்

எப்போதும் கடவுளின் கிருபையால்

Kaṭavuḷ periyavar
eppōtum kaṭavuḷin̄ kirupaiyāl

Figure 10.6 Tamil characters.

10.12.3   Multilingual Characters – Malayalam Language

Multilingual characters - Malayan language as shown in Figure 10.7.

ദൈവം വലിയവനാണ്,
എല്ാം ദൈവകൃപയാൽ

daivaṁ valiyavanāṇ,
ellāṁ daivakrpayāl

Figure 10.7 Malayalam consonants (vyanjanams).

10.12.4   Multilingual Characters – Telugu Language

Multilingual characters - Telugu language as shown in Figure 10.8.

దేవుడుగొప్పవడు ,
అంత భగవంతుని దయవల్ల

Dēvuḍu goppavāḍu,
antā bhagavantuni dayavalla

ಕ	ಖ	ಗ	ಘ	ಜ	ಚ	ಛ	ಜ	ಝ	ಞ
ka	kha	ga	gha	ṅa	ca	cha	ja	jha	ña
[kʌ]	[kʰʌ]	[gʌ]	[gˢʌ]	[ŋʌ]	[ʧʌ]	[ʧʰʌ]	[ʤʌ]	[ʤˢʌ]	[nʌ]
ಟ	ಠ	ಡ	ಢ	ಣ	ತ	ಥ	ದ	ಧ	ನ
ṭa	tha	ḍa	ḍha	ṇa	ta	tha	da	dha	na
[ʈʌ]	[ʈʰʌ]	[ɖʌ]	[ɖˢʌ]	[ɳʌ]	[tʌ]	[tʰʌ]	[dʌ]	[dˢʌ]	[nʌ]
ಪ	ಫ	ಬ	ಭ	ಮ	ಯ	ರ	ಲ	ವ	ಳ
pa	pha	ba	bha	ma	ya	ra	la	va	ḷa
[pʌ]	[pʰʌ]	[bʌ]	[bˢʌ]	[mʌ]	[jʌ]	[rʌ]	[lʌ]	[ʋʌ]	[lʌ]
ಶ	ಷ	ಸ	ಹ	ಅ	ಚೆ	ಜೆ			
śa	ṣa	sa	ha	ṛa	tsa	dza			
[ɕʌ]	[ʂʌ]	[sʌ]	[hʌ]	[ɽʌ]	[tsʌ]	[dzʌ]			

Figure 10.8 Tamil characters.

10.12.5   Multilingual Characters – Kannada Language

Multilingual characters - Kannada language as shown in Figure 10.9.

ದೇವರು ದೊಡ್ಡವನು,

ಎಲ್ಲವೂ ದೇವರ ಅನುಗ್ರಹದಿಂದ

Dēvaru doḍḍavanu,
ellavū dēvara anugrahadinda

ಕ	ಖ	ಗ	ಘ	ಙ	ಚ	ಛ	ಜ	ಝ	ಞ
ka	kha	ga	gha	ṅa	ca	cha	ja	jha	ña
[kɑ]	[kʰɑ]	[gɑ]	[gˢɑ]	[ŋɑ]	[ʧɑ]	[ʧʰɑ]	[ʤɑ]	[ʤˢɑ]	[na]
ಟ	ಠ	ಡ	ಢ	ಣ	ತ	ಥ	ದ	ಧ	ನ
ṭa	tha	ḍa	ḍha	ṇa	ta	tha	da	dha	na
[ta]	[tʰa]	[da]	[dˢa]	[ŋa]	[ta]	[tʰa]	[da]	[dˢa]	[na]
ಪ	ಫ	ಬ	ಭ	ಮ	ಯ	ರ	ಲ	ವ	
pa	pha	ba	bha	ma	ya	ra	la	va	
[pa]	[pʰa]	[ba]	[bˢa]	[ma]	[ja]	[ra]	[la]	[ʋa]	
ಶ	ಷ	ಸ	ಹ	ಳ	ಕ್ಷ	ಜ್ಞ			
śa	ṣa	sa	ha	ḷa	kśa	jna			
[ça]	[ʂa]	[sa]	[ha]	[la]	[kʂa]	[ʤna]			

Figure 10.9 Kannada characters.

10.12.6   Multilingual Characters – Egypt Language

Multilingual characters - Egypt language as shown in Figure 10.10.

الله أكبر ،

كل شيء بـنـعمة الله

allah 'akbar,
kl shay' biniemat allah

بـفـضل مـن الله سبـحـانـه وتـعـالـى

bifadl min allah subhanah wataealaa

IPA	Latin	Name	Final	Medial	Initial	Isolated	IPA	Latin	Name	Final	Medial	Initial	Isolated
[zˤ]	ḍ	dˤɒːd	ـض	ـضـ	ضـ	ض	[ʔ]	(ˈ)	ʔelıf	ـا	—	—	ا
[tˤ]	ṭ	tˤɒː	ـط	ـطـ	طـ	ط	[b]	b	beː	ـب	ـبـ	بـ	ب
[zˤ~ðˤ, dˤ]	ẓ	zˤɑː	ـظ	ـظـ	ظـ	ظ	[t]	t	teː	ـت	ـتـ	تـ	ت
[ʕ]	'	ʕeːn	ـع	ـعـ	عـ	ع	[s, t]	ṯ th	seː	ـث	ـثـ	ثـ	ث
[ɣ~ʁ]	ġ, gh	ɣeːn	ـغ	ـغـ	غـ	غ	[g]	g	giːm	ـج	ـجـ	جـ	ج
[f]	f	feː	ـف	ـفـ	فـ	ف	[ħ]	h	ħɒː	ـح	ـحـ	حـ	ح
[ʔ, q]	q	ʔɒːf	ـق	ـقـ	قـ	ق	[x]	ḫ, kh	xɒː	ـخ	ـخـ	خـ	خ
[k]	k	kaːf	ـك	ـكـ	كـ	ك	[dʒ]	ǧ, j	dʒiːm	ـج	ـجـ	جـ	ج
[l, ɫ]	l	laːm	ـل	ـلـ	لـ	ل	[d]	d	daːl	ـد	—	—	د
[m]	m	miːm	ـم	ـمـ	مـ	م	[z, d]	ḏ, dh	zaːl	ـذ	—	—	ذ
[n]	n	nuːn	ـن	ـنـ	نـ	ن	[r]	r	reː	ـر	—	—	ر
[h]	h	heː	ـه	ـهـ	هـ	ه	[z]	z	zeː	ـز	—	—	ز
[w]	w	wɑːw	ـو	—	—	و	[s]	s	siːn	ـس	ـسـ	سـ	س
[j]	y	jeː	ـى	ـيـ	يـ	ى	[ʃ]	š, sh	ʃiːn	ـش	ـشـ	شـ	ش
		'hamze	ء	—	—	—	[sˤ]	ṣ	sˤɒːd	ـص	ـصـ	صـ	ص

IPA	Latin	Name	Final	Medial	Initial	Isolated	IPA	Latin	Name	Final	Medial	Initial	Isolated
[oː, aʊ̯[4]]	ō/aw		ـو	—	—	و	[ʔ]	(')	ʔɛlɪf	—	—	—	ا
[uː, ʊː~ɔː[2]]	ū'		ـؤ	—	—	ؤ	[ʔa~ʔæ~ʔɛ ʔɑ~ʔɒ[2]]	a-		—	ـأ	أ	—
[eː, aĭ]	ē/ay		ـى	ـيـ	يـ	ى	[ʔu~ʔo ʔʊ~ʔɔ[2]]	u-		—	ـأ	أ	—
[aː~eː]	-aÿ	(ʔɛlɪf maʔˈsuːrɛ)	ـى	—	—	ى	[ʔi, ʔɨ[2]]	i-		—	ـإ	إ	—
[iː, ɨː[2]]	ī		ـي	ـيـ	يـ	ي	[aː~æː ɑː~ɒː[2]]	-ā		ـا	—	—	ا
[ʔiː, ʔɨː[2]]	ī-		—	ـإيـ	إيـ	—	[ʔaː~ʔæː ʔɑː~ʔɒː[2]]	-ā'	(ʔɛlɪf madːɛ)	—	ـآ	آ	—
[iːj]	iyy		ـيّ	ـيّـ	يّـ	يّ	[aː~œː ɑː~ɒː[2]]	-ā'		ـاء	ـأ	أ	اء
[iː, ɨː[2]]	ī'		ـئ	ـئـ	ئـ	ئ	[el-]	el-		—	ـأل	أل	—
							[laː~læː]	lā	laːm ʔɛlɪf	—	ـلا	—	لا

[2] after uvular and pharyngeal (emphatic) consonan
[4] after consonants

10.12.7 Multilingual Characters – Polish Language

Bóg jest wspaniały, Wszystko jest z łaski Boga

Z łaski Boga

A a	Ą ą	B b	C c	Ć ć	D d	E e	Ę ę
a	ą	be	ce	cie	de	e	ę
[a]	[ɔ̃]	[b/p]	[t͡s]	[t͡ɕ/d͡ʑ]	[d/t]	[ɛ]	[ɛ̃]
F f	G g	H h	I i	J j	K k	L l	Ł ł
ef	gie	ha	i	jot	ka	el	eł
[f/v]	[g/k]	[x/ɣ~ɦ]	[i/j]	[j]	[k/g]	[l]	[w/ɫ]
M m	N n	Ń ń	O o	Ó ó	P p	R r	S s
em	en	eń	o	ó	pe	er	es
[m]	[n]	[ɲ]	[ɔ]	[u]	[p/b]	[r]	[s/z]
Ś ś	T t	U u	W w	Y y	Z z	Ź ź	Ż ż
eś	te	u	wu	y	zet	ziet	żet
[ɕ/ʑ]	[t/d]	[u]	[v/f]	[ɨ]	[z/s]	[ʑ/ɕ]	[ʐ/ʂ]
Letter combinations							
ch	cz	dz	dź	dż	rz	sz	
[x/ɣ~ɦ]	[t͡ʂ/d͡ʐ]	[d͡z/t͡s]	[d͡ʑ/t͡ɕ]	[d͡ʐ/t͡ʂ]	[ʐ/ʂ]	[ʂ/ʐ]	
ci	dzi	gi	(c)hi	ki	ni	si	zi
[t͡ɕ]	[d͡ʑi]	[gʲ]	[xʲ]	[kʲ]	[ɲ]	[ɕ]	[ʑ]

Figure 10.10 Polish characters.

Above mentioned are the different languages representations, with their alphabets, consonants and vowels for different languages perspective. Each language has its own script, form, origination, formation, way of being written, encoding format, grammar of the language, way and the representation of the writing and its structures, features, and its patterns. So, on processing of each of these languages its lexicons and skolemization techniques certainly differs. The entity and the protocols differ that needs to be concerned. This leads to the Semantic web analysis and also implementation of NLP along with text Mining aspects.

Here, the results of English character classification results are enclosed here as follows.

10.13 Results

Character	Misclassified	Percentage of misclassifed	Percentage of missed	Correct classification	Accuracy
A	0.0	0	100	120	0.0
B	3.3	4	96.7	116	3.3
C	8.3	10	91.7	110	8.3
D	12.5	15	87.5	105	12.5
E	1.7	2	98.3	118	1.7
F	1.7	2	98.3	118	1.7
G	4.2	5	95.8	115	4.2
H	3.3	4	96.7	116	3.3
I	7.5	9	92.5	111	7.5
J	5.8	7	94.2	113	5.8
K	11.7	14	88.3	106	11.7
L	3.3	4	96.7	116	3.3
M	7.5	9	92.5	111	7.5
N	12.5	15	87.5	105	12.5
O	11.7	14	88.3	106	11.7
P	12.5	15	87.5	105	12.5

(Continued)

(*Continued*)

Character	Misclassified	Percentage of misclassifed	Percentage of missed	Correct classification	Accuracy
Q	4.2	5	95.8	115	4.2
R	7.5	9	92.5	111	7.5
S	5.8	7	94.2	113	5.8
T	4.2	5	95.8	115	4.2
U	11.7	14	88.3	106	11.7
V	0.8	1	99.2	119	0.8
W	5.8	7	94.2	113	5.8
X	5.0	6	95.0	114	5.0
Y	4.2	5	95.8	115	4.2
Z	3.3	4	96.7	116	3.3

Miss-Classification Rate = 5.1%
Total Number of Miss-Classification = 173
Total Number of Correct Classification = 3187

The results above show the classification of the English alphabets for Capital Letters, and the small letters are not considered here in the classification part.

References

1. Lundqvist, F. and Wallberg, O., *Natural image distortions and optical character recognition accuracy*, pp. 21–25, Degree project, KTH Royal Institute of Technology, CSC, KTH20160511, First Cycle, 15 Credits, Stockholm, Sweden, 2016.
2. Al-Marakeby, A., Kimura, M.Z., Rashid, A., Design of an embedded arabic optical character recognition. *J. Signal Process. Syst.*, 70, 3, 249–258, 2013.
3. Anthony, L., Yang, J., Koedinger., K.R., A paradigm for handwriting-based intelligent tutors. *Int. J. Hum.-Comput. Stud.*, 70, 11, 866–887, 2012.
4. Arif, A.S., Pahud, M., Hinckley, K., Buxton, B., Experimental study of stroke shortcuts for a touchscreen keyboard with gesture-redundant keys removed.

Proceedings of Graphics Interface 2014, Canadian Information Processing Society, pp. 43–50, 2014.

5. Azmi, Najwa, A., Nasien, D., Shamsuddin, S.M., A review on handwritten character and numeral recognition for Roman, Arabic, Chinese and Indian scripts. *Int. J. Comput. Sci. Eng.*, 2, 1, 4–8, 2013.

6. Badri, L., Development of neural networks for noise reduction. *Int. Arab J. Inf. Technol.*, 7, 3, 289–294, 2010.

7. Goyal, G. and Dutta, M., Experimental approach for performance analysis of thinning algorithms for offline handwritten devnagri numerals. *Indian J. Sci. Technol.*, 9, 30, 34–39, 2016.

8. Bankar, S. and Nagpure, R., Contextual information search based on domain using query expansion. *Int. J. Emerg. Trends Technol. Comput. Sci.*, 3, 148–151, 2014.

9. Bhoi, K. and Solanki, D.K., Texture segmentation using optimal Gabor filter. Diss. (Doctoral dissertation). Orissa, India, 23–29, 2011.

10. Blaschke, T., Hay, G.J., Kelly, M., Lang, S., Hofmann, P., Addink, E., Feitosa, R.Q. *et al.*, Geographic object-based image analysis–towards a new paradigm. *ISPRS J. Photogramm. Remote Sens.*, 87, 180–191, 2014.

11. Borgo, R., Kehrer, J., Chung, D.H., Maguire, E., Laramee, R.S., Hauser, H., Ward, M., Chen, M., Glyph-based visualization: Foundations, design guidelines, techniques and applications. *Eurographics State of the Art Reports*, pp. 39–63, 2013.

12. Borovikov, E., A survey of modern optical character recognition techniques, *ArXiv*, abs/1412.4183, 31–34, 2014.

13. Chacko, A.M.M.O. and Dhanya, P.M., Handwritten character recognition in malayalam scripts-a review. *Int. J. Artif. Intell. Appl. (IJAIA)*, 5, 1, 6–9, 2014.

14. Chacko, A.M.M.O. and Dhanya, P.M., Multiple classifier system for offline malayalam character recognition. *Proc. Comput. Sci.*, 46, 86–92, 2015.

15. Chaudhari, P.P. and Sarode, K.R., Offline handwritten character recognition by using grid approach. *Int. J. Appl. Innov. Eng. Manage.*, 3, 4, 71–73, 2014.

16. Chen, B.-R., *Design and implementation of MAT-based skeleton and junction detectors for chinese characters*, pp. 98–104, NTUST Department of Electronic Engineering Master Thesis, National Taiwan University of Science and Techonology's, 2015.

17. Manisha, ChN., Sundara Krishna, Y.K., Sreenivasa Reddy, E., Slant correction for offline handwritten telugu isolated characters and cursive words. *Int. J. Appl. Eng. Res.*, 11, 4, 2755–2760, 2016.

18. Joseph, A.D., Laskov, P., Roli, F., Tygar, J.D., Nelson, B., Machine learning methods for computer security (Dagstuhl Perspectives Workshop 12371). *J. Dagstuhl Manifestos*, 3, 1, 1–30, 2013.

19. Frankish, C., Hull, R., Morgan., P., Recognition accuracy and user acceptance of pen interfaces. *Proceedings of the SIGCHI Conference on Human*

Factors in Computing Systems, ACM Press/Addison-Wesley Publishing Co., pp. 109–114, 1995.

20. Borgo, R., Kehrer, J., Chung, D.H., Maguire, E., Laramee, R.S., Hauser, H., Ward, M., Chen, M., Glyph-based visualization: Foundations, design guidelines, techniques and applications. *Eurographics State of the Art Reports*, pp. 39–63, 2013.

21. Chen, G., Li, Y., Srihari, S.N., Word recognition with deep conditional random fields. *2016 IEEE International Conference on Image Processing (ICIP)*, IEEE, pp. 1928–1932, 2016.

22. MacKenzie, I.S. and Zhang, S.X., The immediate usability of Graffiti. *Graphics Interface*, vol. 97, pp. 129–137, 1997.

23. MacKenzie, I.S. and Castellucci, S.J., Empirical research methods for human-computer interaction. *CHI Extended Abstracts*, PHI Learning Pvt. Ltd., pp. 1013–1014, 2014.

24. Rajasekaran, S. and Vijayalakshmi Pai, G.A., *Neural networks, fuzzy logic and genetic algorithm: Synthesis and applications (with CD)*, pp. 15–25, PHI Learning Pvt. Ltd, 2003.

25. Chacko, A.M.M.O. and Dhanya, P.M., Handwritten character recognition in malayalam scripts-a review. *Int. J. Artif. Intell. Appl. (IJAIA)*, 5, 1, 6–9, 2014.

26. Chacko, A.M.M.O. and Dhanya, P.M., Multiple classifier system for offline malayalam character recognition. *Proc. Comput. Sci.*, 46, 86–92, 2015.

27. Jain, A.K. and Farrokhnia, F., Unsupervised texture segmentation using Gabor filters. *Pattern Recognit.*, 24, 12, 1167–1186, 1991.

28. Jain, A.K., Mao, J., Mohiuddin, K.M., Artificial neural networks: A tutorial. *IEEE Comput.*, 29, 31–44, 1996.

29. Jayadevan, R., Kolhe, S.R., Patil, P.M., Pal, U., Automatic processing of handwritten bank cheque images: A survey. *Int. J. Doc. Anal. Recogn. (IJDAR)*, 15, 4, 267–296, 2012.

30. Aggarwal, A., Rani, R., Dhir, R., Handwritten devanagari character recognition using gradient features. *Int. J. Adv. Res. Comput. Sci. Software Eng.*, 2, 5, 85–90, 2012.

31. Patel, U., An introduction to the process of optical character recognition. *Int. J. Sci. Res. (IJSR)*, 2, 5, 155–158, 2013.

11

An Intelligent Agent-Based Approach for COVID-19 Patient Distribution Management

Claudiu-Ionut Popirlan[1], Adriana Burlea Schiopoiu[2]*, Cristina Popirlan[1]
and Ahmed A. Elngar[3]

[1]*Department of Computer Science, Faculty of Sciences, University of Craiova, Craiova, Romania*
[2]*Department of Management, Marketing, Business Administration, Faculty of Economy and Business Administration, University of Craiova, Craiova, Romania*
[3]*Faculty of Computers and Artificial Intelligence, Beni-Suef University, Beni-Suef City, Egypt*

Abstract

The provision of COVID-19 hospital treatment generally entails some individuals, positioned in specific establishments and situations, whose selections and movements want to be classified in order to achieve a powerful and efficient therapy. Artificial Intelligence via wise retailers is used at a large scale and this eases the choice-making leading to a smoothly running coordination technique. This study's painting depicts a wise agent's machine that turned carried out to assist manipulate the care technique in real-international settings. The wise retailers themselves advanced the use of an open-supply platform for peer-to-peer software that is primarily agent based, known as JADE–JAVA Agent Development Framework, which mixes some of wise retailers' techniques: a symbolic choice process for taking decisions with insufficient information; an idea of negotiation, dealing with comprehensible assistance using commitments and conventions; and a fixed verbal exchange primitives for inter-retailers' interactions. The software for this method is tested via an improved software prototype for the scientific control technique of COVID-19 management.

Keywords: Intelligent agents, COVID-19, JADE simulation, multi-agent systems

Corresponding author: adriana.burlea@edu.ucv.ro

Ahmed A. Elgnar, Vigneshwar M, Krishna Kant Singh and Zdzislaw Polkowski (eds.) Handbook of Computational Sciences: A Multi and Interdisciplinary Approach, (225–244) © 2023 Scrivener Publishing LLC

11.1 Introduction

Intelligent agent systems [12–14] and general artificial intelligence [9] support clinical personnel in decision-making in uncertain circumstances (pandemic crisis, treatment, etc.). Therefore, it plays an increasingly decisive part in medicine (test selection and diagnostic decisions). In addition, many medical procedures now involve multiple people from multiple specialty facilities (or departments), and their decisions and actions need to be coordinated for effective and efficient care [16].

In recent years, many types of research have been conducted in the field of AI related to COVID-19 based on the segmentation of computer tomography (CT) images [1, 5].

The pandemic crisis has made a rapid response to the invisible enemy of paramount importance worldwide and the need to provide the healthcare sector with flexible applications for the clinical management process of COVID-19 treatment. Li *et al.* [2] developed an application to detect COVID-19 and distinguish it from other forms of pneumonia. Bo Wang *et al.* [3] developed a generally applicable methodology consisting of a set of models, data collections, annotations, user interface, training tools, testing and processes for clinical delivery. CT images are one of the factors for rapid diagnosis, but multimodal models can be continually improved by adding new data that increase detection accuracy.

Warda *et al.* [4] made an analysis of the three types of COVID-19 diagnosis (e.g., laboratory, RT-PCR and CT tests) and elaborated their Hybrid Diagnose Strategy (HDS) based on data pre-processing, component ranking and classification. Ferguson *et al.* [6] considered two strategies as important for fighting against this enemy: suppression (by reducing the reproduction of the virus) and mitigation (by vaccine or medication). Aggarwal *et al.* [8] based on a critical literature review of COVID-19 arrived at the conclusion that decision-making process using multi-criterion methods is suitable for making the best-informed choices under pressure.

Recently, Gupta *et al.* [7] compared the behavior of the pandemic crisis with the previous healthcare crisis (e.g., Ebola, MERS, SARS, and H1N1) and they elaborated a deep learning model that relies on data collected from the source.

This limitation of the model is also encountered for many AI applications because without high reliability the results are not relevant for diagnosis. This chapter will try to diminish this limitation and build a prototype able to measure in real-time and reduce the uncertainty of epidemiological appearances of COVID-19.

11.2   Intelligent Agent's Architecture Proposal for COVID-19 Patient Distribution Management

The architecture of the proposed intelligent agent system covers multiple knowledge layers, a working memory, a communications manager and a human-computer interface, as shown in Figure 11.1.

For domain efficiency, the intelligent agents need to display both deliberative behaviors (e.g., task decomposition, plan selection, and task allocation) and reactive behaviors (e.g., responding to new data arrival, to

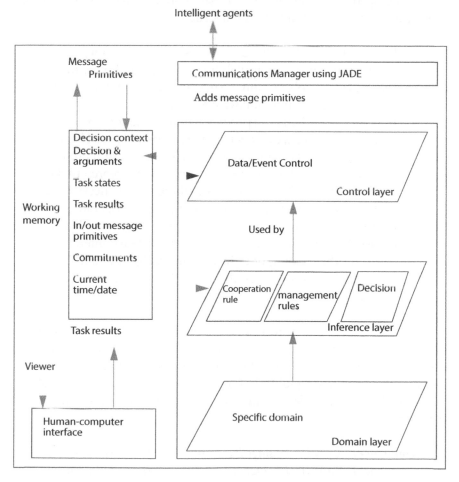

Figure 11.1 Intelligent agents' architecture for COVID-19 patient distribution administration.

current data adjustments and to inconsistent agent commitments in a fast-enough manner).

- The deliberative behavior is accomplished in the proposed architecture by incorporating decision rules for plan selection, task management rules for task decomposition and allocation, and cooperation rules used for commitments.
- The reactive behavior is obtained using the control layer for working memory changes (new task results, goals, messages, changes in existing data, agent commitments, or task states).

The intelligent agent's architecture is based on three layers of knowledge representing the key part of the system structure:

- Domain knowledge – includes, but is not limited to, a patient record and a resource availability database, a clinical management protocols [8] and a specific medical domain (e.g., COVID-19 pandemic) knowledge base.
- Inference knowledge – specify inference relations between domain knowledge, existing patient records and possible new data as generic, declarative inference rules. These represent the essence of the agent system architecture and represent the subdivisions of rules for decision-making under uncertainty, for task management and for operating agent cooperation.
- Control knowledge – is used when new data is added to the working memory generating new knowledge inferences based on the existing ones in the knowledge domain. This meta-level layer manages the execution of inference and domain knowledge.

Detailing, information and facts are stored in the domain knowledge base, not giving any other information about the knowledge usage. For instance, the COVID-19 protocol in the second stage of pandemic can be divided into the following subtasks for patient treatment: 'admit the patient to hospital', 'administer drugs and monitor the patient', and 'discharge the patient':

component ('COVID-19 stage 2', 'admit patient to hospital')
component ('COVID-19 stage 2', 'administer drugs and monitor
the patient')
component ('COVID-19 stage 2', 'discharge the patient').

The inference knowledge base contains rules (implemented as declarative schemas) that stipulate the inference relationship between domain knowledge and current information. For instance, the state of a task is described by the following inference schema:

> becomes 'started' once the state of one of its subtasks becomes 'started':
> schema(conditions(component(Task, Subtask) and state(Subtask, started)), conclusions(state(Task, started))).

The COVID-19 protocol states that, the task 'COVID-19 stage 2' from the above schema should become 'started' when one of its subtasks (e.g., 'admit the patient to hospital') becomes 'started'.

In the control level, after the task becomes 'started', the associated inference rules are executed and the current data is included in the working memory by the following control rule:

> If schema (Conditions, Conclusions) and all true (Conditions)
> then
> add (Conclusions).

Considering this for our model, in the COVID-19 protocol, after the task is 'started' ('admit the patient to hospital' is 'started'), current data are added in the working memory by applying the control rule for the specific inference schema and existing domain knowledge:

> state ('CT 1 stage 2', 'started').

Considering all the above states, an intelligent agent system working session used for COVID-19 protocols can be summarized as follows:

- The intelligent agent launches the goal of finding the best suitable treatment' protocol for a specific COVID-19 infected patient.
- The control layer is activated by the established goal and it implements the decision rule and the existing knowledge for the current patient records in order to obtain a decision associated with arguments that support a particular protocol treatment.
- The doctor is the one that approves the decision and he appeal to the intelligent agent system for execution protocol assistance.

- The control layer is once again activated and it uses the task manager rule to break down the treatment protocol into composing tasks. These subdivided tasks are allocated to an agent and the communication primitives are generated.
- As soon as the intelligent agent confirm the proposal acceptance, the communication manager is the one that transform the primitives into exhaustive messages and send them to the responsible agent. The responsible agent is then included in a dynamic cooperating agents' community.
- The control layer applies the cooperation rules to the commitments generated for the specific agent.
- When the entire treatment protocol turns into a terminal state the cooperation between agents finishes.
- In the same time, the doctor can cooperate in a patient treatment protocol with other agents from the community.

The domain, inference, and control knowledge are logically and functionally separated based on the following two reasons.

First of all, the representation and maintenance of knowledge are clarified in the intelligent system. The architecture of this system is independent related to the medical domain allowing it to be reused in various other domains. Control knowledge and inference knowledge are independent of each other; therefore, control rules can be used for different inference rules.

Finally, the other main reason is that acquiring the information (about patients and treatment protocols) from the knowledge base is convenient. Any adjustment of the domain knowledge doesn't alter the inference and control knowledge.

Temporary data, such as goals to be completed, control states of currently active tasks, completed tasks results, messages and commitments, are generated in different stages by the control layer, by the user, or by the communications manager and are being stored in the working memory of the system's architecture. New data is added in the working memory every moment that the control layer triggers reactions.

The communications manager is the one responsible with sending messages to the other agents from the task management primitives, and receiving messages from other agents translating them into primitives for the cooperation manager.

The human-computer interface facilitates the connection between users and the intelligent system, where the computer has various functions, but it's not completely autonomous and it needs human input in order to be able to use all its functional capabilities. The user receives the results of the inferences from the computer and validates or invalidates them. In case of positive response, the computer will send them to external agents. In case of negative response, the computer will present an alternative solution to the user.

11.2.1   A Clinical Scenario of COVID-19 Patient Distributed Management

When a doctor in a COVID-19 hospital must treat an infected patient, firstly he must decide the appropriate treatment plan for the specific person. Through the human-computer interface the doctor consults the intelligent system which will access one of his decision support systems. When encountering inconsistent or incomplete information, the decision algorithm included in the system builds a particular 'COVID-19 protocol' relying upon various treatment options. The final decision in adopting the protocol belongs to the doctor that authorizes the system to carry out the treatment.

The COVID-19 protocol for stage 2 has three subtasks: 'admit the patient to hospital', 'administer drugs and monitor the patient' and 'discharge the patient'. First task is performed by the doctor, because patient treatment is his main responsibility, while the computer will be involved in following stages. Following the 'admit the patient to hospital' task the system provides two additional subtasks: 'allocate bed' (performed by the hospital's resource management department) and 'obtain patient consent' (performed by the doctor).

After successfully completing the two subtasks, the patient will be allocated a bed and the intelligent system will continue with allocating the next task ('administer drugs and monitor the patient') to a nurse. This task will be further split into other subtasks such as: 'obtain drug', 'administer drug' and 'observe patient' (that can be divided in other subtasks such as: 'measure body temperature', 'take blood samples', and 'analyze blood samples'). The nurse is responsible for completing all these subtasks, that can be divided even further, but this subdivision will not be detailed here.

The nurse reports to the doctor and to the intelligent system about the completion of any of the subtasks performed by her. If all patient indicators are normal, based on all the available data, the system recommends to the doctor (intelligent agent) that he should perform the 'discharge patient' task, split in two subtasks: 'Instruct Patient' and 'Inform'.

Concluding the scenario, there is a constant information exchange (expectations and commitments) between the agents (the doctor, the nurse, the resource management department). The resource management department allocates a bed for the patient to meet the doctor's expectation and the nurse takes the commitment of monitoring and treating the patient in order to complete her assigned tasks.

11.2.2   Communication Management

Communication primitives have been defined considering the interactions between cooperative intelligent agents. Making an extended analysis of the agents' interactions conducted to the following communication management (Table 11.1).

Every communication primitive consists of a type, a content, and an effect over the receiver. The communication primitives are well constructed so that the uncertainty is diminished and the messages between the agents and the system are intuitive and predictable.

The first four primitive types (request, accept, reject and alter) are applied in the task allocation process when the agent's commitments are defined. For the COVID-19 protocol scenario, the doctor (intelligent agent) assign to the nurse (other agent) the task 'administer drugs and monitor patient' with complimentary information. The nurse can accept the doctor request to administrate drugs and to monitor the patient for a number of days starting the next day, or she can reject it (by saying she has to many patients), or she can amend the request notifying the doctor that she will start monitoring the patient in two days.

The inform primitive type can be applied after a task request was accepted and it is used in the result dissemination process. The cancel primitive type is used when an agent modifies its commitment. The acknowledge primitive type is associated to all messages send and received during the communication process.

The task manager associated with the cooperation rules develop different primitives' type when the control layer executes certain task. The primitives are then converted in structured messages by the communication manager. The primitive content is described in Table 11.1 and can be visualized using the following structures.

> *\<message\>::= \<sender\> \<receiver\> \<date\> \<time\> \<patient\>*
> *\<transaction primitive\>**
> *\<sender\>::= \<sender name\> \<contact address\>*
> *\<sender name\>::= \<first name\> \<surname\>*

Table 11.1 Communication management.

Type	Content	Effect on receiver
request	task; response by the date; priority: urgent or not; [provisional schedule]	Receiver agent is the one that decides to commits to the task by accepting the request and informing the sender agent about his decision.
accept	task; [accepted schedule]	Sender agent knows receiver agent is committed to the request. The receiver agent will execute the task and then will inform the sender agent. In this alliance, the manager is the sender agent and the contractor is the receiver agent.
reject	task; [provisional schedule]	If the receiver agent declines the commitment, then the sender agent has to appeal to another agent to solve the task.
alter	task; provisional schedule; acceptable schedule	Sender agent weighs the schedules and elect the one that is suitable for his tasks. The new request is sent to the receiver agent according to the provisional schedule.
propose	task; [proposed schedule]	Receiver agent may or may not adopt the proposal.
inform	any information: data, domain knowledge, or partial plans	Information can be used by receiver agent in order to solve local problem.
query	a question: what, how, whether, and so on	Receiver agent answer the query received and return a response by proposing something new to the sender, informing the sender or reply with unknown in case he has no other valid answer.
cancel	abort the task	Receiver agent should ignore earlier messages.
acknowledge	all of the above	Messages were sent successful via the communication manager.

<first name>::= NAME
<surname>::= NAME
<contact address>::= <email address> | <postal address>| <telephone number> | <fax number>
<email address>::= EMAIL_ADDRESS
<postal address>::= POSTAL_ADDRESS
<mobile number>::= NUMBER
<receiver>::= <receiver name> <contact address>
<receiver name>::= <first name> <surname>
<date>::= <day> <month> <year>
<day>::= NUMBER
<month>::= NUMBER
<year>::= NUMBER
<time>::= <hour> <minute>
<minute>::= NUMBER
<hour>::= NUMBER
<patient>::= <patient name> <date of birth>
<patient name>::= <first name> <surname>
<date_of_birth>::= <year> <month> <day>
<transaction primitive>::= <primitive type> <primitive content>
<primitive type>::= REQUEST | ACCEPT | REJECT | ALTER | PROPOSE|INFORM|QUERY|CANCEL|ACKNOWLEDGE
<primitive content>::= PRIMITIVE_CONTENT.

11.3   Intelligent Agents Task Management

Once the agent's goal is formulated, the clinical protocol is determined in order to obtain the best possible results. The task manager department is used to separate the subtasks and to designate them to agents. The same component handles the management of state tasks.

The clinical COVID-19 protocol is developed by experts as a generic clinical plan. Once the protocol is defined, the task manager divides it into subtask corresponding to the established plan structure. The first subtasks of the plan are usually primitive functions, while the latest are decision tasks that are performed under a decision process. In The COVID-19 protocol, 'allocate bed' is a primitive task, while electing the right drug for a specific patient and administrating it represents a decision task.

For every task or subtask, the intelligent system allocates two agent roles:

- The agent that manages the task accomplishment, he is verifying that the task is executed by an agent and that the task results reach the agent who need it;
- The agent who actually execute the task.

The relationship between these two agents represents a task share, the manager finds the best agent for task execution. The main problem, the one that is solved in the system architecture, is to decide what agent is suitable for a specific task. This relationship is called accountability and, using it, we can define in the system what agent do and to whom he is responsible.

In our system, the nurse (agent) is the one that monitor multiple patients for different doctors (intelligent agents) and she is reporting them the patient's recovery status. Therefore, the nurse agent is in an accountability relationship with doctor agents, she is receiving tasks to execute and she return the execution response to the doctors.

> IF Task is necessary & Task is of type Task Type &
>> Associate agent is accountable to the Agent for tasks of Task Type &
>> Agent prefers to interact with Associate agent concerning Task Type
> THEN request (Agent, Associate agent, perform (Task))

The agents from intelligent system architecture create tasks that at every moment are in a state: scheduled, started, abandoned, canceled or completed. The transition between these states is ensured in the system by the intelligent agent (doctor) who need to be sure that all records are enrolled for the specific patient. The doctor is the one that controls patient records from the bed assignment to the moment when he leaves the hospital and his treatment protocol is written in patient records. The procedure of transition between task states is not simple and the transition management is conscientiously controlled. A case study is presented below:

> schema (conditions(state(Task, cancelled), and component(Task, Subtask) and state(Subtask, started)),
> conclusions (state(Subtask, abandoned)).
> schema(conditions(state(Task, cancelled), and component (Task, Subtask) and state(Subtask, scheduled)),
> conclusions (state(Subtask, cancelled)).

In the system, we implemented the states canceled and abandoned as two different states. The state canceled is when the doctor decides to abort a task in various situations and the state abandoned is when the patient decide to stop the treatment and the doctor cannot modify his decision.

11.3.1   Intelligent Agents Cooperation Management

The cooperative actions described in the intelligent agent's architecture are constructed on commitments. These actions are also influenced by the commitment changes, for example due to resources needed to complete a commitment.

Agents' actions can vary between commitments states from creating to executing it. Therefore, due to the fact that commitments are not irreversible there is a need for conventions that state the conditions for agent behavior regulation towards other agents in the cooperating group.

Because commitments and conventions are the essence of cooperation between agents, two main arguments arise:

- what is involved in establishing a commitment?
- what type of convention is appropriate for monitoring commitments in the given treatment clinic?

11.3.1.1   Establishing Commitments

Commitment is not guaranteed by liability issues, there are other aspects that influence task completion such as availability of mandatory resources. In the considered case, the intelligent agent (doctor) is in an accountability relationship with the patient, because the hospital must have bed vacancy and a nurse that has available time for drug administration and patient monitoring. Only then the agent can commit to starting the COVID-19 treatment protocol. The agent is aware of its available resources, but may need to submit the same task to several other agents from the cooperation group until the task is accepted by one of them, which becomes committed to task execution, informing the manager agent via the subsequent inference rule:

> *IF Associate agent is requested by Agent to perform Task &*
> *Associate agent accountable to Agent for Task Type tasks &*
> *Task is of type Task Type & Task requires Resources &*
> *Resources are available to Associate agent*
> *THEN Associate agent becomes committed to Task, AND*
> *accept (Associate agent, Task, for (Agent))*

The associate agent became the contractor after committing to the task, he performs the task and must inform the manager agent about the results of the task completion and he becomes available to commit to other tasks requested by other agents from the cooperation group. The communication manager triggers the inference rules using primitives to send and receive information between agents.

The message between the contractor and his manager is implemented in the system using the following inference rule:

IF Task is completed and it produces Results &
*   Associate agent is committed to Agent for Task*
THEN inform (Associate agent, Agent, performed (Task),
*   results-produced (Task, Results))*

11.3.1.2   Adaptive Management of Commitment Changes

When committed, the task will almost certainly be executed by the agent, but there are circumstances, independent to the agent, that can influence or even modify the state of the commitment. In the considered COVID-19 scenario, the task could be no longer need due to patient's recovery or sudden death; the task could be adjusted due to unexpected resources reduction (e.g., lack of medication, reduced personnel); the task could be totally modified due to unexpected changes in patient condition (e.g., the patient condition worsens and he needs assisted oxygenation).

Since the commitments can change their states from active to canceled, aborted or modified, the intelligent system must be able to manage the change in conditions locally and also in the cooperating group through the convention. This is important because the system is dynamically built and it can adapt to unexpected modifications in the commitments states.

11.4   Java Agent Development Framework

Multi-agent systems can be implemented via multiple object-oriented programming languages [18], since the agent approach is comparable to object characteristics, such as inheritance, encapsulation or message transmission. Software platforms and frameworks aid the application development providing support and deployment means for communication and coordination of agents in the cooperation group of the multi-agent system [26].

Platforms and frameworks, such as Java Agent Development (JADE) [10, 11] ensure FIPA-compliant features that are essential to the cooperation between intelligent agents. JADE is a user-friendly API built over object-oriented language Java; it creates abstract agents that can be easily modified according to the considered system needs. Agent abstraction simplifies the development of distributed applications using middleware layer facilities.

The ready-to-use and easy-to-customize main features of JADE are:

- Multi-agent distributed system;
- The JADE platform facilitates communication, when possible, deflects assembled/unassembled objects;
- Efficient asynchronous message passing;
- Efficient control over the life-cycle of the agents locally and remotely, via graphical tools;
- Facilitates agent portability, making them always available for commitments in the cooperation group of the multi-agent system;
- The JADE platform has the means to communicate with external applications, sending notifications about agents' status;
- Monitoring and debugging can be easily achieved using a set of graphical tools available in the platform;
- Full compliance with the FIPA specifications [22].

The architecture of the multi-agent system that includes the related components is described below and can be visualized in Figure 11.2 and Figure 11.3.

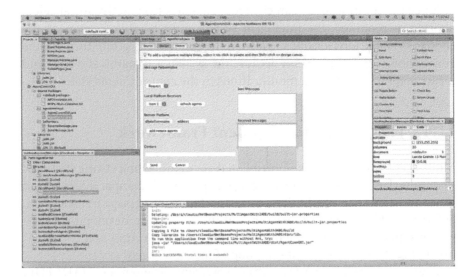

Figure 11.2 JADE implementation 1.

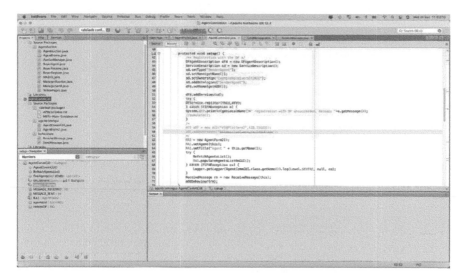

Figure 11.3 JADE implementation 2.

The multi-agent system is capable to control the intelligent agents as described in sections 11.2 and 11.3.

11.4.1   Software Implementation

The multi-agent system in implemented using agent-orientated programming languages due to their focus on handling agents' proprieties and facilities and supports agency attributes such as beliefs, goals, plans, roles, and norms. Agent's structure is well defined and easily accessible in the agent-oriented programming language.

Figure 11.4 and Figure 11.5 present the manner how JADE implementation of multi-agent system defines the best communication statement for sending and receiving messages.

JADE features (see Figures 11.6 and 11.7), like decision making tools and techniques, are used to accomplish different objectives of the intelligent agent system. The set of alternatives for every agent is included in the multi-agent system architecture using parameters and standards.

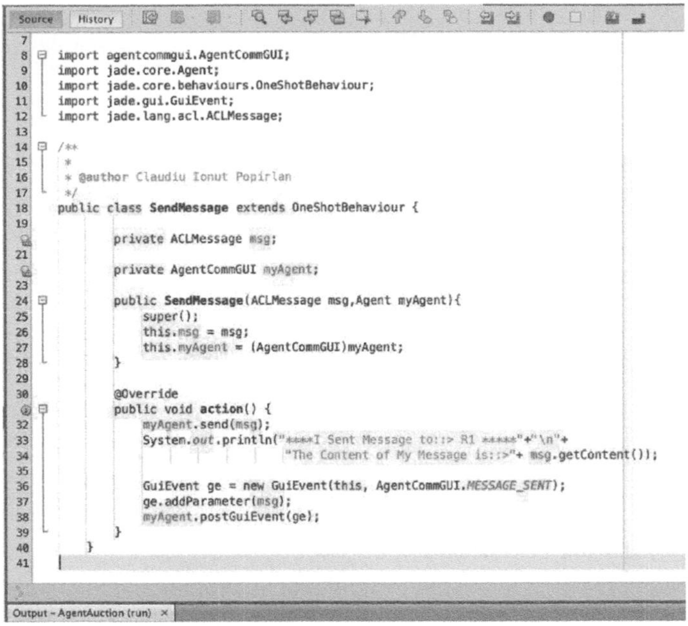

Figure 11.4 Intelligent agent – send message.

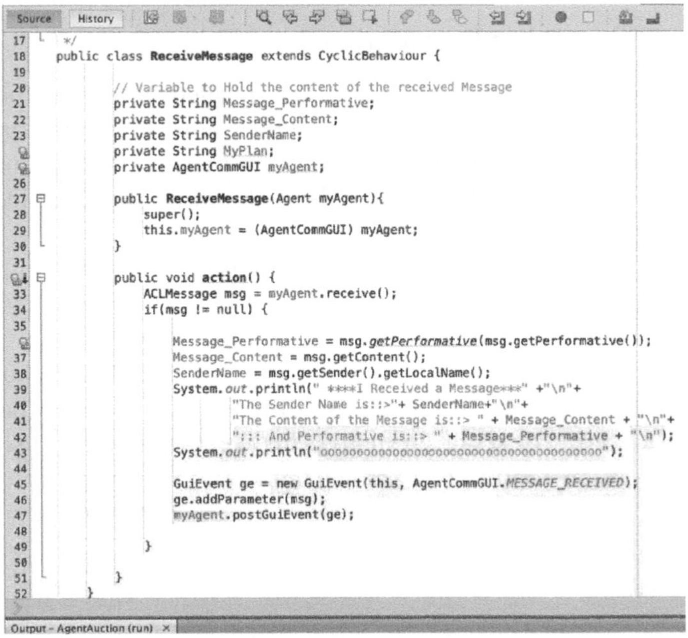

Figure 11.5 Intelligent agent – receive message.

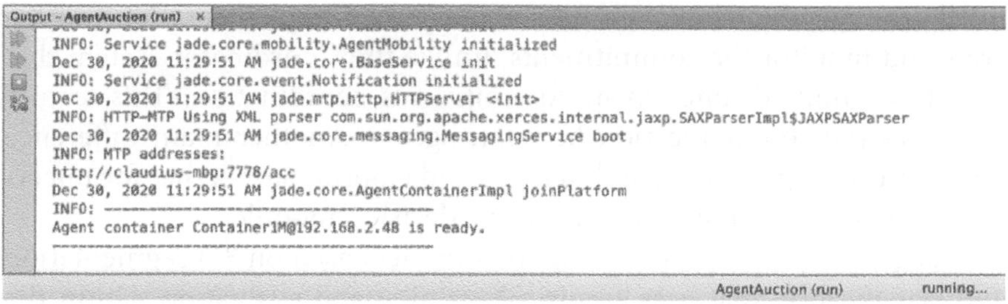

```
Output – AgentAuction (run)   ×
    INFO: Service jade.core.mobility.AgentMobility initialized
    Dec 30, 2020 11:29:51 AM jade.core.BaseService init
    INFO: Service jade.core.event.Notification initialized
    Dec 30, 2020 11:29:51 AM jade.mtp.http.HTTPServer <init>
    INFO: HTTP-MTP Using XML parser com.sun.org.apache.xerces.internal.jaxp.SAXParserImpl$JAXPSAXParser
    Dec 30, 2020 11:29:51 AM jade.core.messaging.MessagingService boot
    INFO: MTP addresses:
    http://claudius-mbp:7778/acc
    Dec 30, 2020 11:29:51 AM jade.core.AgentContainerImpl joinPlatform
    INFO: ------------------------------------------
    Agent container Container1M@192.168.2.48 is ready.
    ------------------------------------------
                                                    AgentAuction (run)        running...
```

Figure 11.6 JADE agent container running.

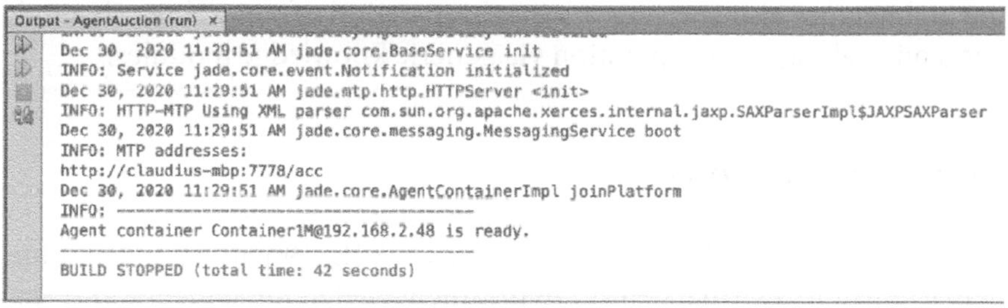

```
Output – AgentAuction (run)   ×
    Dec 30, 2020 11:29:51 AM jade.core.BaseService init
    INFO: Service jade.core.event.Notification initialized
    Dec 30, 2020 11:29:51 AM jade.mtp.http.HTTPServer <init>
    INFO: HTTP-MTP Using XML parser com.sun.org.apache.xerces.internal.jaxp.SAXParserImpl$JAXPSAXParser
    Dec 30, 2020 11:29:51 AM jade.core.messaging.MessagingService boot
    INFO: MTP addresses:
    http://claudius-mbp:7778/acc
    Dec 30, 2020 11:29:51 AM jade.core.AgentContainerImpl joinPlatform
    INFO: ------------------------------------------
    Agent container Container1M@192.168.2.48 is ready.
    ------------------------------------------
    BUILD STOPPED (total time: 42 seconds)
```

Figure 11.7 JADE agent container finish running.

11.4.2   Results Comparison

In this section, our Intelligent Agents-based architecture for COVID-19 patient distribution management, developed in JADE, is summarily analyzed in comparison with other notable multi-agent systems in the literature.

Similar to our COVID-19 system, the multi-layered GRATE [15] architecture uses modules for cooperation, control and situation assessment. But, unlike our Intelligent Agents-based architecture, an uncertainty management tool needed for decision-making in medical treatment is absent in the GRATE architecture. In a formal language like ML2 [17], logical separation of the layers of knowledge implements a proper base for their declaration, verification and validation. GRATE is limited in this area, because its layers have relatively a functional separation and not a logical one.

Like GRATE, there are other comparable layered architectures like INTERMAP [19] and Touring Machines [20] that have similar features.

Searle's speech act theory [21] is used in action coordination that has an important role in the Coordinator conversational system. Our proposed intelligent agent's architecture uses a distributed implementation to generate and monitor the commitments, unlike the Coordinator system that only has a limited function in commitments coordination. This feature facilitates the communication between agents. Another main difference between our implemented architecture and Coordinator is that for uncertainty decision-making we use a generic decision module.

Wang *et al.* [3] proposed a diagnosis model based on 3D segmentation and classification that uses empirical training and evaluation within the diseases and symptoms library.

Our proposed intelligent agent system's working memory uses inference rules modules that are functionally separated and in addition to that, the architecture also specifies a logical separation of knowledge that aids decision-making and cooperation via generic knowledge modules.

11.5   Conclusions

An intelligent agents-based approach for COVID-19 patient distribution management in a virtual reality environment (JADE implementation) was presented in this research. The tasks from COVID-19 protocol stage 2 were controlled using intelligent agents. A very realistic overcome procedure for intelligent agents was created using JADE, their real behavior (interaction between intelligent agents and the environment) evaluated using Java, and its dynamics and results visualized.

Li *et al.* [24] designed a hybrid framework by modifying an original JADE and an original Code with the purpose to increase both exploration and exploitation ability.

Medical decision-making systems were developed using various techniques for specific medical issues, however our JADE implementation for COVID-19 protocol, which has an integrated decision support, can be easily updated for other medical conditions, considering the versatility of mobile-agents and the features of the JADE architecture. Various healthcare aspects can be conveniently integrated in our proposed intelligent agent architecture due to the comprehensive procedures it provides.

The decision procedures implemented in our COVID-19 protocol architecture showed better results in clinical utilization, where it's harder to obtain a quick and accurate diagnosis, compared to conventional methods. This affirmation is in consensus with the results of Badem *et al.* [23] who proposed a method to solve numerical optimization problems and Umar *et al.* [25] who statistically analyzed some genetic algorithms elaborating a new computing paradigm. While our COVID-19 system is being used for treatment protocol, artificial intelligence-based tools in general and multi-agent systems, in particular, lead to improved assistance for medical staff and reform the manner computers are used in the medical field.

References

1. Chen, J. *et al.*, Deep learning-based model for detecting 2019 novel corona-virus pneumonia on high-resolution computed tomography. *Sci. Rep.*, 10, 1, 19196, 2020.
2. Li, L., Qin, L., Xu, Z., Yin, Y., Wang, X., Kong, B., Bai, J., Lu, Y., Fang, Z., Song, Q. *et al.*, Artificial intelligence distinguishes COVID-19 from community acquired pneumonia on chest CT. *Radiology*, 296, 2E65–E71, 200905, 2020.
3. Wang, B. *et al.*, AI-assisted CT imaging analysis for COVID-19 screening: Building and deploying a medical AI system. *Appl. Soft Comput.*, 98, 106897, 2020, https://doi.org/10.1016/j.asoc.2020.106897.
4. Shaban, W.M., Rabie, A.H., Saleh, A.I., Abo-Elsoud, M.A., Detecting COVID-19 patients based on fuzzy inference engine and deep neural network. *Appl. Soft Comput.*, 99, 106906, 2020, https://doi.org/10.1016/j.asoc.2020.106906.
5. Wu, D. *et al.*, Severity and consolidation quantification of COVID-19 from CT images using deep learning based on hybrid weak labels. *IEEE J. Biomed. Health Inf.*, 24, 12, 3529–3538, Dec. 2020.
6. Ferguson, N.M., Laydon, D., Nedjati-Gilani, G., Imai, N., Ainslie, K., Baguelin, M., Bhatia, S., Boonyasiri, A., Cucunubá, Z., CuomoDannenburg, G., Impact of non-pharmaceutical interventions (NPIs) to reduce COVID-19 mortality and healthcare demand, Imperial College London, Report 9, 1-20, UK, 2020, https://www.imperial.ac.uk/mrc-global-infectious-disease-analysis/covid19/report-9-impact-of-npis-on-covid-19/ (Accessed 28 December 2020).
7. Gupta, M., Jain, R., Taneja, S., Chaudhary, G., Khari, M., Verdú, E., Real-time measurement of the uncertain epidemiological appearances of COVID-19 infections. *Appl. Soft Comput.*, 101, 107039, 2021, https://doi.org/10.1016/j.asoc.2020.107039.
8. Aggarwal, L., Goswami, P., Sachdeva, S., Multi-criterion intelligent decision support system for COVID-19. *Appl. Soft Comput.*, 101, 107056, 2021, https://doi.org/10.1016/j.asoc.2020.107056.
9. Russell, S. and Norvig, P., *Artificial intelligence. A modern approach*, Second Edition, Prentice Hall, Upper Saddle River, New Jersey, 2003.
10. Bellifemine, F., Caire, G., Poggi, A., Rimassa, G., JADE. A white paper. *Journal of Telecom Italia Lab*, 3, 3, 6–19, 2003, http://jade.tilab.com/papers/2003/WhitePaperJADEEXP.pdf.
11. Bellifemine, F., Caire, G., Trucco, T., Rimassa, G., *JADE programmer's guide*, JADE 3.3 Edition, Telecom Italia S.p.A., Boston, 2005, http://sharon.cselt.it/projects/jade/.

12. Wooldridge, M., Intelligent agents, in: *Multiagent Systems: A Modern Approach to Distributed Artificial Intelligence*, G. Weiß (Ed.), pp. 27–77, MIT Press, Cambridge, Massachusetts, 1999.

13. Wooldridge, M., *An introduction to multiagent systems*, 3rd Edition, John Wiley and Sons LTD, West Sussex, England, 2005.

14. Wooldridge, M. and Jennings, N.R., Intelligent agents: Theory and practice. *Knowl. Eng. Rev.*, 10, 2, 115–152, 1995.

15. Jennings, N.R., Mamdani, E.H., Laresgoiti, I., Perez, J., Corera, J., GRATE: A general framework for cooperative problem solving. *Intell. Syst. Eng.*, 1, 2, 102–114, 1992.

16. Gordon, C., Herbert, S.I., Jackson-Smale, A., Renaud-Salis, J.L., Care protocols and healthcare informatics. *Proc. of Artificial Intelligence in Medicine Europe 93*, Munich, Germany, pp. 289–309, 1993.

17. van Harmelen, F., ML2: A formal language for KADS models of expertise. *Knowledge Acquisition*, 4, 1, 127–161, 1992.

18. Muller, J.P., Pischel, M., Thiel, M., A pragmatic approach to modelling autonomous interacting systems: A preliminary report, in: *Intelligent Agents, Lecture Notes in Artificial Intelligence*, vol. 890, M.J. Wooldridge and N.R. Jennings (Eds.), Springer Verlag, Heidelberg, Germany, 1995.

19. Ferguson, I.A., Integrated control and coordinated behaviour: A case for agent models in intelligent agents, in: *Lecture Notes in Artificial Intelligence*, vol. 890, M.J. Wooldridge and N.R. Jennings (Eds.), Springer Verlag, Heidelberg, Germany, 1995.

20. Winograd, T. and Flores, F., *Understanding computers and cognition: A new foundation for design*, Ablex Publishing, Norwood, 1986.

21. Searle, J.R., *Speech acts: An essay in the philosophy of language*, Cambridge University Press, Cambridge, UK, 1969.

22. FIPA, 2013. Foundation for intelligent physical agents, IEEE Computer Society, Washington, DC, http://www.fipa.org/.

23. Badem, H., Basturk, A., Caliskan, A., Yuksel, M.E., A new hybrid optimization method combining artificial bee colony and limited-memory BFGS algorithms for efficient numerical optimization. *Appl. Soft Comput.*, 70, 826–844, 2018, https://doi.org/10.1016/j.asoc.2018.06.010.

24. Li, G., Lin, Q., Cui, L., Du, Z., Liang, Z., Chen, J., Lu, N., Ming, Z., A novel hybrid differential evolution algorithm with modified CoDE and JADE. *Appl. Soft Comput.*, 47, 577–599, 2016, https://doi.org/10.1016/j.asoc.2016.06.011.

25. Umar, M., Sabir, Z., Raja, M.A.Z., Intelligent computing for numerical treatment of nonlinear prey–predator models. *Appl. Soft Comput.*, 80, 506–524, 2019, https://doi.org/10.1016/j.asoc.2019.04.022.

26. Popirlan, C.I., Stefănescu, A., Stefănescu, L., A solution based o intelligent software agents to improve the data searching in the contact centers. *6th IEEE Joint International Information Technology and Artificial Intelligence Conference*, 2011.

12

Computational Science Role in Medical and Healthcare-Related Approach

Pawan Whig[1]*, Arun Velu[2], Rahul Reddy Nadikattu[3] and Yusuf Jibrin Alkali[4]

[1]Vivekananda Institute of Professional Studies-TC, New Delhi, India
[2]Director Equifax and Researcher, Atlanta, GA, USA
[3]Department of IT, University of Cumbersome, Kentucky, USA
[4]Federal Inland Revenue Service, Abuja, Nigeria

Abstract

Medical imaging, human genome research, clinical diagnosis, and medical data management are all areas where computer technology plays a critical role in modern medicine, healthcare, and life sciences. Computer science solutions will undoubtedly become a vital element of modern medicine and healthcare as computer technology continues to advance. Computational research and applications in medicine and healthcare on modeling, creating, addressing, and assessing fundamental problems are not only vital but also indispensable! With an emphasis on medical imaging, we describe a collection of key computational challenges and methodologies in current medical research, clinical practice, and applications in this session. Computational issues that emerge in medical imaging, clinical diagnosis, therapy, and other medical applications are discussed in detail. These include immune cell identification and distribution analysis, optimal segmentation, and analysis of many medical objects in 3D images, cancer research and analysis, motion tracking of massive swarming bacteria, and so on. In this book chapter, we show how to formulate difficulties as computational problems using new models, as well as how to solve them effectively. Our methods rely on cutting-edge machine learning, data mining, and geometric optimization techniques, particularly novel deep learning models and algorithms. We also offer experimental data and findings to demonstrate how our ideas may be used in clinical settings. Finally, in the exciting new field of computational medicine and healthcare, we highlight several crucial future research themes and issues.

*Corresponding author: pawanwhig@gmail.com

Ahmed A. Elgnar, Vigneshwar M, Krishna Kant Singh and Zdzislaw Polkowski (eds.) Handbook of Computational Sciences: A Multi and Interdisciplinary Approach, (245–272) © 2023 Scrivener Publishing LLC

Keywords: Computational research, medical, computer science, machine learning

12.1   Introduction

Healthcare is concerned with providing medical treatment to a population, whereas computer science is about computers and their sophisticated computing systems. These two professions could not be more unlike one another [64]. By examining how computer science is applied in the healthcare sector, a relatively young topic effect on physical informatics connects the two. When doctors started looking at how computer logic may aid in the diagnosis and treatment of medical conditions around the beginning of World War II, health informatics initially gained widespread attention. Health informatics didn't take off until the 1950s when computer technology made significant strides. Today, governments all around the world are putting into place laws that encourage the use of health informatics [3].

In the end, health informatics helps to save lives, money, and time. Integrating a doctor's knowledge with a computer's algorithmic output helps minimize mistakes in patient diagnosis and care. Health informatics also makes it easier for patients and clinicians to communicate and allows for the delivery of remote medical treatment [44]. Finally, computer technology improves coordination and administration; tools like digital applications and electronic health records make it simpler for people to keep track of their health and get accurate, dependable medical advice [51].

Public e-health is concerned with healthcare management from the patient's point of view and various factors responsible for healthcare management are shown in Figure 12.1. Computer technologies are employed in this sector to improve the diagnosis and management of healthcare [33].

Data scientists analyze and create the gateways used by hospices to assist people to identify therapeutic wage-earners, book activities, and coordinate conduct regimens. Throughout the new COVID-19 epidemic, for example, infirmaries such as Houston Methodist depended on connected portals to allow patients to book coronavirus vaccination actions. After the affected role got their dosages, these infirmaries used computerized questionnaires to check in with them in the least to safeguard that no serious side belongings occurred [67].

Computer scientists have also coded and built mobile applications and wearable gadgets to assist consumers in monitoring their health. For example, Apple Inc.'s 2014 Apple Watch had a function that allowed customers to measure their pulse when sleeping and exercising. This allowed operators to path their emotion rates at their leisure deprived of the necessity for

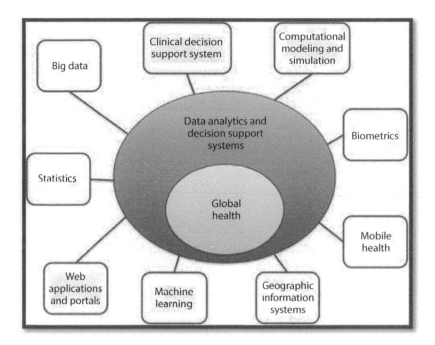

Figure 12.1 Various factors responsible for healthcare management.

a Holter display. In addition, advanced forms of the same watch identified uneven emotional rhythms and warned operators once this discrepancy happened [56]. These notifications complete it easy for consumers to seek medical attention before their health situations deteriorated dramatically. Medical records may also be digitized using computer science to create EMRs, which turn corporeal, complicated therapeutic information into an alphanumeric version, minimizing form-filling for an affected role as shown in Figure 12.2.

EMRs also guarantee that precise patient data is captured and kept on an opportune foundation, allowing clinicians to appropriately identify and luxury affected roles. Assumed with the aid of EMRs, nations such as India are attempting to use the technology in their hospitals to enhance their healthcare systems. Today, the United States has even implemented federal measures to encourage physicians to utilize EMRs [64].

Lastly, data researchers are creating stages such as Zoom Address to encounter modern telemedicine needs. Throughout the COVID-19 epidemic, infirmaries soon hit capacity, resulting in more patients seeking remote care in 2020. Telemedicine is becoming a more handy and important alternative for patients as computers and phones become more widely available [36].

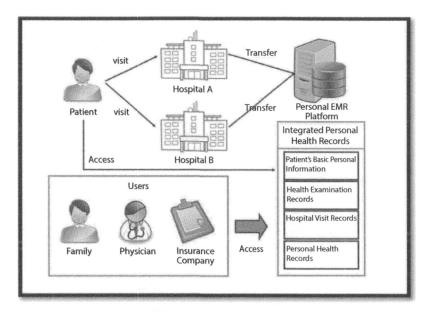

Figure 12.2 Process flow of EMR.

Global health informatics is concerned with using population data discoveries in public healthcare. Large data sets gathered from communities
are collected, analyzed, and responded to using computers. Machines are
mostly rummage-sale to screen global illness eruptions in instruction to
assist users in analyzing present worldwide health situations. Another
instance of this knowledge is Johns Hopkins University's COVID-19 map,
which was created in 2020 throughout the epidemic to show people anywhere they should go. Coronavirus instances remained being reported all
over the world. Johns Hopkins successfully produced a living graphic that
allowable viewers to keep up to current on material about the epidemic
by merging data from dissimilar states concerning coronavirus eruptions
with physical data from cables. These aided users evade parts of the world
anywhere suitcases remained on the rise and informed the public about the
international well-being situation [1, 2, 33].

It is too critical to have computer researchers create systems that collect
data in an efficient, secure, and accurate manner. For example, during the
COVID-19 pandemic, PCR, polymerase chain reaction, and testing results
were improved by the use of algorithms that produced findings in minutes
[60].

Eventually, computers are utilized to assess population statistics and
make public judgments. Algorithms developed to examine global weather

patterns, for example, can alert weather correspondents when a storm is brewing [5, 34, 57]. When computer programs emit this indication, establishments are healthier prepared to grip and react to these unfavorable events, so protecting communities worldwide. This work cannot be completed as rapidly without the use of computer science, and the resulting delay might cost thousands of lives.

Medical computing is the study of how computer programming may aid in the delivery of healthcare services as shown in Figure 12.3. Artificial intelligence and other modern techniques play a crucial role in this area of health computing [61].

Software engineers make it simpler for doctors to identify their patients and cure them by creating software and tools that evaluate certain data. For example, MIT researchers employed machine learning to assist radiologists in detecting various types of cancer. After being fed images of chest X-rays and other data, the algorithm determined which cancer illness was afflicting the patient. The scientists found that combining computer findings with doctor experience resulted in 8% better accuracy, showing that machine learning may have an impact on appropriate medical [4].

Furthermore, computer scientists frequently program medical devices utilized by clinicians. The da Vinci Surgical System, which aids surgeons during operation, for example, needs substantial programming [54]. However, once programmed, the robot can execute a wide range of surgical operations, improving accuracy and efficiency. Coding is also required

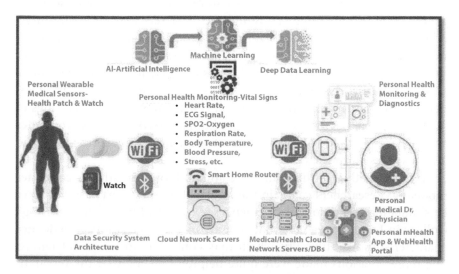

Figure 12.3 Medical computing using artificial intelligence.

for medical imaging devices such as MRIs and X-rays. They give amazing insights that clinicians cannot gain on their own, guiding patients to more accurate and dependable treatment alternatives.

Health research informatics seeks to enhance healthcare by utilizing new data and insights. Computing technologies are utilized to conduct research, evaluate the findings, and apply the findings to the healthcare business [49].

Machines are mostly utilized to conduct clinical trials, which provide researchers with fresh data to work with. For example, computer programs frequently gather, analyze, and interpret data from major trials, such as the one conducted by Neurochem Inc. to examine a novel medicine called Alzhemed, which was supposed to assist patients battling Alzheimer's disease. This enables investigators to guarantee that the medicine is verified the whole thing and can be disseminated safely to the break populace [66].

Computer discipline also facilitates translational investigation. Nowadays, the processer discipline plays an important part in oncology, among the most important sectors undertaking research projects, by identifying DNA mutations that really can lead to vision into the origin of cancer. For instance, Dr. von Mehren developed a medication that attacks metastatic colorectal tumors by targeting particular genetic abnormalities identified only in gastrointestinal people with cancer. Therefore in case, computer programs were utilized to detect Gene mutation and send physician genetic data to researchers like Dr. von Mehren, allowing them to build these ground-breaking remedies [65].

Ultimately, translation informatics stores and analyses biological and genetic data using computers. Simulated data sets may be easily interpreted by researchers using algorithms, modeling, and simulations. As was already established, researchers may examine data and uncover trends using computer algorithms. For instance, Genbank, an NIH genetic sequence database, is often used by researchers to analyze human DNA. Because the human genome includes approximately 3 trillion pairings of nucleotide, a dataset that is too huge for humans to comprehend, computer systems are required to uncover minute variances in genetic issues and diagnose these disorders [52].

Another method utilized in translational bioinformatics is computer modeling. Researchers can gain the information they can't easily observe by simulating certain organs, sequences, or events. Investigators at King's College in London created a model of an affected role emotion to deduce characteristics like difficulty, which may contribute to sentiment failure. The representations made were quite helpful; they allowed the researchers to study the stiffness of the heart and learn new things about various

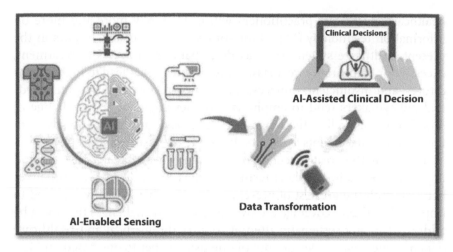

Figure 12.4 Flow diagram for AI-assisted healthcare.

cardiac systems. The Flow diagram for AI-Assisted Healthcare is shown in Figure 12.4.

In addition to the five core areas of health computing, other academic disciplines are also developing as new technologies are developed [50]. For instance, several hospitals throughout the world are implementing nano-medicine. Whenever doctors employ nanomedicine, they utilize nanoparticles to deliver medications to people or study the interior of a body. Bioprinting of human organs via 3D printing is also being developed. As a result, there are fewer organ shortages, and more transplants may be carried out by surgeons.

These two technologies strongly depend on computer engineering: to track particles, computer algorithms must be built, and to 3D print internal tissue, computer modeling should be completed. As new advancements are made, the relationship between computer science as well as the healthcare sector will only grow stronger.

Consumer information systems, public medical technology, medical sciences, medical research computer science, and integrative informatics are the five divisions that frequently make up the large area of information systems.

12.2   Background

A knowledge- and information-intensive industry, healthcare. To gather, manage, analyze, and disseminate information and knowledge about healthcare, healthcare practitioners will need to rely more and more on information technology (IT). Numerous studies have shown flaws in the present healthcare system, such as discrepancies in access to treatment, excessive or inaccurate care, massive inefficiencies that lead to high expenditures, and insufficient, unnecessary, or incorrect care. In response, federal policymakers tend to emphasize the development and exchange of e-health info as well as the usage of IT as crucial infrastructure advancements where placements assist to solve some of these problems [47].

That using the greatest technology currently available to construct and deploy processes in the short term as well as trying to identify the holes between both the greatest of present tech with what is finally required to improve healthcare coverage are two fundamental challenges that must be addressed in any systematic attempt to alter the medical and healthcare data management framework out of one using paper to one based on [46]. The first offers chances for short-term improvement, while the second influence fundamental research and infrastructure projects in the future as shown in Figure 12.5. To clarify how the computer science research community may assist in addressing both of these difficulties, the present study's sponsors commissioned it. Members of this group are knowledgeable about the most recent developments in computer science and can thus provide insight into how they may be used to address current healthcare issues as well as see the potential for new developments [42, 43].

The Committee on Attractive the Processer Discipline Investigate Public in Healthcare Information science activity was time and budget constrained by design. The committee's primary goal in its work was to comprehend the countryside and the effects of the IT savings completed by significant healthcare institutions. Therefore, a wide range of intricate communal, party-political, and economic concerns that make the process of healthcare improvement challenging are not addressed in this research except in the most peripheral manner [39].

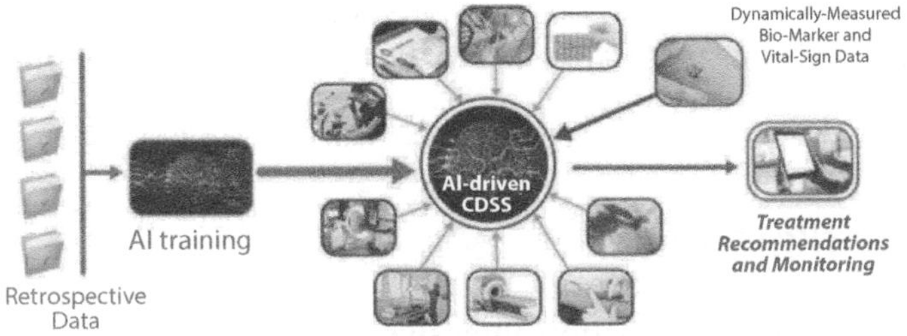

Figure 12.5 Healthcare data management system.

From the committee's point of view, these several pieces of data imply that existing initiatives aiming at the widespread adoption of well-being IT determination non be adequate to realize the goal of 21st-era healthcare and could smooth backfire if they continue entirely on their current track. Researchers in computer science and health/biomedical informatics will need to place more emphasis on providing cognitive support for health-care professionals, patients, and family carers if they are to be successful in this area. The term "cognitive support," refers to computer-founded tools and schemes that give physicians and affected role aid for rational about and addressing glitches connected to particular examples of well-being, will also require attention from vendors, healthcare providers, and the government.

12.3   Healthcare Nowadays

Commonly acknowledged that nowadays healthcare system struggles to provide the best care and agonizes significantly as a result of medicinal mistakes. Many medicinal procedures performed nowadays are unnecessary. These ongoing issues are not due to a lack of competence in health-care labors; rather, result from the intrinsic intelligent difficulty of the field of medicine as a whole and the lack of proper structure in the system that supports clinical decision-making and practice. The environment around healthcare is further complicated by administrative and organizational fragmentation as well as complex, scattered, and ambiguous power and accountability [38].

The duties and workflow of the healthcare industry, the organization and finances of the industry, and the countryside of well-being care IT as it is now applied are three main categories into which many of the important aspects may be divided [35].

12.4   Healthcare Activities and Processes

Making judgments concerning an affected role in medicinal condition and efficacy of previous and upcoming therapies for that specific enduring sometimes requires deliberating under conditions of great ambiguity. In addition, medical processes are frequently complicated and opaque and are characterized by frequent interruptions, ill-defined roles and duties, shoddy scheduling, and little documenting of procedures, goals, and results

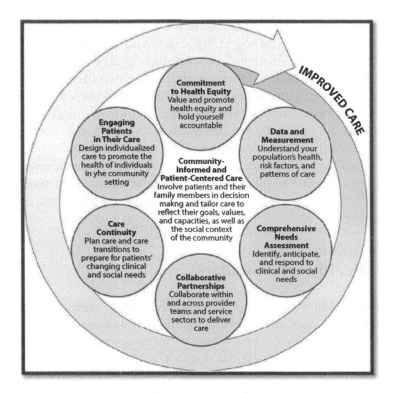

Figure 12.6 Healthcare activities and processes.

as shown in given Figure 12.6. The requirement to deliver complex care to patients in a time- and resource-constrained setting has increased [32].

12.5   Organization and Financial Aspects of Healthcare

The administration is made more difficult by the numerous healthcare spenders and attention tactics, each of which has its standards for attention as shown in Brief in Figure 12.7. Furthermore, financial incentives are sometimes twisted or perverse, resulting, for instance, in more generous remuneration for medical operations than for patient interaction, diagnosis, or preventative treatment [29]. Additionally, upkeep facilities, public infirmaries, hospitals, and main and specialty care physicians must be negotiated by patients and healthcare professionals.

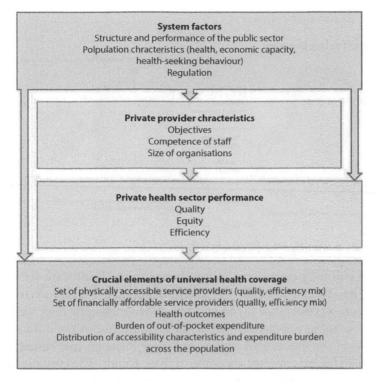

Figure 12.7 Organization and financial aspects of healthcare.

12.6 Health Information Technology is Currently Being Used

Although many healthcare companies do devote a lot of cash to IT, the technology is frequently integrated into schemes in a colossal way that brands smooth simple modifications challenging to adopt. Additionally, it appears that the main purpose of IT applications is to automate operations or business processes as shown in Figure 12.8. They frequently offer insufficient assistance for the reasoning doings of physicians or the system of the individuals who must utilize the system and just imitate current paper-based forms. Additionally, many apps do not make use of the principles of human-computer interaction, resulting in subpar designs that might raise the possibility of mistakes, add to rather than decrease effort, and exacerbate the difficulties associated with carrying out necessary activities [26].

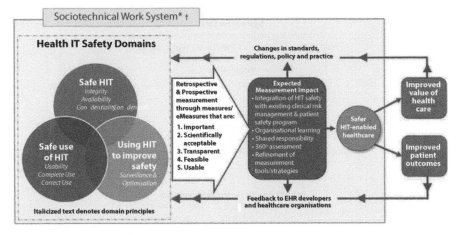

Figure 12.8 Current Health information technology.

There will be greater demand for change in the healthcare setting as a result of several phenomena. The advent of genome founded personalized medication, a greater part for an affected role in managing their well-being upkeep, an aging population with a conforming rise in the difficulty and heaviness of the illness load, and a yet bigger focus on cost and efficiency regulates in health coverage are some of these trends. The pressures put on healthcare practitioners will increase as a result, making healthcare procedures more complicated and time-consuming [7, 8, 22].

12.7   Future Healthcare

The extent to which health services for individuals and populations increase the chances of preferred health outcomes and thus are in line with current expert knowledge [2] is the measure of healthcare quality as shown in Figure 12.9. Healthcare should be egalitarian, timely, fast, safe, and patient-centered, according to the IOM [3]. The efficient use of information is one of several aspects that are necessary to realize this goal (e.g., systemic changes in the way healthcare is paid for, a focus on illness prevention rather than disease treatment [13, 14, 18]. Therefore, the comprehensive information on the ailments, therapies, and results of patients provides healthcare professionals with cognitive assistance to help them assimilate patient-specific facts and take into consideration any lingering ambiguities; as well as, the supporting cognitive integration of evidence-based practice recommendations practice for healthcare practitioners every day. Thus, the tools and

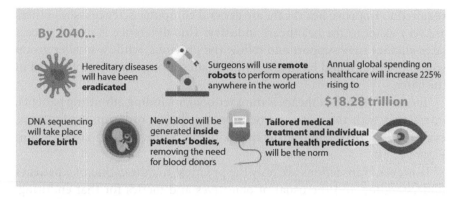

Figure 12.9 Future healthcare.

equipment help doctors manage a patient portfolio and identify issues as they emerge, both for a given patient and populations as a whole. A "thinking" healthcare system that promotes early adoption of promising practices while simultaneously analyzing all patient experiences as experimental data must quickly integrate new technology, biological understanding, treatment modalities, and other developments; Helping patients and families in the effective administration of medical decisions and their implementation, such as the managing of personal health files, information about a patient's ailments and treatment alternatives, and assistance with prompt and level of reporting to physicians, as well as allowing for the expanding diversity of places for care delivery, like the use of home electrical appliances for diagnosis and monitoring, lifestyle interoperability [9, 15–17].

12.8   Research Challenges

The intersection of computer science, healthcare, and biomedical informatics presents complex intellectual research issues. The committee thought it was helpful to think of the required research efforts in terms of two different aspects. The first factor is the requirement for fresh basic, all-purpose research. Some healthcare issues can be considered as having answers on a fairly direct road forward from current technology, while others are complex issues.

The requirement for fresh biomedical and healthcare-related research serves as a second dimension. This second dimension stems from the observation that although some of the technological advancements required to improve healthcare are general computer science issues others are very exact to the healthcare industry. This difference is useful since a large alliance may support and follow the previous, while a smaller group within the health and biomedical informatics groups may be interested in the latter.

The majority of healthcare is transactional, including admitting patients, interacting with them at their bedsides or clinics, ordering medications, evaluating reports, and transferring patients. Some of them are shown in Figure 12.10.

However, transactions are only the practical manifestation of a patient's understanding and the usual of objectives and tactics for that enduring. Clinicians envision a theoretical representation of the patient that reflects their comprehension of the interplaying social, emotional, and additional components. To improve their knowledge of the model they are employing, they utilize fresh discoveries—raw data. They then issue instructions (transactions) that they think may worsen the condition of or even cure the (actual) patient, based on medical expertise, medical reasoning, and mostly heuristic decision-making.

To develop meaningful mental abstractions and associations that are pertinent to the patient's condition, physicians nowadays invest a significant

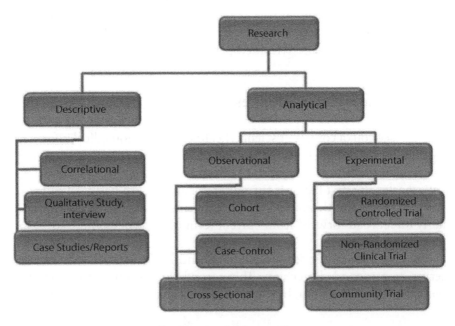

Figure 12.10 Various types of healthcare-related research.

amount of time and effort examining and sorting through raw data about patients. These sorting attempts make doctors focus their limited cognitive resources on the specifics of the data, increasing the likelihood that they may miss some crucial.

The physician interacts with patient models and abstractions that put the raw facts under the committee's concept of patient-centered cognitive support. Although they are still available, raw data are not the clinician's main concern. The computing equivalents of the clinician's mental model of a patient are these virtual patient representations. They provide patient-specific parameterization and multicomponent warnings and show and simulate a hypothesis about interactions occurring in the patient. They are based on submodels of biological, physiological, and epidemiological systems that, for instance, consider the regional prevalence of illnesses.

The physician would be liberated from having to directly interpret raw data by using these models to build clinical context, which would make it much simpler for him or her to define, test, and investigate their working theory. Then, with the use of tools that assist physicians in choosing action to the knowledge of the patient's condition, computers may offer decision assistance. However, even though clinicians may work with abstractions to prevent data overload, with this perspective come numerous difficult research difficulties in computer science. To provide decision assistance that is considerate of workflow and human aspects. Patient utilities, values, and resource restrictions would all be openly incorporated into the decision support systems. They would support comprehensive strategies, goals, and a range of decision-makers. Users might practice interventions on the virtual patient before performing them on the actual one.

There are difficulties in modeling and enabling multiplayer decision-making in addition to the research issues associated with modelling the virtual patient and biological knowledge Methods to link the parts will probably be similarly difficult.

12.9 Modeling

One feature of the virtual patient is the modeling of multiple organ systems, the digestive system, and other subsystems within a real patient to demonstrate how they interact. By properly parameterizing a general model of those subsystems, one method for modeling physiological subsystems in a particular patient is to study that patient. However, determining the proper parameterizations for each particular model and linking the various models with the data used to fuel them present difficult intellectual tasks.

A computational platform must be able to handle various interacting components that may be integrated into bigger, more sophisticated models, for instance, to enable coupling models. One such platform must enable the creation of hierarchical simulation and information structures, which can be produced, used, and adjusted continuously when possible, in addition to supporting the concurrent operation of the data analysis.

12.10   Automation

When automated systems are implemented in a real-world setting, they must cooperate well with one another. However, in reality, they do not since they were each designed independently, which leads to conflicting signals, various monitoring needs, and various safety issues. Most significantly, they pose questions about how much people can trust these systems; too much trust causes people to believe false signs and activities, while not enough trust makes people constantly verify these systems, wasting time. It is still quite difficult to solve the operational integration issues for automated systems.

12.11   Teamwork and Data Exchange

Healthcare-related statistics are quite diverse. Users must be able to perform searches across numerous data sources without the requirement for data standardization or the need to query each database separately to successfully utilize such data. Today, integrating data typically requires a significant effort that costs money.

12.12   Scaled Data Management

Another significant problem is managing the data, assuming there are sizable, connected corpora of data. Annotation and metadata, connectivity, and privacy are a few of the crucial aspects of medical information management.

12.13   Comprehensive Automated Recording of Exchanges Between Doctors and Patients

By doing this, clinicians might spend their time more effectively while also ensuring that patient data are updated and fully accurate and correlating the data from the audio and visual transcripts are some of the significant dimensions in this problem domain.

12.14   Johns Hopkins University: A Case Study

The Gordon and Betty Moore Basis and the Armstrong Institute at Johns Hopkins University have started a two-year project to enhance ICU care. The data is shown in Figure 12.11. This program draws on earlier research from this team, which has shown that systems methods can enhance patient outcomes and safety in high-risk healthcare settings. For instance, a project led by the organization exposed that specifications helped lower the frequency of tube-connected bloodstream infections, a potentially dangerous complication that occurs often in hospitals. These investigations discovered that the checklist eradicated tube-connected circulation infections in the ICUs of the greatest infirmaries, leading to an 80% reduction in contagions per tube diurnal when applied to ICUs throughout an entire state [19, 20, 23, 45]. This kind of instrument might aid in the eradication of these illnesses, which take about 30,000 lives annually and cost the country's healthcare system about $2 billion [24, 25, 27, 48].

The Patient Treatment Program Acute Care Program, which is the current initiative, seeks to improve patient safety and care quality in critical care units. Numerous issues are frequent in critical care settings, including

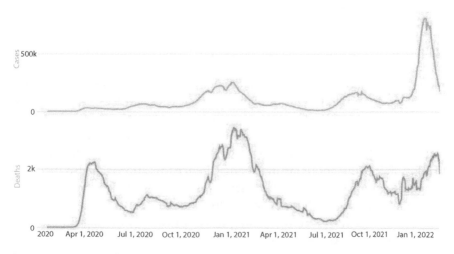

Figure 12.11 Data of number of deaths vs cases.

deep vein thrombosis, injuries from ventilators, and bloodstream infections linked to central lines. A physician would need to carry out several preventative interventions — the majority of which must be carried out several times per day — for each possible harm to avoid these typical harms one at a time. Under this kind of ad hoc strategy, it is predicted that a physician would need to offer up to 200 interventions every day when the quantity of preventative interventions is added together.

The initiative strives to eradicate all forms of enduring damage, counting the damage to self-respect and respect, and incorporate preventative treatments immediately into the therapeutic workflow, in difference to the conventional method of addressing each harm one at a time. To do this, the ICU will be redesigned utilizing an interdisciplinary, patient-centered strategy that combines scientific info systems and scientific gear, redesigns the workflows of the care team, and includes enduring and domestic boxes into regular care. A diagram illustrating how system manufacturing is existing second hand to create and keep improving the healthcare setting. Creating technological platforms that coordinate and integrate multiple technologies and clinical procedures is a crucial component of the project. One podium will feature a dashboard that shows the state of required interferences to avoid harm — interventions that are due and interventions that have already been completed — and makes that status accessible to doctors, patients, and families.

This will increase reliability and consistency. Another platform will include several medical technologies and electronic health data to increase safety and productivity. For patients in critical care units, the first phase of this platform will transmit the instructions from an electronic health record to the dosage in an infusion pump. The initial platform will save a lot of time and work for nurses because the current procedure for changing an infusion dose calls for a nurse to manually enter the new dose level into the infusion pump based on the order in the electronic health record, and a second nurse to manually check the order's accuracy. By removing the possibility of human mistakes, the platform will also offer higher dependability and precision. The surgical ICU at Johns Hopkins will adopt this program in the summer of 2013, and the University of California, San Francisco will do it in the summer of 2014. Technology by itself cannot bring about lasting change, hence this approach also includes cooperation and cultural change activities [28, 58, 59]. For new skills to develop, the project will mix changes to process, technology, and culture. The conceptual framework for the project illustrates the significance of integrating these components.

12.15   Case Study: Managing Patient Flow

Another set of activities employed an approach from the field of operations research to guarantee that resources are accessible to patients in a hospital environment. This is achieved by looking at how patients enter the hospital and proceed from their initial admission through the various hospital units until their discharge. This is crucial since both scheduled cases (like elective procedures) and unscheduled cases (like emergency admissions) affect the hospital census's unpredictability. To reduce unpredictability in the flow of patients to different hospital units, the patient data are evaluated using mathematical models, and the findings of that study are utilized to modify hospital operations, such as the daily operating room schedule [30, 40]. By using these strategies, Cincinnati Children's Hospital was able to enhance patient care while also increasing surgery volume by 7% yearly for two years, all without hiring more personnel or adding more hospital beds [31, 41]. Similar outcomes have been observed at Mayo Clinic in Florida, another institution that adopted this system and was able to boost surgical volumes by 4% while lowering variability by 20%, staff turnover by 40%, and overtime staffing by 30% [37, 53, 55].

12.16   Case Study: Using Electronic Health Records and Human Factors Engineering

By concentrating on how people will interact with technology or processes, human factors engineering may assist in identifying possible safety, quality, and reliability concerns. A human factors analysis of the drug ordering, dispensing, and administration processes — including a computerized physician order entry (CPOE) system — was carried out in one instance of this method. The study's researchers examined the CPOE system's user interface at the Centre Hospitalier Universitaire in Lille, France, and found several problems that restricted the software's use. The Flowchart of the simulation of patient Flow is shown in Figure 12.12. Following that, a simulation of a typical nursing work environment was conducted, and during that test, the participating nurses found 28 usability difficulties [6, 10, 12]. The user interface may support care procedures more effectively and advance the effectiveness and dependability of care by recognizing and resolving any possible usability problems.

As a second illustration, modern medical equipment provides a substantial amount of data for physicians to evaluate and frequently generates

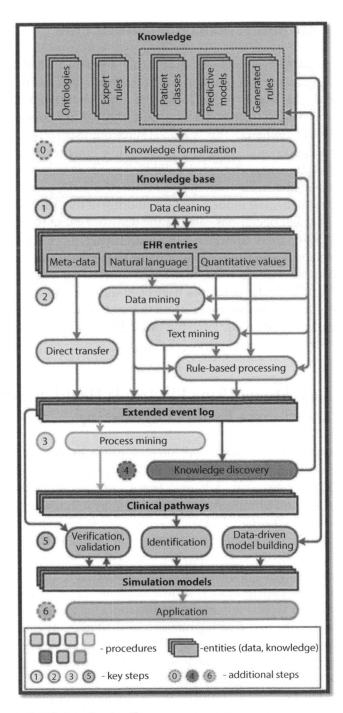

Figure 12.12 Simulation of patient flow.

false alarms. These two elements have produced a challenging work environment where physicians must analyze an excessive amount of data and struggle to determine whether alerts are indeed life-threatening. The Joint Commission and professional associations have urged healthcare executives to look into alarm fatigue and, if required, redesign devices to limit alerts to circumstances when they are clinically essential as a result of the current circumstance.

12.17 Technology, Leadership, Culture, and Increased Learning are Necessary for the Spread of Systems Approaches

The numerous instances where systems tools have been effectively used in the context of health and healthcare highlight the potential of this strategy. However, several obstacles now impede their common adoption. We provide a few of the tactics below to encourage conversation among decision-makers in the health and healthcare fields to solve the impediments.

Boost the production and sharing of systems knowledge. Systems techniques have a greater chance of success when best practices are shared throughout firms and learned from.

- Create resources that list the lessons gained and how other fields have effectively implemented systems ideas.
- Create interdisciplinary learning spaces where engineering and healthcare work closely together to foster dialogue across the fields.
- Create a research agenda to encourage the application of innovative systems techniques and to identify the reasons that restrict their usage.

Give systems approaches the required technological backing. Technology cannot fix problematic processes on its own, but systems tools require an interconnected, integrated technical infrastructure to function.

- Encourage the development of digital records that collect the information required for process improvement, regular care and health maintenance, and success evaluation.
- Adopting standards for the interoperability of medical devices and human factors techniques would enhance the

interoperability, usability, utility, and integration of various technologies.

With correctly designed financial incentives, support system-based efforts. At the moment, financial incentives discourage reform attempts and may render them unsustainable.

- Encourage payment schemes that honor progress and improved medical results.

Expand the health system's knowledge of systems approaches. As technical understanding of systems approaches grows, more of these techniques can be applied, engineering and health experts can communicate better, and these tools can be better tailored to local situations.

- Integrate systems principles into the training of health professionals, including the required courses for doctors, nurses, and other clinical staff, with an emphasis on how these concepts might be used to enhance patient care [69, 70].
- To improve their capacity to integrate into healthcare organizations, increase the educational options available to engineering experts to apply their expertise to health and healthcare delivery [11, 21, 62, 63, 68].

Prioritize the main chances for advancement. Although there are several ways to apply systems approaches to enhance health and healthcare, advancement will be sped up by creating priorities that will receive more focus.

- Determine which medical issues and procedures would be most suited for prevention and management using a systems approach. Given the potential for systems methods throughout the healthcare system, a wide range of applications exists, including general care, the management of chronic conditions like type 2 diabetes, emergency medicine, obstetrics, and mental health.
- Describe how a systems approach may be used to address issues with the patient and family care experience, like the erosion of respect and dignity.

The usage of systems tools can be increased through the use of each of these tactics separately, but further advancement will require a complete strategy that tackles the numerous underlying obstacles impeding their adoption.

12.18   Conclusion

Given the problems with safety, quality, cost, and complexity, it is obvious that the health system needs immediate transformation. A systems approach to improvement is one way to deal with these problems. In other industries, a systems approach has increased quality and value; in the realm of health and healthcare, it might have a similarly revolutionary impact. Their application has helped a small but significant number of healthcare organizations. A systems approach would need to include all the factors impacting health, as well as the interfaces between these various factors, to be applied to health. Due to their comprehensive nature, systems methods face several obstacles that limit their general adoption, including structural, cultural, and technical ones. Additionally, focusing these activities on patients and the general public and including patients as active participants in their usage is necessary for the spread of systems tools to proceed. A wide range of tactics, including technology interoperability, more knowledge, and better distribution of best practices, will be needed to address the obstacles impeding the widespread application of systems methods. By removing these obstacles, systemic methods for enhancing the health of all people and fostering greater health at reduced costs can become standard.

References

1. Alkali, Y., Routray, I., Whig, P., Study of various methods for reliable, efficient, and secured IoT using artificial intelligence, 9, 2022, Available at SSRN 4020364.
2. Anand, M., Velu, A., Whig, P., Prediction of loan behaviour with machine learning models for secure banking. *J. Comput. Sci. Eng. (JCSE)*, 3, 1, 1–13, 2022.
3. Arun Velu, P.W., Impact of COVID vaccination on the Globe using data analytics. *Int. J. Sustain. Dev. Comput. Sci.*, 3, 2, 1–8, 2021a.
4. Arun Velu, P.W., Impact of COVID vaccination on the Globe using data analytics. *Int. J. Sustain. Dev. Comput. Sci.*, 3, 2, 13, 2021b.

5. Braithwaite, S.R., Giraud-Carrier, C., West, J., Barnes, M.D., Hanson, C.L., Validating machine learning algorithms for Twitter data against established measures of suicidality. *JMIR Ment. Health*, 3, 2, e21, 2016.

6. Burton, S., Morris, R., Hansen, J., Dimond, M., Giraud-Carrier, C., West, J., Hanson, C., Barnes, M., Public health community mining in YouTube, in: *Proceedings of the Second International Health Informatics Symposium*, pp. 81–90, 2012.

7. Burton, S., Tanner, K., Giraud-Carrier, C., Leveraging social networks for anytime-anyplace health information. *J. Netw. Model. Anal. Health Inform. Bioinform.*, 1, 4, 173–181, 2012.

8. Burton, S.H. and Giraud-Carrier, C., Discovering social circles in directed graphs. *ACM Trans. Knowl. Discovery Data*, 8, 4, 21, 2014.

9. Chary, M., Genes, N., Giraud-Carrier, C., Hanson, C., Nelson, L.S., Manini, A.F., Epidemiology from tweets: Estimating misuse of prescription opioids in the USA from social media. *J. Med. Toxicol.*, 13, 4, 278–286, 2017.

10. Chew, C. and Eysenbach, G., Pandemics in the age of Twitter: A content analysis of tweets during the 2009 H1N1 outbreak. *PLoS One*, 5, 11, e14118, 2010.

11. Choi, B.C. and Pak, A.W., Multidisciplinarity, interdisciplinarity, and transdisciplinarity in health research, services, education, and policy: 1. Definitions, objectives, and evidence of effectiveness. *Clin. Invest. Med.*, 29, 6, 351–364, 2006.

12. Corley, C.D., Cook, D.J., Mikler, A.R., Singh, K.P., Text and structural data mining of influenza are mentioned on the web and social media. *Int. J. Environ. Res. Public Health*, 7, 2, 596–615, 2010.

13. De Choudhury, M., Gamon, M., Counts, S., Horvitz, E., Predicting depression via social media, in: *Proceedings of the Seventh International AAAI, a Conference on Weblogs and Social Media*, pp. 128–137, 2013.

14. Dredze, M., How social media will change public health. *IEEE Intell. Syst.*, 27, 4, 81–84, 2012.

15. Eichstaedt, J.C., Schwartz, H.A., Kern, M.L., Park, G., Labarthe, D.R., Merchant, R.M., Jha, S., Agrawal, M., Dziurzynski, L.A., Sap, M., Weeg, C., Larson, E.E., Ungar, L.H., Seligman, M.E.P., Psychological language on Twitter predicts county-level heart disease mortality. *Psychol. Sci.*, 26, 2, 159–169, 2015.

16. Eke, P.I., Using social media for research and public health surveillance. *J. Dent. Res.*, 90, 9, 1045–1046, 2011.

17. El-Sayed, A.M., Scarborough, P., Seemann, L., Galea, S., Social network analysis and agent-based modeling in social epidemiology. *Epidemiol. Perspect. Innov.*, 9, 1, 1–9, 2012.

18. Epstein, J.A., Collaborations between public health and computer science: A path worth pursuing. *Am. J. Public Health Res.*, 1, 7, 166–170, 2013.

19. Estrin, D. and Sim, I., Healthcare delivery. Open mHealth architecture: An engine for healthcare innovation. *Science*, 330, 6005, 759–760, 2010.

20. Eysenbach, G., Infodemiology: Tracking flu-related searches on the web for syndromic surveillance, in: *Proceedings of the AMIA, Annual Symposium*, pp. 244–248, 2006.

21. Farmer, A.D., Bruckner Holt, C.E.M., Cook, M.J., Hearing, S.D., Social network sites: A novel portal for communication. *Postgrad. Med. J.*, 85, 1007, 455–459, 2009.

22. Fortunato, S., Community detection in graphs. *Phys. Rep.*, 486, 3-5, 75–174, 2010.

23. Hanson, C.L., Cannon, B., Burton, S.H., Giraud-Carrier, C.G., An exploration of social circles and prescription drug abuse through Twitter. *J. Med. Internet Res.*, 15, 2023.

24. Gorman, D.M., Mezic, J., Mezic, I., Gruenewald, P.J., Agent-based modeling of drinking behavior: A preliminary model and potential applications to theory and practice. *Am. J. Public Health*, 96, 11, 2055–2060, 2006.

25. Hanson, C.L., Burton, S., Giraud-Carrier, C., West, J., Barnes, M., Hansen, B., Tweaking and tweeting: Exploring Twitter for non-medical use of adderall among college students. *J. Med. Internet Res.*, 15, 4, e62, 2013.

26. Hanson, C.L., Cannon, B., Burton, S., Giraud-Carrier, C., An exploration of social circles and prescription drug abuse through Twitter. *J. Med. Internet Res.*, 15, 9, e189, 2013.

27. Heavilin, N., Gerbert, B., Page, J.E., Gibbs, J.L., Public health surveillance of dental pain via Twitter. *J. Dent. Res.*, 90, 9, 1047–1051, 2011.

28. Hesse, B.W., Moser, R.P., Riley, W.T., From big data to knowledge in the social sciences. *Ann. Am. Acad. Pol. Soc. Sci.*, 659, 16–32, 2015.

29. Hindman, M., Building better models: Prediction, replication, and machine learning in the social sciences. *Ann. Am. Acad. Pol. Soc. Sci.*, 659, 48–62, 2015.

30. Hogeweg, P., The roots of bioinformatics in theoretical biology. *PLoS Comput. Biol.*, 7, 3, e1002021, 2011.

31. Jain, S.H., Practicing medicine in the age of Facebook. *N. Engl. J. Med.*, 361, 7, 649–651, 2009.

32. Jashinsky, J., Burton, S.H., Hanson, C.L., West, J., Giraud-Carrier, C., Barnes, M.D., Argyle, T., Tracking suicide risk factors through Twitter in the US. *Crisis: The Journal of Crisis Intervention and Suicide Prevention*, 35, 1, 50–59, 2014.

33. Jiwani, N., Gupta, K., Whig, P., Novel HealthCare framework for cardiac arrest with the application of AI using ANN. *2021 5th International Conference on Information Systems and Computer Networks (ISCON)*, pp. 1–5, 2021.

34. Johnson, G.J. and Ambrose, P.J., Neo-tribes: The power and potential of online communities in healthcare. *Commun. ACM*, 49, 1, 107–113, 2006.

35. Keelan, J., Pavri-Garcia, V., Tomlinson, G., Wilson, K., YouTube as a source of immunization information. A content analysis. *J. Am. Med. Assoc.*, 298, 21, 2482–2484, 2007.

36. Khera, Y., Whig, P., Velu, A., Efficient effective and secured electronic billing system using AI. *Vivekananda J. Res.*, 10, 53–60, 2021.

37. Krieck, M., Dreesman, J., Otrusina, L., Denecke, K., A new age of public health: Identifying disease outbreaks by analyzing tweets, in: *Health Web Science Workshop at the Third International ACM Conference on Web Science*, 2011.

38. Kunkle, S., Christie, G., Yach, D., El-Sayed, A.M., The importance of computer science for public health training: An opportunity and call to action. *JMIR Public Health Surveillance*, 2, 1, e10, 2016.

39. Li, Y., Lawley, M.A., Siscovick, D.S., Zhang, D., Pagán, J., Agent-based modeling of chronic diseases. A narrative review and future research directions. *Prev. Chronic Dis.*, 13, 150561, 2016.

40. McLeroy, K.R., Bibeau, D., Steckler, A., Glanz, K., An ecological perspective on health promotion programs. *Health Educ. Q.*, 15, 351–377, 1988.

41. Merchant, R.M., Elmer, S., Lurie, N., Integrating social media into emergency-preparedness efforts. *N. Engl. J. Med.*, 365, 4, 289–291, 2011.

42. Murugiah, K., Vallakati, A., Rajput, K., Sood, A., Challa, N.R., YouTube as a source of information on cardiopulmonary resuscitation. *Resuscitation*, 82, 3, 332–334, 2010.

43. Mustapha, K. and Frayret, J.-M., Agent-based modeling and simulation software architecture for healthcare, in: *Proceedings of the Sixth International Conference on Simulation and Modeling Methodologies, Technologies and Applications*, pp. 1–12, 2016.

44. Nadikattu, R.R., Mohammad, S.M., Whig, P., Novel economical social distancing smart device for COVID-19. *Int. J. Electr. Eng. Technol. (IJEET)*, 14, 2020.

45. Pandey, A., Patni, N., Singh, M., Sood, A., Singh, G., YouTube as a source of information on the H1N1 influenza pandemic. *Am. J. Prev. Med.*, 38, 3, e1–3, 2010.

46. Paul, M. and Dredze, M., You are what you tweet: Analyzing Twitter for public health, in: *Proceedings of the Fifth International AAAI Conference on Weblogs and Social Media*, 2011.

47. Pelat, C., Turbelin, C., Bar-Hen, A., Flahault, A., Valleron, A., More diseases are tracked by using Google Trends. *Emerg. Infect. Dis.*, 15, 8, 1327–1328, 2009.

48. Pentland, A., Lazer, D., Brewer, D., Heibeck, T., Using reality mining to improve public health and medicine. *Stud. Health Technol. Inform.*, 149, 93–102, 2009.

49. Perez, L. and Dragicevic, S., An agent-based approach for modeling dynamics of contagious disease spread. *Int. J. Health Geogr.*, 8, 50, 2009.

50. Rupani, A., Saini, D., Sujediya, G., Whig, P., A review of technology paradigm for IoT on FPGA. *IJARCCE-Int. J. Adv. Res. Comput. Commun. Eng.*, 5, 9, 61–64, 2016.

51. Rupani, A., Whig, P., Sujediya, G., Vyas, P., A robust technique for image processing based on interfacing of Raspberry Pi and FPGA using IoT. *2017 International Conference on Computer, Communications, and Electronics (Comptelix)*, pp. 350–353, 2017.

52. Rupani, A., Whig, P., Sujediya, G., Vyas, P., Hardware implementation of IoT-based image processing filters. *Proceedings of the Second International Conference on Computational Intelligence and Informatics*, pp. 681–691, 2018.

53. Scanfeld, D., Scanfeld, V., Larson, E.L., Dissemination of health information through social networks Twitter and antibiotics. *Am. J. Infect. Control*, 38, 3, 182–188, 2010.

54. Schwartz, H.A. and Ungar, L.H., Data-driven content analysis of social media, a systematic overview of automated methods. *Ann. Am. Acad. Pol. Soc. Sci.*, 659, 78–94, 2015.

55. Senge, P.M., *The fifth discipline: Is the art & practice of the learning organization*, Doubleday, New York, 2006.

56. Sharma, A., Kumar, A., Whig, P., On the performance of CDTA-based novel analog inverse low pass filter using 0.35 μm CMOS parameter. *Int. J. Sci. Technol. Manage.*, 4, 1, 594–601, 2015.

57. Silverman, B.G., Hanrahan, N., Bharathy, G., Gordon, K., Johnson, D., A systems approach to healthcare: Agent-based modeling, community mental health, and population well-being. *Artif. Intell. Med.*, 63, 2, 61–71, 2015.

58. Sood, A., Sarangi, S., Pandey, A., Murugiah, K., YouTube as a source of information on kidney stone disease. *Urol.*, 77, 3, 558–562, 2010.

59. Steinberg, P.L., Wason, S., Stern, L.J.M., Deters, B., Seigne, J., Kowal YouTube as source of prostate cancer information. *Urol.*, 75, 3, 619–622, 2010.

60. Velu, A. and Whig, P., Protect personal privacy and wasting time using Nlp: A comparative approach using Ai. *Vivekananda J. Res.*, 10, 42–52, 2021a.

61. Velu, A. and Whig, P., Protect personal privacy and wasting time using Nlp: A comparative approach using Ai. *Vivekananda J. Res.*, 10, 42–52, 2021b.

62. West, J.H., Hall, C.P., Hanson, C.L., Prier, K., Giraud-Carrier, C., Neeley, E.S., Barnes, M.D., Temporal variability of problem drinking on Twitter. *Open J. Prev. Med.*, 2, 1, id17410, 2012.

63. Whig, P., Exploration of viral diseases mortality risk using machine learning. *Int. J. Mach. Lear. Sustain. Dev.*, 1, 1, 11–20, 2019.

64. Whig, P. and Ahmad, S.N., Simulation of a linear dynamic macro model of the photocatalytic sensor in SPICE. *COMPEL Int. J. Comput. Math. Electr. Electron. Eng.*, 33, 1/2, 611–629, 2014.

65. Whig, P. and Ahmad, S.N., Fuzzy logic implementation of the photocatalytic sensor. *Int. Robot. Autom. J.*, 2, 3, 15–19, 2017.

66. Whig, P. and Ahmad, S.N., Comparison analysis of various R2R D/A converters. *Int. J. Biosens. Bioelectron.*, 4, 6, 275–279, 2018.

67. Whig, P., Nadikattu, R.R., Velu, A., COVID-19 pandemic analysis using the application of AI, in: *Healthcare Monitoring and Data Analysis Using IoT: Technologies and Applications*, p. 1, 2022.

68. Zamith, R. and Lewis, S.C., Content analysis and the algorithmic coder: What computational social science means for traditional modes of media analysis. *Ann. Am. Acad. Pol. Soc. Sci.*, 659, 307–318, 2015.

69. IOM (Institute of Medicine). *Crossing the quality chasm: A new health system for the 21st century.* Washington, DC: National Academy Press, 2005.

70. Spear, S. J., Fixing healthcare from the inside: Teaching residents to heal broken delivery processes as they heal sick patients. *Acad. Med.*, 81(10 Suppl):S144–149, 2006.

13

Impact of e-Business Services on Product Management

Sanchit Sarhadi[1] and Priyadarshini Adyasha Pattanaik[2]*

[1]Department of Sales, Container Xchange, Hamburg, Germany
[2]LaTIM INSERM U1101, IMT Atlantique, France

Abstract

Smart products e-business services impact the manufacturing market in industry 4.0 in international e-business transactions based on smart product service which is booming day by day and gaining prominence value by transforming into the digital realm. The international e-business trade is the most important center of the logistics hub and is one of the main pillar continents of the world. The wave of smart product-service systems (PSS) has enhanced the road to a better international trade environment, to reduce product risks and individual customer satisfaction. This paper explains the strengths and weaknesses of the growing servitization challenges of e-business transactions worldwide by studying two cases of multinational companies which are working smart in the manufacturing sector and by taking interviews with their managers. Smart product servitization has become a key e-business and moved up to the value chain to overcome several barriers associated with the design, management, and delivery of the product. The paper tries to address these challenges by presenting a study and simple flexible multi-faceted assessment model of international e-business product service innovation to provide an effective means for enterprises to enhance their e-business, by taking interviews with the respective managers of the company and to address what is the complexity and challenges faced in the process of product service, notably by the host country, challenges associated with political sector, geographical type, the economical sector, and investment sector.

Two interviews were held and the results were analyzed in assessing the impacts or challenges of the smart products in the manufacturing market. The qualitative method used in this paper for the research purpose explored to impress an impact

---

Corresponding author: ppattanaik055@gmail.com

Ahmed A. Elgnar, Vigneshwar M, Krishna Kant Singh and Zdzislaw Polkowski (eds.) Handbook of Computational Sciences: A Multi and Interdisciplinary Approach, (273–298) © 2023 Scrivener Publishing LLC

that creates in the manufacturing industries and qualitative methodology is quite pragmatic.

Keywords: Product service system (PSS), smart products, manufacturing market, Industry 4.0, international e-business, smart machines, e-business services, Internet of Things (IoT)

13.1   Introduction

The manufacturing market in India and also other countries nowadays is huge and with the implementation of smart products or the industrial 4.0 evolution expanding in the manufacturing market and making the industry smart by adopting better product service systems or the e-business models for the smart connectivity and thus making the international e-business denser with the expansion of the markets in manufacturing by becoming smarter and making the industry smarter by adopting better smarter versions of their machinery for making the products or for the manufacturing [1]. The smart connected products and their e-business worldwide [2] becoming at international levels giving the hopes for the markets to expand their e-business uniquely and immensely for developing the e-business and expanding at a huge market-making possible profit in the international environment.

Our main motivation for this paper is to assess the industry dynamics of the smart products used in the manufacturing market and analyze the complete industry dynamics in smart manufacturing, it is a relevant topic to be researched as in India and the worldwide smart products in the manufacturing sector in the future booming industry and to be completely adopted by 2025 and so it is expanding and tremendously increasing to discover. Hence, we would be analyzing various factors, challenges, and impacts of the smart products used in the manufacturing market and discussing the models of PSS used here by taking two companies' interviews.

International e-business in the smart connected products in the manufacturing market is a booming industry and has great international markets with huge implications on various factors like transactions, other e-business services issues, product issues, etc. In this paper, we are studying the implications of smart e-business services in the manufacturing market or the so-called Industry 4.0 concept [3] which has been properly explained in this paper. India being the developing smart country in the smart manufacturing e-business services and dealing with international e-business also and planning to expand internationally, it is a relevant topic to study in our paper to find the link between international e-business services in the smart e-business services in the big developing market in India and ever-growing market and we are studying the implications and the complexity of challenges faced in the process of product service, notably by the host country, and the implications on the political sector, geographical and the economical sector [27].

13.2   Literature Review

A. Product Service System (PSS)

PSS is a special case of servitization and integrated PSS, also it is known as a functional-oriented e-business model for the companies. It is a combination of products and services. This is associated with a series of new market trends and market strategies for the companies to perform and earn profits. According to Mont 2002 [4], it is a growing trend in today's world competition in E-business that the combination of products and services is leading in the present scenario for the manufacturing companies. The companies which are investing more in rising industrial services of their products are following the above-mentioned trend i.e. the trend of PSS for product-centric [5, 6]. So, to gain, social, economic, and environmental benefits, PSS is a great solution for many companies. Also, the product-service system is in other terms, defined as a system of products, services, and supporting networks and infrastructure that is built as more competitive, fulfills customer needs, and have lesser environmental problems or impacts on it [4]. We will study in the next parts of the paper the detailed version of all the aspects of PSS and the Challenges faced in the servitization of PSS by companies, In the next part of the literature review, we will study more about this topic with more comprehensive information that has been researched previously and what more to be done in future, with our observation and opinions in the other respective parts [7].

According to Baines *et al.* 2007 and Tukker 2004, PSS are three types that are product-oriented, user-oriented, and result-oriented [8–10].

Result-oriented PSS – Where the company's main objective is to sell their results instead of their product that are tangible. The companies take the responsibility which delivering the product that including services, maintenance, and the delivery of the product, so the product owner is with the company. One of the examples [8–10] of result-oriented service is the printing services, they have a contract with the provider company (customers) that provides service to do their printing services. So basically they deliver the printing services with quality and also provides them the printers to print, this is all a result-oriented PSS.

User-Oriented PSS – User-oriented PSS [9, 10] is different than result-oriented PSS, as in this classification of PSS, the product has a more role of the product than the service and so the service manufacturer sells the accessible service and the use of that specific product. Their main focus is on the use and the increased life-span of the product [9]. An example of this classification is the manufacturer which makes the tools of some machinery at different factories in the different locations and customer may select a location which is suitable to them to buy from there and so after using the tools they can return the tools in the same location after using the service but consumers are responsible for the tools in maintaining them, cleaning them, etc.

Product-Oriented PSS – In Product-Oriented PSS [10], the product which is sold and the ownership of that product is being transferred, also in this kind of PSS, the other extra services are being given to the customer for its more lifespan and better working of the product, The Best example for this is the after-selling services that are being offered by the companies like managing the customer care for LG company so that to tell them how to use the product or if the consumer is getting problems in using the product (Tomiyama 2003). This is how product-oriented PSS works, by mainly focusing on the product and the services associated with it to give them the more focused services to the consumer for better usage of the product.

The Product-Oriented PSS [10] applies the limited value of services to the consumer for example if any product purchased from a company, say LG electronics and they give you the Guarantee of that product for at least one year for changing the parts if there some problem in some part of the product, So this guarantee does not influence in increasing the value in using the product.

So, all the types of PSS [8–10] we studied above have been used by different companies according to the PSS models they have for their profits and for their more selling of the product based on the services they provide to customers. They work on the principles of eco-efficiency of their products and increase the life of the products. Also furthermore in this thesis, we would study the smart PSS and the design of the model which can be suited for the companies along with the e-services it can provide to the consumers with the involvement of international business transactions globally.

Development of Well-Designed PSS

Making of well-designed PSS [11] plays a crucial thing for companies, to make a better business model with the good implementation of the better PSS plan which can be beneficial for the company and also better for the consumers who use the products and use the services. The perfect PSS business plan is required to get smooth products and services for both companies and customers. There were many different aspects of the approaches of PSS like some are product-centered and some are Service-centered, there were many studies in the past on the PSS studies and they have something in common like few phases in it like implementation, ideation, and inspiration but usually, it consists more like initiation and evaluation also and with the perfect PSS design model. Figure 13.1 represents the 5 phases of a well-designed product service system. It defines the to and from the process from initiation to implementation and vice versa.

The first stage i.e. initiation in which the opportunity is created about the consumer or the manufacturer and this opportunity is defined as the requirement or the market in which the technology has to be implemented or we can say the need of the PSS process and once it is found it is being followed by the other process like the inspiration of the Model and in this phase, all the technological trend or what is being popular in the market has to be followed and also the tools used in that field or the products needs and the most important is the customer's needs, what they demand or what are their expectations and which can be observed by interview, or taking the observations from the past research about the products used or how much is being used by the number of consumers and how that technology has been used for the products [11].

After the inspiration phase, there comes the ideation phase, in which the solutions have to be created according to the demands or the requirements of the consumers to satisfy them and fulfilling the needs that were observed in the phase previous to them and also there are many ways for creating a solution by benchmarking or the patents or the literature prevailing or it can be done by searching it internally like brainstorming when the solutions are created in meetings and all the ideas and solutions are to be noted with no barriers or criticism and then later the best solutions are to be finalized by various evaluations, for example, morphological boxes or Pugh matrix in which the needs of customers and the criteria is to be noted and further arises for the evaluations.

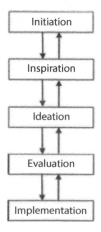

Figure 13.1 Design of well-designed product-service-system.

Then, the final stage arrives i.e. implementation and in this phase the final testing and analyzing of all the models or the concepts, and the simulation or the testing is performed to check the model to be in a success and to ensure that this concept or the model is worth proceeding further for getting live for the PSS.

Hence the whole five-phase process [11] for the development of PSS which is well designed and on which companies can rely on has been discussed above and which has to be allowed to succeed for the companies and so for the consumers.

Business Process Modeling Notation (BPMN)- It is a method to develop and to analyze the PSS, It is a graphical notation [12] which is a standard or general form which has been accepted internationally and it shows all the process activities of the business models of different stakeholders and also the flowing of messages or other activities it follows, It is a simpler way to illustrate the flow between them and to analyze the process of PSS but currently this process is not used much in the software development sectors.

Also, in the EU, there is a German project called SusProNet [12, 13] that aims to create a very strong network of all the EU investors and experts from industry, institutes, and others to develop product service research. Figure 13.2 shows that the project work is influenced by the systematic program for the Product Service System (PSS) for creating and sharing of the knowledge related to it. Many organizations, people, investors and many companies associated with it are working together on different methods of the product-service system, to get better business plans for their own companies to enhance their business whether any industry says manufacturing industry or any other. It helps in the problems associated with the PSS or whether to develop more knowledge and giving or taking advice for their methods and products services model are to be discussed here in the SusProNet model [13].

It is the easiest and clear way of communicating and illustrating the business from its initial stage to the last stage where the managers of operations

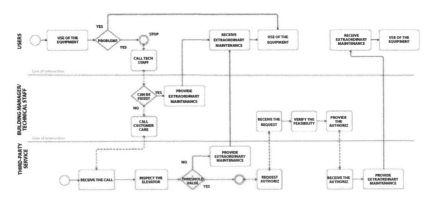

Figure 13.2 Description of SusProNet networking with investors.

check the process and approve it. BPMN1.0 was created for the first time in 2004 and currently, BPMN2.0 is used and other versions will be there soon [13]. It consists of several elements that are graphical for example flow objects, connection objects, artifacts, swim Lanes. They all have different functions to follow in the representation to create a complete process.

B. Smart Manufacturing and Smart Products – Industry 4.0

Industry 4.0 is a term coined by the German government and this concept is immensely derived as a driver to play in the digital Industries and this type of industry is completely dependent on the products which are customized and are manufactured in a great way of the facile manufacturing environment [3, 18]. It is the digital transformation of manufacturing industries that make the products in a completely smart environment, it believes in the process of value creation. It is written as Industry 4.0 because it is known for the fourth industrial revolution which has led the manufacturing companies to change their usual process of production to change it to more smart manufacturing ways with the use of more smart technology. The smart products have the ability is not just the internal-external features of the product showing it to be smart but also better customer and supplier or manufacturing experience [18]. Figure 13.3 shows the structure of Industry 4.0 which includes the whole relationship between the Internet of Things, Smart Sensor, Advanced Robotics, Big Data Analytics, 3D Printing, Augmented Reality, Cloud Computing.

INDUSTRY 4.0 FRAMEWORK - THE DIGITAL TECHNOLOGIES

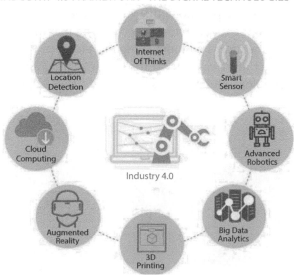

Figure 13.3 Structure of Industry 4.0.

C. Manufacturing Market – New Smart Industry

As we discussed above in Industry-4.0, that one of the major new industries in the smart technology is the manufacturing market only, it is the largest market in the industrial IoT (Internet of Things) or the smart market [19]. There are many other markets as well in the smart industries like retail market, utility market or smart education, etc. Figure 13.4 describes the whole work process in a smart manufacturing industry. The manufacturing market is the largest market among all as it is the market in which the smart machinery or the smart process is being done and making the industry to be the best one to make them smart with the use of more smart technologies or using of IoT i.e. Internet of Things.

The use of advanced data analytics and the processing of the data help in the increase in the growth of the IoT which is globally in the manufacturing market. With the use of more IoT applications in the manufacturing market, it helps in increasing the overall experience of the manufacturing processes or in the production of the products, with the machines more reliable and more life of its working, the better control over the processing of the manufacturing work with the applications of IoT, also increase in the better quality, the compliance of the company, the reduced costs or the better product output and so getting better operations with more quality in the process of the manufacturing operations [19]. With the increasing use of technology in the enterprise which is also more innovative and focusing more on the R&D i.e. research & development, can help it better growth or the improvement in the market of IoT in the manufacturing domain. Also, with various machine applications that help in the making of more facile the IoT industry in the manufacturing sector. The manufacturing sector is increasing by having more and more companies to open their manufacturing process and get more easiness by making it to the best with the use of more smart technology and products to make it easier to produce [19, 25].

Figure 13.4 Description of the working process in a smart manufacturing industry.

There are many companies as well which are becoming the main key companies who are creating better IoT solutions for the manufacturing sectors to make it better and smart and examples of them are IBM corporations, Bosh software, Zebra technologies, Siemens, Cisco, etc. and many more companies are creating best IoT solutions for the manufacturing sector so that this sector grows and make it global smart manufacturing solutions. It has been analyzed that the IoT manufacturing markets will tend to grow in the next few years and which will rise to the more economical with this sector. In the future, the genetic regulation of compliance helps in the emergent growth of the manufacturing market in the following years. Several factors like data security or data privacy are some of the factors that can be a hindrance to the growth of IoT in global manufacturing markets. The Industrial IoT or the smart manufacturing firms has many advantages as well [19].

Also, as mentioned above that the largest market in smart products is the manufacturing market only and mainly the technology used in smart products is the Internet of Things (IoT). The industries which are based on the Internet, the products, software, and data are connected over the Internet is known as Internet of Things and this technology when used in the Industries are known as industrial IoT (IIoT) or smart products or industries, the manufacturing market is the most popular and ever-growing industry in smart Products after the retail, utility or other industries. There have been many initiatives that take place to make the smart factories and also it has been predicted that by 2023, smart factories or smart manufacturing industries could add more than $2.2 trillion of the economy in the total economy in the manufacturing industry. The digital platform and the latest technologies are providing them to enhance their functioning and profits by making the manufacturing firms more productive and smart.

Also, there is research which was given by Capgemini Research Institute [20] that if there would be more smart factories but the right one then more and more economy would be added by 2023 as discussed above i.e. 2.2 trillion dollars of the economy. So the smart factories are scaling up and in the period from 2019 to 2023 there would be a great increase in the set-up of the more and more smart factories scaling up will be the fore coming challenge for industry 4.0 with the graphical representation of benefits of IoT is shown in Figure 13.5. It is said that around 55% of companies say that their smart factories involve the Greenfield projects and it is more in the mid-size and small scale industries, and also 33 percent of the companies are doing the processes in their factories more digitally now [20].

Sixty-eight percent of companies that are manufacturing have already the smart initiatives in their factories presently whereas in 2017 it was

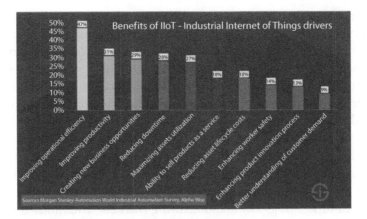

Figure 13.5 Graphical representation of benefits of IoT.

around 43%. This information was gathered by the Capgemini Research Institute [20]. The manufacturing firms are adapting themselves onto more and more into smart factories making themselves digitalized and making their processes smarter and getting more smart industries to create a huge market in smart industries and forecasting more and more investments in the upcoming years in this market of smart industries.

Henceforth, smart products in the manufacturing market were having huge impacts on the industry on their industrial dynamics and forecasting the global smart manufacturing economy. Presently there are not very much industries in manufacturing which have adopted the system of the smart product or technology worldwide or in India, hence there can be tremendous profits and business in the field of manufacturing as India has started the concept of make in India project in which huge investments are made in the smart manufacturing of India and already there have been many companies which have been involved with government initiative and with the trust of government they are moving forward [19, 20]. There are a great demand and impacts on smart products, benefits, or the challenges as well which all we will be studying in this thesis and analyze the impacts and challenges. Companies are innovating more and more with new technologies to adopt smart factories or the products, which is long term, there will be a huge global gain in this industry, below is a graph which will show by 2025, what will be the impact on business in manufacturing industries. Rest, we will be studying and analyzing all the industrial dynamics and innovation of the company by interviewing the companies as well to get an insight and to analyze in the latter part of this thesis. Here is the figure graph of the predicted economic impact of the IoT in 2025 by Mckinsey & Company.

D. Connection between PSS and Smart PSS

PSS are made smarter by involving technology into it Like IoT, wireless communication, internet, etc. The first-ever smart PSS Process with the involvement of information technology (IT) was made in 1999 from Goedkoop. It states the few phases in it which as follows in the below figure as well. There were three types of PSS i.e. conventional, IoT-enabled, and smart PSS and they are according to the innovation in the IT sector and based on how smart and connected it is. So at the start when conventional PSS came, it was internet-based and used to work with human intelligence and with the use of data transmission efficiency like 3G services [18–20]. Also in this phase Crowdsourcing was to be done to solicit contributions from many crowds online or outside.

Then in the IoT-based PSS, for example, GPS google and traffic data to be collected from various phones via internet from users and various devices gets connected through IoT. With machine intelligence and the use of connectivity it works.

In the Smart-PSS [17, 20] that is the latest to be used and that is being the combination of the human and machine-based intelligence which consists of the digital online and offline smartness with the connectivity of both human as well as smart connectivity for example the smart product's technology. There are many examples of smart PSS products like smart cars, smart doorbells, smart speakers, etc., one of the most popular smart products examples by amazon is Alexa, which takes human voice recognition and transform command into functions and can be connected to any other home devices like TV, speakers or the other amazon smart products, etc shown in Figure 13.6 [21]. So in all these smart connected products, The PSS is built in such a way that it acts smartly while the proper services and safe product to be used by consumers. It all consists of smart PSS.

13.3   Data Collection and Method Details

A. Methodology

A smart product-service system is recognized as a key business strategy for international investors willing to move up the value chain. The purpose of this unit is to discuss the methodology and the data collections through certain content analysis that is being done in the past, all the researches and data available and interviewing two managers with his team members of the related firms of smart products in manufacturing industries. So, we are using the qualitative methodology for our research in this thesis for smart products and to know the impacts of smart products on the manufacturing

Figure 13.6 Examples of smart products.

industry dynamics. However, several hurdles have to be conquered to successfully integrate business with products and services. The integration of eco-efficiency and eco-design product service leads to a minimum negative environmental impact with increase economic added value [18]. This study particularly aims at three objectives: 1) Rigorous customer satisfaction, combined with creativity, and gaining profit with compatible ideas; 2) PSS should be smart, practical, simple, economic viability, and understandable; 3) sustainability development causing maximum social well being with economic added value; 4) good network coordinator; 5) efficient infrastructure and governance structure needed to produce a product service.

The qualitative method which we are using in this thesis for the research purpose that is we are doing some interviews from the managers along with his team members of the companies which are using the smart connected products while doing their manufacturing process, to explore the dynamics of smart product business service and the challenges and the impact it creates in the manufacturing industries and qualitative methodology is quiet pragmatic for this kind of research when we do [18–21]. To build a smart product business model, we used some different levels of international business analysis. The interviews with the managers are done to know the impact and challenges of these companies at the industrial level. Also, we identified the content-based papers related to the international and domestic business for the manufacturing market for the smart products and we discussed it in the previous topic of literature review also. Moreover, the entire approach of this study results in data collection, network construction, and analysis with block designing of the PSS model also for the companies for their PSS model who manufactures the smart products and sells to the manufacturing companies to manufacture their products smartly.

In our master research thesis, we have chosen the method of interviewing the managers with his team that is we call them to group interviews or discussing the case studies of two organizations. In this method, we interviewed the managers of two organizations of manufacturing industries with the team members of the company as well. So, the two companies which we interviewed and we shall discuss their case studies in this thesis are Sphoorti machine tools and Tata Motors [22, 23]. Also, we selected these manufacturing firms because these companies are working on the thesis research topic that we are doing and these manufacturing companies in different industries are working on smart products. Fortunately, these companies and the associated persons from these industries are already part of the research program and they have been sanctioned by the government of India to support the research on the specific government site related to smart manufacturing in India and so they were easily being contacted without much hustle and so we talked in-depth about the process and the topic or the problem statement of this thesis. The interview is being done by the managers and their team members of both companies and discussing the case studies about their own companies. The managers and the team members of both the companies were chosen from the same industry working in the smart environment and we asked few questions from each of them to assess the impacts of the challenges of the products or machines formed smart [14–18].

Both cases studies were led by the managers of the two associations where managers and two of their colleagues were interviewed. The interview questions were done independently, which means every part was met independently. The strategy helped in causing the group and task chief to feel allowed to communicate their suppositions and not having pressure from any side. Each meeting was around 30 to 20 minutes of duration.

Through this contextual analysis or the interview process, we were able to understand the views of the employees and how they perceived their thoughts about the manufacturing process for smart machines or the products used. The case study is a suitable method as we were able to analyze teams working in the same methodology but under different working conditions having a different perspective and having divergent organization thinking as every firm has different cases and also a different way of reaching the client. These two case studies could have given two different results, and we were looking for some similarities in our case studies that could prove our research question.

B. Data Collection

The case studies or the interviews are done by taking the semi-structured interview questions and openly asking them to prove our thesis problem statement and then to analyze the data [22, 23]. The interviews were done on Skype calls and they are well transcribed. Also, we were provided the company brochure for the industry related to smart tech before the interviews so that we could be specific to ask the questions and get a little information about the company beforehand, this helps the managers of the companies and also for us to reduce the time or to save the time and directing only towards the main focus of the thesis. The interview guide was made before asking them the different questions which were formed based on the literature review.

A semi-structured interview was conducted to gain a better insight and in-depth knowledge of the topic we were researching. A semi-structured set of some questions were prepared for the interview. They were able to talk about the topics asked freely and open-ended questions, and in cases where the answers were not clear enough, we were able to explain further and ask more in-depth questions. While the interview was taking place, the questions were elaborated or asked questions based on the answer received from the interviewee to get a complete explanation for the data analysis. All the information based on the industry dynamics of the smart manufacturing or the smart machines or the products, they produce later to send them to the manufacturing companies for the production, is being done and the relevancy of the questions asked was directed to the research problem statement of our topic (Table 13.1).

Table 13.1 Case study of manager and team members.

Case study	Subjects	Company	Smart solutions provider	Methodology
Case study- 1	Manager and 2 Team members	Sphoorti machine tools Pvt. Ltd.	Ace micromatic group	Semi-structured Group Interview questions
Case study- 2	Manager and 2 Team members	Tata Motors	Rockwell Automation India	Semi-structured Group Interview questions

Hence, the data is collected based on the interviews done from the companies and also by the content on the internet through previous researches and the articles associated on the smart products as well as on the smart manufacturing of the companies and getting to know the challenges associated with it and how it impacts the industry dynamics for the firms at the industrial level and how the sales and profits of these companies are getting more focused and what will be the future aspect of the manufacturing industry is all being analyzed in this thesis and the data analyzed is being written in the next part of data analysis. Also, we have shown in the brief as a content grid as the details of all the data collection method involved in our thesis below (Table 13.2).

Table 13.2 Survey of questionnaire session in Sphoorti Machine Tools Pvt. Ltd.

Measures that were supposed to be analyzed for the research under the impacts and challenges	Observations from the interview
Any challenges for smart Technology products.	Data Security fears Lack of system Integration and knowledge issues Proper Wireless telecommunications infrastructure Standardization required for interoperability
Smart technology or the product adopted successfully	Real-time Tracking of data TPM-Track e-Shopx smart concept
Positive Impacts	More operational efficiencies Cost-saving
Innovation dynamics	Seeking for more innovating solutions from smart machines manufacturer or smart solutions provider
Political problems	No political issues stated
Industry Life	Better efficiency and working methodology
Economical management (Sales & profits)	30% more profits after adopting smart

(Continued)

Table 13.2 Survey of questionnaire session in Sphoorti Machine Tools Pvt. Ltd. (*Continued*)

Measures that were supposed to be analyzed for the research under the impacts and challenges	Observations from the interview
Marketing	After being smart, Marketing led more e-business
International e-business	Indian & Europe and expanding
Improvement	Consistently innovating and the cost incurred
Knowledge for the smart technology	Requirement and training of smart technology is a challenge too.
Future of the firm	Expanding more and adopting more smart solutions in 2022

C. Data Analysis and Results

As the interviews conducted and each case study of the company was discussed to them and was asked questions to their managers and team members of the company or firm, we analyzed several opinions for the thesis research problem statement of our master thesis topic i.e. we try to analyze or understanding the impact of the smart products on the manufacturing industry dynamics, we studied several impacts or challenges faced by the companies of manufacturing firms and also how the industry dynamics depend on the market, also we studied the impacts on 5 porter forces, the industry evolution in the past or how it is moving forward in future like in the upcoming part of the thesis in the future aspects of the results section in detail, we will discuss how the manufacturing market going to work and act accordingly in the smart products. The industry life cycle is being discussed in the results analysis part as well in the detailed version of the discussion of whatever has been found by the interviews. The industry innovation plays a huge role in the market for the industry dynamics growth in the manufacturing market, as we discussed in the literature part of this thesis that innovation in the industry of smart products is they by involving the new technology to adapt it the products and make it smart products and this managers and team managers to get the all the impacts on all industry evolution and the challenges if any they face.

As we interviewed our first company that is Sphoorti Machine Tools Pvt. Ltd. [22] (Table 13.2), which is using smart product technology in their company for the manufacturing and this company is doing the business in India and expanding outside India as well now after being getting smart, It took the smart technology adoption from a company, Ace Micromatic Group which is the largest conglomerate in the country which been expanding in a great constant and increasing growth rate for 3 decades now. While interviewing the company we asked them certain on-point questions for asking about the impacts and challenges of the company they are facing and about the industry dynamics. Below is the table (Table 13.3) where we can find some of our analysis of our interview from Sphoorti Machine Tools Pvt. Ltd.

The above content grid analysis (Table 13.3) is used for depicting what we talked in an interview with the manufacturing company which has adopted smart manufacturing methods and what has been the impacts and challenges if any for the company to work and all types of impacts whether positive or negative were been discussed in the interview. The interview process was quite smooth for us and as this company started adopting the smart technologies or products in 2015 when the company was facing few challenges on working on its own, as said by the manager that the company was initially a small enterprise in the manufacturing of tool disc and tool holders and it is India's global manufacturer and around 40% of the sales are to be done globally as they have the sales market in Germany as well, we were told by the team member during the interview when we asked for the international business-related question that how your company is adapting to expand your business globally or it has been working already. Also, earlier before deciding to be smart adopted, this company was facing several challenges as well as managing their manual data and so they decided to get smart and do the real-time methodology by the Ace Micrometric group, which provides high-end Manufacturing automation solutions, Also, we talked about the company of their manufacturer that 'what roles do smart machine or smart technology builder plays in the process of smart manufacturing for your firm?' Team member answered this question as he was then in charge of dealing with the company's innovative technology advisors of ace.

Micrometric group and what he told us regarding that was the companies which provides engineered solutions for us plays a huge role and with their invented ideas and technology [19, 28], 'it boosts our process which thereafter help the business of the company' and later told to us that

Table 13.3 Survey of questionnaire session in Tata Motors.

Measures that were supposed to be analyzed for the research under the impacts and challenges	Observations from the interview
Any challenges for smart Technology products	Operational risks Project management issues Change risks Interoperability implementation issue Lack of knowledge/Training
Smart technology or the product adopted successfully	Implementing new MES (manufacturing execution system)
Positive Impacts	Standardized MES landscape Enabled the enterprise fully connected Timesaving
Political problems	Required authorizations from government
Industry Life	Better efficiency and working methodology
Economical management (Sales & profits)	More profits & better sales dynamics
Marketing	After being smart, Marketing led more e-business
Improvement	Consistently innovating and the cost incurred
Knowledge for the smart technology	Requirement and training of smart technology is a challenge too
Future of the firm	Planning to automate other plants of Tata motors as well

after adopting smart solutions, 'our company got 30 % of more profits in their sales after and also we started doing more marketing to gather other customers and were also attracted for the smart technology manufacturing' and since they are the tool discs manufacturer and doing in the smart way by reducing the time for making and also for doing business abroad, they adopted real-time tracking data smart technology in order to achieve more operational efficiency in their processes and the [24, 29, 31] manager said that they decided this to operate for the smart technology solution for Amit's (smart solutions provider) of TPM-track technology suite to increase the efficiency that helped them to gain more data analytics solutions. Since they have varied machines line around 21 machines manufacturing and in all the machines they implemented this but then when we asked that '*do you still happy for this solution or do you still think there should be some improvement or which you think as a challenge?*' their team member replied that '*data security is still a concern, and sometimes there is a lack of system integration and machines with a real-time data could not connect and then sometimes it does not relate to the machines and as well as the Real-time calculator*', so He said when there is some bug, it becomes a huge problem for the company for making it a time-consuming process to operate on it. When we asked for the '*training procedure of the smart products*', they said that the '*training or the knowledge is the other challenge for the industry*' as if they want to adopt smart technology then, there should be provided proper training modules to the existing workers and then they have to spend on training for the company working, Although they are still working for the future smart technology with a complete manufacturing firm in a smart way so that they can enhance the company business as they concluded that at an end way question they were happier except for some small issues which can be managed thereafter. They have adopted some other smart solutions as well for example e-SHOPx smart product and that is being used for the paperless procedure and it is well implemented but he said the factory cannot be fully paperless because on some or other way the paper is used. This was being analyzed by the interview and rest detailed version or the explanations will be done in the results part of the book chapter.

So, Sphoorti Machining Tools Private Ltd. company has stated the above distinguishments in their smart procedures and between which the challenges or the impacts whether positive or negative have been discussed above and more will detail discussed in the next part of the Thesis after cumulating of both interviews discussion and analyzing of both the interviews to answer proper solutions for our thesis problem statement. Hence the company has adopted many smart solutions, which have been given a huge topic of discussion for the company being smart and talking about the repercussions of the smart technologies being adopted in positive or negative ways. Starting from Real-time tracker, visual factor and on, online inspections or e-Shopx paperless solutions with little challenges as well as successfully discussed with us and we analyzed successfully the impacts at the industrial level [25, 26, 30 31].

For the second Interview with Tata Motors, i.e. the vehicle plant of Tata Motors in Pune, we interviewed the manager and the 2 team members of that vehicle plant. There is a manufacturing unit of some Tata cars like zest, bolt, Indicia, and some other models as well. In 2011, the company top engineers and managers decided to change the manufacturing operation to adopt smart products or technology to be more efficient for the company as told in the interview. Tata motors were facing severe system failures of their servers from the sporadic server failures (this term was being taken by them in the interview). The main motive of all time was the quality to its customers hence they took support to make their manufacturing with smart solutions of getting MES (Manufacturing Execution System) with automated real-time, information sharing process with quality gates in which when the defect occurs or detected then the measures were to be taken with the automatic alerts systems and communication which is traceable or it is also said as Meta smart factory. Tata Motors bought this technology and made a contract with the most popular Rockwell automation solutions for building a new MES for their manufacturing plant in Pune. During the interview, we analyzed the impacts of the smart products used by them in the content grid below that will be giving us, in brief, the analyzed version from the interview about the impacts of smart products or the technology in the manufacturing unit or the industry [31–33].

Performing the tasks and also they said in the future they will be planning to automate their other plants as well, When it was asked all the *challenges they face* with the current MES which they have right now because our research thesis focus on the challenges of the smart products as well so that we can get the full insight of the current smart manufacturing scenario so that in future problems could be solve by the research and companies get full overview of all the impacts and challenges of the current system and they can build on using some of the other or their own manufacturing firms as their own smart by adopting them as the new smart manufacturing processes easy. Through the interview firstly our main focused topic was the challenges and impacts, so we first got to know the challenges they feel it still has in their new MES. The challenges that were being discussed with the manager of Tata motor smart plant of Pune was not so complex but we did our research through in-depth interview, market content analysis approach and industry insights knowledge and we saw that operational risk are always the first challenge they found in their new MES apart from having many new positive impacts on the system, we found it as an operational risk in which it can be any unforeseen circumstances like the improper implementation of the process and it can be the software or the hardware issues, or It might be possible that there is no certain training to provide to the employees and the process can't be learned or implemented as it is supposed to do and so there must be a regular inspection at every stage of the manufacturing process in a smart manufacturing system that they followed in their plant to check them as a smoothly going process. Sometimes, It can also incur some of the Project management issues as sometimes due to some unrelated problems occur may be due to technical or some working scenario related then in that case, the length of the project or the work associated i.e. the manufacturing got incurred as well. Also, we have been told in the interview by a team member that *'Change Risk is also a risk factor the challenge for them in the start of the new MES system that they followed as in the start'*, they tend to know related issues, workers could not really perform the actions according to the process and so they were supposed to give the workers or employees into training and knowledge and which led to a little bit of cost-incur to them but in overall it was a happy process for them as well moreover, that was the reason they started the smart technologies or adopting smart products in their company.

Also, when we discussed some of the pros and the success of the smart project they implemented in their company by adopting the new MES system and hence made their whole company with other two plants fully connected enterprise and it helps the manufacturing process easily influenced connected and with tracking all the data and information and hence they up-graded their data floor with having a lot of benefits and so their new MES system collects the data turns them into actionable information, it was told in the interview that since it was already in other two plants there was Factory talk system in their other plants as well and now in this plant also and so it was so easy for them when the defect was detected a quality gate and so the alarm is ringed, and making it a huge connected and smart manufacturing company or a manufacturing plant, Also now less time to be given to the process of their manufacturing. Also, it was told to us in the interview that for *the future we have more plans to make their other plants connected as they have the more sales and markets and due to less time consuming for manufacturing and more customer-oriented*, the company is having more profits since the last years which is helping them to succeed. As it was smarter, less time consuming and better market industry dynamics and sales or profits scheme they are following.

13.4   Results

After, the complete analysis we have observed that both the companies which we interviewed in this paper tends to have our problem statement resolved and researched regarding finding the impacts and challenges of their smart connected products at the manufacturing industrial level and we have seen that two firms adapted the process to have smart connected technology for their manufacturing process and we have analyzed in detail after having the in-depth interviews from the firms' managers and their team members associated in the project to know the complete impacts by smart products on their industry. We studied or analyzed after having both the interview with the firms and analyzed the impact on the following- 5 porter services, their industry evolution, their life cycle of manufacturing unit, and about their innovation dynamics.

While interviewing the managers of both the companies, we got tremendous response and which helped us in developing our paper, the way they responded to us and told us each and every challenge, issues or the things they see in their manufacturing market was to be studied and researched in our paper. Following our interviews we got noted various points and analysis which we also shown in the tables of analysis in the above section.

After getting information from the companies' managers, we made a final pact after looking at both the cases that several factors depending on the company's e-business enhancement especially by making or adapting to smart products or the smart technologies in their firms. Both the companies after taking the decisions for making it smart, the companies were in the direction of gaining more e-business driven by the customer because of the smart technology they have adopted, by talking about the innovation dynamics, that is since they took services from the other companies for making more innovative decisions to make them smarter and to get a smart model for their e-business, Likewise both companies with adopting smart technologies, later tend to have many e-businesses in the market and making their e-business manufacturing process facile and effective.

Smart products or machines is the new future of the manufacturing industries to produce their end products smartly or efficiently and this new industrial revolution will increase the e-business of smart builders of machines or the manufacturers who want to adopt a new process of the smart manufacturing and so adopting technologies like IoT (Industrial Internet of Things), connectivity of the devices, flexibility and the safety or security of the industrial happenings.

13.5 Conclusion

We thereby can conclude in-detail that we successfully related and accomplish our initial motivation that was by understanding the impacts of smart products e-business services in the manufacturing market in India or the industrial 4.0. Our initial motivation was to assess the challenges and impacts of the smart products in manufacturing market and what challenges do companies face by adopting the smart products and to assess the industry dynamics and the manufacturing industry dynamics of smart products on how to be used or adopted by the companies and how it is to be implemented in future for the growth for the manufacturing industry in using the smart products as the smart machines. In this paper we researched various industry dynamics factors notably by the host country, challenges associated with political sector, geographical type, the economic sector and investment sector.

Two interviews were held and the results were analyzed in assessing the impacts or challenges of the smart products in the manufacturing market. The qualitative method which we used in this paper for the research purpose that is we are doing some interviews from the managers along with his team members of the companies which are using the smart connected products while doing their manufacturing process, to explore the dynamics of smart product e-business service and the challenges and the impact it creates in the manufacturing industries and qualitative methodology is quiet pragmatic for this kind of research when we do.

Hence, the observations from both the interviews with the companies have let us conclude that there are few impact and few challenges of smart products in the manufacturing market industries and after studying the complete industry dynamics, we were able to conclude and prove our intension to satisfy research needs and motive.

References

1. Daniels, J.D., Radebaugh, L.H., Sullivan, D.P., Salwan, P., *International business: Environments and operations*, Pearson, 2016.
2. Mohelska, H. and Sokolova, M., Smart and connected product changes company's strategy of business orientation. *Appl. Econ.*, 48, 47, 4502–4509, 2016.
3. Oztemel, E. and Gursev, S., The review of literature of industry 4.0 and other related technologies. *J. Intell. Manuf.*, 31, 1, 127–182, 2020.
4. Mont, O.K., Clarifying the concept of product–service system. *J. Cleaner Prod.*, 10, 3, 237–245, 2002.

5. Reim, W., Parida, V., Ortqvist, D., The Product Service Systems (PSS) business models - A systematic literature review. *J. Cleaner Prod.*, 97, 61–75, 2015.

6. Smith, K.J., Rosenberg, D.L., Timothy Haight, G., An assessment of the psychometric properties of the Perceived Stress Scale-10 (PSS 10) with business and accounting students. *Account. Perspect.*, 13, 1, 29–59, 2014.

7. Chow, D.C. and Schoenbaum, T.J., *International business transactions: Problems, cases, and materials*, Wolters Kluwer Law & E-business, 2020.

8. Chowdhury, S., Haftor, D., Pashkevich, N., Smart Product-Service Systems (Smart PSS) in industry firms: A literature review. *Proc. CIRP*, 73, 26–31, 2018.

9. Baines, T.S., Lightfoot, H.W., Evans, S., Neely, A., Greenough, R., Alcock, J.R., Peppard, J., State-of-the-art in product-service systems. *Proc. Inst. Mech. Eng., Part B: J. Eng. Manuf.*, 221, 10, 1543–1552, 2007.

10. Tukker, A. and Tischner, U., Product services in the research field: Past, present and future. Reflections from a decade of research. *J. Cleaner Prod.*, 14, 17, 1552–1556, 2006.

11. Scherer, J.O., Kloeckner, A.P., Ribeiro, J.L.D., Pezzotta, G., Pirola, F., Product-Service System (PSS) design: Using design thinking and business analytics to improve PSS design, in: *8th CIRP IPSS Conference. Product-Service Systems Across Life Cycle*, vol. 47, pp. 341–346, 2016.

12. Abramowicz, W., Filipowska, A., Kaczmarek, M., Kaczmarek, T., Semantically enhanced business process modelling notation. *Semantic Technologies for Business and Information Systems Engineering (Concepts and Applications)*, pp. 259–275, 2012.

13. Tukker, A., Eight types of product–service system, experiences from SusProNet. *Bus. Strategy Environ.*, 13, 4, 246–260, 2004.

14. Rijsdijk, S.A. and Hultink, E.J., How today's consumers perceive tomorrow's smart products. *J. Prod. Innov. Manage.*, 26, 1, 24–42, 2009.

15. Davis, S. and Botkin, J., Coming of knowledge-based business. *Harv. E-bus. Rev.*, 72, 5, 165–70, 1994.

16. Rust, R.T. and Kannan, P.K., E-service: A new paradigm for business in the electronic environment. *Commun. ACM*, 46, 6, 36–42, 2003.

17. Wang, Z., Chen, C.H., Zheng, P., Li, X., Khoo, L.P., A novel data-driven graph-based requirement elicitation framework. *Adv. Eng. Inf.*, 42, 100983, 2019.

18. Lorenz, M., Rüßmann, M., Strack, R., Lueth, K.L., *Man and machine in industry 4.0: How will technology transform the industrial workforce through 2025*, p. 2, The Boston Consulting Group, 2015.

19. Gilchrist, A., *Industry 4.0: The industrial Internet of Things*, Press, 2016.

20. Karabegovic, I., Karabegovic, E., Mahmic, M., Husak, E., Implementation of industry 4.0 and industrial robots, in: *International Conference "New Technologies, Development and Applications"*, pp. 3–14, June 2019.

21. Pazienza, A., Macchiarulo, N., Vitulano, F., Fiorentini, A., Cammisa, M., Rigutini, L., Trevisi, A., *Novel integrated industrial approach with cobots in*

the age of industry 4.0 through conversational interaction and computer vision, Press, 2019.

22. Purohit, S.R. and Shantha, V., Implementation of 5s methodology in a manufacturing industry. *Int. J. Sci. Eng. Res.*, 6, 8, 225–231, 2015.

23. Yerpude, S. and Singhal, T.K., IoT & supported SMART supply chain management for online retail management (e-retail)-empirical research. *Int. J. Logist. Syst. Manage.*, 36, 3, 441–461, 2020.

24. Al Omoush, K.S., Understanding the impact of intellectual capital on E-business entrepreneurial orientation and competitive agility: An empirical study. *Inf. Syst. Front.*, 24, 2, 549–562, 2022.

25. Setiawan, A.B., Dunan, A., Mudjianto, B., Policies and innovations of financial technology business models in the digital economy era on the E-business ecosystem in Indonesia, in: *Handbook of Research on Green, Circular, and Digital Economies as Tools for Recovery and Sustainability*, pp. 22–42, IGI Global, 2022.

26. Alsheyadi, A., A contingent perspective on the development of e-business tools and performance: A review. *Asian J. Bus. Manage.*, 10, 2, 17–26, 2022.

27. Minhas, A. and Emilsson, S., *How can an organization with B2B experience enter a new market utilizing a B2C e-commerce strategy instead?: A case study of a fragrance company*, 2022.

28. Li, J. and Zhang, X., The export operation mode and optimization strategy of crossborder e-commerce enterprises integrating data mining algorithms. *Wireless Commun. Mobile Comput.*, 2022, 1–13, 2022.

29. Kittlaus, H.-B., Management of software as a business, in: *Software Product Management*, pp. 7–50, 2022.

30. Toffel, M.W., The growing strategic importance of end-of-life product management. *Calif. Manage. Rev.*, 45, 3, 102–129, 2003.

31. Gorschek, T., Gomes, A., Pettersson, A., Torkar, R., Introduction of a process maturity model for market-driven product management and requirements engineering. *J. Softw.: Evol. Process*, 24, 1, 83–113, 2012.

32. Xu, F., Li, Y., Feng, L., The influence of big data system for used product management on manufacturing–remanufacturing operations. *J. Cleaner Prod.*, 209, 782–794, 2019.

33. Li, C.Z., Chen, Z., Xue, F., TR Kong, X., Xiao, B., Lai, X., Zhao, Y., A blockchain and IoT-based smart product-service system for the sustainability of prefabricated housing construction. *J. Cleaner Prod.*, 286, 125–391, 2021.

14

Analysis of Lakeshore Images Obtained from Unmanned Aerial Vehicles

Ivana Čermáková[1*] and Roman Danel[1,2]

*[1]Faculty of Economics, VSB – Technical University of Ostrava,
Ostrava, Czech Republic*
*[2]Department of Mechanical Engineering, Institute of Technology and Businesses in
České Budějovice, Ostrava, Czech Republic*

Abstract

Water bodies and their surrounding areas are often problematic when it comes to remote sensing. However, unmanned aerial vehicles (UAVs) can be used for both emergency events (e.g. floods) and for studying specific issues in small water bodies, such as shoreline changes or invasive plant growth. This chapter discusses the possibilities of analyzing lakeshores using UAVs and presents a case study focused on current issues in the area of lakeshore studies.

Keywords: Unmanned aerial vehicles, lakeshore images, remote sensing

14.1 Introduction

Unmanned Aerial Vehicles
Unmanned aerial vehicles (UAVs) are defined as aerial vehicles that do not have pilots and are categorized into three main groups [1], namely,

- UAVs,
- Remotely piloted vehicles (RPVs) and
- Drones.

Corresponding author: ivana.cermakova@vsb.cz

Ahmed A. Elgnar, Vigneshwar M, Krishna Kant Singh and Zdzislaw Polkowski (eds.) Handbook of Computational Sciences: A Multi and Interdisciplinary Approach, (299–322) © 2023 Scrivener Publishing LLC

In general, the public at large does not recognize the term unmanned vehicles, and all three groups are seen as UAVs. More technical communities traditionally recognize the terms RPV and UAV. RPVs are remotely piloted vehicles controlled from a remote position. RPVs are always UAVs, but UAVs are not always RPVs, as UAVs can fly autonomously, and flights can be pre-programmed. The term drone describes a UAV that tends to be an automatized part of a monitoring system, which, for example, discharges the direction (scans the area of interest) based on system instructions [2].

In the context of aerial vehicles, the term unmanned aerial systems (UAS) has been introduced. UAS can be explained as a system composed of aerial vehicle, control station and necessary flight components [3].

The cost of buying aerial vehicles was initially high, but with increased interest and production, the price has decreased (specialized UAVs, e.g. with laser scanners added for use in agriculture, are still produced to order and have high prices). Moreover, in many cases, the use of this technology by public administrations has led to a reduction in cost and producer prices. The total cost of mapping landscapes using UAVs is negligible these days, especially when the mapping is repeated. Using a UAV that is remotely piloted by a human is a fast and safe method of acquiring images that does not pose a risk to human health, as areas that would be dangerous to monitor using field monitoring, such as marshes, can also be monitored [4].

Primarily, the cost of using UAVs is divided into two groups: one-time and recurring costs. One-time costs are expenses that are incurred only once and are not dependent on the number of hours of operation of the equipment. A typical example of this type of cost is the cost of transporting the UAV to the customer. One-time costs also include [4]

- Costs related to the equipment placed on the UAV. These costs are often the highest. However, it depends on the equipment because, in the case of an unusual vehicle modification, the price will undoubtedly be high.
- Transportation costs. For one-time imaging, the UAV must usually be moved from its base to the desired location.
- Costs for travelling technical support. These costs arise if it is necessary to use a technical support team during mapping. This team usually performs most of the operations related to the entire imaging mission, such as setting up the UAV and controlling the UAV when in flight. These costs are typically included in the mission cost.

- The cost of acquiring a drone. Many users do not take advantage of the opportunity to own a UAV. In the case of photography, these users tend to rent a UAV and carry out the mission either by themselves or with the help of a specialized company. The exception is organizations that repeatedly carry out imaging, as it is more advantageous for them to purchase their own UAV and not only from a financial point of view.

Recurring expenses explain why the cost is proportionally high to the number of UAV flight hours. Usually, these expenses are also called costs per hour of operation. Recurring costs are divided into [5]

- Direct costs. Usually, these include fuel, batteries, oil and routine equipment maintenance. In addition, the cost of hiring UAV operators is also included in direct costs.
- Insurance cost. The insurance cost is determined by the degree of insurer risk and the number of persons insured.
- Communication support costs. Communication costs must be included for each hour of operation and include the cost of team member communications.
- Mission planning and data analysis costs. These costs are also calculated proportionally according to flight hours.

It should be mentioned that the cost of military UAV missions is many times greater than the cost of civilian missions [4].

It is also necessary to mention the influence that the weather has on flight planning. If the temperature drops below 0°C, launching a UAV is not recommended for two reasons: ice can form on the propellers, and the equipment can be damaged as it contains electronic elements, including the battery. Furthermore, the lens can mist up when it is foggy or if the temperature is below 0°C, leading to poor-quality images. In addition, orientation is difficult in fog. It should also be noted that flying in strong winds is not recommended because of the inability to reliably control the UAV and the possibility of damage being caused to the UAV. The same applies to flying in heavy rain. The limitations are similar for every UAV, but each UAV can have its own additional restrictions, and the limitations are listed in the UAV's handbook [3].

14.2   Possibilities of Processing Images Acquired from Unmanned Aerial Vehicles

First, the purpose of the study must be defined. Available data and methods depend on the purpose of the study. To increase the effectiveness of image processing, the process should be divided into sub-steps: define the purpose, location and users of the study; define the relevant and available data and vehicle; determine usable image processing methods; evaluate and interpret the results.

14.3   Defining Purpose, Location and Users of the Study

First, it is necessary to determine the purpose of the research, i.e. what the researcher wants to achieve and what the aim of the research is. The choice of location depends on the purpose of the research. It is necessary to eliminate areas where flying is not permitted. These areas can be found on the Civil Aviation Authority website, which has up-to-date information. If the chosen location is in an area where it is not possible to fly, it is necessary to determine whether the ban on flying is temporary or permanent (e.g. in national parks). If the area has a permanent prohibition on flights, it will be necessary to look for another suitable location. If the site has a temporary prohibition on flights, the period when it is possible to fly needs to be determined. If this period is satisfactory, the contracting authority gathers all other necessary information (e.g. by contacting the managers of the relevant area and asking about the necessity of a flight permit), and the selection of the location is then successfully completed by obtaining a permit. In the event of unsuitable flight times, it would be necessary to find another location. After determining the availability of the site for the given flight, it is advisable to evaluate other risk factors in the given location, e.g. the nearby presence of power lines or densely concentrated built-up areas. If there are no risk factors in the given location or the level of risk is considered negligible, the selected location is suitable. If the risk factors are significant, another location must be chosen. Risk factors depend on the area in question and are both general (e.g. the nearby presence of power lines) and specific to each research purpose (e.g. in the case of shoreline monitoring, it is not appropriate to map a lake whose bank is densely covered with vegetation because the vegetation, including treetops, can then be seen, and the shoreline would not be identifiable).

The users are defined after the location has been determined and acquired. The type/types of users of the research results are defined. Defining the users is helpful in terms of further steps; for example, in some cases, a different type of sensor can be used for mapping when, for a given group of users, lower image quality is sufficient. This consideration can lead to considerably less expense.

14.4   Suitable and Available Data and Vehicle

This sub-step depends on the ownership of the UAV. When the researcher has their own UAV and primarily uses only this vehicle with a fixed/integrated camera, the possibility of recording different types of data is low. On the other hand, if the researcher does not have a UAV or needs a specialized UAV and camera, the supply of relevant and available data and vehicles becomes more plentiful.

In the case of the purchase of data by an external company, the entire process after the initial defining purpose, location and users continues with the determination of available companies and devices. A market analysis of companies that provide land surveying/mapping using UAVs is carried out. The type of device, the type of sensor, the cost-effectiveness of image acquisition, and the prestige of or satisfaction of customers with the given company are taken into account.

If multiple devices are available, the research must take, at a minimum, the following factors/questions into account. First, what data is to be captured (data from the RGB band, thermal band, other band or a combination of these bands)? This factor applies to a UAV with an integrated camera. Second, at what resolution is the data to be captured? This factor applies to a UAV with an integrated camera. How large is the area? In the case of a large area of interest, for example, from two UAV devices providing the same quality data thanks to a camera with the same specification, the battery capacity and other factors will logically be taken into account. If it is possible to fly over the entire area with one device at once (without battery change), while in the case of another device should it be necessary to interrupt the acquiring and replace the battery and then complete the acquiring, the first device will be the obvious choice.

The choice of a camera is also a decision that has to be taken. Here, it is appropriate to distinguish between UAVs with integrated cameras and UAVs (often custom-made vehicles) to which a camera or cameras can be attached. In both cases, it is necessary, at a minimum, to take the following factors/questions into account: first, what data is to be captured (data from the RGB band, thermal band, other band or a combination of these bands)? Second, at what resolution is the data to be captured? What other outputs, such as video, must be created? What additional information needs to be gathered during the flight? For example, in some cases, it is necessary to have a device available that has global navigation satellite system capability with real-time kinematics technology (GNSS RTK), which saves this information to the data during the flight.

From this initial study, a few firms that appear suitable for the imaging process should be selected. From these companies, it is necessary to select one that will perform the image acquisition; therefore, the requirement is to select a suitable machine and company. The choice of device and company can take different forms. The process can start with a straightforward comparison, e.g. according to price, a more sophisticated method, such as Fuller's triangle method, or a pairwise comparison. The second variant, as well as other variants used in managerial decision-making, is very often used by public administrations and is financed by national and international grants, where the process of selecting a suitable company and machine using sophisticated decision-making methods is a requirement. In the second variant, several criteria are usually compiled, which are ranked according to importance. For example, when choosing a UAV and a company, the criteria could be the following: the band in which the data is provided, the type of sensor, the spatial resolution of the resulting images, the price and the reliability/prestige of the company. The weight of individual criteria depends on the nature of the contract. Subsequently, the available options and the companies that provide them are evaluated within the framework of particular criteria and ranked accordingly. The vehicle and company with the highest scores are then selected to implement the contract.

14.5   Usable Image Processing Methods

The methods that can be used depend on the purpose of the research. This sub-chapter contains the most practical methods: classification methods, spectral indices and invasive plant detection by UAV.

Classification. Classification methods are divided into two main groups [6]: traditional approaches and modern approaches. Traditional approaches are divided into supervised classification (i.e. classification with a teacher or user-controlled classification) and unsupervised classification (i.e. classification without a teacher or automatic classification). Modern approaches are divided into neuron networks, textural classification, fuzzy logic classification and contextual classification.

Classification is a technique for obtaining more detailed information about the spatial distribution of the investigated phenomenon from the existing image recording. This process produces an output dataset based on the input data. Each element in the input file is assigned a characteristic value, usually a collection of spatial elements that can be raster cells, points, lines or polygons. A classified input image is created if the number of these characteristic values is small compared to the range of input data. In addition, the result of the classification can be used as input for the next classification, and the concept of the reclassification would then be discussed [7].

In supervised classification, the researcher pre-defines the so-called training areas, which specify numerical descriptions of the elements in the algorithm that need to be classified. The guided classification consists of four subsequent steps [8].

- First, the training area needs to be defined. A training area must be created for each category to be identified in the image. The choice of training areas is up to the researcher and affects the success and failure of the classification. Therefore, the selection of training areas should be supported by supporting data, e.g. information gained from processing of the area from a landscape survey. Training data must be complete and representative. Completeness means that all classes to be defined must be characterized. Representativeness means that the areas selected for training should represent the given class or category.

- Additionally, spectral features need to be generated. Using statistical characteristics, the training surfaces are assessed in terms of whether they appropriately characterize the given classes and whether the trained classes differ sufficiently in their spectral behavior. An evaluation of the suitability of training areas can be carried out using various methods, such as by using a histogram or spectrogram.

- Moreover, a suitable decision rule needs to be created. A decision rule, also called a classifier, assigns individual image elements to one of the classes. The most used classifiers are minimum cluster center distance, rectangle, 'K' nearest neighbor, maximum likelihood and Bayesian classifiers.

- Finally, a specific class needs to be assigned to the elements of the resulting image. The subsequent evaluation of the classification is still related to this step since it is not possible to end the classification without an assessment. For example, the evaluation can be completed using an error matrix or a kappa coefficient.

In contrast to supervised classification, unsupervised classification does not use training surfaces for its own classification [8]. Instead, its principle is based on examining unknown pixels and aggregating them into groups based on their tendency to form clusters. The basic assumption is that pixels belonging to the same class are close to each other in the multidimensional space, while pixels of different groups are well separated. Multivariate statistical methods, known as cluster analysis, are then used to define clusters in the multispectral space. The results of the first stage are the spectral classes. When these classes are given some geographic content, they become informational classes. The K-means algorithm and iterative self-organizing data analysis algorithm are among the most used unsupervised classification algorithms. It is also necessary to evaluate the classification, for example, by an error matrix or kappa coefficient.

The above methods, whether supervised or unsupervised, are referred to as per-pixel classification methods. As these classifications always evaluate a given pixel without using any information about its surroundings, modern approaches were developed [8].

- Neural networks can be used for the classification of data as they are able to combine different types of input data. The algorithms are based on the idea of neurons running in the nervous system. Individual neurons are interconnected in a network. Thus, a neuron that becomes a node in this network can have several inputs but only one output. The output of the given node is generated only if the set of inputs generates an output higher than the selected threshold value. Otherwise, output from another node is generated. Neural networks usually contain hidden layers in addition to input and output layers. Usually, the output values are represented by the probability of belonging to a given class.
- Textural classifiers are based on the spatial variability of values in an image, as the variability of certain classes is described by the texture. Textural classifiers are based on the spatial variability of values in an image. These classifiers

are usually used in the case of heterogeneous data when, for example, the area consists of different surfaces – concrete, water bodies, tree crowns and others.

- Fuzzy logic relates to algorithms and decision rules that are not precisely defined at every step and allows a certain degree of uncertainty. The classification of pixels is carried out based on the probability of the pixel belonging to a specific class, which is defined by a membership function. A particular element belonging to a given class acquires either a value between 0 (the pixel certainly does not belong to the given class) and 1 (the pixel certainly belongs to the given class) or a percentage. The result of this method can be a multi-band image, where the image elements of the given band carry probability values of their belonging to one particular class.

- Contextual classifiers are based on the principle of object recognition and classification into individual classes based on studying individual parts of the image in their context. The effort is, therefore, to describe the spatial arrangement of objects in the entire picture. These classifiers attempt to describe and quantify structure and context.

Currently, the use of machine learning techniques and deep learning techniques is on the rise. Because these methods are new, the support of commercial software is still lower than the support of other classification methods. These techniques are often programmed as packages in Python.

The primary purpose of any classification is to classify the given image as efficiently as possible so that it is divided into the appropriate classes with the greatest possible accuracy.

Spectral indices. The vegetation's spectral reflectance is used as a characteristic of its spectral behavior. The different reflectivity in different parts of the electromagnetic spectrum (EM) is used to calculate spectral indices. A subgroup of spectral indices consists of vegetation indices [9]. Vegetation indices use combinations of images from different parts of the spectrum, which highlight the vegetation or show its state of health – suitable if the lakeshore has vegetation cover. The normalized excess green index (NExG), normalized green-red difference index (NGRDI), red-green-blue vegetation index (RGBVI), visible atmospherically resistant index (VARI) and vegetation index of excess green (ExG) are primarily used.

NExG highlights the vegetation (in the formula, subtract and impute from the green part of the EM spectrum) – Formula 14.1 is

$$NExG = \frac{2 \times G - R - B}{G + R + B},$$
(14.1)

where G = values of pixels in the green part of the EM spectrum,
    R = values of pixels in the red part of the EM spectrum and
    B = values of pixels in the blue part of the EM spectrum.

The explanation of variables in Formula 14.1 is similar for all vegetation indices.

NGRDI is an index that highlights vegetation cover from other cover [10], so a shore with vegetation is easily visually separated from water cover. Formula 14.2 is

$$NGRDI = \frac{G - R}{G + R}.$$
(14.2)

RGBVI is mainly used for ascertaining the current state of vegetation and predicting its future state [11]. Formula 14.3 is

$$RGBVI = \frac{(G \times G) - (R \times B)}{(G \times G) + (R \times B)}.$$
(14.3)

VARI is the same as NExG – it highlights the vegetation in the image [12]. Formula 14.4 is

$$VARI = \frac{G - R}{G + R - B}.$$
(14.4)

Finally, ExG is also based on the highlights of the vegetation in the image, but it multiplies the green part of the electromagnetic spectrum to increase the given information [13]. Formula 14.5 is

$$ExG = 2 \times G - R - B.$$
(14.5)

14.6   Invasive-Plant Detection

Invasive plant species contribute to environmental changes, and some can adversely affect the health and safety of residents. Regulation No. 1143/2014 of the European Parliament and the Council of the EU [https://www.legislation.gov.uk/eur/2014/1143] on preventive measures regarding the spread of invasive and alien species has been in force since 01 Jan 2015. One of the tasks the UAVs' image processing capability is used for is the detection of invasive plants and the speed of their spread.

The occurrence of invasive plants can be divided into three categories:

- Point occurrence relates to self-growing individuals that do not form any structures.
- Linear occurrence primarily relates to vegetation on roads, riparian vegetation, vegetation in water reservoirs dams and vegetation that borders agricultural land.
- Widespread occurrence relates to compact spatial structures; the invasive species has a high coverage rate that is either spontaneous or anthropogenically conditioned.

Detection by UAV is characterized by low costs when covering an area of up to 30 ha. At low-flying altitudes, it is possible to achieve higher accuracy than with competing sensing methods (aerial or satellite images). The problem is still the low availability of spectral detectors and their high price.

An analysis of photographs taken by UAVs shows that not all plant stands are easily identifiable. The evaluation can only be carried out where the plants to be detected are not covered by a higher layer (shrubs or trees). An *Impatiens parviflora* stand is a typical example of a plant that cannot be detected by UAVs. *Impatiens glandulifera* is an example of growth that is only partially detectable; it grows in the gaps of bushes or along the edges of forests. Some plants are only highly detectable in the flowering period (*Solidago gigantea*). Other species whose flowers are the same color do not form such dense and extensive stands, and the issue of ID mistakes can also be solved by using optimal flight dates.

Ortho maps are created by photogrammetric processing of a series of vertical RGB photos. These maps enable the identification of plant communities in inaccessible places by field survey. The identification of invasive plants in UAV images (ortho map) requires a certain knowledge of their characteristic features. Unfortunately, a method of fully automated detection of individual species of invasive plants is not yet available.

Based on the analysis of repeated imaging of an area over time, it is possible to evaluate the severity and danger of the spread of invasive plants (Figure 14.1). For selected species that may threaten the environment, analysis can serve as a basis for deciding whether to proceed with the direct disposal of these plants and for establishing a strategy to prevent their further spread.

Some spectral indices can be used for monitoring invasive plants. However, it depends on each type of plant. UAV imaging mostly uses a combination of images from the near infra-red (NIR) part of the EM spectrum, e.g. in invasive plant monitoring focused on *Heracleum mantegazzianum, Fallopia japonica, Ailanthus altissima* and *Robinia pseudoacacia* [14]. The unavailability of NIR images is problematic and can be solved by supervised classification methods when the cover is heterogeneous (when

Figure 14.1 Example of potential *Solidago* invasion directions on a fragment of an orthophoto map from Mszana, Poland [15].

other vegetation has different colors from invasive plants) or by spectral indices when there is low-density vegetation cover in the area of interest.

14.7 Evaluation and Interpretation of the Results

Classification methods are often evaluated using an error matrix and/or kappa coefficient. An error matrix (also known as a confusion matrix) represents the difference between observed and classified values [6]. It is constructed in the form of a square matrix and calculates the overall accuracy of the chosen classification method. It is helpful not only for achieving overall accuracy but also for using multiple classification methods on the same imagery. The error matrix shows if each cover (when using the supervised classification method) was trained well; if not, the difference between observed and classified values will be significant. If that happens, it will be necessary to change the problematic training data, define them again and execute the classification again. The form of the error matrix is shown in Table 14.1.

User accuracy indicates the probability that a pixel assigned to a certain class actually represents that class. It is calculated for each class separately as a proportion of correctly classified pixels (value on the main diagonal) to the number of pixels included in this category (sum in the row corresponding to the assessed class).

Producer accuracy is the ratio between the correctly classified pixels (again, the value on the main diagonal) and the pixels used for testing the given class (the sum in the column, i.e. the total number of pixels of the training areas of the given class or the number of points used for testing the given class).

Table 14.1 Error matrix for evaluation of classification methods.

		Reference data (observed data)		
		Cover 1	**Cover 2**	**Total**
Classified data	Cover 1	True/True	True/False	**Classified Cover 1**
	Cover 2	True/False	True/True	**Classified Cover 2**
	Total	**Observed Cover 1**	**Observed Cover 2**	**Overall**

Finally, *overall accuracy* is given for the entire classification. It is calculated as the proportion of all correctly classified pixels (sum of values on the main diagonal) to the total number of classified pixels. User, producer and overall accuracy is recalculated as a percentage, while the rest of the table provides values in points [6].

The Kappa coefficient (Formula 14.6) compares the accuracy determined from the error matrix with the accuracy achievable by purely randomly assigning pixels to individual classes. The value of the Kappa coefficient can range from zero to one. Higher values mean a better result (agreement), and above 0.75 is a good classification result. A value of one would mean that for a given classification, 100% of the errors that were created during the purely random classification of pixels into individual classes have been avoided [16].

$$\kappa = \frac{N \sum x_{ii} - \sum x_{i+} x_{+i}}{N^2 - \sum x_{i+} x_{+i}}, \qquad (14.6)$$

where: N – number of elements, x_{i+} (x_{+i}) – elements in the *i*th row (column).

When there are available GNSS RTK coordinates, it is possible to compare the classified shoreline to measured coordinates [17–19].

Interpretation of the results is inherent in the visualization of the results [20]. Both, interpretation and visualization, depend mainly on the users of the study. In the first case (interpretation), it will be necessary to decide whether, for example, map output or raster output is appropriate and understandable. Often, the information obtained, e.g. a change in the size of the shoreline, is easier to interpret with the help of graphs and tables, especially if the study is aimed at the general public. In the case of distribution to GIS workers (it means staffs able processed the data in GIS software), the outputs will likely be distributed in the form of map or raster outputs (with standard cartographic information such as legend or scale). From the point of view of detected changes to water bodies or their shorelines, information is provided on the detected extent of changes. For example, from the graphs of changes made earlier, it was found that in the next period, the value changed by 20%, and it is, therefore, necessary to interpret the finding as, for example, a decrease in the water area by 20%. This information should be easy to understand, even for laypeople. Separate graphs and tables do not inform laypeople; it is still necessary to interpret the results so that it is clear what findings were gathered from the monitoring of the water's surface.

14.8 Analysis of Lakeshore – Koblov Lake

This sub-chapter shows the process analysis of lakeshore images obtained from a UAV and applied to concrete research/case studies. Koblov Lake was used as an area of interest for shoreline detection, and the study of changes used the classification method. For the detection of invasive plants, the spectral index was used. The results and their interpretation were chosen for general computer users via images and written descriptions.

14.9 Area of Interest

The area of interest is located in the Silesian Ostrava district of the city of Ostrava in the Moravian-Silesian Region (Figure 14.2). The size of the lake is 0.2 km², The lake was established 35 years ago and is used for breeding carp, which is released in the winter months [21].

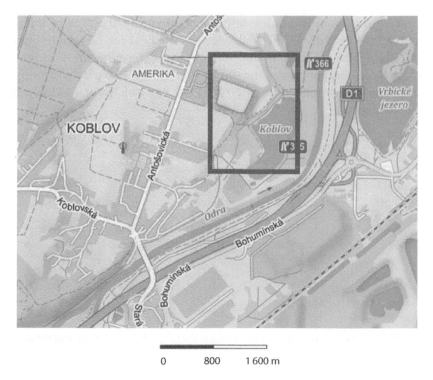

0   800   1 600 m

Figure 14.2 Location of Koblov lake [22].

14.10   Data Acquisition

Koblov Lake is partly surrounded by inaccessible vegetation in the summer months. Therefore, observation using the in-situ method would be difficult. However, the available part of the shoreline was surveyed using the GNSS RTK technique (Figure 14.3a). The entire area of interest, i.e. a section of Koblov Lake, was scanned using a UAV. DJI MAVIC 2 (Figure 14.3b) was used for Koblov Lake.

A DJI MAVIC 2 has propeller drives and four engines and weighs 907 g. The maximum flight duration is 31 minutes, and the maximum distance is 18 km. This UAV cannot be used under these conditions: temperature below -10°C; wind speed faster than 10 m/s; fog with visibility below 100 m; icing on propellers; drizzle, rain or snow.

In all cases, the flight height was 65 m, and the flight height was set in the UAV's software before each flight. The images were taken with 80% overlap in both directions. The time horizon was chosen according to weather and other conditions to cover a long period of time, namely, 19 May 2021 to 29 Sep 2021, with flight dates of 19 May 2021, 27 Jul 2021 and 29 Sep 2021.

During the acquisition, dovetail targets placed in the area of interest were used (an example of dovetail targets in the field can be seen in Figure 14.4). The GNSS RTK technique was used to determine the position of drifting targets and points on the shore. The Trimble R10 geodetic receiver and online corrections from the CZEPOS network were used for the implementation.

(a)   (b)

Figure 14.3 (a) Koblov shoreline surveyed using the GNSS RTK technique and (b) DJI MAVIC 2 [Source: Authors, 2022] [23].

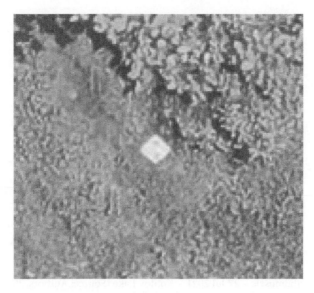

Figure 14.4 Dovetail target placed on the shore of Koblov Lake [Source: Authors, 2022].

14.11   Data Pre-Processing

The camera integrated into the DJI MAVIC 2 provided images from the visible part of the EM spectrum. An orthomosaic was created from the images in the Agisoft Metashape software (version 1. 7. 4). First, all images were uploaded to the software. This was followed by removing reprojection errors and other necessary operations before importing the tracking points. The tracking points are the points that the RTK uses to focus on the targets (Figure 14.3) so that their positions are accurate. The next step is the marker placement step. The targets are found in the images, and the researcher places markers at these locations to create the image references (which is the next step) as accurately as possible. Then, one random point is selected as a control point. Root mean square error during georeferencing is a maximum of 9 cm (in the case of control points) and a maximum of 3.7 cm in the case of other points. Then, the data is optimized. After that, it is possible to create other outputs, such as point cloud, Digital Model of Terrain (DMT) or an orthomosaic. After creating an orthomosaic, it is advisable to crop the output only to the area of interest. An orthomosaic from 27 Jul 2021 is shown in Figure 14.5.

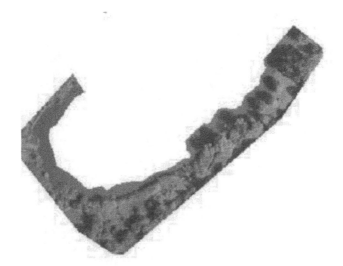

Figure 14.5 Orthomosaic – 27 Jul 2021 – Koblov Lake [Source: Authors, 2022].

14.12   Data Processing and Evaluation

Due to the availability of exact coordinates for parts of the shoreline, thanks to RTK, it is possible to use these data as verification data. Thus, the classified image and the shoreline extracted from it are measured relative to the coordinates obtained from the Trimble R10. First, it is advisable to define the area to which this process will apply. Due to the inaccessible shore due to vegetation (left part of Figure 14.6), the area of interest is reduced to a smaller section of Koblov Lake (right part of Figure 14.6).

The area was classified by the interactive supervised classification algorithm in ArcGIS Desktop (version 10. 8. 1) because the unsupervised

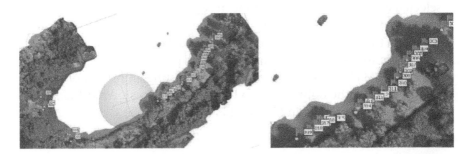

Figure 14.6 Reduction of the area of interest [Source: Authors, 2022].

classification methods provided unsuitable results. Interactive supervised classification is one of the supervised classifications.

The methodology is based on the maximum likelihood classification. Since this is a controlled classification method, it is necessary to determine the training classes first. The training data contained a total of two classes: water (green objects in Figure 14.7) and cover (red objects in Figure 14.7). The water class contained 10 training samples, and the cover class contained 20 training samples.

The chosen classification (interactive supervised classification) was calculated based on the training data. The classified image was converted to a polygon using the Raster to Polygon tool. Subsequently, the created polygon representing the water surface was selected. In this case, more polygons representing water cover were selected and merged. The water surface extracted was imported into the original image containing the coordinates from the RTK (Figure 14.8 – the blue polygon represents the classified water cover, and the orange points represent the shoreline coordinates measured by GNSS RTK Trimble R10).

The resulting shoreline (in this case, the edge line of the resulting polygon in the area of interest) is compared with the coordinates, and the difference between the actual (measured) value of the coordinates (coordinates acquired from Trimble R10) and the value obtained by classification is determined. The calculation is based on the statistical method of least squares.

For detection of the invasive plant can be used only methods using the visible part of the EM spectrum because only images from UAVs are

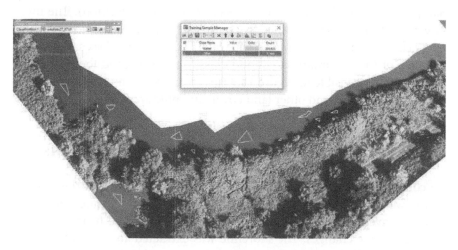

Figure 14.7 Creating training samples from the orthomosaic from 27 Jul 2021 [Source: Authors, 2022].

Figure 14.8 Classified water cover combined with an orthomosaic and the RTK coordinates - 27 Jul 2021. [Authors, 2022].

available. NGRDI, one of the spectral indices focused on highlighting vegetation, was used first. Because of other vegetation inherence, the invasive plant cannot be distinguished from other vegetation, and, consequently, the whole problematic vegetation was highlighted. Supervised methods of classification were used instead. The best results were achieved using the maximum likelihood classification. Because of the base of the method and different land cover in the images, three training classes were chosen: invasive plants, other vegetation and land cover on the shore and water. Before the classification was chosen, training classes were chosen in Training Sample Manager (the same process was used for classification). The invasive plants training set contained five samples; the other vegetation and land cover class contained six samples; the water class contained six samples. An example of the maximum likelihood classification method focused on an invasive plant is visible in Figure 14.9 (green areas are invasive plants, grey areas are vegetation and other land cover, and blue areas are water areas).

14.13   Evaluation and Interpretation of the Results

By comparing the two types of coordinates, it was found that the classification was 95% accurate in the shoreline area (the area defined in Figure 14.6), on average. The classified images can therefore be further used to study shoreline changes. The shoreline was extracted and smoothed from the polygons. The original polygon and the smoothed shoreline are shown in Figure 14.10. Individual periods are distinguished by color. Green shows

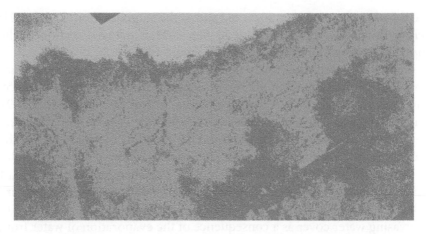

Figure 14.9 An invasive plant classified using the maximum likelihood classification - 27 Jul 2021 [Source: Authors, 2022].

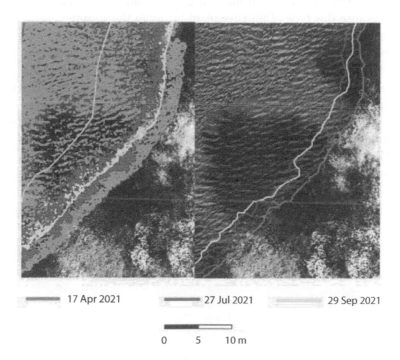

17 Apr 2021   27 Jul 2021   29 Sep 2021

0   5   10 m

Figure 14.10 The original polygon and the extracted and smoothed shoreline of Koblov lake [Source: Authors, 2022].

the shoreline from 19 May 2021; red shows the shoreline from 27 Jul 2021; yellow shows the shoreline from 29 Sep 2021; a detailed section of the shoreline is shown in the entire area in Figure 14.10.

Some fluctuations are clearly visible in Figure 14.10. For exact information, the information about the shoreline was exported to Microsoft Excel and then recalculated. The change between 19 Apr 2021 and 27 Jul 2021 was 5%. The first date was chosen as a rudimentary value (100%). The second date had decreased water cover, and the shoreline moved to 95% of the water area. The last monitoring date, 29 Sep 2021, showed decreased water cover, and the shoreline had moved another 3%. Therefore, during the last survey, the water area consisted of 92% of the water cover from the primary value. These values are the norm (determined by hydrologic); a factor of decreasing water cover as a consequence of the evaporation of water from open water bodies must also be considered [24].

The second part of the assessment consisted of results from the detection of invasive plants. The invasive plants were detected in parts of the area (shown in Figure 14.9). The images from 19 May 2021 did not contain the invasive plant because this type of invasive plant grows in the summer. Growth and difference between 27 Jul 2021 (the left part of Figure 14.11) and 29 Sep 2021 (the right part of Figure 14.11) are shown in Figure 14.10, where the green parts are invasive plants, the blue part is water, and the green parts are other vegetation and land cover. The acquisition image from 29 Sep 2021 was taken after it had rained, which is why most of the area is classified as water.

The difference between 27 Jul 2021 and 29 Sep 2021 was calculated by the number of pixels classified as invasive plants (the green pixels in Figure 14.11). The image from 27 Jul 2021 is 82% invasive plants; the image from 29 Sep 2021 is 21% invasive plants. The last date was past the blooming period of these types of invasive plants. The size of the area with invasive plants was enormous. For the research providing detailed information

Figure 14.11 An abundance of invasive plants on the shore of Koblov Lake, 27 Jul 2021 and 29 Sep 2021. [Source: Authors, 2022].

should be the area monitored in the next years in the same period to finding the changes. If the area covered by invasive plants is growing, it can be predicted, and the areas where protective cover should be implied can be known. A concrete definition of invasive plant/plants should be provided by the specialist. These future works are in progress now.

14.14   Conclusion

This chapter focuses on the possibility of analyzing lake images acquired from UAVs. The chapter first explains the basic methodology, namely, the term UAV. Then, a process of image processing is proposed. The process is divided into subsequent steps: defining the purpose, location and users of the study; relevant and available data and vehicle; usable methods of image processing (classification, spectral indices and invasive plant detection); evaluation and interpretation of the results. The whole process is demonstrated using one case study, Koblov Lake, with an emphasis on shoreline changes and invasive plant detection.

References

1. Work, Jr., E.A. and Gilmer, D.S., Utilisation of satellite data for inventorying prairie ponds and lakes. *Photogramm. Eng. Remote Sens.*, 42, 5, 685–694, 1976.
2. Fahlstrom, P.G. and Gleason, T.J., *Introduction to UAV systems*, 4th ed., vol. xxv, p. 280, John Wiley & Sons, Chichester, 2012.
3. Civil Aviation Authority, 2011, Accessed 02 Mar 2018. [Online]. Available: http://www.caa.cz.
4. Civil UAV Assessment Team, Earth observation and the role of UAVs: A capabilities assessment, 2010, Accessed 14 Feb 2018. [Online]. Available: https://www.nasa.gov/centers/dryden/research/civuav/index.html.
5. Baker, P. *et al.*, Using shorelines for autonomous air vehicle guidance. *Comput. Vision Image Understanding*, 114, 723–729, 2010.
6. Lillesand, T.M., Kiefer, R.W., Chipman, J.W., *Remote sensing and image interpretation*, 7th ed, John Wiley & Sons, Inc., Hoboken, 2015.
7. De By, R.A. *et al.*, *Principles of geographic information systems*, Netherlands: The International Institute for Geo-Information Science and Earth Observation, 2001.
8. Lillesand, T.M. *et al.*, *Remote sensing and image interpretation*, 6th ed, John Wiley & Sons, Inc., Hoboken, 2008.
9. Qi, J. *et al.*, View-atmosphere-soil effects on vegetation indices derived from SPOT images, in: *Physical Measurements and Signatures in Remote Sensing*,

Presented at 5th International Colloquium, J.J. Hunt (Ed.), pp. 785–790, Courchevel, France, CRC Press, February 1991.

10. Tucker, C.J., Red and photographic infrared linear combinations for monitoring vegetation. *Remote Sens. Environ.*, 8, 127–150, 1979.

11. Bendig, J. *et al.*, Combining UAV-based plant height from crop surface models, visible, and near infrared vegetation indices for biomass monitoring in barley. *Int. J. Appl. Earth Obs. Geoinf.*, 39, 79–87, 2015.

12. Gitelson, A.A. *et al.*, Novel algorithms for remote estimation of vegetation fraction. *Remote Sens. Environ.*, 80, 76–87, 2002.

13. Woebbecke, D. *et al.*, Color indices for weed identification under various soil, residue, and lighting conditions. *Trans*, 38, 259–269, 1995.

14. Müllerová, J. *et al.*, *Metodika mapování invazních druhů pomocí dálkového průzkumu [Methodology for invasive species mapping using remote sensing]*, Botanický ústav AV ČR [Botanical Institute of the Academy of Sciences of the Czech Republic], Průhonice, 2017.

15. INVARO, Hodnocení zdrojů a rizik spojených s invazivními druhy rostlin [Assessment of resources and risks associated with invasive plant species]. Output from the scientific project INVARO. Accessed 20 Jun 2022. [Online]. Available: http://invaro.vsb.cz/results, 2019.

16. Dobrovolný, P., *Dálkový průzkum Země. Digitální zpracování obrazu* [Remote land survey. Digital image processing], 1998.

17. Papakonstantinou, A. *et al.*, Coastline zones identification and 3D coastal mapping using UAV spatial data. *IJGI*, 5, 75, 1–14, 2016.

18. Templin, T., Popielarczyk, D., Kosecki, R., Application of low-cost fixed-wing UAV for inland lakes shoreline investigation. *Pure Appl. Geophys.*, 175, 3263–3283, 2018, [Online]. Available: https://doi.org/10.1007/s00024-017-1707-7.

19. Javernick, L. *et al.*, Modeling the topography of shallow braided rivers using structure-from-motion photogrammetry. *Geomorphology*, 213, 166–182, 2014, [Online]. Available: https://doi.org/10.1016/j.geomorph.2014.01.006.

20. Čermáková, I., Komárková, J., Sedlák, P., Using UAV to detect shoreline changes: Case study - Pohranov Pond, Czech Republic. *Int. Arch. Photogramm. Remote Sens. Spat. Inf. Sci.*, 23, 803–808, 2016.

21. Koblov, R., 2022, Accessed 29 May 2022. [Online]. Available: http://www.rybolovkoblov.cz/.

22. Mapy.cz, *OpenStreetMap*, Seznam.cz, Czech Republic: Prague, 2022, Accessed 24 Aug 2018. [Online]. Available: www.mapy.cz.

23. DJI, 2022, Accessed 29 May 2018. [Online]. Available: https://www.dji.com/cz/mavic-2/info A. Beran et al., "Ztráta vody výparem z volné vodní hladiny" [Loss of water by evaporation from the water surface], Vodohospodářské technicko-ekonomické informace, vol. 61, pp. 12–18, 2019.

24. A. Beran *et al.*, "Ztráta vody výparem z volné vodní hladiny" [Loss of water by evaporation from the water surface], *Vodohospodářské technicko-ekonomické informace*, vol. 61, pp. 12–18, 2019.

15

Robotic Arm: Impact on Industrial and Domestic Applications

Nidhi Chahal[1], Ruchi Bisht[1], Arun Kumar Rana[2]* and Aryan Srivastava[1]

[1]Electronics and Communication Engineering, Chandigarh Engineering College, Landran, Mohali, Punjab, India
[2]Computer Science & Engineering, Galgotias College of Engineering and Technology, Greater Noida, Uttar Pradesh, India

Abstract

Industrial robotic arms help organizations gain a competitive advantage and reduce costs by automating important activities that contribute to worker safety, faster production, and higher productivity. Automation is getting overpowered day by day and the industry is growing in the field of automatic and user-friendly tools, a day-to-day problem that we thought of was to get rid of those devices which are user-friendly but too exhausting to control. An automatic device could be the real-time boss, and the idea is to create a robotic arm using the principle of the internet of things, artificial intelligence, mechanics, and the basics of electrical engineering. We have an ideological and implementable design for a robotic arm. This arm is programmed so that it could work on voice commands and facial recognition technology (other than facial recognition we can take for, by using infrared rays' software could catch the exact gazing point where the eyes are looking, the image processing algorithm is the basic working of the system in that case). By interpreting the image, the user and device could communicate more effectively. (In simple terms we will change the signals or be exact the reading in some specific color codes for the detection and communication) Also, it has some other qualities like being helpful in many tasks for mankind. Our innovation can be helpful in various fields such as healthcare, industries, household, etc. The problem behind the idea was to simplify the work done and make it more effective and less time-consuming with the help of technology. That brought us to the idea that this would help every industry in a significant manner.

*Corresponding author: ranaarun1@gmail.com

Ahmed A. Elgnar, Vigneshwar M, Krishna Kant Singh and Zdzislaw Polkowski (eds.) Handbook of Computational Sciences: A Multi and Interdisciplinary Approach, (323–340) © 2023 Scrivener Publishing LLC

Keywords: IoT - Internet of Things, ML - Machine Learning,
AI - Artificial Intelligence

15.1   Introduction

The robotic arm is used for many purposes like automating some processes like collecting and sorting goods from the pallets, whereas it can
also be used for household purposes. A robotic arm also helps to reduce
the chances of getting hurt by human workers in some dangerous tasks. A
basic robotic arm is made up of seven metal segments linked by six metal
joints and is frequently used in manufacturing. The computer regulates the
operation of stepper motors, allowing the computer to operate the device.
It works on the principle of the Internet of Things (IoT). Robotic arms are
important in space exploration programs; NASA uses some tools like this
in their programs running in outer space for collecting samples from different planets. The robotic arm is used for many purposes like automating
some processes like collecting and sorting goods from the pallets, whereas
it can also be used for household purposes and in many other industries
like the healthcare sector, textile industry, and many other industrial purposes. Robotic arm also helps to reduce the chances of getting hurt by
human workers for some industrial purposes [1–7].

Robotic arms are important in space exploration programs; NASA uses
some tools like this in their programs running in outer space for collecting
samples from different planets. This can be made using Arduino UNO,
Arduino NANO, Bluetooth module, and some other devices. These devices
are used to connect the hardware to the software and the cloud as well as
the input and delivery of the output. The arm can be made at a convenient
cost and be easily affordable for most the industries and help them in their
causes if being specific then, the innovation could be very helpful in the
healthcare when it can easily be useful in the contactless transfer of food
and contactless carriage of clothes, also in sanitization process. Whereas
the industries are wide and serve in the various sectors so is our robotic
arm. Robotic arms are basically and widely are also known as industrial
robots, and often described as mechanical arms. A device that acts similar
to a human arm moves similarly, including some joints, that either move
in a direction or rotate around the axis and helps in various tasks. These
types of devices are usually programmable, and more of a complex mechanism. This is also helpful in tasks like welding, gripping, snipping, etc.,
depending on the application. These human-like arms are easy to operate
and handle [8–12]. Because they only function in a limited space, robotic

arms are extremely simple to construct and program. When you put a robot out into the world, things become a little more complicated. First, the robot needs a functional movement mechanism. Wheels are frequently the best option when the robot merely needs to move over smooth ground. Wheels and tracks can also be used on rocky terrain. However, because legs are more versatile, they are frequently used by robot designers. Building legged robots also aids researchers in their understanding of natural loco- motion. Designers frequently look to the animal kingdom for inspiration for robotic mobility. Six-legged insects have great balance and can adapt to a wide range of terrain. Four-legged robots like Boston Dynamics' Spot resemble dogs, and the resemblance inspires comparisons as they do peril- ous tasks like construction inspection. Balancing two-legged robots is dif- ficult, but people have become better with practice.

This works on the basic principles of friction. This can be used in han- dling chemical laboratories and also for security purposes. This program- ming arm can be handled for automatic industrial processes. The robotic arm can be used for underwater applications in the underwater subma- rine due to its lightweight structure and design processes. Very high-speed manipulation, snippy manipulation owing to a highly high weight design, and very low inertia are the four main advantages of this design as shown in Figure 15.1.

Figure 15.1 Prototype of a mechanical arm.

15.2 Circuit Diagram

The voltage across variable resistors will be noisy since it is not perfectly linear. As a result, capacitors are put across each resistor to filter out the noise, as indicated in the diagram as shown in Figure 15.2. Now we'll feed the variable resistor voltage (the voltage that represents position control) into Arduino's ADC channels. We'll use the UNO's four ADC channels, A0 through A3, for this. Following the startup of the ADC, we will have a digital value of pots representing the user's chosen location. This number will be utilized to match the location of the servo [13–15].

Six ADC channels are available on the Arduino. For our Robotic Arm, we employed four. The integer numbers vary from 0–1023 (210 = 1024 values) due to the 10-bit resolution of the UNO ADC. This implies that input voltages ranging from 0 to 5 volts will be converted to integer values ranging from 0 to 1023. As a result, for every (5/1024 = 4.9 mV) unit.

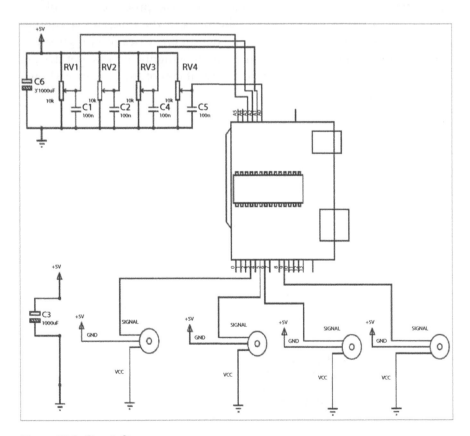

Figure 15.2 Circuit diagram.

15.3   Literature Survey

This historical assessment will take a different perspective than earlier published studies of the rapidly expanding robotic technology [16]. This inquiry will focus solely on the robotic arm, which will be examined in the same manner as the human arm. The emphasis will be on a history of sequential development and how we came to build a piano-wire based, seven degrees of freedom surgical system for urology that is currently being used extensively throughout the United States. The intention is to fully depict a scenario in which humans crave for an enhanced, human-like effector that would provide all the advantages of mechanization while removing all the potential drawbacks of the human actuator. We'll look at historical initiatives that came before modern electrical systems first [17]. Joints in mechanical systems are anthropomorphic representations of the human arm. The shoulder joint of the contemporary mechanical arm will then be discussed. The wrist will then be examined, and finally the elbow joint. The hand will then be examined across all iterations, serving as a bridge between historic and contemporary surgical systems [18]. Even though it is still in its infancy, this technology has a history that is almost as fascinating as the contemporary hardware and software that power these wonders of modern engineering. A robotic arm is usually similar to a human arm, made with programming languages and some hardware.

The arm may or may not be a total part of mechanics or too complex robotics, depending upon the user's interpretation [19]. A robotic arm could be defined as a chain of links that are operated by motors. Market is filled with different types of robotic arms, the majority of robotic arms have six joints and seven sections, mostly controlled by the help of a stepper motor and basic programs. These are used for some specific actions like assistance in factories and labs [20]. We can use hand gestures to control the arm and send the required signals to the device. Using Arduino and connecting the arm with proper functionality to make it work. Engineers are now working on robotic systems that may be related with operational hazards [21]. They must protect themselves while working on these by employing techniques such as repetition and backup systems, and the entire process should be overseen by a human operator. There are two controllers: a servo and a non-servo, because the entire system will be controlled by electrical devices [22]. The usage of a servo controller provides a lot of information about the robotic system and constantly checks the robot axes, which are connected with position and velocity, and the data is stored in the robot's memory. The system is controlled by extremely limited switches since non-servo controllers lack feedback requirements. In our instance, the servo controller is the ideal way to start since we require the backup system [23].

Today we live in a world where not only human is competing with human but also technology is a competitor for a human being, assistants are being replaced by artificial intelligence, also the world is heading towards self-governed robotics, which can work on single command independently to perform their given tasks. Militaries and the medical sector are some of the fields where these robots are now being used. They work for assignments involving high temperatures, and tasks like defusing bombs, and handling molten metal might be fatal for people. Hence, Robots can replace humans to perform these kinds of dangerous tasks [24]. Robots are becoming more and more interwoven into our daily lives, and they are trying to replace manpower. A service robot, according to the International Federation of Robotics (IFR), is a fully automated robot that may operate in a variety of disciplines. Currently, these mobile robots are employed in offices, military activities, hospital operations, hazardous settings, and agriculture [25].

There are many robotic arms in the present commercial market times, some of them are very excellent and of top-notch in quality if considering their work and accuracy ratio. Also, the tech is growing faster in current times and not stopping for anyone to grow at a slow pace, the growth curve in terms of robotic technology is exponential. Types of robotic arms are available in the commercial market. In standard versions of robots, are not capable of doing work that efficiently but the current advanced mechanism is capable of doing various tasks efficiently and effectively. Creating a robot that is not just more like a human being than industrial-grade robots but also more accessible, affordable, and "hackable" than high-end prototypes or readily available robotic arms. It benefits from its similarity to a human arm in terms of scale and form, as well as in terms of motor capabilities and joint structure. Robotics applications are widely employed in the fields of research, laboratory-based work, and industrial work to automate processes and eliminate human mistakes [26].

The mechanical construction of a robotic arm is described in this work. This robotic arm is frequently used to transport objects from one location to another. This application might be used in an industrial setting to move a weighing object like as a tank, container, or other object. An automated procedure has the benefit of completing tasks faster and with fewer mistakes. The implementation of a robotic arm with switching control is also described in this study. The use of the force-controlled function may be seen in industrial and manufacturing settings [27]. Robotic arms are a necessity for the International Space Station's construction and maintenance, support of external International Space Station experiments, capture of free-flying objects or modules, support of extravehicular activity, and participation in other scientific endeavors. These robotic devices can handle difficult, sophisticated activities like moving and installing 100,000-kg modules as well as easy, everyday chores like placing cameras [28].

15.4   Operation of Robot

The word "robot" comes from the Czech word "robota," which translates to "forced labor." The great majority of robots are appropriately represented by this. Most robots in use today are designed to do laborious, repetitive manufacturing jobs. They perform tasks that are challenging, dangerous, or boring for people. For instance, the robotic arm is frequently used in industrial operations. A standard robotic arm is made up of seven metal segments joined at six different points. Using stepper motors attached to each joint, the robot is rotated by the computer (some larger arms use hydraulics or pneumatics). Step motors move in exact increments as opposed to conventional motors. This makes it possible for the computer to move the arm precisely and repeatedly. The robot uses motion sensors to make sure it moves precisely the right amount [29].

A six-jointed industrial robot resembles a human arm in that it has the same joints as the shoulder, elbow, and wrist. Instead of a moving body, the shoulder is frequently linked to a foundation structure that is immovable. Six degrees of freedom allow this robot to turn in six different directions. A human arm, in contrast, has seven degrees of freedom. Moving your hand from one place to another is the function of your arm. Similar to this, the robotic arm's function is to move an end effector from one place to another. Robotic arms may be fitted with a variety of end effectors, each of which is designed with a specific function in mind. One form of common end effector is a scaled-down hand that can pick up and carry different things. Pressure sensors are widely used in robotic hands to inform the computer of how firmly the robot is grasping an object. As a result, the robot is unable to drop or damage anything it is holding. Examples of end effectors include blowtorches, drills, and spray paint. Likewise is meant for commercial robots. For instance, a robot may screw the lids of peanut butter jars as they go along a production line. The arm is guided by the programmer using a portable controller as they instruct a robot how to do a task. Every time a new unit leaves the assembly line, the robot repeats the exact same set of movements that it has learned through memory. The bulk of industrial robots assemble automobiles on auto assembly lines. Robots can perform a lot of this job more efficiently than humans since they are so precise.

15.5   The Benefits of Industrial Robotic Arms

Robotic arms, often referred to as articulated robotic arms, are nimble, trustworthy, and accurate machines that can be trained to carry out a limitless number of tasks under various circumstances. They are used in warehouses to choose, chose, or sort products from distribution conveyors to fulfil customer orders, in factories to automate repetitive tasks like painting machinery or components, and in farms to select and transfer ripe crops into storage trays. Additionally, as industrial settings become more networked and robotic technologies develop, new commercial operating models and use cases are made possible by the expanding capabilities of robotic arms.

It used to be essential to train a robotic arm to carry out very particular tasks, including picking up a single sort of object from a precise location with a specific orientation. Robots are unable to discern between different types of objects, put objects with some degree of tolerance (in an area rather than in a precise location), or change their grip according to the orientation of the object.

Improved safety. Robotic arms do tasks that are dangerous and have a high potential for human damage, protecting employees.

Increased effectiveness and productivity. Robotic arms can work nonstop for 24 hours a day, 7 days a week, enabling businesses to continually conduct production, inspections, or other tasks to enhance productivity.

Increased accuracy. Robotic arms, by definition, do tasks requiring great accuracy or consistency more regularly and precisely than humans.

15.6   Component Details

- Mechanical Gripper
  Things are gripped and held by a mechanical gripper when they are moved from one location to another. A built-in micro servo on the gripper enables it to open and close its jaws to grasp objects. Using laser cutting technology, acrylic is used to make the gripper. The second jaw's gear meshes with the servo shaft, which is fastened to the end of the first jaw.

The gear moves as the motor turns, moving the mesh gear and the jaws open or shut to release or hold the items.

- Bearing Base
  The base is fashioned to balance the center of gravity of the entire arm and be strong enough to support the complete assembly. The arm can cover the hemispherical volume and the base enables the arm to move smoothly in the necessary directions. Installed in the base, the bearing supports the full weight of the base and transfers rotational movement from the base to the robotic arm.
- Motor Servo
  Three main servo motors are used in the robotic arm, one for base movements and two on either side of the base plate to transfer motion via the many connections that make up the arm. Because the servo motor is fastened to the base plate, it is sturdy and operates without vibrations.
- Controller
  Delivering servo signals, a series of repeated pulses with varying width, allows one to operate a servo. The width of the pulse (most common for current hobby servos) or the duty cycle of a pulse train (less common nowadays) determines the position that the servo will reach. The controller translates the digital instruction signal into an analogue parameter, such the rotation of a servo motor shaft. Using the controller, we can upload the software controlling the servo motions.

Both the Arduino(s) are for the uploading and execution of the program, and transferring of signals from glove to robotic arm. Codes for facial recognition, Bluetooth module, and all the sensors are used, whereas the hardware material is required to make the outer body. Servo motors are typically employed when precise shaft movement or location is required. It is not advised to use them for high-speed applications. For low-speed, medium-torque, and accurate location applications, servo motors are advised. These motors are therefore perfect for building robotic arms. There are several shapes and sizes available for servo motors. Three wires are typically included on a servo motor: a positive voltage wire, a ground wire, and a position setting wire. The BLACK wire connects to the ground, the YELLOW wire to the signal, and the RED wire to the power. The pieces of an industrial robot must be energized to move because they cannot move on their own. As a result, elements such as robotic arms are outfitted with

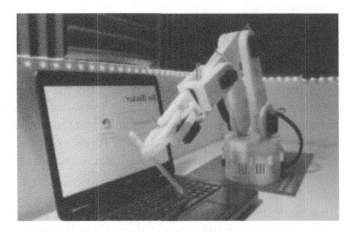

Figure 15.3 Robotic arm and its components.

motors to aid mobility. A motor is an electronic device with linear and rotary actuators driven by electric, hydraulic, or pneumatic energy. The actuators push and spin robotic elements into action as they move at fast speeds.

Sensors in robots are devices that detect or measure specified characteristics and initiate a response in response. They are embedded in robot constructions for safety and control. Safety sensors identify barriers in order to avoid human-robot and robot-robot accidents. They are a relatively new addition to robot structures, notably in collaborative robotics. Control sensors, on the other hand, are used to receive commands from an external controller, which are subsequently executed by the robot. Consider the controller to be the brain of a robot. It is the primary operating system that governs how all of the robot's components function [30–32]. It has software that allows it to receive, understand, and execute orders. In increasingly advanced robots, the controller may also contain a "memory" from which it may do repetitive tasks since it "remembers" how things function. Artificial intelligence is also embedded into the controller of smart robots via software. Figure 15.3 depicts one example.

15.7   Working of Robotic Arm

The Figure 15.4 shows the connection of the mechanical arm and the working principle behind the arm is the same, as explained above the Arduino gives the command to the device for the rotating of motors and that rotation helps the arm to operate. Whereas, the camera identifies the image of the user with the help of python codes in the system that recognizes the

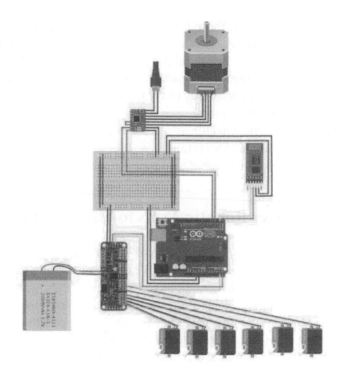

Figure 15.4 Circuit using components.

user identity and move accordingly [33–38]. The default reference value for Arduino ADC channels is 5V. This indicates that for ADC conversion at any input channel, we can provide a maximum input voltage of 5V. Because certain sensors offer voltages ranging from 0-2.5V, we gain less precision with a 5V reference, thus we have an instruction that allows us to modify this reference value. So we have "analogReference ();" to change the reference value. The maximum board ADC resolution is 10 bits by default; this resolution may be adjusted using the instruction ("analogue read resolution (bits)"). We have left this reference voltage to the default in our Robotic hand circuit, therefore we may read the value from the ADC channel directly by invoking the method "analogRead(pin);", where "pin" denotes the pin where we attached the analogue signal, say "A0". The value from the ADC may be recorded as int SENSORVALUE0 = analogRead (A0).

Let's speak about the SERVO now. The Arduino Uno includes a capability that allows us to control the servo position by simply entering the degree value. For example, if we want the servo to be at 30, we may represent the value directly in the program. Internally, the SERVO header (Servo.h) file handles all duty ratio computations. The user is given with four pots. And by rotating these four pots, we can deliver varied voltage to UNO's ADC channels. As a result, the user has control over the digital values of Arduino. These digital values are mapped to modify the servo motor position; hence, the servo position is under the user's control; thus by rotating these Pots, the user may move the joints of the Robotic arm and pick or grasp any object. A tool device connected to the wrist of a robotic arm is known as an end-effector. It improves the robotic arm's dexterity and makes it more suitable for certain jobs. They are a more practical alternative than designing a new robot arm for each task.

15.8   Intel Takes Robotic Arms to The Next Level

Industrial robotic arms may be designed and deployed using Intel's hardware, software, and ready-to-use solutions, which range from free algorithms, middleware, and reference implementations to CPUs and GPUs with built-in AI inference acceleration. The computing power needed for automated operation is provided by Intel® processors for IoT and embedded applications [39].

Robotic arms can recognize objects and their environment thanks to Intel® RealSenseTM technology. A wide array of depth cameras are necessary to enable depth mapping, which is essential for enabling robotic arms to operate in a variety of environments. Additionally, the Intel® Distribution of OpenVINOTM toolkit enables developers to streamline the development process and enable a write-once, deploy-anywhere model by enabling them to optimize, tune, and run comprehensive AI inference using a built-in model optimizer as well as runtime and development tools. For the intake of video and time series data, Intel® Edge Insights for Industrial provides a prevalidated, ready-to-deploy software reference architecture. It may publish to local or cloud apps and includes AI analysis. Because it's based on Docker, apps may be easily modified and customized.

A software-defined reference platform for industrial controls called Intel® Edge Controls for Industrial is accessible and cost-free. Functional safety, real-time, deterministic computation, standards-based industrial communication, and management are all included in one system.

15.9   Robotic Arm Applications

One of the primary benefits of industrial robotic arms is their adaptability to a wide range of applications, from simple to complicated tasks in the safest or harshest conditions. Automating these duties not only removes human workers from potentially hazardous situations, but also allows those workers to focus on higher-value tasks such as client interaction [40].

Here are some of the most prevalent applications for robotic arms in manufacturing today:

- Palletizing
  Robotic arms can be used to automate the process of loading items into pallets. Palletizing becomes more accurate, cost-effective, and predictable by automating the process. The employment of robotic arms also relieves human workers of jobs that pose a danger of bodily harm.
- Handling of Materials
  Material-handling robotic arms can aid in the creation of a secure and efficient warehouse by ensuring that goods and materials are appropriately kept, easily found, and delivered. Automating these operations can aid in the delivery of items to clients, the prevention of workplace accidents, and the overall efficiency of a facility.
- Welding
  Welding is a skill that robots can undertake in advanced industrial settings like vehicle manufacture. Welding is a great option for sophisticated robots with vision and AI augmentation for inline quality inspection due to its essential impact on product quality.
- Inspection
  Quality inspection is often conducted at the end of a production line, delaying the detection of manufacturing quality issues. Businesses can profit from real-time inspection by augmenting robots with vision and AI systems, reducing waste and downtime.
- Pick Place
  In modern production and logistics, pick-and-place robots are commonly used. They are outfitted with modern machine vision systems that let them to rapidly and efficiently recognize an object, grip it, and move it from one spot to another [41, 42].

15.10 Conclusion

The effect of industrial robotic arms in the manufacturing business is expanding, with benefits like as cost savings, increased production, and efficiency. Many companies that use robotic arms save money on low-skilled human labor by reducing waste and human mistake. The chapter's objectives, which included creating the hardware and software for an accelerometer-controlled robotic arm, were met. The observation clearly demonstrates that its movement is exact, accurate, easy to regulate, and user-friendly. The robotic arm has been created effectively because the robot's movement can be accurately controlled. This robotic arm control approach is anticipated to solve difficulties like placing or picking things away from the user, as well as picking and placing dangerous goods quickly and easily. The robotic arm may be used for both industrial and domestic applications. This might be an overly corporeal aide with some virtual features. This robotic arm comes in handy at a time when we need it. The robotic arm may be used for both industrial and domestic applications. This might be an overly corporeal aide with some virtual features. This robotic arm comes in handy at a time when we need it. In the future, robots will be able to operate securely next to people and will frequently be far less expensive than their industrial counterparts. Collaborative robots will become more widely used by firms with stringent ROI criteria as they become more effective in challenging industrial environments.

References

1. Shabaz, M., Singla, P., Jawarneh, M.M.M., Qureshi, H.M., A novel automated approach for deep learning on stereotypical autistic motor movements, in: *Artificial Intelligence for Accurate Analysis and Detection of Autism Spectrum Disorder*, pp. 54–68, IGI Global, UK, 2021.
2. Srivastava, R., Mallick, P.K., Rautaray, S.S., Pandey, M. (Eds.), *Computational intelligence for machine learning and healthcare informatics*, vol. 1, Walter de Gruyter GmbH & Co KG, France, 2020.
3. Jimson, E.R., Nisar, K., Bin Ahmad Hijazi, M.H., Bandwidth management using software defined network and comparison of the throughput performance with traditional network, in: *2017 International Conference on Computer and Drone Applications (IConDA)*, 2017, November, IEEE, pp. 71–76.
4. Kumar, A., Sharma, S., Goyal, N., Singh, A., Cheng, X., Singh, P., Secure and energy-efficient smart building architecture with emerging technology IoT. *Comput. Commun.*, 176, 207–217, 2021.
5. Muratore, F., Ramos, F., Turk, G., Yu, W., Gienger, M., Peters, J., Robot learning from randomized simulations: A review. *Front. Rob. AI*, 9, 220–231, 2022.
6. Radoglou Grammatikis, P., Sarigiannidis, P., Moscholios, I., Securing the Internet of Things: Challenges, threats and solutions. *Internet Things*, 5, 41–70, 2019.

7. Lv, Q., Zhang, R., Liu, T., Zheng, P., Jiang, Y., Li, J., Xiao, L., A strategy transfer approach for intelligent human-robot collaborative assembly. *Comput. Ind. Eng.*, 168, 108047, 2022.

8. Kumar, A., Sharma, S., Singh, A., Alwadain, A., Choi, B.J., Manual-Brenosa, J., Goyal, N., Revolutionary strategies analysis and proposed system for future infrastructure in Internet of Things. *Sustainability*, 14, 1, 71, 2021.

9. Aloqaily, M., Boukerche, A., Bouachir, O., Khalid, F., Jangsher, S., An energy trade framework using smart contracts: Review and challenges. *IEEE Network*, 11, 1–7, 2020.

10. Zhang, A. and Lin, X., Towards secure and privacy-preserving data sharing in e-health systems via consortium blockchain. *J. Med. Syst.*, 42, 8, 140, 2018.

11. Rana, A., Chakraborty, C., Sharma, S., Dhawan, S., Pani, S.K., Ashraf, I., Internet of Medical Things-based secure and energy-efficient framework for healthcare. *Big Data*, 10, 1, 18–33, 2022.

12. Xie, S., Zheng, Z., Chen, W., Wu, J., Dai, H.N., Imran, M., Blockchain for cloud exchange: A survey. *Comput. Electr. Eng.*, 81, 106526, 2020.

13. Sun, W., Cai, Z., Li, Y., Liu, F., Fang, S., Wang, G., Security and privacy in the medical Internet of Things: A review. *Secur. Commun. Netw.*, 2018, 300–317, Mar. 2018, Art. no. 5978636.

14. Sahi, M.A., Abbas, H., Saleem, K., Yang, X., Derhab, A., Orgun, M.A., Iqbal, W., Rashid, I., Yaseen, A., Privacy preservation in e-healthcare environments: State of the art and future directions. *IEEE Access*, 6, 464478, 2017.

15. Kumar, A. and Sharma, S., Internet of robotic things: Design and develop the quality-of-service framework for the healthcare sector using CoAP. *IAES Int. J. Robot. Autom.*, 10, 4, 289, 2021.

16. Wang, W., Tian, W., Liao, W., Li, B., Hu, J., Error compensation of industrial robot based on deep belief network and error similarity. *Robot. Comput.-Integr. Manuf.*, 73, 102220, 2022.

17. Wang, W., Tian, W., Liao, W., Li, B., Hu, J., Error compensation of industrial robot based on deep belief network and error similarity. *Robot. Comput.-Integr. Manuf.*, 73, 102220, 2022.

18. Hatzivasilis, G., Soultatos, O., Ioannidis, S., Verikoukis, C., Demetriou, G., Tsatsoulis, C., Review of security and privacy for the Internet of Medical Things (IoMT), in: *Proc. 15th Int. Conf. Distrib. Comput. Sensor Syst. (DCOSS)*, May 2019, p. 457464.

19. Dhawan, S., Chakraborty, C., Frnda, J., Gupta, R., Rana, A.K., Pani, S.K., SSII: Secured and high-quality steganography using intelligent hybrid optimization algorithms for IoT. *IEEE Access*, 9, 87563–87578, 2021.

20. Alsubaei, F., Abuhussein, A., Shiva, S., Security and privacy in the Internet of Medical Things: Taxonomy and risk assessment, in: *Proc. IEEE 42nd Conf. Local Comput. Netw. Workshops (LCN Workshops)*, p. 112120, Oct. 2017.

21. Rana, S.K. and Rana, S.K., Blockchain based business model for digital assets management in trust less collaborative environment. *J. Crit. Rev.*, 7, 19, 738–750, 2020.

22. Sun, Y. and Lo, B., An articial neural network framework for gait-based biometrics. *IEEE J. Biomed. Health Inform.*, 23, 3, 987998, Aug. 2018.

23. Rana, S.K., Kim, H.C., Pani, S.K., Rana, S.K., Joo, M.I., Rana, A.K., Aich, S., Blockchain-based model to improve the performance of the next-generation digital supply chain. *Sustainability*, 13, 18, 10008, 2021.

24. Stern, A.D., Gordon, W.J., Landman, A.B., Kramer, D.B., Cybersecurity features of digital medical devices: An analysis of FDA product summaries. *BMJ Open*, 9, 6, 11–28, 2019, Art. no. e025374.

25. Rana, A.K. and Sharma, S., Internet of Things based stable increased-throughput multi-hop protocol for link efficiency (IoT-SIMPLE) for health monitoring using wireless body area networks. *Int. J. Sens. Wirel. Commun. Control*, 11, 7, 789–798, 2021.

26. Kumar, N.M. and Mallick, P.K., Blockchain technology for security issues and challenges in IoT. *Proc. Comput. Sci.*, 132, 1815–1823, 2018.

27. Haghi, M., Neubert, S., Geissler, A., Fleischer, H., Stoll, N., Stoll, R., Thurow, K., A flexible and pervasive IoT-based healthcare platform for physiological and environmental parameters monitoring. *IEEE Internet Things J.*, 7, 6, 5628–47, June 2020.

28. Baker, S.B., Xiang, W., Atkinson, I., Internet of Things for smart healthcare: Technologies, challenges, and opportunities. *IEEE Access*, 5, 26521–44, 2017.

29. Kumar, A., Sharma, S., Goyal, N., Gupta, S.K., Kumari, S., Kumar, S., Energy-efficient fog computing in Internet of Things based on routing protocol for low-power and lossy network with contiki. *Int. J. Commun. Syst.*, 35, 4, e5049, 2022.

30. Ibrahim, A.A.A., Nisar, K., Hzou, Y.K., Welch, I., Review and analyzing RFID technology tags and applications, in: *2019 IEEE 13th International Conference on Application of Information and Communication Technologies (AICT)*, 2019, October, IEEE, pp. 1–4.

31. Bangyal, W.H., Nisar, K., Ibrahim, A., Bin, A.A., Haque, M.R., Rodrigues, J.J., Rawat, D.B., Comparative analysis of low discrepancy sequence-based initialization approaches using population-based algorithms for solving the global optimization problems. *Appl. Sci.*, 11, 16, 7591, 2021.

32. Sabir, Z., Nisar, K., Raja, M.A.Z., Ibrahim, A.A.B.A., Rodrigues, J.J., Al-Basyouni, K.S., Rawat, D.B., Heuristic computational design of Morlet wavelet for solving the higher order singular nonlinear differential equations. *Alexandria Eng. J.*, 60, 6, 5935–5947, 2021.

33. Laghari, A.A., Wu, K., Laghari, R.A., Ali, M., Khan, A.A., A review and state of art of Internet of Things (IoT). *Arch. Comput. Methods Eng.*, 33, 1–19, 2021.

34. Chegini, H., Naha, R.K., Mahanti, A., Thulasiraman, P., Process automation in an IoT–fog–cloud ecosystem: A survey and taxonomy. *IoT*, 2, 1, 92–118, 2021.

35. Zhang, Y., Sun, Y., Jin, R., Lin, K., Liu, W., High-performance isolation computing technology for smart IoT healthcare in cloud environments. *IEEE Internet Things J.*, 1–1, 2021.

36. Jacob, T.P., Pravin, A., Ramachandran, M., Al-Turjman, F., Differential spectrum access for next generation data traffic in massive-IoT. *Microprocess. Microsyst.*, 82, 103951, 2021.

37. Kuwahara, Y., Aihara, N., Yamazaki, S., Ohuchi, K., Mizuno, H., Energy-efficiency comparison of ad-hoc routings in a shadowing environment for smart IoT. *International Conference on Information Networking (ICOIN)*, IEEE, pp. 801–804, 2021.

38. Xingmei, X., Jing, Z., He, W., Research on the basic characteristics, the key technologies, the network architecture and security problems of the Internet of Things, in: *Proceedings of 2013 3rd International Conference on Computer Science and Network Technology*, 2013, October, IEEE, pp. 825–828.

39. Ojanperä, T., Mäkelä, J., Majanen, M., Mämmelä, O., Martikainen, O., Väisänen, J., Evaluation of LiDAR data processing at the mobile network edge for connected vehicles. *EURASIP J. Wireless Commun. Networking.*, 1, 112, 1–23, 2021.

40. A., Sargent, C.S., Nord, J.H., Paliszkiewicz, J., Internet of Things (IoT): From awareness to continued use. *Int. J. Inf. Manage.*, 62, 102442, 112, 2022.

41. Oktian, Y.E., Witanto, E.N., Lee, S.G., A conceptual architecture in decentralizing computing, storage, and networking aspect of IoT infrastructure. *IoT*, 2, 2, 205–21, 2021.

42. Almezhghwi, K., Serte, S., Al-Turjman, F., Convolutional neural networks for the classification of chest X-rays in the IoT era. *Multimedia Tools Appl.*, 45, 1–15, 2021.

16

Effects of Using VR on Computer Science Students' Learning Behavior in Indonesia: An Experimental Study for TEFL

Muthmainnah[1], Ahmad Al Yakin[1], Luís Cardoso[2]*, Ahmed A. Elngar[3],
Ibrahim Oteir[4] and Abdullah Nijr Al-Otaibi[5]

[1]Universitas Al Asyariah Mandar, Polewali Mandar, Sulawesi Barat, Indonesia
[2]Polytechnic Institute of Portalegre and Centre for Comparative Studies of the University of Lisbon, Portalegre, Portugal
[3]Faculty of Computers and Artificial Intelligence, Beni-Suef University, Beni-Suef City, Egypt
[4]Batterjee Medical College, Jeddah, Saudi Arabia
[5]Majmaah University, Jeddah, Saudi Arabia

Abstract

Virtual reality is one of the technological innovations in education that is very popular and favored by young people. Future of technology in language learning (FUTELA) like VR, educators can take advantage of the many features included in VR apps to help their students learn more effectively. However, it remains unclear how VR can help students become more engaged in their studies. To close this hole, we conducted a pre-experimental study with the experimental group to find out how the learning outcomes obtained with the application of VR and their behavior influence the involvement of students' Online learning classes. At a time when Online learning is so widely used, it is very important to know which ones involve the student's behavior the most. In this study, we focused on learning models of behavioral, emotional, and cognitive dimensions. The experimental group results have shown the students are more active, more engaged, increase retention, and positive emotions, and have higher effectiveness, attractiveness, participation, task completion, and level of interaction in discussion activities as evidenced by research findings. For the emotional evaluation of students, of course, interaction, attractiveness, and

*Corresponding author: lmcardoso@ipportalegre.pt

Ahmed A. Elgnar, Vigneshwar M, Krishna Kant Singh and Zdzislaw Polkowski (eds.) Handbook of Computational Sciences: A Multi and Interdisciplinary Approach, (341–364) © 2023 Scrivener Publishing LLC

satisfaction, there were statistically significant differences in pre-test and post-test learning outcomes. On the other hand, VR appears a positive effect on deep learning, students' autonomy in learning, and intrinsic motivation. The application of VR shows that students are more active in thinking, critical thinking, and maximum problem-solving. VR seems to encourage more "creative", imaginative, inspiring activities by facilitating the exchange of ideas and confidence in learning.

Keywords: Virtual reality, behavior, blended learning, and language teaching

16.1 Introduction

VR is a system designed based on a computer system with appropriate hardware and software to implement the concept of virtual reality. Virtual world is the term we use to describe what a VR system represents. Object models and descriptions of their behavior are examples of virtual world content such as models and their spatial arrangements and virtual environments for one or more users is what we mean by VR systems.

Since the worldwide pandemic, virtual reality has gained more and more attention and popularity in education. Virtual reality has a significant impact on learning motivation and autonomy [1], spatial ability [2], communicative ability development [3], vocabulary [4] and productive language skills for special purposes in students of all ages [5]. This reality caused lecturers and students in universities to have to switch from traditional classroom instruction to online learning after the COVID-19 pandemic, and virtual reality (VR) has emerged as an important tool for this transition to digital technology-based learning [5].

Today around the world, educational movements and reforms have taken various forms. When it comes to change in education, innovation has played an important role, especially as technology has advanced over the last few decades. Educators have worked hard to leverage these technological advances to open new possibilities for innovative, creative, and alternative forms of learning [6]. Educators have faced many challenges and opportunities due to the rapid advancement of technology. For some time now, academics have been very interested in the educational applications of mixed reality and artificial intelligence (AI).

Virtual reality (VR) has many unique advantages for distance education. Virtual and learner-centered language learning environments [7]. [8] as well as fully immersive physical and mental experiences are part of this package that no other technology can offer students. Learners can engage with virtual objects and avatars in a three-dimensional (3D) world through VR technology while also enhancing their sensory perception, especially visual (especially depth perception) and auditory (especially depth perception). Curiosity and enthusiasm for learning are piqued in this way. As a result, students are open to full participation in online learning activities where various authentic contexts are available [9, 10].

English-language professionals have worked to improve students' English-language proficiency by continuously innovating, for example, with mobile technology augmented reality, [11] and robots [12]. Virtual learning environments have features that align with language learning instructional strategies. [13] Learners can practice speaking a foreign language in a virtual reality environment, for example, by posing as an avatar and interacting with other avatars. Interaction with robots makes it easier to learn a new language. Role-playing, for example, is a common method of teaching languages. It is critical to tailor English courses to the specific communication needs of workers in a given workplace [14]. Because robots are interactive, language and communication can take place in a simulated environment like VR. Students can interact with robots and experience realistic simulations.

Students and educators alike are faced with the urgent need to switch to online education today. Many college students' study habits are thrown off by the stress and anxiety that comes with online learning. Some young people are unable to take advantage of this new learning environment, while others are simply struggling to keep up with their education and remain motivated and engaged in their studies [15]. As a result, the modern learning environment is unable to effectively incorporate technology. Assuming agency in learning, initiating, and maintaining meaningful multimodal communication, and developing conceptual understanding through active engagement both physically and emotionally with digital resources will be hindered without direct and direct teacher support in online learning. No matter how well-intentioned they may be, a teacher who has never taught online or undergone relevant training is doomed to failure.

According to [16] it can take a long time for new users to become comfortable with VR equipment and virtual learning environments, which can be frustrating for beginners. This technology has the potential to distract students from their studies if they are not familiar with it. Students tend to become distracted by the brightly colored, but artificial world, which can lead to a lack of focus on their academic work [17]. To further complicate matters, virtual objects cannot be physically perceived by learners if the course content is relevant to technology practice. Virtual reality (VR) devices can cause dizziness or loss of balance in some users [18].

An investigation into RALL is needed to gain new insights into how application systems and educational content can be designed to encourage students' learning and retention. Artificial intelligence (AI) robots have been integrated into only a handful of research studies, such as the ones conducted by [19, 20]. There are, however, few studies on the acquisition of a foreign language through virtual reality immersion. Incorporating virtual reality into the classroom can inspire students' interests, motivations, attitudes, and participation (VR). In order to learn vocabulary in context, multiple VR exposures are required, and the overall impression of VR learning is positive. There are also new developments in VR technology and how it is used to teach languages, as well as how students themselves perceive the experience to improve their own learning habits and the quality of their education. When it comes to learning a foreign language, the effectiveness of VR instruction relies heavily on the effectiveness of the lesson plans that teachers create. The findings of this study can help educators, researchers, and developers of virtual reality applications.

16.2 VR as FUTELA

According to [21] virtual reality (VR) technology allows students to engage in authentic learning activities in simulated, immersive, and interactive virtual environments. Virtual reality (VR) has proven to be particularly useful for second language acquisition (L2A). However, VR research has tended to focus on desktop-based VR rather than mobile-rendered HMDs, leaving the potential of mobile-rendered HMDs unexplored. The purpose of this study is to examine the impact of mobile-rendered HMD VR on EFL learners' vocabulary learning by using a commercial VR app. In Taiwan, 49 seventh graders were selected from two classes and randomly assigned to one of two groups: the experimental group (who used virtual reality headsets) or the control group (who watched videos). Mobile-rendered HMDs were used by VR players to interact with the Mondly VR app and have conversations with virtual characters. It was through a personal computer that they watched the walkthrough video signal of the VR player's app. Vocabulary tests, a perception questionnaire, and interviews were used to evaluate the participants' vocabulary acquisition.

Virtual reality (VR) technology, according to [21] allows students to participate in real-world learning activities in simulated, immersive, and interactive virtual spaces. Using virtual reality (VR) has proven to be extremely beneficial in the acquisition of a second language (L2A). In contrast, most of the VR research has focused on desktop-based VR, leaving the potential of mobile-rendered HMDs largely unexplored. It is the goal of this study to examine the impact of mobile-rendered HMD VR on EFL learners' vocabulary learning by using a commercial VR app. There were

49 seventh graders from two classes in Taiwan who were randomly assigned to one of two groups: experimental or control (who watched videos).

VR players interacted with the Mondly VR app and had conversations with virtual characters using mobile-rendered HMDs. They watched the walkthrough video signal of the VR player's app on a personal computer. The participants' vocabulary acquisition was assessed using vocabulary tests, a perception questionnaire, and interviews. In general, augmented reality (AR), virtual reality (VR), and mixed reality (MR) are used to support language learning (MR). They aid students in learning the target language in a simulated or enhanced setting as stated by [22].

Student's motivation in online/distance learning is strongly influenced by teacher practices, and this includes encouraging student autonomy while also ensuring that students learn and engage in interpersonal relationships [23]. Personal goals and student learning behaviors are supported by providing support for autonomy, which encourages and facilitates students to pursue these goals [24]. [25] students' perspectives are considered by teachers who support autonomy in online learning, choices around learning are allowed, reasons are given when choices are limited, language control is avoided, and unnecessary pressure and demands on students are reduced.

Personalized learning opportunities that respect and accept students' individual interests and allow flexibility to tailor learning activities are recommended by [26] for students who have access to multiple languages and navigation support in order to choose from a variety of educational resources. By using their own voice, students will be able to make their own decisions and decisions about personal goals and self-efficacy, and they will feel empowered in learning [25]. Inspiring students to take charge of their learning increases their level of engagement. Students who had teachers who supported their autonomy also reported higher levels of emotional involvement, in addition to improved concentration and time management [27, 28]. Students who are more engaged in class and communicate frequently with their instructors about their progress in class (agent engagement) are more likely to succeed [29]. However, this has not been studied, it is possible that having more control over one's educational goals will lead to more cognitive engagement [26].

According to [27] getting teachers to show more warmth, affection, and enjoyment in their work has been shown to improve the quality of the teacher–student bond. Pedagogical care, involvement, closeness, acceptance, and help [30] are just a few examples of the emotional and motivational support that involved teachers can offer to students in online learning. They can also help students build trusting relationships in collaborative learning environments [31] and small gatherings for debate [25].

If this is done, students will feel more welcomed, safe & effective, and they will internalize their experience and participate more actively. Students' participation in class activities (behavioral engagement), their feelings toward the class and its activities (emotional engagement), their confidence in their ability to complete difficult tasks (cognitive engagement), and their willingness to speak up about their learning needs are all influenced by good teacher-student relationships. Students' levels of behavioral, emotional, and agentic engagement can be predicted by their level of relatedness, as a result of this correlation [32, 33].

16.3   Using the Internet to Study and Learning Behavior

Even if we reject the resignation of tech-determinists completely, it seems inevitable that we will face VR and invitations to meet in the metaverse as workers, educators, learners, and social beings. Human-computer interaction and computer-supported collaborative work in exploring how VR can enable new forms of learning and teaching are increasingly finding exciting venues in the metaverse. It is easy to see that, in many ways, virtual classrooms do not provide the same genuine relationships between students as traditional classroom settings where students are not restricted to physical locations. To avoid mistaking maps for reality, [34] warns that when simulacra take their place, they can be misinterpreted as reality. Therefore, instructional learning using VR should take into account the duration of interaction with VR, be facilitated with appropriate learning outcomes, and design interactive learning environments.

Behavioral psychology theory argues that students' behavioral data can be used to provide feedback about their characteristics and psychodynamics [35]. Students' online operational behavior can be observed directly during online learning and stored as part of the student's personal profile. In addition, observing how students learn when engaged in online learning, students' operational behavior is considered as their learning behavior and can represent exploratory learning behavior or learning engagement patterns. Students' online learning behaviors can be reflected in their behavior when interacting with these online learning media and technologies, once they are understood correctly [36].

There are many ways to measure online learning behavior, but the most common are using frequency and time. This includes tracking how many times courses or resources were accessed [37], how many times resources were accessed and for how long [38], how many times teaching videos were accessed [39] and how long it takes to complete a test [39]. Then, [40] suggests behavioral data should be cleared to avoid bias caused by abnormal values, and the adequacy of behavioral data collection should be verified after data collection.

This study will examine how students intentionally engage in learning behaviors such as accessing material through VR repeatedly to improve the quality of their language; how they provide direct, structured feedback; synergize with their classmates; build harmony with lecturers; form teamwork; discuss, think critically, and improve problem solving and collaborate during treatment with VR, not only getting fun Do not play games for learning only.

16.4   Methods

This study used a pre-experimental design, namely the design that I covered was only one group or class that was given pre and post tests. One group pretest and posttest design were carried out in one group without the presence of a control or comparison group, [41]. The author uses analytical techniques to analyze the data obtained from the research results. It aims to obtain accurate data according to the research objectives and to find out the difficulties faced by students in producing drama review texts based on moral values by using the note-taking pair technique. The research pattern used is the one-group pretest and posttest design research pattern.

In this study, we used one class taught by the instructor for one consecutive semester with an identical syllabus, subject matter, and class activities to ensure that the treatment conditions were valid. In terms of course-related discussions, students in the experimental group used virtual reality in learning English (TEFL). A blended learning system was used at the university during the research.

An ecologically valid real class in which the VR platform is used in natural educational practice was used in this study in a computer science faculty student laboratory environment where strict control of experimental conditions to investigate the effects of VR was applied. There were limitations placed on how participants used VR services in this study. All students in the computer laboratory use VR because their smartphone capacity is not sufficient to access VR. Because of this, we can better understand what is happening in the actual classroom and draw conclusions from real-world examples. We chose VR for this study, but the aim was to examine the impact of various language learning content built as teaching materials on student participation. Student learning activities are supported by a VR forum accessed via the CoSpaces Edu link. When blended learning attracts the attention of students, it is very important to know which learning behaviors attract the students' attention the most. We wanted to find out which of VR many features would be best at getting students to pay attention in real-world classrooms.

16.5   Research Participants

Participants in this study were students at the faculty of computer science on Information system study program in the Eastern Indonesia region, and 30 students were enrolled in the 2021–2022 academic year (Figure 16.1). The students studied English classes with class meetings once a week for two hours per week and a total use of VR for six weeks. Instructors teach courses in a reverse approach by distributing YouTube-based instructional videos via WhatsApp group social media accounts before each class and guiding students to apply what they have learned in class. The first two weeks include knowledge of linguistic content, and for six weeks use VR with teaching materials, namely exploring the airport with the following steps:

1. Through a VR link on CoSpaces Edu, students can see what is going on at the airport.
2. The next activity in groups, they read dialogues, listen to conversations, and they explore airports; they determine vocabulary related to airports; they determine directions for recording new vocabulary.

Figure 16.1   VR treatment in the class and students' English performance.

3. Next, in groups (consisting of five students), they design a dialogue related to the airport, then they discuss and determine the character and topic of the dialogue.

4. After the dialogue is finished, they present the dialogue in front of the class. The lecturer provides feedback and corrects the errors contained in the dialogue.

5. The knowledge they gain from the VR platform is put into practice in the form of group role play.

6. After doing the role play, each student is asked to then present his resume about the airport, which is recorded using his smartphone and uploaded on the YouTube account of each student.

16.6   Techniques for Analyzing Data

The data analysis technique used by the researcher is descriptive and inferential statistics. Descriptive statistical analysis used the percentage, average, and standard deviation formulas. Meanwhile, for inferential statistical data analysis, normality, homogeneity, and significance tests were used. The researcher employs descriptive and inferential statistics for data analysis. The percentage, average, and standard deviation formulas were used in descriptive statistical analysis. Normality, homogeneity, and significance tests were used for inferential statistical data analysis.

1. Descriptive Statistical Analysis
   Statistical data is statistical data used to analyze data by describing or describing the data collected, not drawing conclusions that are generally accepted or generalized. This technique yields the following data: mean, mode, range, minimum, maximum, standard deviation, variance, and frequency distribution table. The data is to describe the students' English skills. The descriptive statistical process is done manually by the amount of data.

2. Inferential Statistical Analysis
   Inferential statistics is a statistical technique used to analyze sample data, and the results are applied to the population. Inferential statistics are used to determine whether the null hypothesis is accepted or rejected. For the purposes of this inferential statistical analysis, the normality test, homogeneity test, and hypothesis testing were first performed.

16.7   The Indicator of Efficiency

The effectiveness criteria determined in this study are:

1. Learning outcomes
   To determine the efficacy of providing VR applications, consider whether the student's acquisition value is greater than the value of the maximum completeness category. It is said to be very effective if the level of completeness reaches 85% of the total number of students.
2. Student activities (learning behaviors)
   The activity referred to here is if students are able to achieve success with VR as the learning media applied at least in the good category.
3. Student response
   In learning activities students can give a positive response at the stage of learning methods, which is where this result is calculated from being said to be effective if 50% of students give a positive response (based on the questionnaire asked).

16.8   Results and Discussion

Analysis of experimental class pre-test data are shown in Table 16.1.

Based on Table 16.1, using SPSS Version 28, It can be explained by the number of students. As many as 30 people have an average score of 60.65. where the median value is 60.00 and the highest score achieved by students is 60. The standard deviation of 13,440 ranges from a minimum score of 33, a maximum of 80 from the lowest possible score of 30, and a maximum of 80 from the highest possible score of 100.

Based on Table 16.2, using SPSS Version 28, it can be explained by the number of students. As many as 30 people have an average score of 78.00. where the mean score is 77.50 and the most achieved score is 70. The standard deviation is 8.794. The minimum score range is 65. The maximum is 98 from the lowest possible score, which is 30. The maximum is 98 from the highest possible score, which is 100. Inferential statistics is a statistical technique used to analyze sample data, and the results are applied to the population. Inferential statistics are used to determine whether the null hypothesis is accepted or rejected. A normality test was conducted to determine whether the sample under study was normally distributed or

Table 16.1 Pre-test.

	Valid	30
N	Missing	0
Mean		60.67
Median		60.00
Mode		60
Std. deviation		13.440
Variance		180.644
Range		47
Minimum		33
Maximum		80
Sum		1820

Table 16.2 Post-test.

	Valid	30
N	Missing	30
Mean		78.00
Median		77.50
Mode		70
Std. deviation		8.794
Variance		77.328
Range		33
Minimum		65
Maximum		98
Sum		2340

not. The acceptance criteria that a data set is normally distributed or not are as follows:

1. If the significance is 0.05, then the data is not normally distributed.
2. If the significance is greater than 0.05, then the data is normally distributed.

Table 16.3 shows that the results of the analysis or normality test at the pre-test stage have the value of sig. = 0.123 and at the post-test stage the value of sig. = 0.136. The data for the second stage of this study is normally distributed because the test results are more significant than the alpha (0.05). Paired samples t-test is a test that is used to compare two means of two paired samples with the assumption that the data is normally distributed. samples that come from the same subject variable, each taken during different situations and circumstances. This test is also called the paired t-test. Furthermore, to answer the hypothesis in this study, can be seen in the Table 16.4.

Table 16.4 shows that the difference in the average value for the two stages is -32.700 and the standard deviation value is 15.745. From the results of the t-test conducted, the data shows a negative value. This is because one stage has a lower yield. In a phenomenon like this, negative values can be changed or considered to be positive values. The results of the t-test showed t-count =-11.376, the value of degrees of freedom was 29, and the significance (2 tailed) was 0.001. Because the significance (2-tailed) is less than alpha (0.05), it can be said that VR influences the first semester of English classes at the Faculty of Computer Science in Indonesia.

In English, students can access a Google form to complete a questionnaire regarding their response to the use of VR after treatment for 6 meetings. Before starting the survey, participants were asked to read the questionnaire, and if there was an item they did not understand, they were given time to ask. The questionnaire was distributed via WhatsApp.

Table 16.3 Tests of normality.

	Kolmogorov-Smirnov[a]			Shapiro-Wilk		
	Statistic	df	Sig.	Statistic	df	Sig.
Pre-test experiment	.200	30	.004	.945	30	.123
Post-test experiment	.134	30	.177	.947	30	.136

Table 16.4 Paired samples test.

		Paired differences					t	df	Significance	
					95% Confidence interval of the difference					
		Mean	Std. deviation	Std. error mean	Lower	Upper			One-sided p	Two-sided p
Pair 1	Pre-test - Post-test	-32.700	15.745	2.875	-38.579	-26.821	-11.376	29	<.001	<.001

Although students are urged to complete the survey in one sitting, they can save their answers and continue the survey whenever they need to because they are given one week to complete the survey.

Based on the data on Figure 16.2, students' likeability with positive statement by using VR it is easy to learn English of 15.6% participants strongly agree and 34.4% agree. The second statement asked about they had felt fun learning by using VR 34.4% strongly agree position and 34.4 agree position.

The data from Figure 16.3, it can be seen that most of the students' interactiveness with VR fall into positive position about their happiness

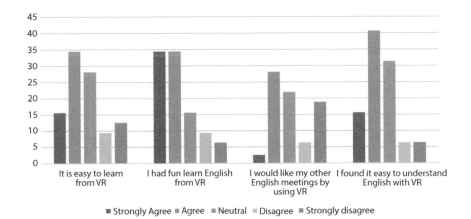

Figure 16.2 Likeability on VR.

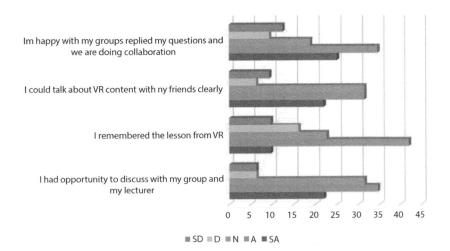

Figure 16.3 Interactiveness.

in doing feedback and collaboration. Most of them choose strongly to agree 21.9% and 34.4% agree. Students looked more confident to share about their experiences and tell their friends about the materials (Airport, Animal words, Roman House, End of dinosaurs, theater camp) clearly. They also claim the TEFL materials by using VR it is memorable. Previous results showed that participants in the current study agreed with the items on the questionnaire and giving their recommendation to use VR.

Of 15.6% respondents strongly agree and 43.8% choose to agree about VR better to use in learning and their retention (Figure 16.4) about VR in positive responses. VR materials easy to understand and they can imagine the real (Airport, Animal words, Roman House, End of dinosaurs, theater camp) from VR.

The statement about effectiveness and attractiveness the first statement asked about the materials from VR platform is easy to understand most of the students choose strongly agree 22.5% and agree with this statement is 35.5%. They also have new experience and felt enjoy by using VR in learning process. So, they felt happy and can learn better.

Previous studies have shown that VR content goes hand in hand with student behavior in learning because students have more freedom to come up with new ideas when working in a group. In order to be recognized as the best group in the class, they feel a personal responsibility to gather enough ideas to write and speak essays that will work. The item in Figure 16.5 was the last one to be graded, and it was clear that students did not

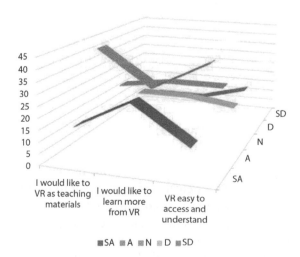

Figure 16.4 Retention.

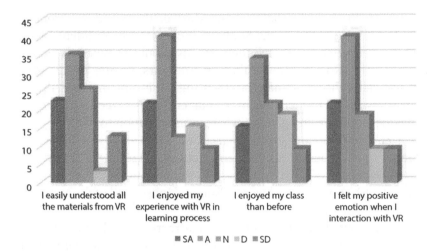

Figure 16.5 Effectiveness and attractiveness.

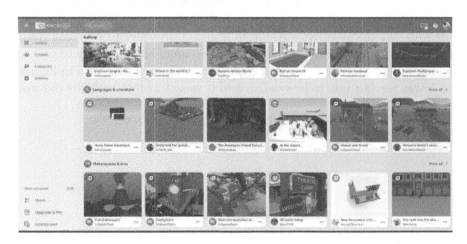

Figure 16.6 VR platform from Co Space Edu.

hesitate to complete their assignments on time, present their resumes and share their knowledge with their teams. They want to devote all their time to high quality academic papers. According to them, doing more than one thing while working together is impossible because of the large amount of time spent discussing and conversing. The positive atmosphere fostered by working in groups with like-minded individuals impresses and delights students, the study found. Because students can work more easily and with fun, English composition classes become more interesting. For all that they had to fear at first, students gradually gained confidence and lost the fear of making mistakes as they found the activity motivating and encouraging.

However, spelling and grammatical errors still interfere with students' writing. When students seek clarification about their spelling or grammatical structure, pronunciation and movement in speech, researchers must step in to ensure that they receive the feedback they need to improve their skills. Students benefit from participating in small groups and find VR with elective activities valuable and useful in improving their English skills and developing positive attitudes towards their use in class and their participation in small groups (Figure 16.6).

16.9 Discussion

The Indonesian Ministry of Education announced that online learning or eLearning would be used to allow students to continue their education during the pandemic COVID-19 period and after and teachers are expected to use technology and be creative when teaching online also adopt *Merdeka Belajar Kampus Merdeka (MBKM)* curriculum. It was quite a challenge for teachers to adjust to the new norm because of this sudden digital demand. Most lecturers in Indonesia had a difficult time handling the responsibility of ensuring that students were able to learn effectively and efficiently.

This COVID-19 period, however, students were more responsive and supportive when they were able to learn from the comfort of their own homes. According to previous research, students enjoyed and appreciated the novelty and novelty of this experience, and we can incorporate this FUTELA in the classroom blended or hybrid.

Students were compelled to participate in online group discussions as a means of learning. There are many reasons why technology has made it easier to teach and learn the target language in today's digital era. Universitas students should be taught the English language using technology because it provides for more information than can be found in a traditional textbook. In addition, technology can aid students in their ability to learn and enhance their language skills, as well as aid teachers in meeting the needs of their students in language learning environments. Moreover, lecturers now have a plethora of new tools at their disposal thanks to the positive impact of technology on the teaching and learning process.

There is no doubt in the results presented here, however, that the use of gamification in the classroom, as well as Virtual Reality, allowed students to gain real-world experience while also building social skills and actions. As a result, students were able to learn a second language in a new and exciting way thanks to these possible confounding factors.

VR is found to be a successful medium and technology to improve students' ability in foreign languages. Due to this approach, students of different levels can support, encourage, and provide feedback to one another, which leads to an increase in their post-test scores. The use of this approach creates a more engaging, comfortable, memorable, and enjoyable learning environment where students can share and exchange ideas to achieve their goals. The EFL skills of students in small groups may have improved significantly. Consequently, these processes include critical thinking, problem solving, mind mapping, analyzing and criticizing, planning, drawing outlines, and finding solutions to specific problems in groups rather than undertaking these processes individually or in the context of a larger class. Another study corroborates the success of VR in helping students improve their English according to [42, 43] findings about the need to improve learning performance, interactively in language learning [44] memorable, focus and pay attention in learning [45]. Autonomy in learning and the students can control their own learning pace, motivation, participations [46] the findings of the same time.

It should be noted that VR as FUTELA allows students to take on some responsibilities of English skills. Everyone on every team feels a personal responsibility and does their best to live up to expectations. Students can communicate, observe, feel confident, self-directed in learning, autonomy and collaborate more as a result of VR, which helps foster social communication. VR also develops students' ability to provide feedback on their writing and pronunciation errors, be they spelling, punctuation, grammar, or errors related to organization, pronunciation, accuracy, volume, and gestures. With this VR method, students feel more in control of their work as creators and builders of ideas and knowledge in online classes. They collaborate, brainstorm, confident to express their knowledge and exchange ideas in a more collaborative and student-centered environment. It is as if the lecturer has faded into the background, allowing students to take control of their own learning. Several other studies in the same area have reached similar conclusions. [47, 48] VR can be used to improve students' communication, critical thinking, behavior and motivational skills, according to students. Anxiety was reduced when students interacted with each other in interesting groups using VR in studying EFL findings as this was found in the same place as other similar findings by [49].

Some students did not like the VR method used at the beginning of the treatment, which was one of the difficulties and challenges that the researcher faced during this research. The computer lab is not supported with high internet bandwidth, some computers don't work and the Wi-Fi in this lab suddenly disconnects. In addition, most of the male students were reluctant to work in small groups because at first the weaker male students were afraid of being negatively absorbed by group activities, also they were not confident in English. They feel unmotivated, three good students believe that they are more competent than lower level students and they choose their own team and as a result, working in groups will distract them. Some of them initially expressed their reluctance to work in groups, but after the researcher explained the steps of the procedure to them in the first lecture, they began to change their minds. When one of the students chose his team members, the lecturer had chosen randomly, then if the group members wanted to take the whole assignment, some students complained that their group members were inactive and indifferent because they saw it as an opportunity to sit and do nothing. Students' inability to come up with original ideas for their projects such as writing dialogues, resumes or summaries, conversations and role-playing scripts assigned to them is another source of frustration. The researcher acts as a facilitator, offering suggestions to help students generate new ideas and develop a general outline for their project. When one of the five groups lost members, it caused some disruption to the project as a whole, but the researcher tried to solve this problem by giving other group members to help them. Sometimes two groups have discussions and if the other group is less working or by working with this group the lecturer will ask them to study together and solve problems.

Research into how English language teachers can use VR to implement blended learning lessons based on the lesson's objectives was also recommended. Future studies examining secondary school students' use of mobile devices in second language learning will do well to consult interviews and observations. A small number of VR applications are geared specifically toward higher university students attempting to improve their English language proficiency. For this reason, it is strongly recommended that future lecturers in the educational sector conduct further research and experimentation with this technology to better understand how it can be used by language teachers and students to meet their needs during this ongoing digital era situation.

This study has several limitations that point to various future research avenues. Undergraduate students of higher education were used for this research. Our findings may not be generalizable to other settings such as elementary schools, high schools and junior high schools, due to these contextual factors. A variety of disciplines and locations can be examined in future research, as well as in non-academic contexts. For the second part of the investigation, the researcher looked at student usage for one semester (eight weeks). It is possible that the results could be influenced by the "novelty effect", i.e. the tendency of students to perform better when new technology is introduced. It's possible that researchers could see how long-term VR adoption affects student learning and engagement over time. This study, however, shows how different levels of engagement ultimately lead to different qualities of learning. It is not possible to separate out the effects of mobility and synchronicity on the reported outcomes. Future research may consider varying the experimental conditions while controlling for confounding variables to determine possible individual effects of mobility and synchronicity. It is possible that one group used asynchronous online discussion and asynchronous quasi-synchronous VR communication via mobile phones.

16.10   Conclusion

Researchers conducted a study to find out VR because FUTELA prefers to be used to teach and improve the target language of higher education students. As a result of the announcement of the Ministry of Education and Culture that all education sectors in Indonesia will implement *Merdeka Belajar Kampus Merdeka (MBKM),* this has a major impact on the education system, especially for teachers to be free to create, design and develop materials that is why innovative teaching methods will help them to learn better and their behavior in learning. It is inevitable that lecturers become restless if they cannot quickly adjust to the virtual nature of the syllabus, lesson planning, and delivery. Even so, the students have a sense of purpose during this COVID-19 pandemic outbreak because they can learn from the comfort of their own homes using technology and they hope to be in the same situation after COVID-19. It facilitates the acquisition of the desired language by creating a favorable learning environment. Because of this, high school teachers will need help and training as they try to incorporate technology into their lessons. Students will be given the opportunity to improve their language skills in a meaningful way if these ICT tools are successfully integrated.

New insights and better understanding of how this VR technology should be used to improve students' language learning skills, especially in developing creativity, self-confidence, critical thinking, problem solving, autonomy in learning, collaborative, expressing ideas, building teamwork, and improving their skills. engagement to learn the target language (EFL) is provided in this paper.

References

1. Molina-Carmona, R., Pertegal-Felices, M.L., Jimeno-Morenilla, A., Mora-Mora, H., Virtual reality learning activities for multimedia students to enhance spatial ability. *Sustainability*, *10*, 4, 1074, 2018.
2. Salah, K., Rehman, M.H.U., Nizamuddin, N., Al-Fuqaha, A., Blockchain for AI: Review and open research challenges. *IEEE Access*, *7*, 10127–10149, 2019.
3. Yang, F.C.O., Lo, F.Y.R., Hsieh, J.C., Wu, W.C.V., Facilitating communicative ability of EFL learners via high-immersion virtual reality. *J. Educ. Technol. Soc.*, *23*, 1, 30–49, 2020.
4. Tai, T.Y., Chen, H.H.J., Todd, G., The impact of a virtual reality app on adolescent EFL learners' vocabulary learning. *Comput. Assisted Lang. Learn.*, *35*, 4, 892–917, 2022.
5. Arnó-Macià, E., Aguilar-Pérez, M., Tatzl, D., Engineering students' perceptions of the role of ESP courses in internationalized universities. *English Specif. Purp.*, *58*, 58–74, 2020.
6. Howard, S., Serpanchy, K., Lewin, K., Virtual reality content for higher education curriculum, in: *VALA2018 Proceedings: 19th Biennial Conference and Exhibition*, VALA-Libraries, Technology and the Future Inc., pp. 1–15, 2018.
7. Ma, Q. and Yan, J., How to empirically and theoretically incorporate digital technologies into language learning and teaching. *Biling.: Lang. Cogn.*, *25*, 3, 392–393, 2022.
8. Rawat, K.S. and Sood, S.K., Knowledge mapping of computer applications in education using CiteSpace. *Comput. Appl. Eng. Educ.*, *29*, 5, 1324–1339, 2021.
9. Makransky, G., Borre-Gude, S., Mayer, R.E., Motivational and cognitive benefits of training in immersive virtual reality based on multiple assessments. *J. Comput. Assisted Learn.*, *35*, 6, 691–707, 2019.
10. Petersen, G.B., Klingenberg, S., Mayer, R.E., Makransky, G., The virtual field trip: Investigating how to optimize immersive virtual learning in climate change education. *Br. J. Educ. Technol.*, *51*, 6, 2099–2115, 2020.
11. Lin, C.C., Lin, V., Liu, G.Z., Kou, X., Kulikova, A., Lin, W., Mobile-assisted reading development: A review from the activity theory perspective. *Comput. Assisted Lang. Learn.*, *33*, 8, 833–864, 2020.
12. Van den Berghe, R., Verhagen, J., Oudgenoeg-Paz, O., Van der Ven, S., Leseman, P., Social robots for language learning: A review. *Rev. Educ. Res.*, *89*, 2, 259–295, 2019.
13. Rintjema, E., Van Den Berghe, R., Kessels, A., De Wit, J., Vogt, P., A robot teaching young children a second language: The effect of multiple interactions on engagement and performance, in: *Companion of the 2018 ACM/IEEE International Conference on Human-Robot Interaction*, pp. 219–220, March 2018.
14. Malicka, A., Gilabert Guerrero, R., Norris, J.M., From needs analysis to task design: Insights from an English for specific purposes context. *Lang. Teach. Res.*, *23*, 1, 78–106, 2019.

15. UNESCO, National education responses to COVID-19: Summary report of UNESCO's online survey, Paris, 2020.

16. Adedoyin, O.B. and Soykan, E., COVID-19 pandemic and online learning: The challenges and opportunities. *Interact. Learn. Environ.*, 28, 1–13, 2020.

17. Ceha, J., Law, E., Kulić, D., Oudeyer, P.Y., Roy, D., Identifying functions and behaviours of social robots for in-class learning activities: Teachers' perspective. *Int. J. Soc. Rob.*, *14*, 3, 747–761, 2022.

18. Turner, C., Augmented reality, augmented epistemology, and the real-world web. *Philos. Technol.*, *35*, 1, 1–28, 2022.

19. Xue, Y., Ju, Z., Xiang, K., Chen, J., Liu, H., Multimodal human hand motion sensing and analysis—A review. *IEEE Trans. Cognit. Dev. Syst.*, *11*, 2, 162–175, 2018.

20. Chen, Y.L., Hsu, C.C., Lin, C.Y., Hsu, H.H., Robot-assisted language learning: Integrating artificial intelligence and virtual reality into English tour guide practice. *Educ. Sci.*, *12*, 7, 437, 2022.

21. Tai, T.Y., Chen, H.H.J., Todd, G., The impact of a virtual reality app on adolescent EFL learners' vocabulary learning. *Comput. Assisted Lang. Learn.*, *35*, 4, 892–917, 2022.

22. Li, K.C. and Wong, B.T.M., A literature review of augmented reality, virtual reality, and mixed reality in language learning. *Int. J. Mob. Learn. Organ.*, *15*, 2, 164–178, 2021.

23. Hartnett, M.K., Influences that undermine learners' perceptions of autonomy, competence and relatedness in an online context. *Australas. J. Educ. Technol.*, *31*, 1, 86–99, 2015.

24. Assor, A., Kaplan, H., Roth, G., Choice is good, but relevance is excellent: Autonomy-enhancing and suppressing teacher behaviours predicting students' engagement in schoolwork. *Br. J. Educ. Psychol.*, *72*, 2, 261–278, 2002.

25. Alamri, H., Lowell, V., Watson, W., Watson, S.L., Using personalized learning as an instructional approach to motivate learners in online higher education: Learner self-determination and intrinsic motivation. *J. Res. Technol. Educ.*, *52*, 3, 322–352, 2020.

26. Bedenlier, S., Bond, M., Buntins, K., Zawacki-Richter, O., Kerres, M., Facilitating student engagement through educational technology in higher education: A systematic review in the field of arts and humanities. *Australas. J. Educ. Technol.*, *36*, 4, 126–150, 2020, https://doi.org/10.14742/ajet.5477.

27. Skinner, E., Furrer, C., Marchand, G., Kindermann, T., Engagement and disaffection in the classroom: Part of a larger motivational dynamic? *J. Educ. Psychol.*, *100*, 4, 765, 2008.

28. Froiland, J.M., Parents' weekly descriptions of autonomy supportive communication: Promoting children's motivation to learn and positive emotions. *J. Child Fam. Stud.*, *24*, 1, 117–126, 2015.

29. Khajavy, G.H., MacIntyre, P.D., Barabadi, E., Role of the emotions and classroom environment in willingness to communicate: Applying doubly latent

multilevel analysis in second language acquisition research. *Stud. Second Lang. Acquis.*, *40*, 3, 605–624, 2018.

30. Berchiatti, M., Ferrer, A., Galiana, L., Badenes-Ribera, L., Longobardi, C., Bullying in students with special education needs and learning difficulties: The role of the student–teacher relationship quality and students' social status in the peer group. *Child Youth Care Forum*, *51*, 3, 515–537, Springer US, June 2022.

31. Shin, S., Kwon, K., Jung, J., Collaborative learning in the flipped university classroom: Identifying team process factors. *Sustainability*, *14*, 12, 7173, 2022.

32. Mystkowska-Wiertelak, A., Teachers' accounts of learners' engagement and disaffection in the language classroom. *Lang. Learn. J.*, *50*, 3, 393–405, 2022.

33. Reyes, B., Jiménez-Hernández, D., Martínez-Gregorio, S., De los Santos, S., Galiana, L., Tomás, J.M., Prediction of academic achievement in Dominican students: Mediational role of learning strategies and study habits and attitudes toward study. *Psychol. Sch.*, *60*, 3, 606–625, 2022.

34. Baudrillard, J., Simulations. *New York*, 1983.

35. Hu, Y.H., Effects of the COVID-19 pandemic on the online learning behaviors of university students in Taiwan. *Educ. Inf. Technol.*, *27*, 1, 469–491, 2022.

36. Shang, J., Xiao, R., Zhang, Y., A sequential analysis on the online learning behaviors of Chinese adult learners: Take the KGC learning platform as an example. in: *Blended Learning. Education in a Smart Learning Environment: 13th International Conference, ICBL 2020, Proceedings 13*, Springer International Publishing, Bangkok, Thailand, August 24–27, 2020.

37. Asarta, C.J. and Schmidt, J.R., Access patterns of online materials in a blended course. *Decis. Sci. J. Innov. Educ.*, *11*, 1, 107–123, 2013.

38. Morris, L.V., Finnegan, C., Wu, S.S., Tracking student behavior, persistence, and achievement in online courses. *Internet High. Educ.*, *8*, 3, 221–231, 2005.

39. Lin, S.Y., Aiken, J.M., Seaton, D.T., Douglas, S.S., Greco, E.F., Thoms, B.D., Schatz, M.F., Exploring physics students' engagement with online instructional videos in an introductory mechanics course. *Phys. Rev. Phys. Educ. Res.*, *13*, 2, 020138, 2017.

40. Dumais, S., Jeffries, R., Russell, D.M., Tang, D., Teevan, J., Understanding user behavior through log data and analysis, in: *Ways of Knowing in HCI*, pp. 349–372, Springer, New York, NY, 2014.

41. Campbell, D.T. and Stanley, J.C., *Experimental and quasi-experimental designs for research*, Ravenio Books, Chicago, Rand McNally & Company, 1963.

42. Hoang, D.T.N., McAlinden, M., Johnson, N.F., Extending a learning ecology with virtual reality mobile technology: Oral proficiency outcomes and students' perceptions. *Innov. Lang. Learn. Teach.*, 16, 1–14, 2022.

43. Chang, C.Y., Sung, H.Y., Guo, J.L., Chang, B.Y., Kuo, F.R., Effects of spherical video-based virtual reality on nursing students' learning performance in childbirth education training. *Interact. Learn. Environ.*, *30*, 3, 400–416, 2022.

44. Harris, C.E., *Assessing the effect of interactivity on virtual reality second language learning*, Doctoral dissertation, Rowan University, New Jersey, 2022.

45. Ma, W. and Luo, Q., Pedagogical practice and students' perceptions of fully online flipped instruction during COVID-19. *Oxf. Rev. Educ.*, *48*, 3, 400–420, 2022.

46. Azar, A.S. and Tan, N.H.I., The application of ICT techs (mobile-assisted language learning, gamification, and virtual reality) in teaching English for secondary school students in Malaysia during COVID-19 pandemic. *Univers. J. Educ. Res.*, *8*, 11C, 55–63, 2020.

47. Alwafi, G., Almalki, S., Alrougi, M., Meccawy, M., Meccawy, Z., A social virtual reality mobile application for learning and practicing english. *Int. J. Interact. Mob. Technol.*, *66*, 8, 55–73, 2022.

48. Chen, Y.L., Hsu, C.C., Lin, C.Y., Hsu, H.H., Personalized english language learning through a robot and virtual reality platform, in: *Society for Information Technology & Teacher Education International Conference*, 2022, April, Association for the Advancement of Computing in Education (AACE), pp. 1612–1615.

49. Thrasher, T., The impact of virtual reality on L2 French learners' language anxiety and oral comprehensibility: An exploratory study. *CALICO J.*, *39*, 2, 10–1558, 2022.

17

Satisfaction of Students Toward Media and Technology Innovation Amidst COVID-19

Muthmainnah[1]*, Ahmad Al Yakin[1], Saikat Gochhait[2], Andi Asrifan[3], Ahmed A. Elngar[4] and Luís Cardoso[5]

[1]Universitas Al Asyariah Mandar, Polewali Mandar City, Indonesia
[2]Symbiosis Institute of Digital and Telecom Management, Constituent of Symbiosis International Deemed University, Polewali Mandar City, India
[3]Universitas Muhammadiyah Sidenreng Rappang, Chennai, Indonesia
[4]Faculty of Computers and Artificial Intelligence, Beni-Suef University, Beni-Suef City, Egypt
[5]Polytechnic Institute of Portalegre and Centre for Comparative Studies of the University of Lisbon, Lisbon, Portugal

Abstract

This study looks at how English as a Foreign Language (EFL) instructors at Al Asyariah Mandar University feel about their participation in the creation of digital resources. The author bases this opinion on the assumption that creating high-quality educational resources for use online is a top priority. In keeping with the university's new philosophy of customized education, concerns were identified through the student experience and level of satisfaction in developing online course materials. As the internet and digital technologies increase, more opportunities will emerge for teachers to use technology to aid in the learning and teaching of a second or foreign language. Educational institutions need to carefully assess the implications of implementing any form of new technology in the classroom. The purpose of this study was to better understand how EFL students feel about using internet resources in the classroom. This chapter uses a mixed methods strategy to investigate whether the online EFL teaching mode meets the needs of their students or not. The majority of students prefer to use digital tools such as Zoom, Google Classroom, WhatsApp Groups, and Padlet for lectures; e-books, blogs, Mangatoon, NovelToon, AnimeTv, Pinterest, Instagram, YouTube, movies

*Corresponding author: muthmainnahunasman@gmail.com

Ahmed A. Elgnar, Vigneshwar M, Krishna Kant Singh and Zdzislaw Polkowski (eds.) Handbook of Computational Sciences: A Multi and Interdisciplinary Approach, (365–390) © 2023 Scrivener Publishing LLC

and songs for course materials; and Quizziz, Wakelet, and Quizlet for online assessments. As the study authors point out, educators' own expectations, motivations, and worldviews have a significant impact on how well they implement technology tools in the classroom. Teachers who favor a more conventional approach to language teaching tend to favor mixed methods. Almost all (97%) of the 109 respondents agreed that EFL teachers use technology in the classroom appropriately. WBL Almost all respondents (97%) felt that the quality of the resources delivered was reflected in the amount of time and effort expended in designing a learning center setting that supports the curriculum. 94% of people who took the survey felt the same way. It was said that 93.9% of the feedback students received was of sufficient quality, that 85.7% of the time students spent working together in groups or with friends was productive, and that 99.0% of respondents would recommend a learning situation that encourage synthesis and analysis for another. As a result, constructivists in the field of education are vying for power in the EFL class that utilizes technological tools. The findings of this study can inform the efforts of education authorities to improve media literacy of ESL students.

Keywords: Innovation in teaching, EFL, media and technology, online learning, english language teaching

17.1   Introduction

The global spread of the COVID-19 pandemic has severely curtailed educational opportunities for students all over the world. Emergency online and remote learning have been forced upon students and teachers alike. It's difficult for them to switch from a face-to-face learning model to an online one that relies on a variety of different kinds of technology. Teachers' pedagogical expertise and students' learning repertoire must be expanded considering the current pandemic's urgent demand for technological infrastructure improvements in the educational system. As a result of these circumstances, educational researchers and practitioners should re-examine the roles of educators and students in online learning as well as the technological environment.

As [1, 2] as the outbreak spread, it became evident that there were other factors at play that affected the success of online instruction. Even though online classes no longer require face-to-face interaction, professors are still expected to provide learning materials and connect directly with students. Teachers and students both benefited from the ability to access materials and classroom "space" at any time from any location, even when they weren't prepared for the new medium. Many countries, including Indonesia, are experimenting with the implementation of EFL online classes in response to the COVID-19 pandemic that is expected to begin in early 2020. Because of a decision made by Indonesia's education policymakers, online classes will be implemented across the country beginning in mid-March, 2020. Following the outbreak of COVID-19, this decision was made. As a result of the outbreak, the Ministry of Education has proposed online courses for K-12 and postsecondary institutions. First, schools and universities were told to switch out traditional classes for 14 days at a time with online classes.

The Circular Letter of the Minister of Education and Culture Indonesia No. 4 Year, issued by the Ministry of Education and Culture [3] Kemendikbud (2020), established policy. Education policies in an emergency period deployment of Coronavirus disease 2019 (COVID-19) are described in detail in 2020, including the use of online and home-based learning methods to implement them. As a result, no new academic year can begin in Indonesia's educational institutions. Most of the teaching and learning takes place online and over the phone. While COVID-19 can provide university lecturers and students with new challenges when conducting online learning, Students must quickly adapt to the new method and learn something new because of this. Originally a face-to-face system, it was transformed into an online one.

[4] Due to today's challenging and unprecedented circumstances, it is imperative that our educational system be completely overhauled. In addition to formal education, the impact on informal and non-formal education is significant. It is generally agreed that one-on-one time spent teaching and learning in the classroom cannot be replicated elsewhere. But after the COVID-19 crisis, online education has become a pedagogical movement from the old way to the new way of teaching and learning. This trend has moved from the classroom to Zoom, from the personal to the virtual, and from seminars to webinars. E-learning and distance education have been seen as non-formal education in the past, but if current trends continue, they may replace them. There is a high probability that COVID-19 in Indonesia will have a global impact on the education sector, and some of the most popular online communication platforms are listed above. Popular options include Google Classroom, Google Meet, and Google Hangouts/Hangouts on Air, while WhatsApp can be used in the classroom to help with teaching.

There is evidence that students' opinions about the effectiveness of online learning technologies and, by extension, their attitudes towards technology as a whole have been influenced by the fact that students find online learning more attractive because of this amount of flexibility. The comfort of teachers and students with new technologies and their level of engagement largely determine whether an online course will be successful or not. The following works have been cited extensively [5–10]:

It is possible that students may benefit from rethinking their approach to learning with the help of online tools and strategies. Studying the shift to online education during COVID-19 and even after COVID19 can help us reduce the global disruption it causes. As an education team in the teaching and educational sciences faculty, we are very concerned about the factors affecting students at our university who were unfamiliar with online learning prior to the pandemic response. In 2020, asynchronous class discussion forums, video lectures, and live activities with weekly posts will all be available to students from around the world. As a higher education institution or university, we quickly address student and faculty concerns about the sheer amount of data and communication available through e-learning platforms. We aimed to investigate how these factors affect students' impressions and overall satisfaction with the virtual classes provided by our institution.

Online learning, or "e-learning," refers to the use of digital tools for teaching and learning, as defined by [11]. Technology has enabled students to study whenever and wherever they like. The goals of online education include instruction, dissemination of knowledge, and the promotion of student-to-student communication. Current research, however, presents some unique challenges for online education. Due to the outbreak of COVID-19 in Indonesia, educational institutions have shifted their teaching methods to rely solely on online interactions, so students can take classes from anywhere in the country on a predetermined schedule. Indonesian students and teachers may not always be ready for online learning because of differences in how online learning is done and other things.

Given the speed with which the pandemic is spreading, full online training should be introduced soon. One of the most pressing issues in online education is how to foster a sense of belonging among participants. That's why it's so important for online education to emphasize the value of social presence, engagement, and collaboration. Given the differences between electronic learning (e-learning), mobile learning (m-learning), and distance learning (d-learning), the phrase "online learning" used here is more of a combination of the three.

Email and instant messaging by WhatsApp, like in Indonesia, can be used in online learning activities. As a result, while the locations can be accessed from any location, the time is still largely determined by the school or university's schedules. Exchanges with other students are encouraged, but the learning process is still structured and paced (not ad hoc).

Asynchronous or synchronous online learning can be high-quality if the courses are well-prepared.

Three dimensions of online pedagogy were proposed by [12] elaborate educational principles, educational functions, and educational variables. Interaction is facilitated by the formation of a triangle between these three points. An emphasis on student-centered learning and teaching is reflected in pedagogical principles. Students are now expected to be self-organized, self-directed, and independent learners rather than passive recipients of traditional instruction. This has meant that traditional classroom instruction has been replaced by the creation of learning environments. In addition, the emphasis has shifted away from acquiring specific knowledge and toward developing general skills and knowledge outcomes. Cooperative and collaborative learning has become critical in today's classrooms. International and intercultural communication has been added to CBE (Computer Based Education) because of its global nature. The concept of authentically situated learning has evolved in the virtual classroom. The online environment favors problem-oriented, case-oriented, and inquiry-oriented learning.

Content, objectives, design approach, methods, strategies, and evaluation are all pedagogical aspects of web-based learning (WBL). [13] proposed a model for the educational aspects of WBL. It acknowledges similar influences on the study by [12] in online environments, and it adds a comprehensive framework that includes technological, interface design, online support and management, and resource support to try to understand design issues in flexible and distributed learning systems. The Effective Dimensions of Interactive Learning are a Groundbreaking Study in Instructional Technology, Cognitive Science, and Adult Education. The authors have used [14] work as a starting point to analyze the Training and Development Program's instructional efficacy. Its "wholeness," the continuity of its dimensions, and the complexity of what it has to say about online instruction are its strengths.

This chapter details the findings of a survey conducted between January 2021 and January 2022 at a university making the switch from traditional classroom instruction to fully online learning. Teachers at this institution were asked to place a greater emphasis on asynchronous teaching content, such as YouTube-based instruction, online discussions, and the sharing of ideas through platforms like WhatsApp Group (WAG) and Padlet, Comics (MangaToon), e-books (Google Play books), Weblogs, Virtual Reality, Artificial Intelligence, Pinterest, Instagram, and movies; Anime (AnimeTV), Novel (NovelToon), and MindMeister; online meetings by using Zoom and Google Meet; online assessment by using Wakelet,

Quizziz, Tubequiz, and Quizlet rather than synchronous lectures or tutorials. The survey results were analyzed by taking into account both the qualitative and quantitative answers from our students. This was done with the goal of improving the materials that English Foreign Language Lecturers (EFLL) used during COVID-19.

17.2   Literature Review

17.2.1   Accelerating Digital Transformation in the Education Sector

Integrating digital solutions into our daily lives is a crucial part of a process known as "digital transformation." As a result of digital transformation, more people are able to get a quality education; the educational system can be developed in accordance with international standards; the quality of education can be enhanced; and educators and students can grow into people who are eager to learn, think critically, and create new solutions. Using cutting-edge tools like VR/AR, deep learning/AI, and the IoT are all a part of this shift [15]. It's no secret that the prevalence of digital technologies such as big data, analytics, the cloud, mobile apps, and social media platforms has led to a sea change in many businesses [16].

[17] argues that the term "digital transformation" encompasses much more than just the introduction of cutting-edge ICT tools like the cloud, the IoT, big data, blockchain, AI, and machine learning. Digital transformation in educational institutions relies heavily on electronic learning. To better serve their students, faculty, and other institutions in the future, universities work to adopt e-learning practices [18]. In order to better prepare students for the workforce of the future, educational institutions are emphasizing the importance of developing students' digital competence [19].

These days, online education is all the rage. To put it simply, this educational system is unified and focused on the individual learner. Learners process, transmit, save, evaluate, communicate, administer, and manage their education with the help of electronic learning forms [20]. Students develop a sense of autonomy in their approaches to schoolwork, information acquisition, and interactions with faculty and classmates. E-learning encourages independent study because of this. By providing students with opportunities for immediate and constructive feedback and interaction, digital learning environments foster intrinsic motivation and encourage students to take charge of their own education. A learner with a good mental attitude finds studying English fun and is willing to put in the time and effort necessary to become fluent [21, 22]. On the other hand, argues that students' negative attitudes can hinder their ability to fully participate in class. Because of these negative ideas about the value of education, some students start to dislike learning and their teachers.

In addition, by using new technology, digitizing curricula places students at the center of an educational environment that is more positive, dynamic, accessible, and engaging. As a result, students' horizons broaden and their capacity for independent study grows. The reason people like studying English as a foreign language (EFL) is because it creates an environment that is appealing and encouraging.

Beginning in early 2020, COVID-19 mandated a digital transformation in Hungarian schools. Distance learning and employment is not a new concept, but it is still relatively uncommon in Hungary, which presents new issues for educators and their students. Due to the epidemic, many schools, including Universitas Al Asyariah Mandar University, had to close in the middle of March and switch from traditional face-to-face instruction to online learning.

The term "digital transformation" refers to an innovative approach to using digital technology to address real-world issues. Instead of only perpetuating and bolstering established methods, it enables brand-new forms of inventive and original ways. By the end, "digital transformation" has occurred when "established digital usages enable innovation and creativity and stimulate considerable change within the professional or knowledge arca [23]. The heart of digital transformation, then, is not the digitalization or digitization of established procedures but rather the development and implementation of technological responses to pressing problems.

17.2.2   Digital Media and Technology in English as a Foreign Language (EFL)

Previous studies have shown that digitization presents both risks and potential for universities and colleges. The increased need for trained professionals is good news for universities, but they still face challenges in meeting students' learning needs [24]. There have been several requests for digital transformation to be incorporated into ELT courses, but only a small number of papers by [25] provide any kind of practical assistance. Therefore, no established best practices exist. Teachers of EFL who want to include discussions of digital transformation in their classes will need to begin from scratch by familiarizing themselves with a wide range of pedagogical approaches, evaluating their efficacy in the classroom, developing a comprehensive curriculum, and finally introducing the new material to their students. Teachers and classroom settings play a significant role in teaching as a foundation. This could require a lot of time and effort [26].

In this study, we don't talk about how to educate about digital transformation; rather, we talk about how to teach and practice media and technology in an online or blended classroom. This is in line with studies on English education, which emphasize the development of concrete media and technology to improve English abilities over theoretical understanding. In contrast to studies focusing on English skills and the students' confidence in English, ours stands apart for one key reason. This chapter addresses the education of future English as a Foreign Language (EFL) learners, whose role in driving digital transformation was previously underestimated by integration media and technology as MobiTech in learning that a successful digital transformation requires well-trained leaders, but it also requires the participation of workers who possess the necessary skills.

Managing the many issues that arise during a digital transformation requires both theoretical and practical expertise. In the not-too-distant future, university students will face a complex set of challenges, including rising expectations for 21st century skills, rapid technological advancements, and mobile learning. To better equip students with the necessary skills, it is necessary to update both the delivery and content of education [27]. Students are better equipped to deal with the realities of digital transformation thanks to advances in teaching methodology. Learning through projects seems sufficient in the face of the digital revolution.

It is multidisciplinary and built on the principles of self-direction, initiative, and collaboration. The chosen project challenges are developed in advance of the course by teachers with modern instructional design. The projects that go along with the topic classes require the students to put their knowledge to use. The students are tasked with balancing multiple priorities, including the allocation of time and materials. Thus, students can gain exposure to the routine tasks of English, acquire necessary context, and learn to recognize important drivers and impediments in the path to digital transformation. Students' efforts and the answers they find are very helpful to the municipalities and practitioners concerned. The suggested course adopts a project-based learning approach because it acknowledges that students of English as a foreign language (EFL) have too few chances to develop their skills in problem solving and teamwork [28].

As Nayyar, [29] explains, "digital media" refers to anything that originates in the media, entertainment, or information industry or any of its various subindustries. Accessible and consumable via various digital devices, it consists of digital platforms (such as websites and applications), digital content (such as text, audio, video, and photos), and digital services (such as information, entertainment, and communication). Personal, organizational, and societal effects of digital media

The increased use of digital media nowadays is altering people's daily lives as well as their ability to connect and collaborate in the workplace and the community at large. The findings from this project's investigation of five countries representing different areas indicate that this is a worldwide occurrence. Increased use has both positive and negative effects on people's lives and on society as a whole. People are no longer passive bystanders or consumers of the effects of the digital revolution. Instead, they are actively changing digital media and what it means in society because digital media has given them power.

An increase in digital media consumption has many positive effects on both individuals and society. One, it facilitates communication and gives people more agency by bridging geographical and other divides—bringing together people who have similar interests and values and bringing together people who might otherwise never meet [29]. It provides resources that can be used to encourage more people to get involved in their communities and build groups around shared interests and causes and increases productivity and work-life balance by giving employees and employers more leeway in scheduling and working arrangements. Thirdly, it makes it easier to get an education and keep learning throughout one's life, both of which are crucial for developing and acquiring expertise [30].

1. Literacy

Many different conceptions of what it means to be literate can be found in published works. Literacy now has a very different meaning than it once had. Traditional literacy skills such as reading, writing, speaking face-to-face, and arithmetic are no longer necessary. The scope of the concept keeps expanding to encompass new domains of expertise [31]. As a result of this process of adaptation, literate learning is now inextricably intertwined with material goods. Literacy today means something different depending on a wide range of circumstances, including but not limited to 1) the prevalence of new technologies; 2) the impact of these technologies on social norms (e.g., the rise of online social networks); 3) the changing demands of a given population; 4) the evolution of means of communication; and 5) the difficulties brought about by the spread of globalization. The concept of "literacy" has recently impacted how English is taught and learned in our modern day. Thus, it will be quite useful to discuss recent literacy theories or methods that have impacted language instruction [32].

2. Competence with digital media.

The key to digital literacy is "mastering concepts, not keystrokes." There are many competing definitions of digital literacy, and one way to tell them apart is by the emphasis placed on either mastery of ideas or evaluation of information and intelligent analysis and synthesis, or on the provision of lists of specific skills and techniques that are seen as necessary to qualify as digitally literate [33]. When it comes to digital literacy, [34 p. 43]; identifies eight key components.

1. Cultural

   According to [34], it is essential to understand the background of a phenomenon in order to fully appreciate it. For what reasons does it serve as an excellent launching pad? It is through experience in a variety of online communities that one acquires the cultural competence necessary for effective digital literacy. Locations with their own set of problems, norms, and thought patterns should be among those considered. This ensures that behavior modification will be necessary. The ease with which people can shift between these various virtual environments is, therefore, a useful barometer of development. Thirty digital literacies can be positively transformed by emphasizing its cultural component. Learning about other people's digital cultures and contexts can broaden one's perspective in much the same way that learning a new language can.

2. Cognitive

   The ability to think critically in the digital realm is also essential. Literacy's positive effects on one's mind are comparable to or even greater than those on one's ability to interact and express oneself with others. In the previous section's final paragraph, it was alluded to that having access to a wider variety of resources (or "lenses") allows people to appreciate and make sense of a larger chunk of the Internet. Belshaw [34] to return to the language learning metaphor, there is a very real sense in which technical and cognitive processes must be mastered in order to become "fluent." Not only is it necessary to become technologically literate, but mastering these processes is also a valuable end in and of themselves. The cognitive component of digital literacy is best illustrated by the pervasive "software menu." Branched logic, which is required by this idea, does not exist in the real world.

3. Constructive

The ability to use technology for constructive purposes is the third pillar of digital literacy. Literacy, as mentioned by [35], is always about reading and writing. Literacy can be measured by one's ability to construct anything. [36, 37] elaborate by saying that, in the digital world, literacy is knowing how to make effective use of digital resources to promote positive social change. What it means to "build" something shifts when exact copies of other people's work can be made with minimum effort. To control how their content is used, publishers and people can now employ new kinds of licenses like Creative Commons. To be constructive, one should not start from scratch but rather build upon the work of others, giving appropriate credit where it is due. Mastering this constructive facet of digital literacy entails understanding the contexts and methods for appropriating, reusing, and remixing content. It's just as important to know how the digital and physical worlds are different as it is to be able to put together the work of others in a creative way.

4. Communicative

The goal of one's communication is essential to the practice of communicative literacy. The communicative component of digital literacies is inseparable from the constructive component, as both require the creation of what could be called a social object. The nuts and bolts of literacies in digital networked contexts are the knowledge, skills, and understanding necessary to accomplish this. The communicative component of digital literacies is becoming increasingly important as the number of digital channels for human interaction grows [38]. Despite the interrelated nature of all the "fundamental parts," the close relationship between the cultural and communicative elements stands out.

After all, it takes familiarity with the established norms and assumptions of a certain digital technology in order to successfully utilize it. Subtle differences exist between, say, mobile and landline phone use or among various social networks. How can young people be expected to behave correctly if they have not been guided through the communication protocols and conventions of a certain platform? Although there is no single defining feature of digital literacies that is more important than the others, Communicative

Competency is unquestionably foundational. In other words, while any of the parts can be combined with others to foster growth, the communicative aspect is virtually required for any such endeavor. In light of the fact that using a given digital technology for effective communication requires familiarity with and application of a set of established norms and assumptions, it may be wise to plot out future development of this component with a view toward delving ever so slightly deeper into a specific area with each passing iteration [39].

5. Confidence

Instead, the confidence factor is something that, like the others, can be concentrated on. Confidence, like the other elements, should not be practiced in isolation. However, this element requires making connections between previously learned material. To do this, one must learn to recognize and take advantage of the digital world's distinctive features compared to the analog one [40]. Confidence in one's ability to use digital tools and resources to find solutions to problems and direct one's own education is a key component of developing digital literacy. Fortunately, this can be facilitated by methods proven effective in a wide range of educational settings. With the combination of mentoring and reflective self-analysis learners are not only asked to think about their methods, but also to build a community.

6. Creative

For the purposes of the creative component of digital literacies, the goal is to create something new and useful. In this context, "digital" refers to the use of digital tools and methods to produce or accomplish goals that were previously unachievable or, at the very least, out of reach for most people. According to [34] Belshaw (2014:52–54), "creativity in digital domains emerges through generating something new (not necessarily "original") that is of value in a particular context." As can be seen in the SAMR model, there are two main components to developing students' creative skills in the context of digital literacy. To begin with, traditional forms of education need to be rethought extensively in light of the opportunities presented by digital tools. Second, for true creativity to grow, the traditional power structure between teacher and student needs to change.

7. Critical

To be critical of literacy practices means examining the assumptions and power dynamics that underpin them. Communication in the online, digital world is very different from the analog world. When thinking about what it means to be media literate in the digital age, the critical component comes closest. The questions, "Who is the audience?" and "Why does it matter?" are pertinent here. What people are included and what people are not? I'm curious as to the text's underlying assumptions. Moreover, etc. Many methods exist for teaching this facet of computer literacy. Improving your proficiency in the critical subcomponent of digital literacies requires you to reflect on the ways in which you now engage with literacy. Thinking about their origins, influences, and the consequences of one's actions is an important part of this process.

8. Civic

Lastly, we get to the topic of digital literacies. As such, this section focuses on literacy habits that help civil society grow. Understanding how to consume the media produced by corporations and governments is only part of what it means to be digitally literate. The Civic element, which is closely related to the Critical one, focuses on self-organization in digital settings [34]. Students can more easily translate identified challenges and solutions into technological concepts if the curriculum is adapted to help them increase their digital literacy and understand the processes involved in digital transformation. Since students of English are not likely to be technology experts, the new curriculum should focus on two types of critical competencies: (a) digital and (b) non-digital [40]. Some examples of digital competencies are the ability to read and write digitally, interact and collaborate digitally, understand and use data digitally, learn and work quickly and effectively online, and utilize digital learning and working methods. Competencies outside of the realm of technology include independent thought, flexibility, originality, persistence, problem solving, and project management. We sorted through several definitions of digital transformation [41] and "digital maturity" to determine what would be covered in the class.

17.3 Methods

Mixed qualitative methods are used in this research. Research that employs a mix of quantitative and qualitative approaches is known as a mixed method because it allows researchers to collect more accurate, reliable, and comprehensive data. Combining exploratory sequential design with a combination model of research was used in this study (sequence of discovery). One of the most used research models is known as the sequential explanatory design or combination research technique model. This model uses both quantitative and qualitative methods in a sequential manner [42].

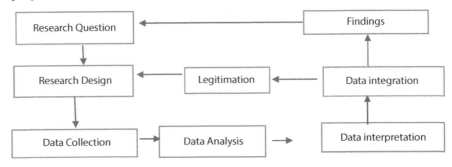

Figure 17.1 Mix method flow chart.

This research was carried out in Indonesia, which included Al Asyariah Mandar University students who were active in the semester of the Academic Year 2021–2022 as respondents. The research was conducted online using Google Form and the questionnaire used was adjusted from Dixon, K., & Dixon, R. (2010 p.18-20). As many as 109 EFL students were recorded as respondents in this study. Supervision will take place from January 20, 2021 to January 20, 2022, and will be conducted at the English I and English II courses. The selection of research subjects is carried out using a purposive sampling technique. The criteria for students involved in this research are Universitas Al Asyariah Mandar students who are active in the active semester of the academic year 2021–2022, who are taking online learning. In the COVID-19 phase, the data from the questionnaire is shown as pictures to find out how students feel about online learning.

Students are given a monthly overview of the implementation of online learning using a questionnaire via a Google form. This kind of analysis can be done in a number of ways, both quantitative and qualitative (descriptive and inferential data analysis). Preparing the data to be analyzed, exploring the data, analyzing it to answer research questions, and displaying and validating it are all steps in this study's data analysis procedure. The quantitative and qualitative approaches are used to analyze the data that has been gathered. According to this, numbers and percentages are used to convey descriptive information in sentences. Data reduction, data visualization, and conclusion drawing/verification are the next steps.

17.4   Results and Findings

In this study, we introduce this course to demonstrate that English-language students can influence digital transformation in the classroom by integrating relevant media and technology and student-centered learning approaches. College students can learn in classes that solving problems in a digitally transformed world needs to be done in a completely new way, not just by making the status quo stronger with technology.

A number of those who were given access to the updated digital procedure have even started using it. Students gain the ability to take a comprehensive view of a problem and apply that lens to real-world scenarios where they have to consider not only technological innovations but also the learning process and improve their metacognitive skills. The course promotes ICT and RALL (Robot-Assisted Language Learning, like VR and AI) through the students and their ideas.

The solutions created have demonstrated that students have the necessary competencies and abilities for digital transformation, and their responses show that they value content. We think that the proposed course will help students develop these important skills and learn how to use media and technology to meet their needs. It will do this by combining practical instruction with exercises.

Ninety-seven percent of 109 respondents replied that EFL lecturers use technology appropriately. The EFL students agree that lecturers combine cutting-edge visual learning principles and the most up-to date information and communication technology tools into creative learning resources.

Based on Figure 17.2, 98 respondents stated that the lecturer at the beginning of learning conveys the learning objectives, learning tools, materials, and skills that will be applied.

A total of 97% of respondents felt lecturers were highly creative in matching between materials, learning styles, and learning contexts. The respondents believe lecturers understand their conditions and listen to their choices in collaborating EFL with matching e-materials using film, songs, comics, novels, VR, AI, Anime, blogs, YouTube, Pinterest, Instagram, and Tubequizard. The result was shown by using

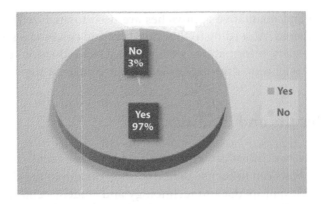

Figure 17.2 Constructivist approach to teaching/learning.

this application or WBL 97% of respondents agreed that quality planning into the curriculum paid for the quality of materials delivery. The result on Figure 17.3 question number 3 on the statement learner center environment was that 94% of respondents agreed and 6% said no. Flexible and technologically competent respondents perceived both learning and satisfaction as 76% stated their flexibility to access the materials due to internet connection problems and devices. Figure 17.4 is the online learning and teaching strategy. The seventh statement range of appropriate teaching strategies in online learning, as shown above, 86.7% stated yes and 13.3% stated not appropriate. While the next question concerns learning strategies, 97% took yes. The statement of reliability of access was 70% categorized as yes and 30% no. The result indicates internet access is a big challenge during online and accessible materials. On the question of respondents' level of engagement with online materials, the results showed

Figure 17.3 Effective online pedagogy.

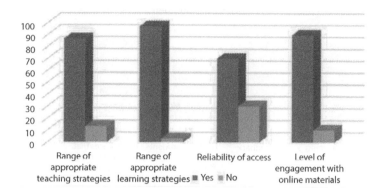

Figure 17.4 Online learning and teaching strategy.

a high percentage of agreement. 89.9% of respondents engaged with these materials.

In Figure 17.5 interrogates knowing about pedagogical dimension in online class. As displayed in the above figure, the frequency rate is high, the opportunity for deep learning is 92.99% in the strong belief category, the quality of feedback is 93.9%, the level of interactivity between students in a team or collaborating with their friends is 85.7%, and learning experiences that encourage synthesis and analysis are highly recommended by 99% of the respondents.

Figure 17.6 illustration of specific assessment by e-learning Highly recommended is assessment discussion-based using Tubequizard, shown in Figure 17.6 of 85.6% of respondents highly recommended by using Quizziz 76.8%, using Quizlet 76.3%, and Mindmister 37.1%.

The interview results show a positive response, and sometimes students need the help of lecturers in conducting internet searches for relevant content. The difference between true and false information was beyond their comprehension. The educational process is unlikely to function successfully under these conditions. In addition, it was found that students said, "Because their experience with browsing in cyberspace using the internet only for entertainment needs causes students to find it difficult to determine which website is reliable. However, today's learning using collaborative media and technology really helps them learn more. Problems can also come from the facilities that are already there, like not having a Wi-Fi connection or enough tools, though students' mobile devices can now fill that role.

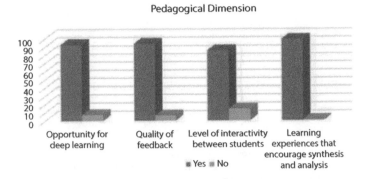

Figure 17.5 Pedagogical dimension.

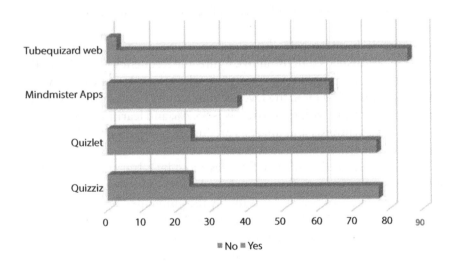

Figure 17.6 Media and online technology for assessment.

According to Nurnadifa, "The majority of the problems I feel in promoting digital literacy come from the infrastructure that will be used. We are aware that there are times when the Wi-Fi signal is weak. In addition, some classmates even have platform constraints that are accessed on their cellphones, sometimes hampered by inadequate connections. A further barrier to learning, such as accessing VR or AI applications, is the inadequate availability of equipment in the computer laboratory; for example, a broken computer. As expected, this will hinder students' ability to learn while their smartphones are not supported. "Zulkifli has a different opinion. Zulkifli claims that the most significant obstacle to using media and technology in the classroom is not the lack of resources in the classroom, but rather the attitudes and beliefs of the students themselves. Since every student now has their own android device, they don't have to worry about learning that requires access to multiple platforms or the web.

17.5 Discussion

The internet has enormous potential to be utilized in the delivery of education to various groups. There are many online resources available to educators today. The Internet is increasingly being used to deliver educational materials to students at a "distance," including those who may never be able to attend a class in person. An overview of Web-based learning materials for distance learners is presented in this study.

Though the COVID-19-induced digital revolution was bumpy and fraught with difficulties, a majority of students surveyed said they preferred it and would do so again. As a result of our investigation, we have some observations and hypotheses to share. One, nearly half of students who tried out an online course liked it enough to keep going that route. A second reason is that students who aren't having any problems with technology would rather utilize their own gadgets throughout the lessons. Finally, technical challenges and other worries have split the students who will not favor online education.

About half of the students surveyed said they would choose online education in the future, making it a successful model. Almost everyone who responded acknowledged the need for regular class meetings. As a result, they favor self-paced online education organized around semesters rather than the traditional academic year. There were no direct inquiries concerning whether or not postponed training, such as intensive courses, would be accepted. Students currently believe that weekly lessons are essential. These students did not report any technological difficulties and already possessed enough facilities.

Online teaching and learning tools such as Zoom, Google Meet, Facebook, and YouTube streaming are used according to the needs of students and lecturers. They have difficulty adapting to new teaching strategies [43] during COVID. In this study, most students chose that lecturers use WhatsApp to conduct online curriculum transactions instead of messengers and telegrams. Students are used to using WhatsApp in their daily lives, and it is also convenient for students to use it anytime. In this study, English lecturers facilitate students with various variants of teaching materials using songs, Pinterest, Instagram, movies, comics, anime, and e-books. In addition, lecturers also use VR, AI, and Tubequizard to increase teachers' efficacy and confidence in applying students' motivation theory by strengthening their design beliefs. While many theories and principles exist to help teachers engage online learners more effectively [44] and [45]. This study puts e-learning into practice in the classroom and the results demonstrate efficient learning.

As a result of [46] recommendations, effective online learning can be achieved in higher education (HE) institutions Students and teachers must be prepared to use ICT tools, and HE institutes must have basic ICT infrastructure, as well as ICT tools and access to learning platforms and all online studies have shown that online learning is at least as effective as traditional learning. This study also found that 97 percent of 109 respondents replied to their high satisfaction category when online that EFL lecturers use technology appropriately. The EFL students agreed that lecturers combine cutting-edge visual learning principles and the most up-to-date information and communication technology tools into creative learning resources. Also, 98 respondents stated that a lecturer at the beginning of learning conveys the learning objectives, learning tools, materials, and skills that will be applied. There are, however, problems with how the repository chooses what to keep because everyone who puts something on the site does so on their own time.

According to the findings of this study, good materials, learning designs, and appropriate e-learning platforms are needed to support online education. It is the responsibility of lecturers at universities to develop and create online learning materials using applications that do not take long, but must have planning, choose the right material according to the curriculum, have good TPACK knowledge, identify student needs and conditions that must be overcome by making learning instructions online in English, and incorporate various variants of e-materials into the curriculum. The global pandemic and future online learning activities are two examples of how these digital teaching materials can be used to develop appropriate media and technology-based teaching materials. Online teaching and learning can also be hampered by problems with digital infrastructure, such as a limited number of students or a connection that keeps going down.

Students also argue that teachers of English as a second language that incorporate digital literacy into their lessons will need to be resourceful in their use of media and technology or applications or the web to construct or design engaging and engaging lessons for their students. Also, other students claim that "teachers must be creative in employing both software and hardware to develop or design materials," demonstrating their understanding that such originality is essential for successfully incorporating digital literacy into EFL instruction.

Students' opinion also argues that "when it comes to teaching English as a foreign language, I find it difficult to incorporate digital literacy into the curriculum. To successfully include digital literacy into EFL instruction, teachers must be fluent in both the subject matter and information technology. "The researcher understood from one of the students (Harjuni) responses that she found it difficult to include digital literacy in the EFL classroom. It's clear from what she said. Her opinion on the matter was stated directly, "In my opinion, the integration of digital literacy into teaching English as a foreign language is tough." This was her opinion on the matter. Then, in the following sentence, she clarified why this task is so difficult: "This is due to the fact that combining subject matter expertise with IT know-how is essential for those teaching English as a foreign language in the digital age."

Amazing resources and techniques lose their appeal if they can't be accessed online. The worldwide pandemic should serve as a call to action for the development of a fully functional online learning environment suitable for both students and educators. The lack of student motivation is another issue that can hinder online education. Teachers are urged to redesign their lessons to include more engaging, learner-centric activities in light of the findings of this study. Motivating and enriching students' learning experiences can be achieved through the use of engaging content [47]. Students in the sample were also less reliant on their "teachers" because they had developed greater self-confidence and felt more in control of their own education. They also thought it was important to interact with their fellow students. High-quality online programs that center on authentic learning experiences may be fostering a new generation of learners who are truly self-reliant and proactive. If this is the case, educators and designers must concede that students have agency over their own education and can employ prior knowledge and interests to personalize their learning. What this shows is a change in educational philosophy.

It's also possible that unintentional "worlds" of online learning are emerging. They are less likely to be carbon copies of the traditional lecture halls we are used to. Sims, R. [48] claims that today's students have a strong preference for independent study. The way that education is provided, and the roles played by the various stakeholders in the education process are likely to be affected by this. Incorporating the pedagogies of online, learner-centered environments into our current models and practices requires new models and frameworks.

This study's findings show that students agree that online education is increasingly focused on the individual learner. They experience joy, enjoyment, and fun as a result of their time spent watching, listening to, and playing content found online. Teachers' responsibilities here include, among other things, making visually appealing materials and troubleshooting technical issues that arise frequently during online instruction.

17.6 Conclusion

The face-to-face study highlights the satisfactions faced by university EFL students during the global pandemic, as well as insights into online teaching activities. E-learning platforms are diverse, integrating games and e-materials as creativity to prepare effective, practical, efficient online learning materials, and students are highly motivated or engaged in online teaching, according to research findings. In addition, participants reported that they faced problems with unstable internet connections, especially for students, and the need for ICT integration training programs. The participants also shared their thoughts and ideas on how to improve their technology skills. An e-learning platform that represents the university is highly recommended for online learning activities. It's also a good idea to incorporate technology into university curricula and create engaging online resources and student e-books or cloud materials. To be fair, this study's participants' perceptions of the challenges and insights of online teaching are not representative of all perspectives of Indonesian EFL students. Although the findings are interesting in and of themselves, it is recommended that future studies recruit a diverse group of participants from around the world.

References

1. Unger, S. and Meiran, W.R., Student attitudes towards online education during the COVID-19 viral outbreak of 2020: Distance learning in a time of social distance. *Int. J. Technol. Educ. Sci.*, 4, 4, 256–266, 2020.

2. VanLeeuwen, C.A., Veletsianos, G., Johnson, N., Belikov, O., Never-ending repetitiveness, sadness, loss, and "juggling with a blindfold on:" Lived experiences of Canadian college and university faculty members during the COVID-19 pandemic. *Br. J. Educ. Technol.*, 52, 4, 1306–1322, 2021.

3. Kemendikbud, Pusat Pendidikan dan Pelatihan Pegawai Kementrian Pendidikan dan Kebudayaan. Ministry and Education Indonesia, 2020, https://pusdiklat.kemdikbud.go.id/surat-edaran-mendikbud-no-4-tahun-2020-tentang-pelaksanaankebijakan-pendidikan-dalam-masa-darurat-penyebaran-corona-virus-disease-covid-1-9/.

4. Huang, R.H., Liu, D.J., Tlili, A., Yang, J.F., Wang, H.H., *Handbook on facilitating flexible learning during educational disruption: The Chinese experience in maintaining undisrupted learning in COVID-19 outbreak*, p. 46, Smart Learning Institute of Beijing Normal University, Beijing, 2020.

5. Ellis, R.A. and Bliuc, A.M., An exploration into first-year university students' approaches to inquiry and online learning technologies in blended environments. *Br. J. Educ. Technol.*, 47, 5, 970–980, 2016.

6. Oliveira, G., Grenha Teixeira, J., Torres, A., Morais, C., An exploratory study on the emergency remote education experience of higher education students and teachers during the COVID-19 pandemic. *Br. J. Educ. Technol.*, 52, 4, 1357–1376, 2021.

7. Wei, H.-C. and Chou, C., Online learning performance and satisfaction: Do perceptions and readiness mat-ter? *Distance Educ.*, 41, 1, 48–69, 2020, https://doi.org/10.1080/01587 919.2020.1724768.

8. Korhonen, A.M., Ruhalahti, S., Veermans, M., The online learning process and scaffolding in student teachers' personal learning environments. *Educ. Inf. Technol.*, 24, 1, 755–779, 2019.

9. Mitchell, L.D., Parlamis, J.D., Claiborne, S.A., Overcoming faculty avoidance of online education: From resistance to support to active participation. *J. Manage. Educ.*, 39, 3, 350–371, 2015.

10. Vladova, G., Ullrich, A., Bender, B., Gronau, N., Students' acceptance of technology-mediated teaching–how it was influenced during the COVID-19 Pandemic in 2020: A Study From Germany. *Front. Psychol.*, 69, 12, 636086. 2021.

11. Seiradakis, E.V. and Spantidakis, I., Online course design and materials development for teaching reading of research articles to EFL undergraduate students at a Greek Technical University. *J. Teach. English Specific Acad. Purp.*, 6, 2, 285–296, 2018.

12. Heiner, M., Schneckenberg, D., Wildt, J., Online pedagogy–innovative teaching and learning strategies in ICT-environments. *Workpackage*, vol. 1, pp. 001–001, 2001.

13. Khan, B.H., The people-process-product continuum. *Educ. Technol.*, 44, 33–40, 2004.

14. Reeves, T.C. and Reeves, P.M., Effective dimensions of interactive learning on the World Wide Web, in: *Web Based Instruction*, B.H. Khan (Ed.), pp. 59–66, Educational Technology Publications, Springer Nature, 1997.

15. Elgohary, E., The role of digital transformation in sustainable development in Egypt. *Int. J. Inf. Media Commun. Technol.*, 4, 1, 71–106, 2022.

16. Nwankpa, J.K. and Roumani, Y., IT capability and digital transformation: A firm performance perspective, 2016.

17. Petkovics, I., Digital transformation in higher education. *J. Appl. Tech. Educ. Sci.*, 8, 4, 77–89, 2018.

18. Zabadi, A.M. and Al-Alawi, A.H., University students' attitudes towards e-learning: University of Business & Technology (UBT)-Saudi Arabia-Jeddah: A case study. *Int. J. Bus. Manage.*, 11, 6, 286–295, 2016.

19. Bond, M., Marín, V.I., Dolch, C., Bedenlier, S., Zawacki-Richter, O., Digital transformation in German higher education: Student and teacher perceptions and usage of digital media. *Int. J. Educ. Technol. High. Educ.*, 15, 1, 1–20, 2018.

20. Gluchmanova, M., Creation of e-courses in english for students of production technology. *TEM J.*, 6, 3, 613, 2017.

21. Alamer, A., Basic psychological needs, motivational orientations, effort, and vocabulary knowledge: A comprehensive model. *Stud. Second Lang. Acquis.*, 44, 1, 164–184, 2022.

22. Zhang, Z., Learner engagement and language learning: A narrative inquiry of a successful language learner. *Lang. Learn. J.*, 50, 3, 378–392, 2022.

23. Frennert, S., Hitting a moving target: Digital transformation and welfare technology in Swedish municipal eldercare. *Disabil. Rehabilitation: Assist. Technol.*, 16, 1, 103–111, 2021.

24. Karlberg, M. and Bezzina, C., The professional development needs of beginning and experienced teachers in four municipalities in Sweden. *Prof. Dev. Educ.*, 48, 4, 624–641, 2022.

25. de la Peña, E., The reading experience for children and young adults: A territory of transformation in TEFL, in: *Using Literature to Teach English as a Second Language*, pp. 142–173, IGI Global, 2020.

26. Maatuk, A.M., Elberkawi, E.K., Aljawarneh, S., Rashaideh, H., Alharbi, H., The COVID-19 pandemic and E-learning: Challenges and opportunities from the perspective of students and instructors. *J. Comput. High. Educ.*, 34, 1, 21–38, 2022.

27. Chen, R.H., Fostering students' workplace communicative competence and collaborative mindset through an inquiry-based learning design. *Educ. Sci.*, 11, 1, 17, 2021.

28. Al-Busaidi, S. and Al-Seyabi, F., Project-based learning as a tool for student-teachers' professional development: A study in an Omani EFL teacher education program. *Int. J. Learn. Teach. Educ. Res.*, 20, 4, 116–136, 2021.

29. Nayyar, S., Digital media and society implications in a hyperconnected era, in: *USA: World Economic Forum*, 2016, January.

30. Abdallah, M., Teaching english as a foreign language from a new literacy perspective: A guide for egyptian EFL student teachers. *Online Submission*, 2021.
31. Mills, K.A. and Unsworth, L., *Multimodal literacy*, Oxford University Press, 2017.
32. Mitchell, S.A. and Walton-Fisette, J.L., *The essentials of teaching physical education: Curriculum, instruction, and assessment*, Human Kinetics, SHAPE America set the Standard, 2022.
33. How, R.P.T.K., Zulnaidi, H., Rahim, S.S.A., The importance of digital literacy in quadratic equations, strategies used, and issues faced by educators. *Contemp. Educ. Technol.*, *14*, 3, ep372, 2022.
34. Belshaw, D., *The essential elements of digital literacies*, Doug Belshaw, Eavi, Media Literacy for Citizenship, 2014.
35. Hull, G.A. and Moje, E.B., What is the development of literacy the development of. *Commissioned Papers on Language and Literacy Issues in the Common Core State Standards and Next Generation Science Standards*, vol. 94, p. 52, 2012.
36. Livingstone, S., Critical reflections on the benefits of ICT in education. *Oxf. Rev. Educ.*, *38*, 1, 9–24, 2012.
37. Almaiah, M.A., Al-Khasawneh, A., Althunibat, A., Exploring the critical challenges and factors influencing the E-learning system usage during COVID-19 pandemic. *Educ. Inf. Technol.*, *25*, 6, 5261–5280, 2020.
38. Pegrum, M., Hockly, N., Dudeney, G., *Digital literacies*, Routledge, 2022.
39. Murray, L., Giralt, M., Benini, S., Extending digital literacies: Proposing an agentive literacy to tackle the problems of distractive technologies in language learning. *ReCALL*, *32*, 3, 250–271, 2020.
40. Qiao, S., Yeung, S.S.S., Zainuddin, Z., Ng, D.T.K., Chu, S.K.W., Examining the effects of mixed and non-digital gamification on students' learning performance, cognitive engagement and course satisfaction. *Br. J. Educ. Technol.*, 61, April 2020, 2022.
41. Yu, H., Fletcher, M., Buck, T., Managing digital transformation during re-internationalization: Trajectories and implications for performance. *J. Int. Manage.*, *28*, 4, 100947, 2022.
42. Johnson, R.B. and Onwuegbuzie, A.J., Mixed methods research: A research paradigm whose time has come. *Educ. Res.*, *33*, 7, 14–26, 2004.
43. Mishra, L., Gupta, T., Shree, A., Online teaching-learning in higher education during lockdown period of COVID-19 pandemic. *Int. J. Educ. Res. Open*, *1*, 100012, 2020.
44. Chiu, T.K.F. and Lim, C.P., Strategic use of technology for inclusive education in Hong Kong: A content-level perspective. *ECNU Rev. Educ.*, *3*, 4, 715–734, 2020, https://doi.org/10.1177/2096531120930861.
45. Ryan, R.M. and Deci, E.L., Intrinsic and extrinsic motivation from a self-determination theory perspective definitions, theory, practices, and future directions. *Contemp. Educ. Psychol.*, 61, 2020, https://doi.org/10.1016/j.cedpsych.2020.101860.

46. Ali, W., Online and remotes learning in higher education institutes: A necessity in linght of COVID-19 pandemic. *High. Educ. Stud.*, 10, 3, 16–25, 2020, Retrieved March 17, 2008, from http://www.jld.qut.edu.au.

47. Thadphoothon, J., *Online language learning survey*, Special report, Dhurakij Pundit University, 2020.

48. Sims, R., Beyond instructional design: Making learning design a reality. *J. Learn. Des.*, 1, 2, 1–9, 2006.

Index

Printed and bound by CPI Group (UK) Ltd, Croydon, CR0 4YY

27/10/2024

14580177-0002